Drawing Thought

How Drawing Helps Us Observe, Discover, and Invent

Andrea Kantrowitz

The MIT Press
Cambridge, Massachusetts
London, England

The MIT Press
Massachusetts Institute of Technology
77 Massachusetts Avenue, Cambridge, MA 02139
mitpress.mit.edu

The MIT Press would like to thank the anonymous peer reviewers who provided comments on drafts of this book. The generous work of academic experts is essential for establishing the authority and quality of our publications. We acknowledge with gratitude the contributions of these otherwise uncredited readers.

This book was set in hand-drawn fonts by Andrea Kantrowitz and Skolar Sans by Rosetta. Printed and bound in the United States of America.

Library of Congress Cataloging-in-Publication Data

Names: Kantrowitz, Andrea, author.
Title: Drawing thought : how drawing helps us observe, discover, and invent / Andrea Kantrowitz.
Description: Cambridge, Massachusetts : The MIT Press, 2022. | Includes bibliographical references.
Identifiers: LCCN 2021060536 | ISBN 9780262544320 (paperback)
Subjects: LCSH: Drawing--Psychological aspects. | Cognition.
Classification: LCC NC715 .K36 2022 | DDC 741.01/9--dc23/eng/20220509
LC record available at https://lccn.loc.gov/2021060536

10 9 8 7 6 5 4 3

EU product safety and compliance information contact is: mitp-eu-gpsr@mit.edu

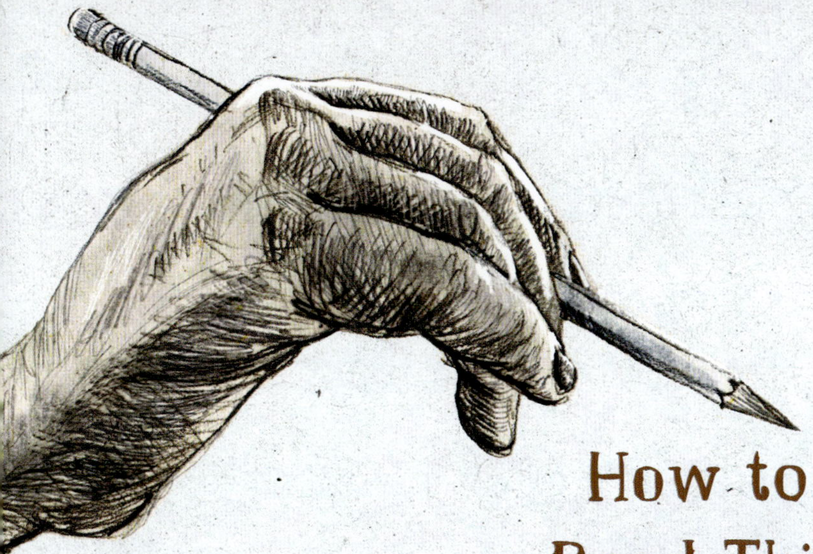

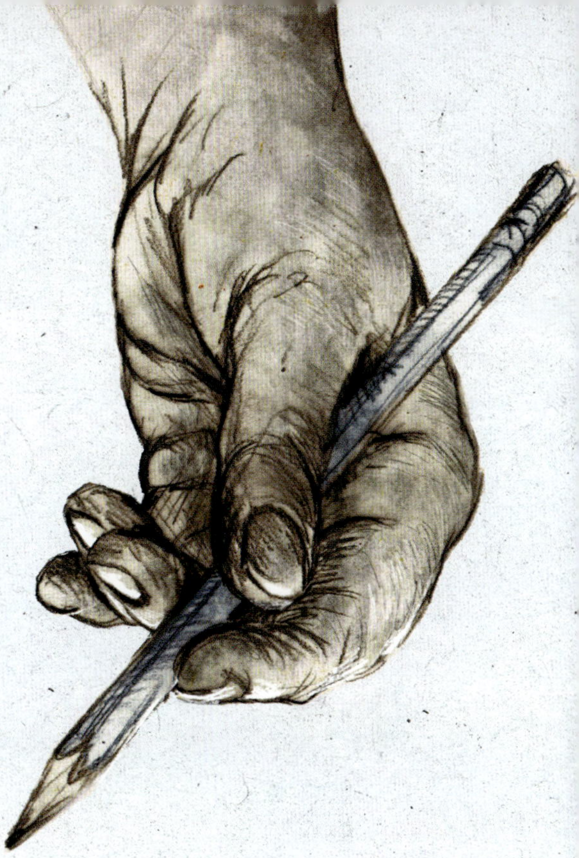

How to Read This Book

In these pages, I investigate the relationship between the art of drawing and the science of cognition.

Keep a pen or pencil and a sketchbook handy. Drawing can give you new tools to examine the worlds, real and imagined, inside and outside your own mind and help you discover hidden treasures and invent new ones.

From time to time, I suggest a short drawing exercise or thought experiment. To learn more about the science referenced in the main text, I invite you to explore the resources listed in the endnotes.

No prior experience or knowledge of drawing (at least since kindergarten!) required.

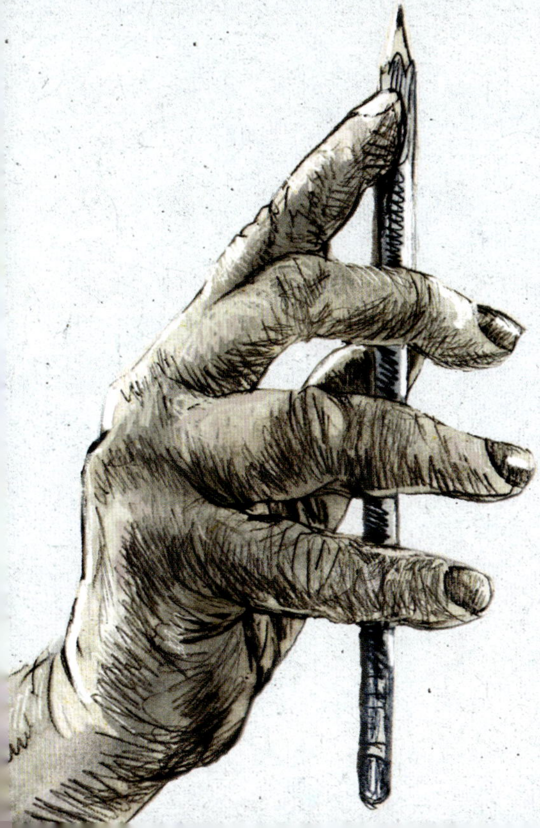

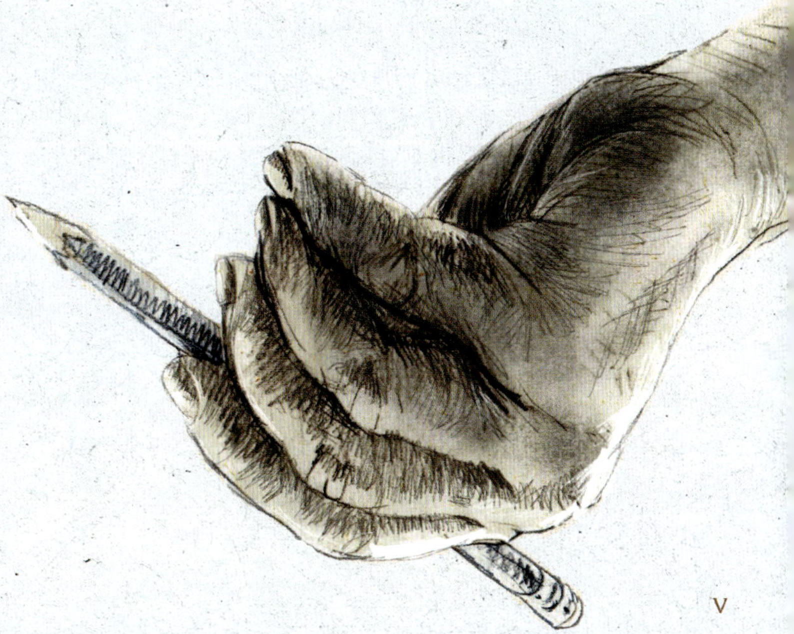

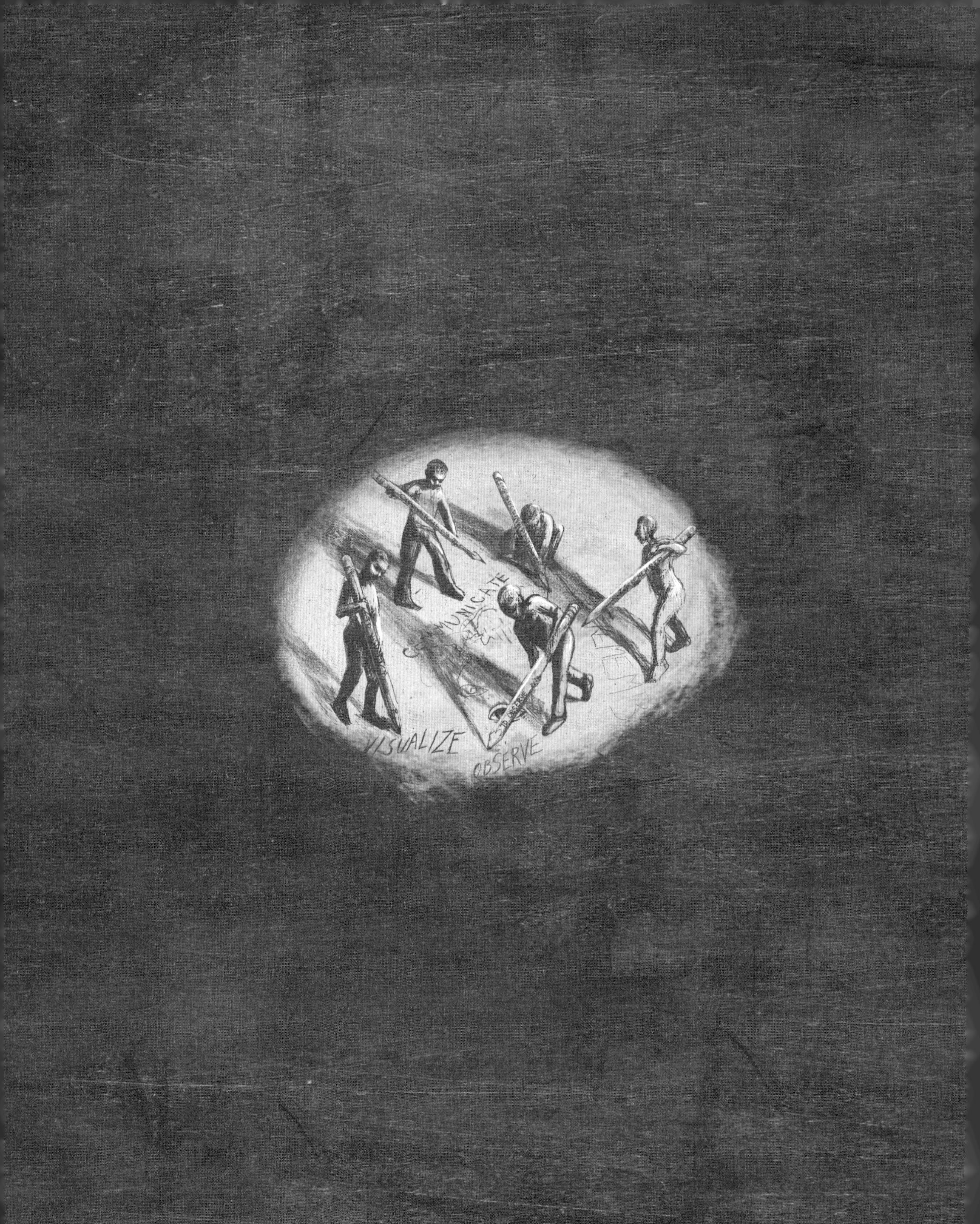
VISUALIZE
TO OBSERVE
OBSERVE

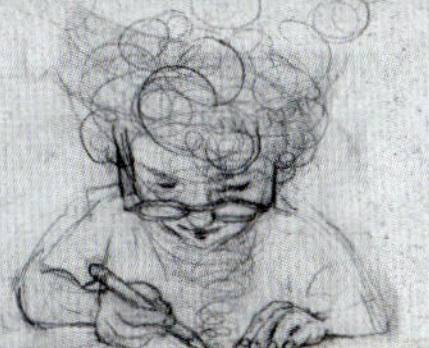

Prelude

Drawing, I locate my THOUGHTS, my SELF, in time and space.
Marks on paper connect inner and outer worlds.

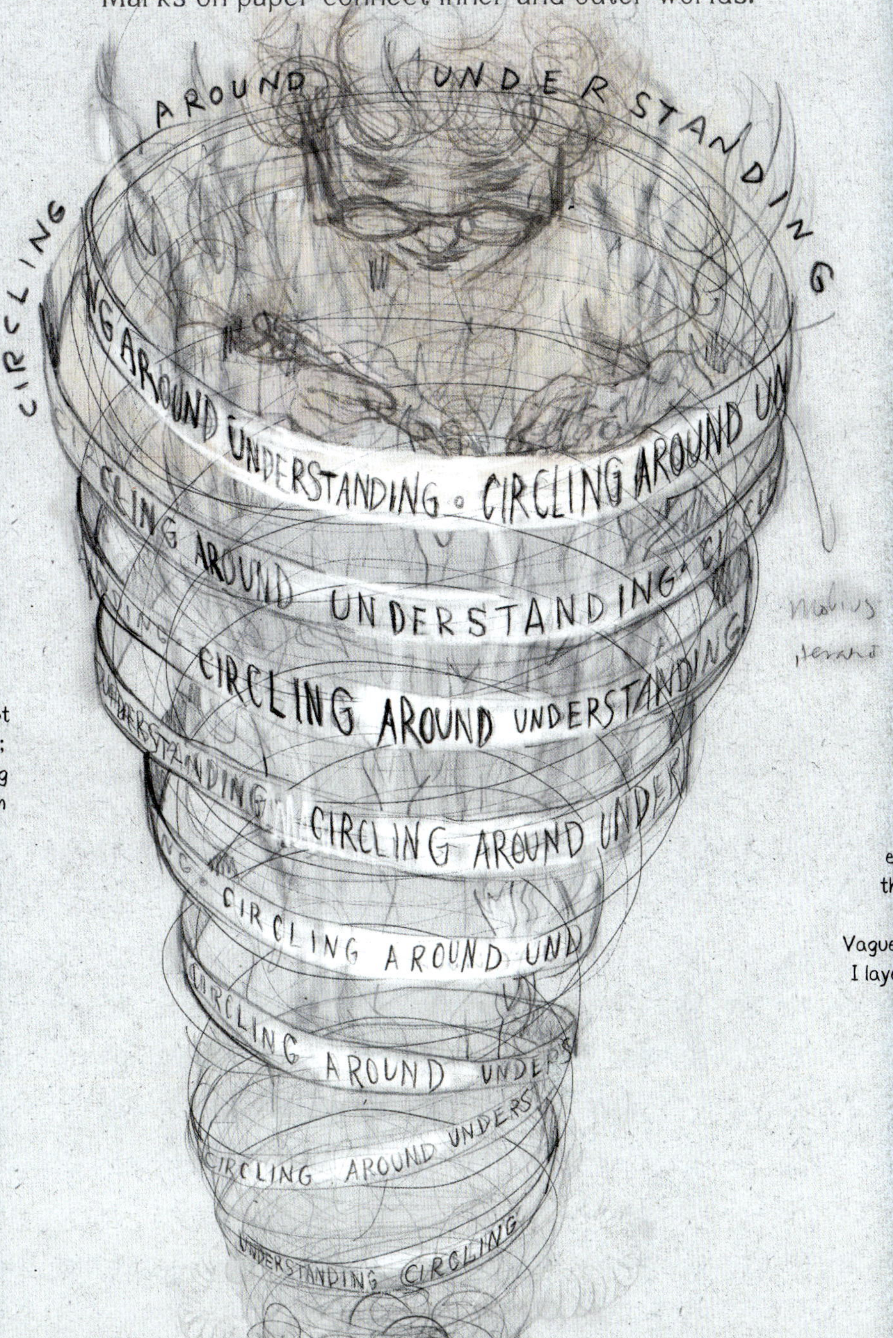

OBSERVING,
I draw IN the world, becoming aware of the place in which I find myself; sounds, smells, the temperature of the air...
When looking back at my sketchbooks days, weeks, even years later,
I feel the breeze on my cheek, hear the conversation at the next table, the dog barking in the distance.
I notice details I was not conscious of at the time; a child quizzically looking up at her dad, an unseen passageway.

From INSIDE my own mind I draw OUT images, fuzzy and indistinct at first, slowly taking shape on the surface before me.
Ideas, feelings, memories, and insights I didn't know I had appear on the page. I play, exploring forms, pulling them apart and putting them together again...
Vague impressions coalesce.
I layer and revise lines and shapes until something unforeseen emerges.

I draw what IS,
what IF, and
what MIGHT BE.

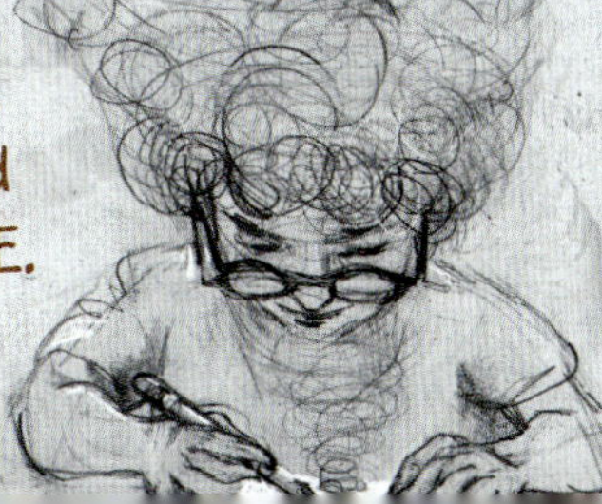

I draw to make the
world and my own
thoughts NEW again...

CONTENTS

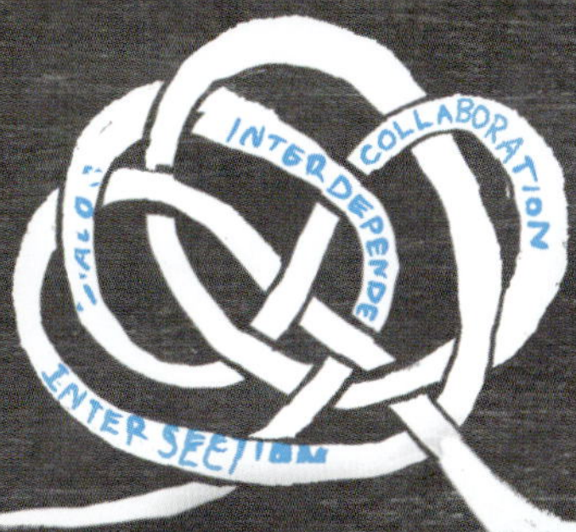

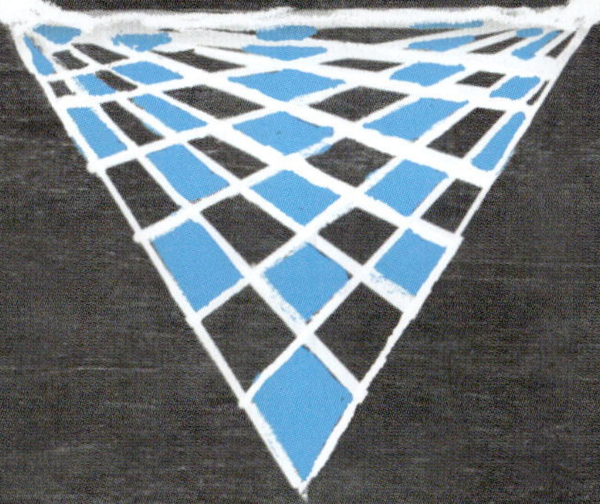

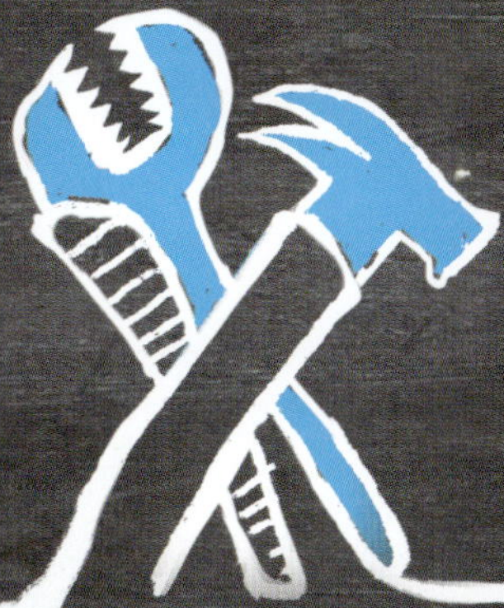

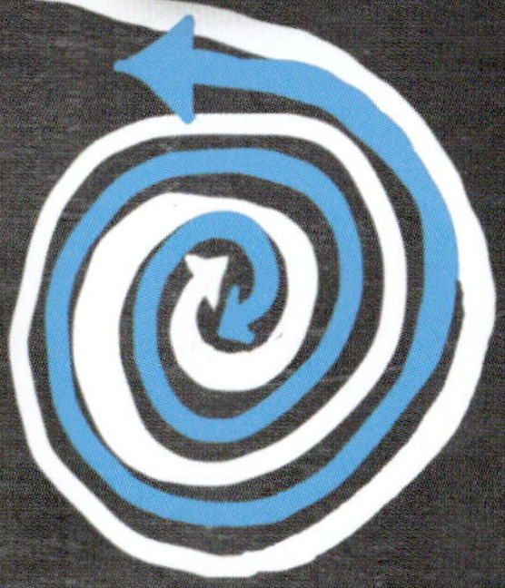

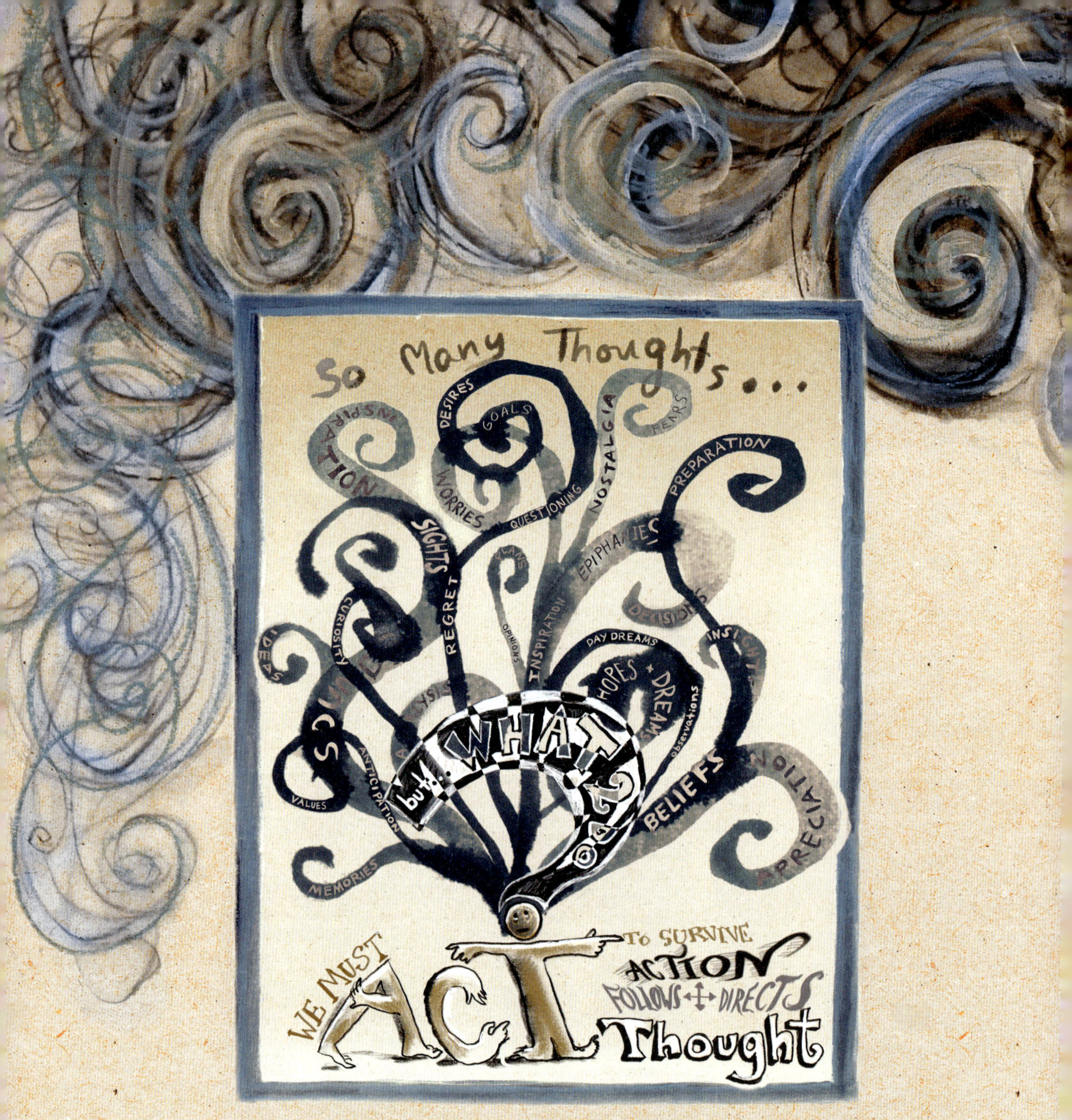
So Many Thoughts...
INSPIRATION
DESIRES
GOALS
NOSTALGIA
FEARS
PREPARATION
WORRIES
QUESTIONING
SIGHTS
REGRET
PLANS
EPIPHANIES
DECISIONS
INSIGHT
IDEAS
CURIOSITY
OPINIONS
INSPIRATION
DAY DREAMS
HOPES
DREAMS
OBSERVATIONS
BELIEFS
VALUES
ANTICIPATION
MEMORIES
APRECIATION
but... WHAT?
WE MUST ACT
TO SURVIVE
ACTION
FOLLOWS ↔ DIRECTS
Thought

chapter one

The Evolution of Thought

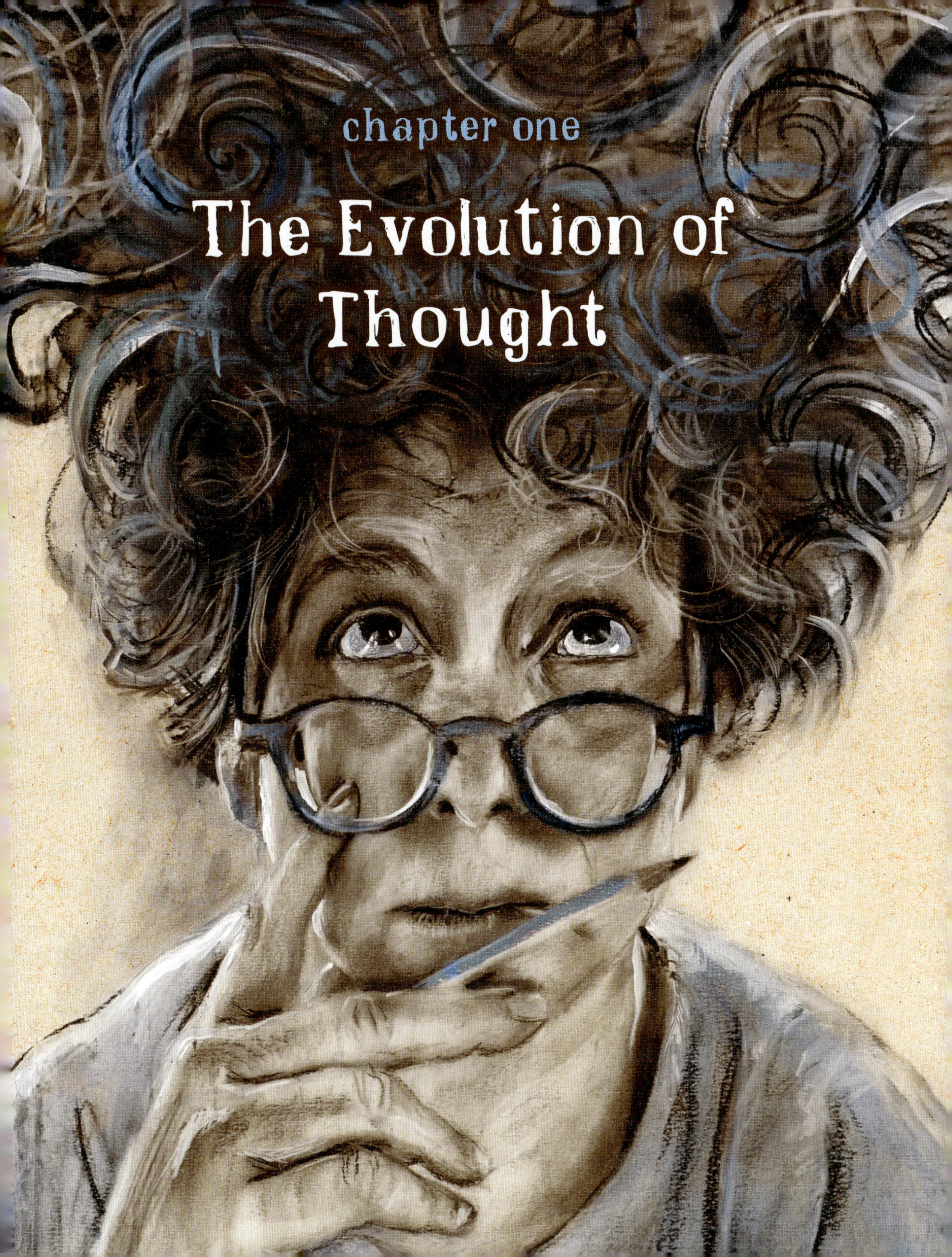

Drawing out the varied and variable evolution of our thoughts.

Our ability to think formed under the pressures of natural selection. We THINK to figure out what to DO in order to SURVIVE. Entangled patterns of thought and behavior evolved together to help us navigate the various environments in which we find ourselves. Myriad (sometimes contradictory) streams of thought FLOW together to guide our way through the world.

Drawing makes thought visible. It slows down thinking and helps the drawer pay attention to ambiguities that might otherwise be missed. Marks and lines elicit new thoughts as a drawing EVOLVES over TIME.

The practice of drawing is found across almost all known human cultures and time periods. We can imagine our ancient ancestors' thought processes based on the traces of their beliefs, ideas, and experiences left behind on cave walls.

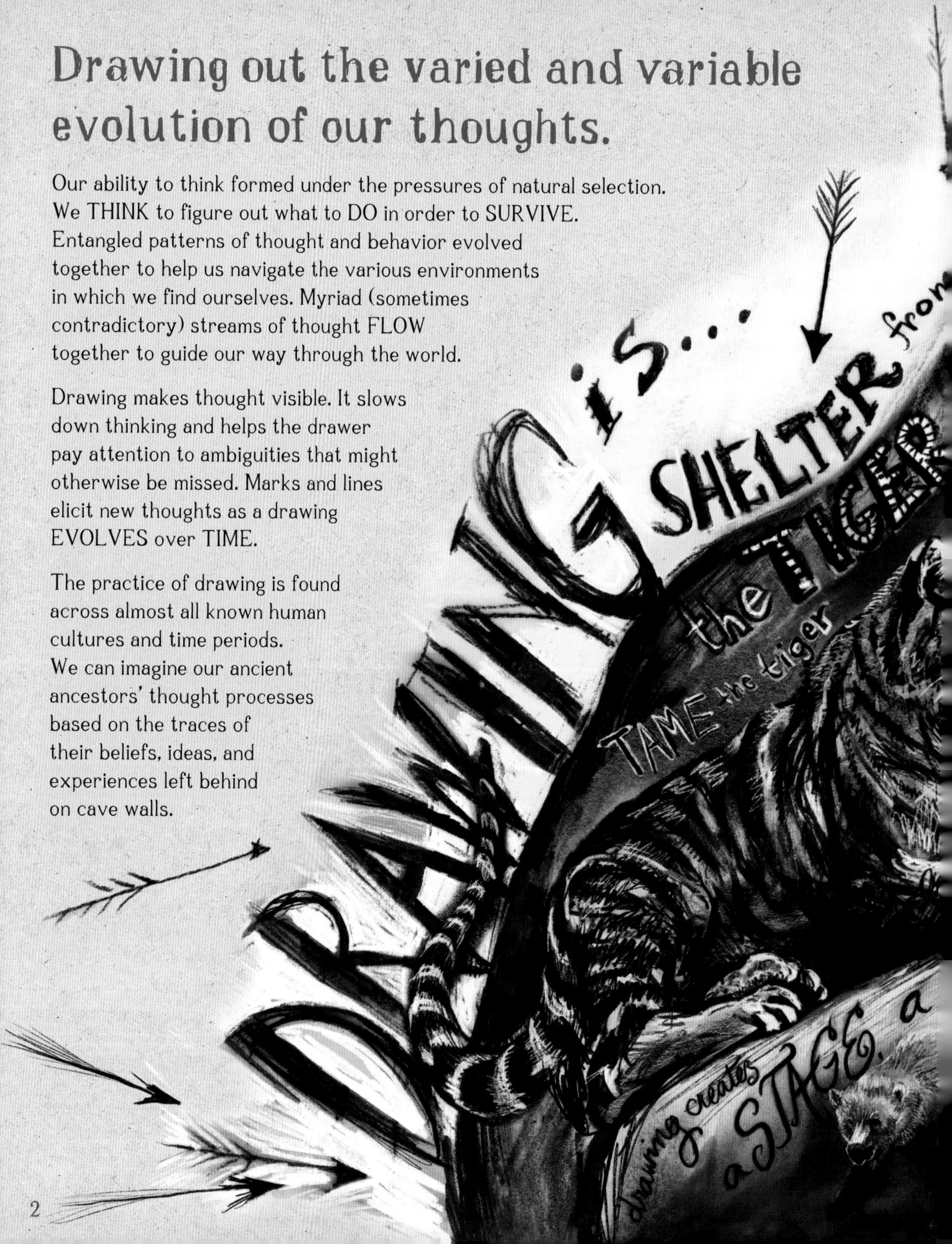

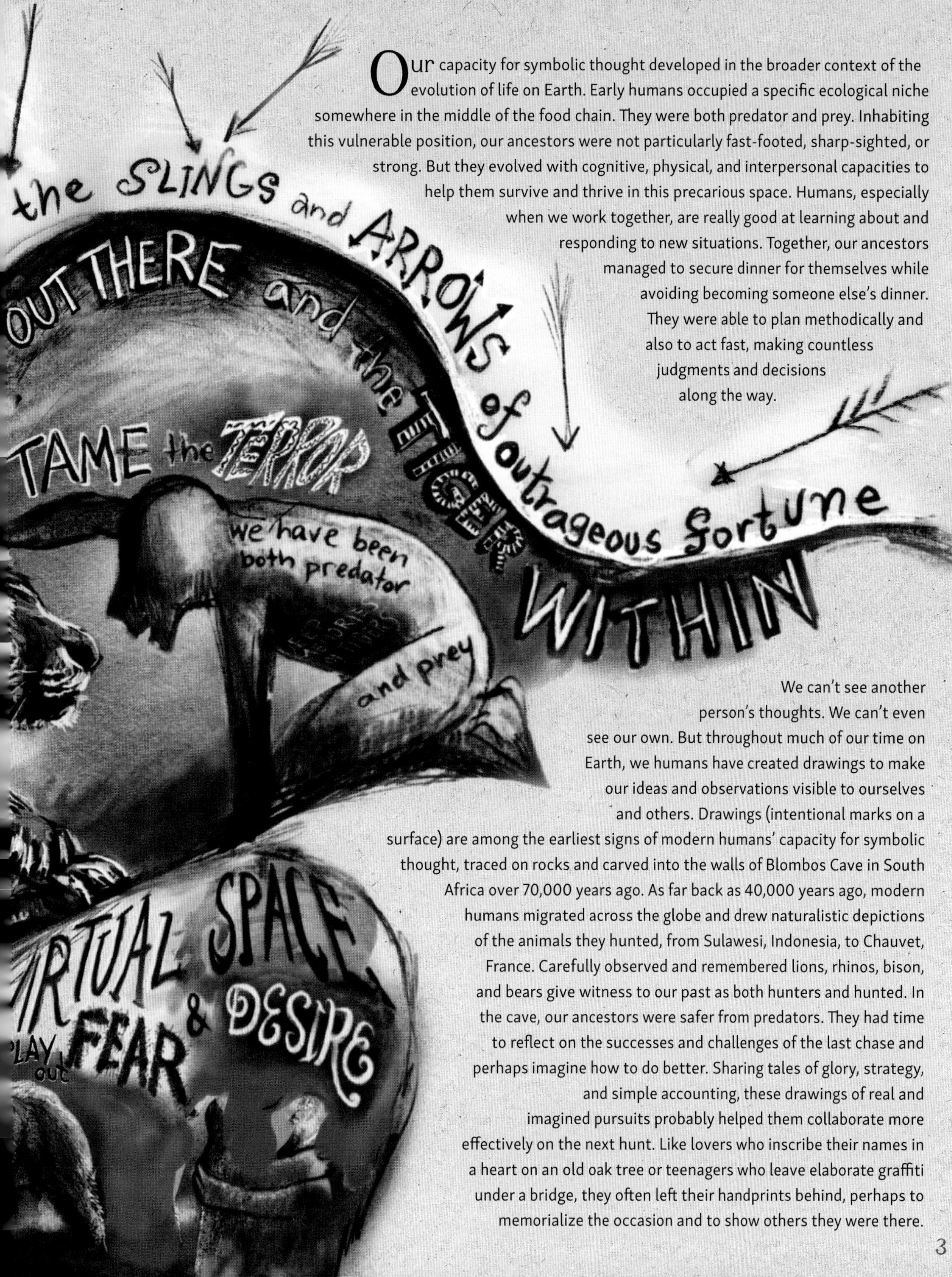

Our capacity for symbolic thought developed in the broader context of the evolution of life on Earth. Early humans occupied a specific ecological niche somewhere in the middle of the food chain. They were both predator and prey. Inhabiting this vulnerable position, our ancestors were not particularly fast-footed, sharp-sighted, or strong. But they evolved with cognitive, physical, and interpersonal capacities to help them survive and thrive in this precarious space. Humans, especially when we work together, are really good at learning about and responding to new situations. Together, our ancestors managed to secure dinner for themselves while avoiding becoming someone else's dinner. They were able to plan methodically and also to act fast, making countless judgments and decisions along the way.

We can't see another person's thoughts. We can't even see our own. But throughout much of our time on Earth, we humans have created drawings to make our ideas and observations visible to ourselves and others. Drawings (intentional marks on a surface) are among the earliest signs of modern humans' capacity for symbolic thought, traced on rocks and carved into the walls of Blombos Cave in South Africa over 70,000 years ago. As far back as 40,000 years ago, modern humans migrated across the globe and drew naturalistic depictions of the animals they hunted, from Sulawesi, Indonesia, to Chauvet, France. Carefully observed and remembered lions, rhinos, bison, and bears give witness to our past as both hunters and hunted. In the cave, our ancestors were safer from predators. They had time to reflect on the successes and challenges of the last chase and perhaps imagine how to do better. Sharing tales of glory, strategy, and simple accounting, these drawings of real and imagined pursuits probably helped them collaborate more effectively on the next hunt. Like lovers who inscribe their names in a heart on an old oak tree or teenagers who leave elaborate graffiti under a bridge, they often left their handprints behind, perhaps to memorialize the occasion and to show others they were there.

OBSERVE your THOUGHTS

Take a moment to sit quietly and pay attention to your own mind at work. What do you notice? Sitting at my desk in the early morning, I hear birds announcing the day's arrival. Looking out the window, I see a jogger go past, and infer that he's getting in his daily run before his workday begins. I could be wrong ... (maybe he's chasing a dog that ran out without its leash ... maybe his child forgot their lunch and he is trying to catch up with the school bus ...) It's spring and flowers are starting to bloom, which reminds me of my mother's delight at the first daffodils and crocuses of the year. As I take a break from writing, I think about the laundry that needs to be folded and put away, emails that need to be written,
yesterday's walk in the park.
What are your thoughts?

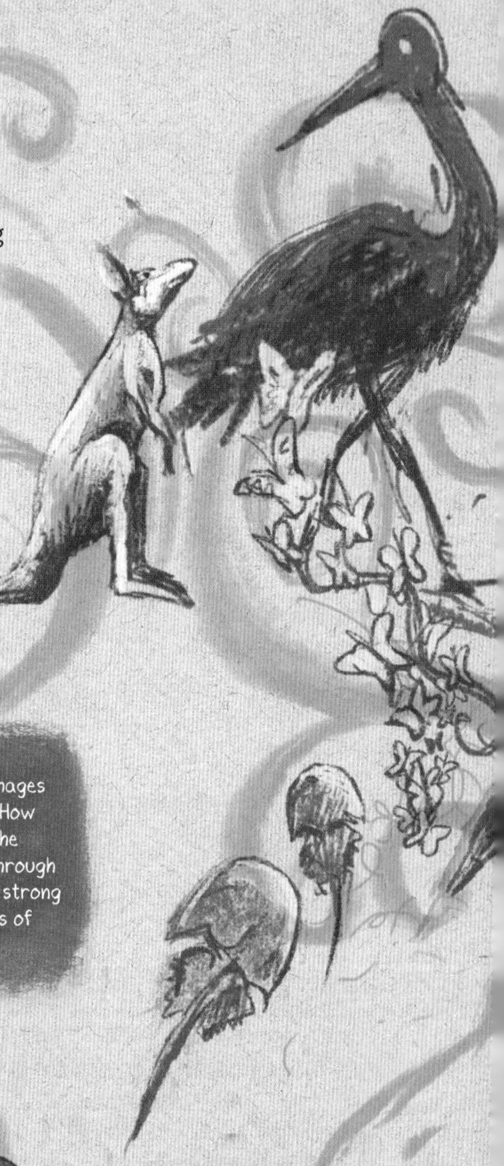

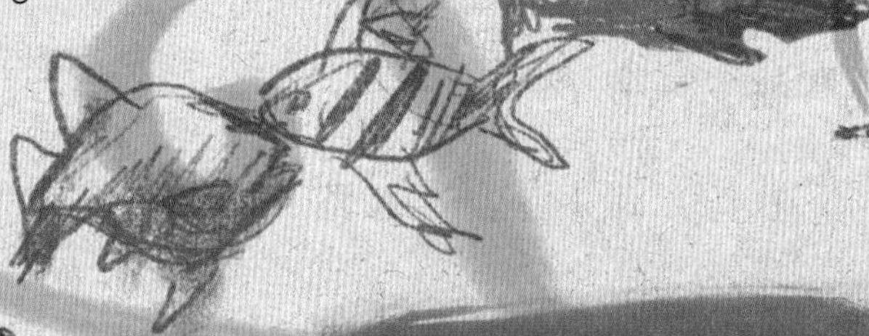

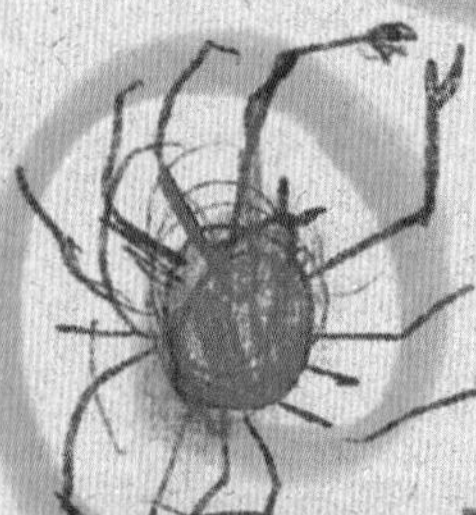

SKETCHNOTE YOUR THOUGHTS

Without overthinking it, try using very simple images or symbols to indicate a few of your thoughts. How does one idea lead to another? Try to mirror the quality of the relationship between two ideas through the quality of your line. (Is it shaky or loopy or strong and direct?) Sketchnoting can be a useful means of generating and elaborating on our thoughts.

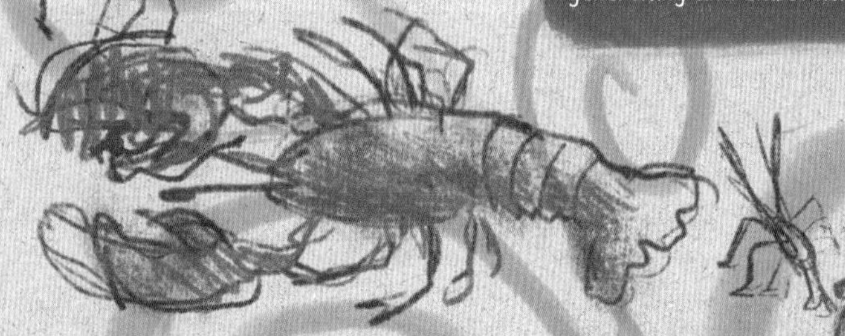

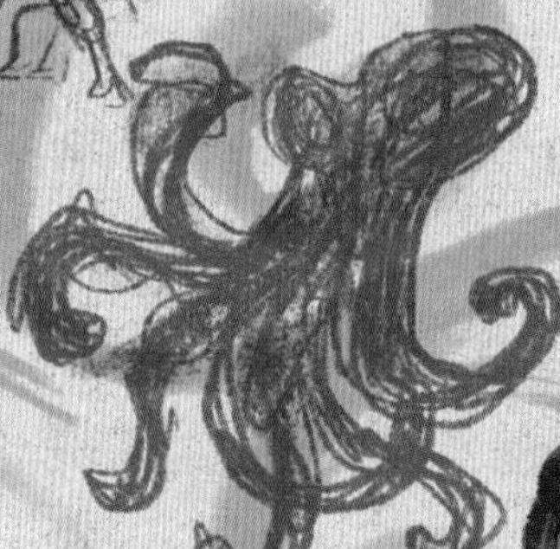

Our THOUGHTS are NOT always under our direct CONTROL.

Chances are, when you took a moment to observe, you noticed how your thoughts tended to float from past to future and back again, moving swiftly and naturally between ideas and perceptions, memories and plans. We might sometimes wish our minds were better organized, with our thoughts neatly tucked and stacked into tidy boxes, to be pulled out and opened at will. Like my laundry at the moment, they are anything but. We don't always know what we are thinking, or why we are thinking it. It can feel like our thoughts have minds of their own.

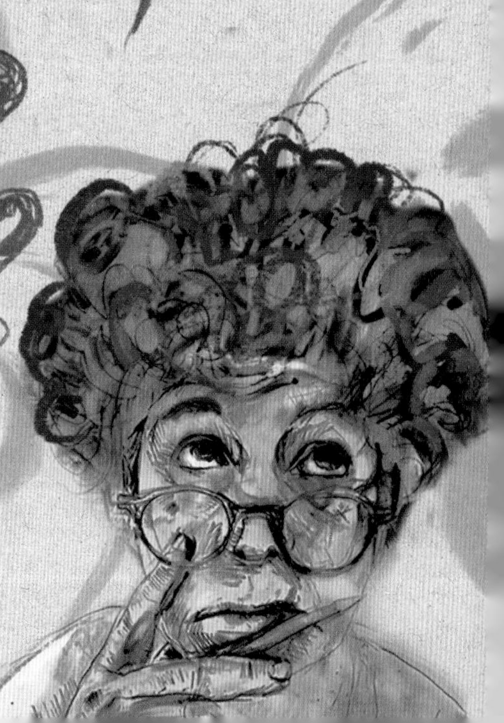

What we experience as MIND arises from structures and processes of the BRAIN.

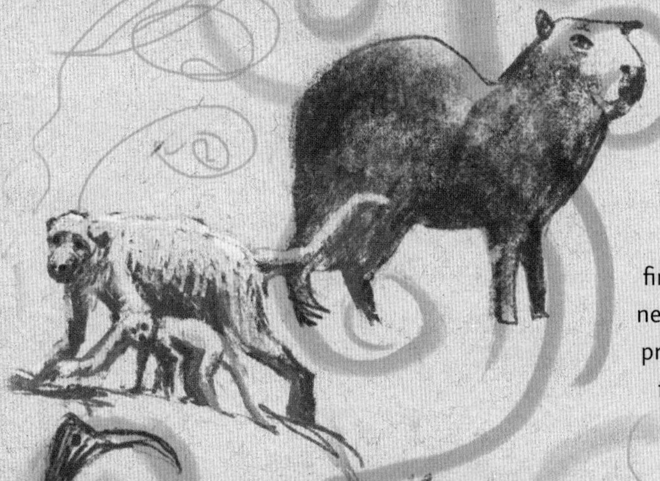

INFORMED by millennia of evolutionary processes, the workings of the human brain are COMPLEX and EXTRAVAGANT. Our capacity for symbolic thought (which underlies our proclivity for drawing out our thoughts) may be a distinctive feature of our species. The human brain evolved over eons; it was not designed in a lab. We have inherited equipment that originally served ancient physical imperatives to cooperate, find food, and successfully reproduce. Through chance mutations and necessities of survival in a dangerous world, the cerebral cortex of our primate ancestors expanded exponentially. The resulting neocortex is full of alternative pathways, fault lines, and work-arounds. That rich proliferation of interconnections in our expanded neocortex is one of the secrets of our remarkable ADAPTABILITY.

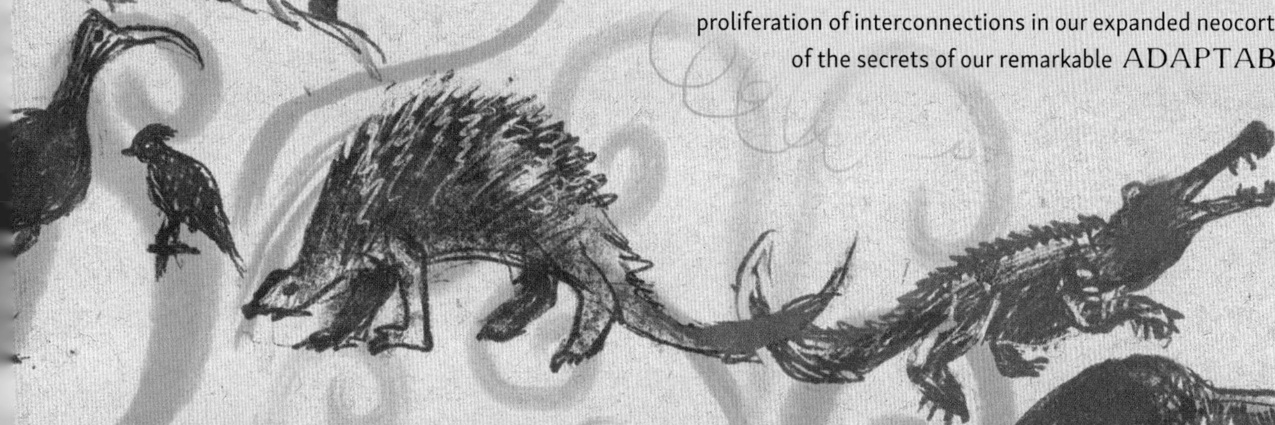

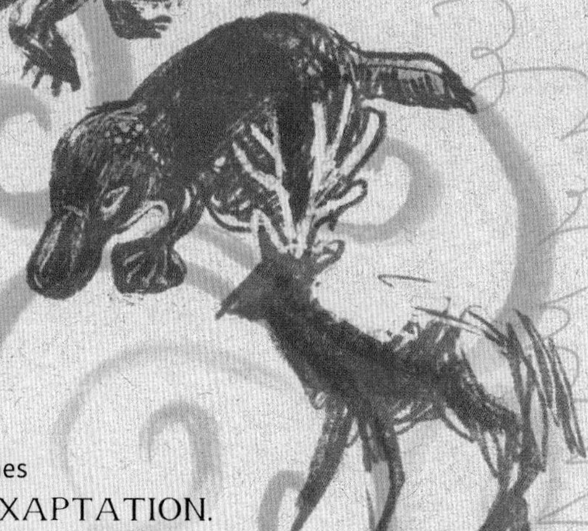

EVERYTHING that IS, WAS once something ELSE.

The rock in my hand was once molten lava deep below the earth's crust. Million-year-old glaciers in Antarctica are now melting into the ocean. In daily life, something that was useful in one context can become useful in another. I bring my ceramic coffee mug outside as I look through some papers, but as I finish my coffee, I realize the heavy mug makes a great paperweight.

Among living things, a trait that evolved in response to certain conditions sometimes becomes useful in a different way. Evolutionary biologists call this phenomenon EXAPTATION. Some dinosaurs possessed feathers long before they developed the ability to fly. The sutures in skulls of all young vertebrates allow for growth, but in mammals they facilitate birth by allowing for compression. Once they no longer needed to use their thumbs and strong grip to swing through trees, early humans used their opposable thumbs for new purposes: to make and use tools.

New abilities are both facilitated and constrained by the circumstances of their historical genesis. Many of humankind's exceptional cognitive, physical, and social capacities can be traced back to those we inherited from our ancestors and then put to new purposes. Among the higher primates, only our species had the cognitive and collaborative ability to spread in large numbers across the planet, learning to survive and thrive in environments from the Arctic to the Equator.

Thought is EMBODIED and SITUATED in the environments in which we find ourselves.

Human thought consists of a complex series of interactions between our brain, bodies, and the environment. As we move through the world, we make sense of current experiences based on prior knowledge and innate cognitive predispositions. We are aware of much less than we realize at any given moment. Our attention may be limited, but it is flexible and responsive, constantly adjusting to external and internal changes.

Our understandings and perceptions are continually updated from multiple sources of information flowing between the central nervous system (including the brain), the whole body, and our surroundings.

We LEARN from EXPERIENCE.

Our thoughts are not bounded by instinct or innate predisposition: they are malleable. We learn by trial and error. (Babies will often throw their spoons or dishes on the floor, just to see if someone will pick them up again!) We respond flexibly to new experiences, by virtue of our remarkable ability to learn from one another and the environment in which we find ourselves. We can respond to opportunities that may become available in unfamiliar or ambiguous situations. We are able to work together to adapt to whatever might happen next: we can "GO with the FLOW."

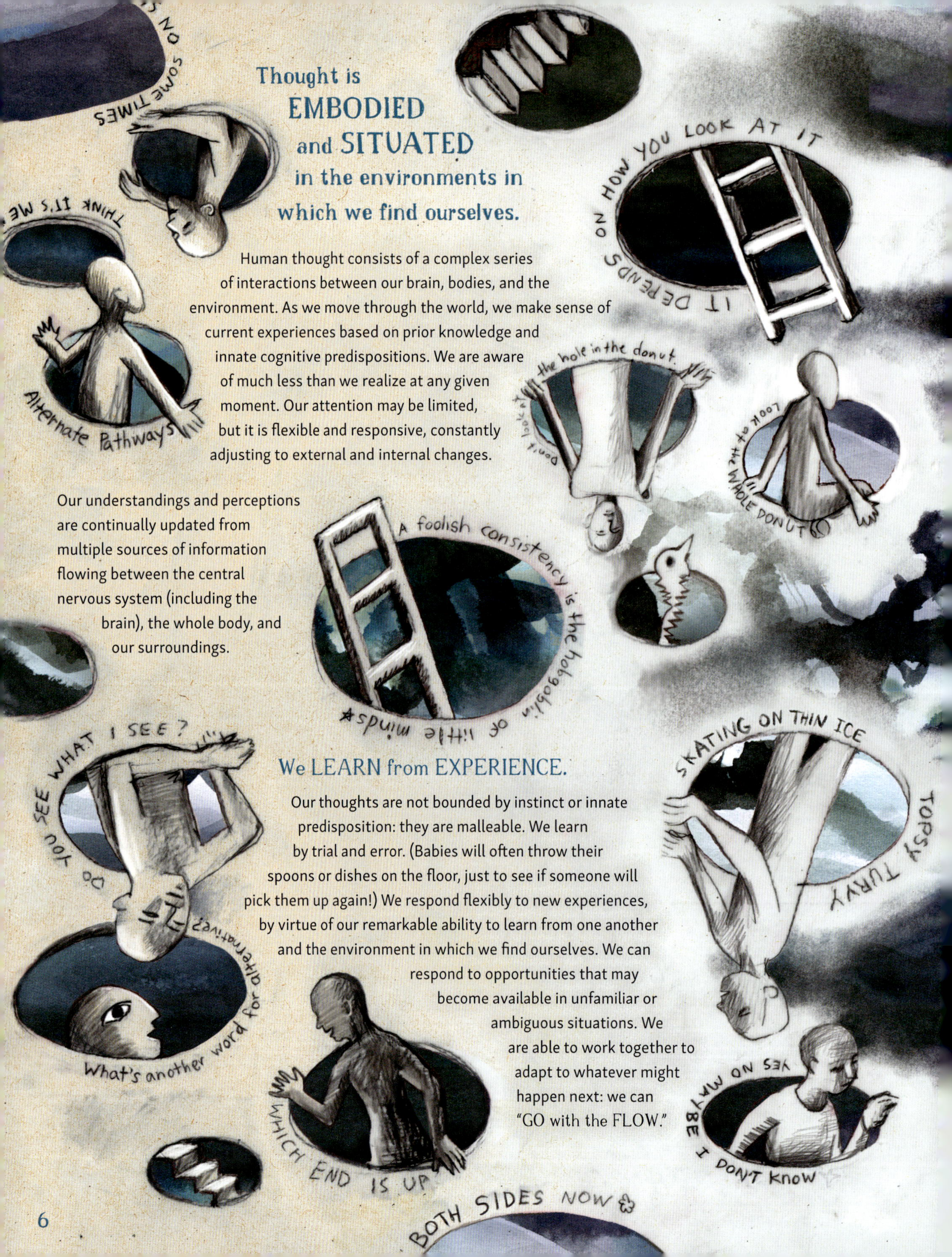

Consciousness is FLUID and continuous.

The nineteenth-century philosopher William James first coined the expression "stream of consciousness." He argued against what was (and remains) a popular mechanical model of the brain/mind. His fluid analogy conveys that thoughts are not contained in discrete boxes neatly stacked together to form our understanding of the world and ourselves. Instead, James proposed that thought is continuous and infinitely variable, a river in which waters are always changing. We can never experience exactly the same thought twice. Yet the clean and rational metaphor of the brain as machine persisted, appealing to human preferences for orderly and systematic explanations.

"Consciousness, then, does not appear itself CHOPPED UP in BITS. ... It is NOTHING JOINTED; It flows. A 'river' or 'stream' are the metaphors by which it is most naturally described. In talking of it hereafter, let us call it the stream of Thought, of consciousness, or of subjective thought."

~ William James, The Principles of Psychology 1890

We have built thinking machines.

Our minds calculate well enough to invent and build computers millions of times faster and more precise at calculation than we are. Engineers design computational systems that teach themselves to solve well-defined problems much faster and better than humans. We have even built instruments that can measure the flow of our thoughts.

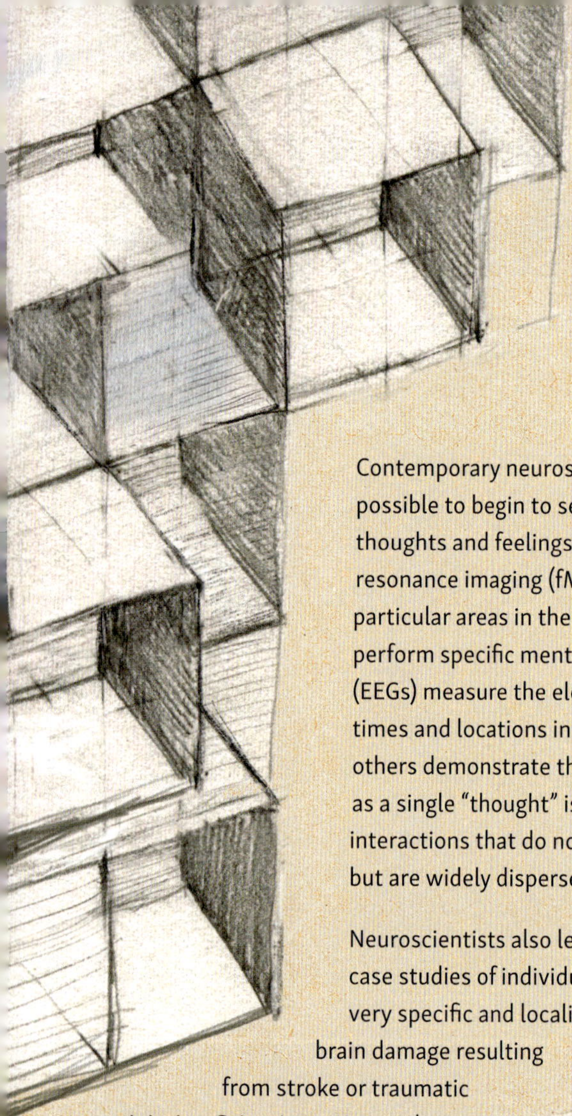

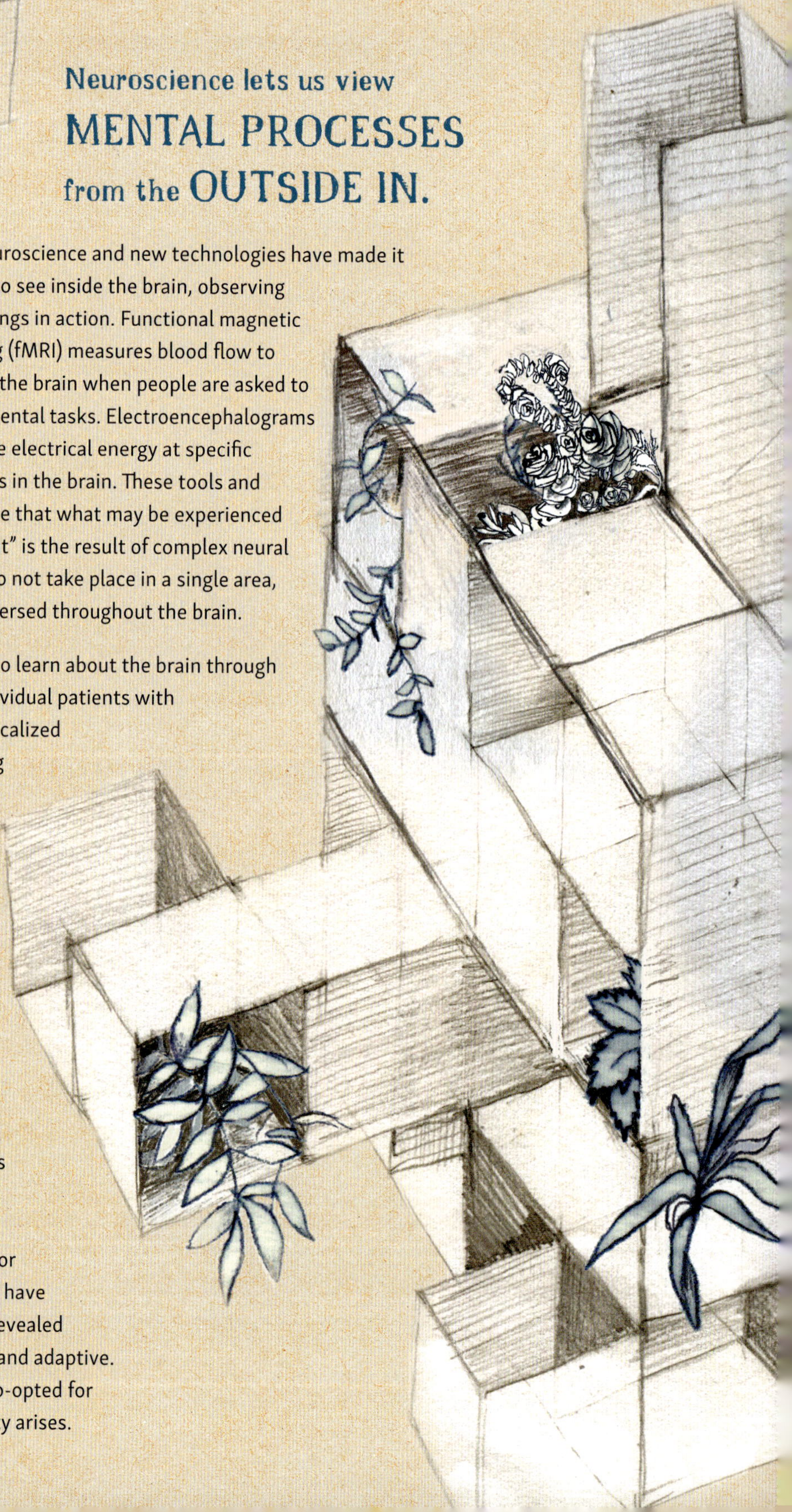

Neuroscience lets us view MENTAL PROCESSES from the OUTSIDE IN.

Contemporary neuroscience and new technologies have made it possible to begin to see inside the brain, observing thoughts and feelings in action. Functional magnetic resonance imaging (fMRI) measures blood flow to particular areas in the brain when people are asked to perform specific mental tasks. Electroencephalograms (EEGs) measure the electrical energy at specific times and locations in the brain. These tools and others demonstrate that what may be experienced as a single "thought" is the result of complex neural interactions that do not take place in a single area, but are widely dispersed throughout the brain.

Neuroscientists also learn about the brain through case studies of individual patients with very specific and localized brain damage resulting from stroke or traumatic injuries. Scientists gain insight into healthy brain function by finding out what these patients can and cannot do.

When an area of the brain that performed a certain function becomes damaged, a different part of the brain may take over that job. With appropriate interventions, patients with severe injuries can sometimes regain important functions over time.

The brain changes in response to experiences and opportunities moment by moment. It's possible to learn to walk or talk again after a stroke that left a person, at first, speechless or unable to walk. Case studies of patients who have experienced a variety of brain injuries have revealed how neural circuits are flexible, interwoven, and adaptive. Brain areas used for one purpose are often co-opted for other functions when the need or opportunity arises.

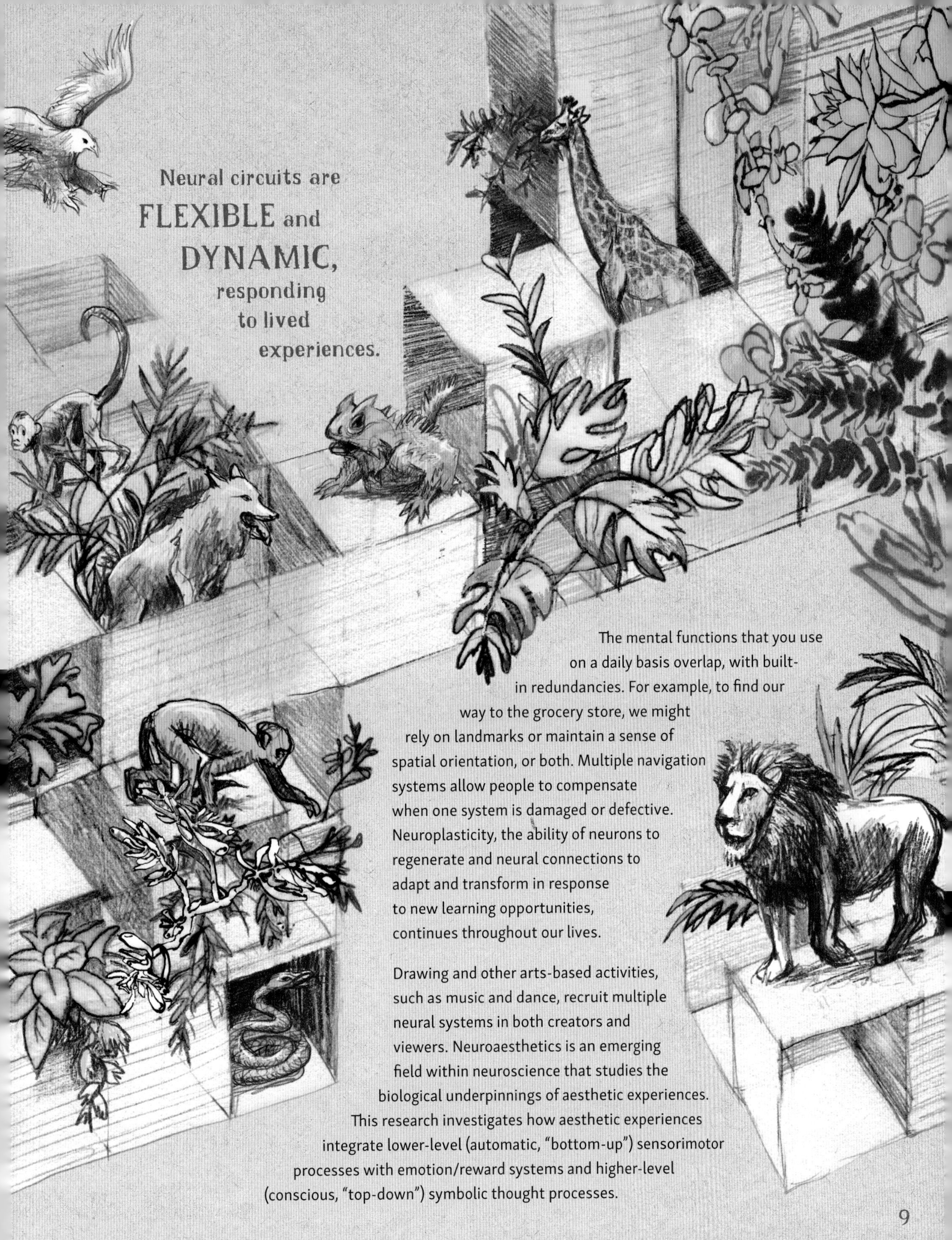

Neural circuits are **FLEXIBLE** and **DYNAMIC,** responding to lived experiences.

The mental functions that you use on a daily basis overlap, with built-in redundancies. For example, to find our way to the grocery store, we might rely on landmarks or maintain a sense of spatial orientation, or both. Multiple navigation systems allow people to compensate when one system is damaged or defective. Neuroplasticity, the ability of neurons to regenerate and neural connections to adapt and transform in response to new learning opportunities, continues throughout our lives.

Drawing and other arts-based activities, such as music and dance, recruit multiple neural systems in both creators and viewers. Neuroaesthetics is an emerging field within neuroscience that studies the biological underpinnings of aesthetic experiences. This research investigates how aesthetic experiences integrate lower-level (automatic, “bottom-up”) sensorimotor processes with emotion/reward systems and higher-level (conscious, “top-down”) symbolic thought processes.

Thought flows in TWO DIRECTIONS

Conscious, goal-directed thought proceeds from the TOP DOWN. When we are thinking hard, our eyebrows knit together or we might gaze upward. We tend to point toward the part of the brain directly behind our forehead, which is called our prefrontal cortex (PFC). This region is essential to what cognitive scientists label "executive function." The human PFC is more developed than that of other mammals, including our closest cousins, not just in the volume of neurons but also in the amount of glial cells, which connect neurons in different parts of the brain and nervous system.

Executive function, anchored in the prefrontal cortex, recruits other brain regions associated with attention and information processing. It includes goal-directed tasks, such as planning, analyzing, evaluating, and self-regulation, which are initiated by an explicit reasoning process. We set agendas, schedule events, and keep appointments. Metacognition, the awareness and understanding of one's cognitive processes (thinking about thinking), is also a conscious top-down process. If the prefrontal cortex is damaged, it's possible to survive, but a lot can go wrong. It might no longer be possible to make plans or consider the consequences of one's actions. The ability to function independently in the world could be lost.

Much thought flows from the BOTTOM UP. That song you can't get out of your head, the brownie you are craving, the person sitting at the next table who looks a lot like your long-lost friend: so many of our thoughts have little to do with our conscious goals. Initiated by external or internal stimuli, thoughts float through our minds unbidden, such as memories triggered by a smell or sound.

Bottom-up processes happen in real time, in response to situations as they occur. These include learned and automated habits, routines, and skills, like those used for driving a car and riding a bicycle, which are deployed as needed in the moment. Unwelcome, intrusive, frightening thoughts and sudden, illuminating insights into seemingly impossible situations all flow from the bottom up.

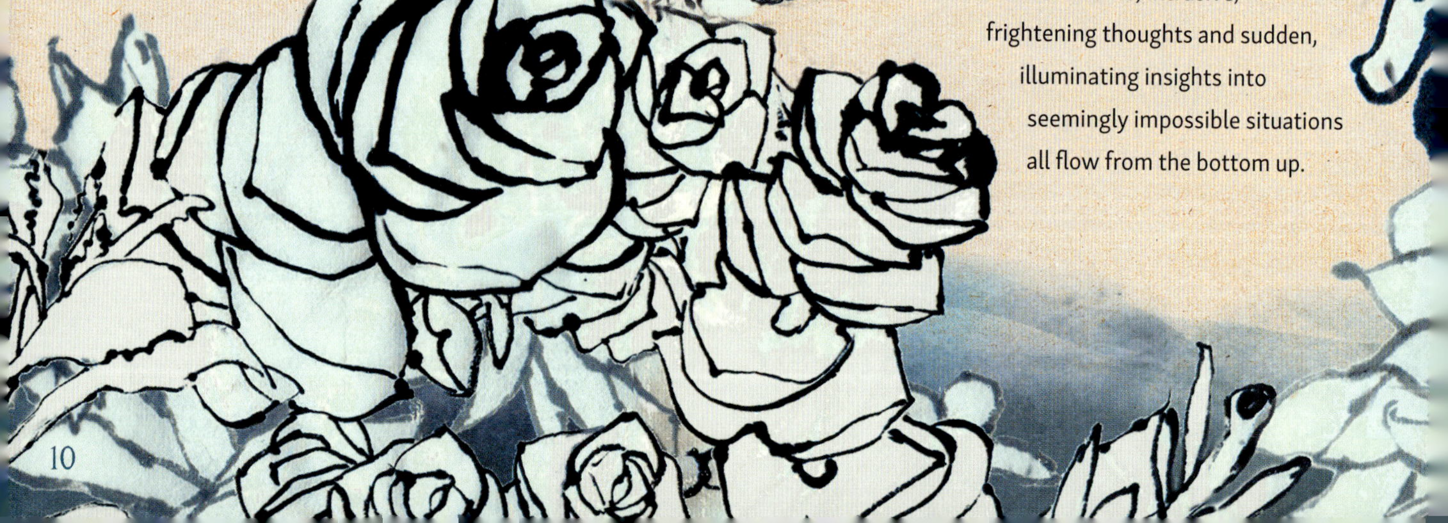

EMOTIONS are bodily responses to change, to both external events (such as a loud noise) and internal cues (such as hunger). The basic emotions of joy, sadness, fear, anger, surprise, and disgust each have distinct neural signatures. These basic emotions are universal across cultures and even shared with other animals. We intuit them in other people's involuntary facial expressions and body language.

Emotions can be generated and regulated by both TOP-DOWN and BOTTOM-UP processes. If I suddenly hear a sudden loud bang, I experience (feel) fear, resulting from bottom-up sensory cues. As I read the latest news reports on melting glaciers and forest fires, I might also experience (feel) fear, based on top-down judgments I make based on prior knowledge of the significance of those reported events.

In common parlance, emotions and feelings are interchangeable concepts. Neuroscientists, however, make an important distinction: emotions are universal, involuntary physical responses that we share with other animals; FEELINGS are nuanced, subjective EXPERIENCES of emotional states, mediated by personal history and the larger cultural context. Neuroscientist Antonio Damasio explains, "The ability to 'feel' feelings extends the reach of the emotions by facilitating the creation of new forms of adaptive response."

As I relax in the sunshine, a sudden loud BANG activates a mixed emotional response of surprise and fear. I feel apprehensive and look around. I realize it was just a car backfiring as it started up. I feel satisfied there is nothing to worry about and return to enjoying a beautiful day at the park. Or perhaps I look up at the sky and see storm clouds gathering. I feel worried, quickly gather my things, and seek shelter before the rain starts.

Emotions put us in MOTION. Our feelings help us pay attention, make sense of emotions, and figure out what to do next. We learn to FEEL OUR WAY through changing and sometimes challenging situations and environments.

"The life of REASON…demands…a LOVE of TRUTH and a CONTEMPT for lying, a CONCERN

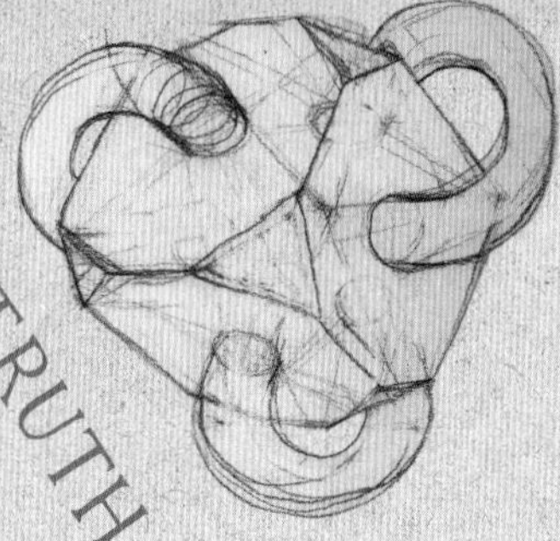

FEAR and anger, JOY and contentment, sadness and disgust recruit different neural processes and feedback loops between raw bodily sensations, emotions, feelings, and conscious thoughts. Emotions are universal, but feelings (how we interpret and what we do with our emotions) are unique to the individual. We can learn to sit with difficult emotions like fear and anger that might otherwise stir us to fight or flight. Instead, we can consider what prompted our negative emotions, transforming our felt experience and response.

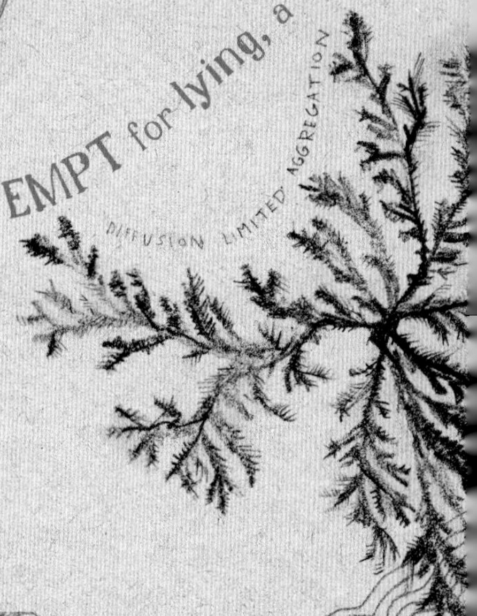

EMOTION and REASON are in a dynamic relationship of feeling and knowing that help us negotiate between inner and outer worlds. If we ignore our fears while walking down a dark alley at night, we might miss shifting shadows or muffled footsteps that could signify danger. In broad daylight, ignoring joy, we might miss the opportunity for the quiet pleasure a clear blue sky offers. If we only pay attention to our emotions, we could miss fun adventures out of fear or never make it to work on time due to our happiness, sitting at home drinking our morning coffee. Our emotions alert us to changes in ourselves and surroundings, and feelings and thoughts help us figure out what to do about it. According to Damasio (an expert on the intimate relationship between emotion and reason), consciousness itself is simply the feeling of knowing that we have feelings.

We are INFOVORES. There is nothing more human than the hunger for information, whether it's neighborhood gossip, sports scores, or the latest political news bulletin. We can easily get addicted to scrolling through our phones to discover the latest gossip among our online "friends." Neuroscientists Ed Vessel and Irving Biederman discovered that opioid-driven pleasure receptors in our brains respond to fresh understandings of complex phenomena. There are more opioid receptors at higher levels of understanding and this very real chemical underpinning extends to aesthetic experience. Once we satisfy our immediate physical needs, we are driven to pursue our favorite flavor of cognitive delight, whether it is insight into a difficult mathematical equation or a hike to a spectacular mountain top view. There is real pleasure in "drawing out" new meaning from what we thought we knew.

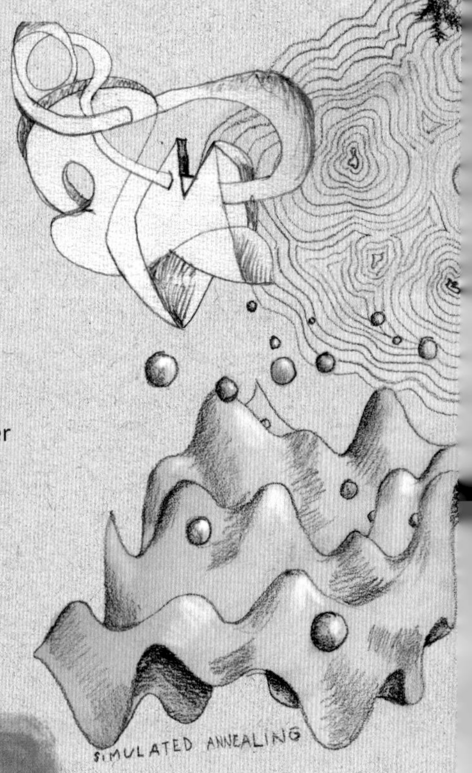

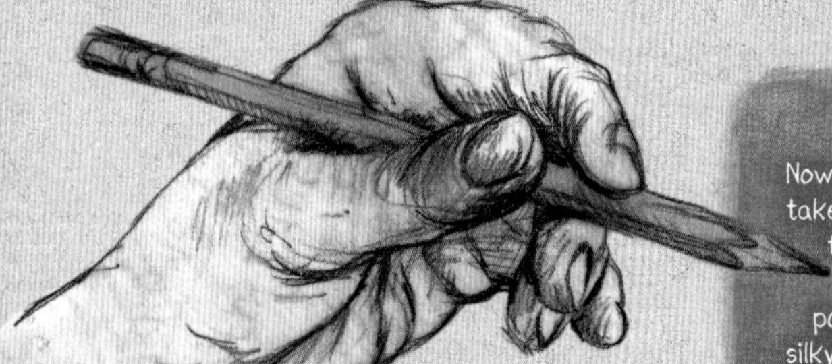

FEEL YOUR THOUGHTS…

Now that we are near the end of this chapter, take a minute to feel the qualities of your thoughts. What is their rhythm (staccato or legato?), their shape (round or pointy?), their texture (fuzzy, rough, or silky?) Are they heavy or light? Perhaps contradictory thoughts are going through your mind. Make a quick sketch that expresses some qualities of your thoughts **RIGHT NOW.**

Philosopher of science and education Israel Scheffler identified cognitive emotions such as "concern for accuracy in observation and inference, and a corresponding repugnance at error in logic or fact" that are intrinsic to the drawing process.

r accuracy in observation and inference, and a corresponding REPUGNANCE at error in LOGIC or FACT…”

— Israel Scheffler, *In Praise of the Cognitive Emotions*

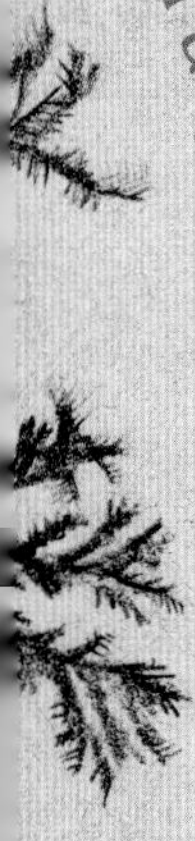

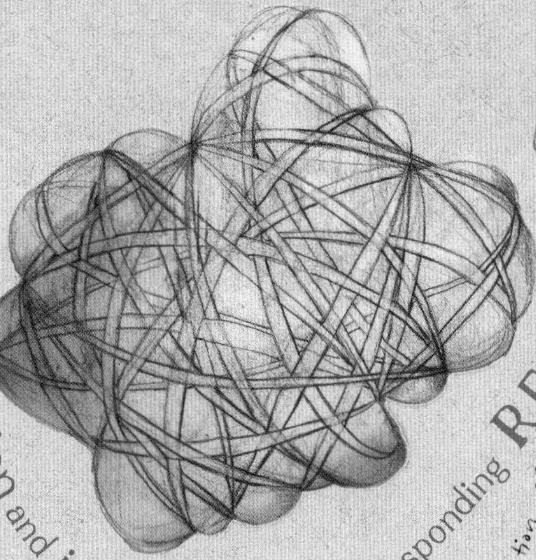

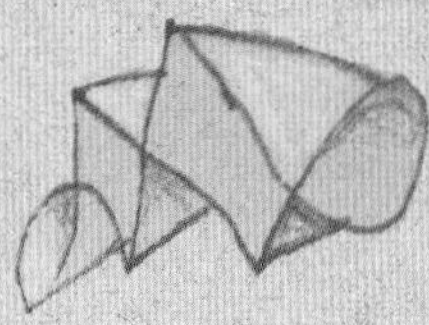

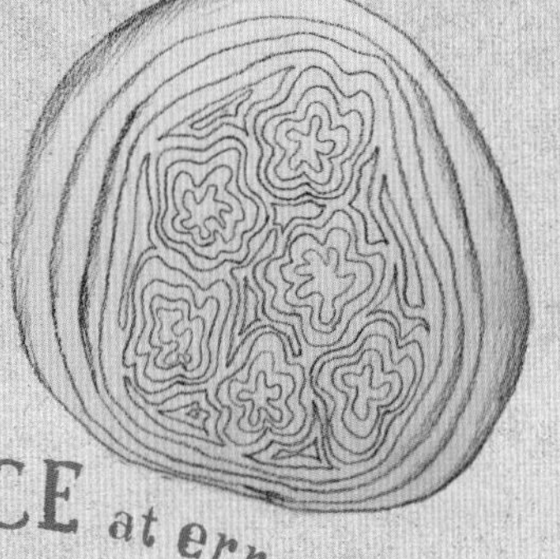

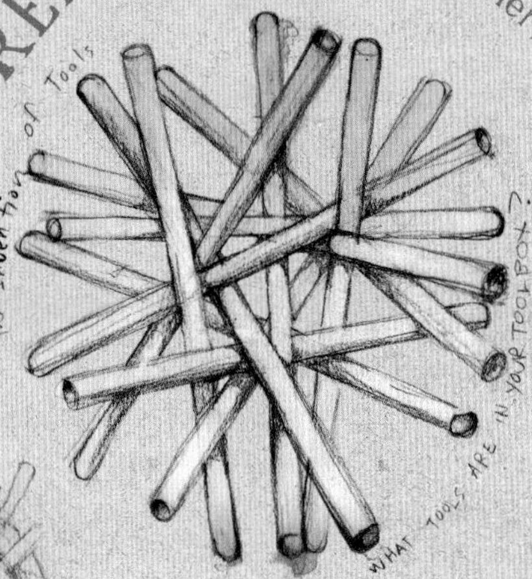

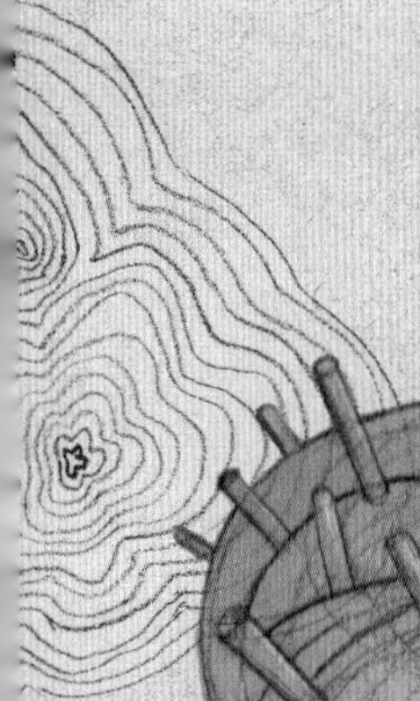

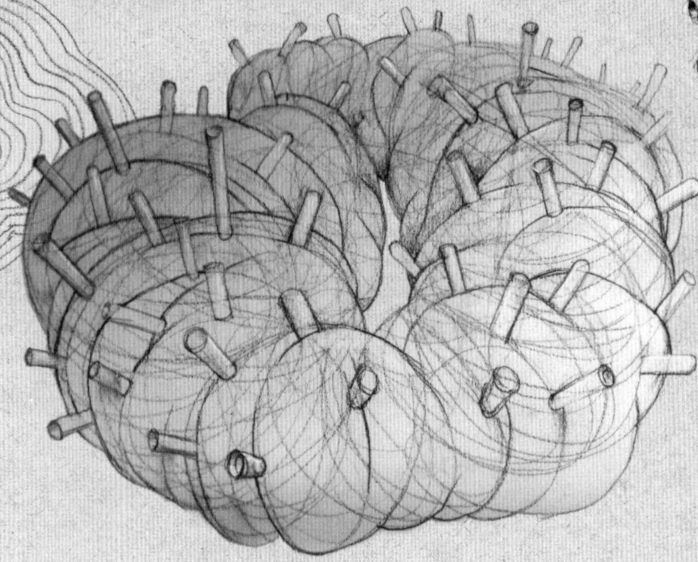

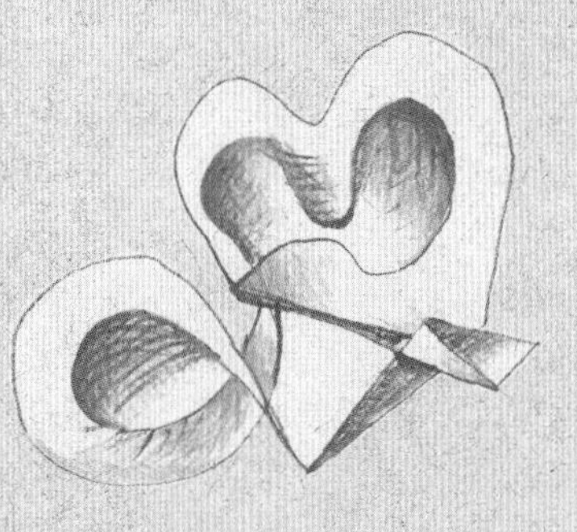

Drawings make our thoughts visible from the INSIDE OUT.

Our minds naturally wander. When confronted with an ambiguous or unknown situation, it can help to let go of preconceived ideas and goals, for a moment at least. Whether we are drawing or daydreaming or even when we are moved by a work of art, we often find personal meaning in unexpected places. Neuroscientists call this state of mind activation of the default mode network. Loosening top-down, executive control of thinking processes and allowing thoughts to wander widely over the landscape of our minds, we sometimes happen upon a solution where we least expect it. On a leisurely walk, the work-around for a stubborn computer glitch or an idea I couldn't put into words before suddenly occurs to me. It could be the result of seeing things from a different angle, coming at a problem from the opposite direction.

The nature of thought is dynamic, always in flux, always moving forward. Drawing materializes the fluid, continuous, iterative, and action-oriented nature of human thought. We can record the paths our minds take and revisit, revise, and reconstruct these mental journeys. We can play with alternatives.

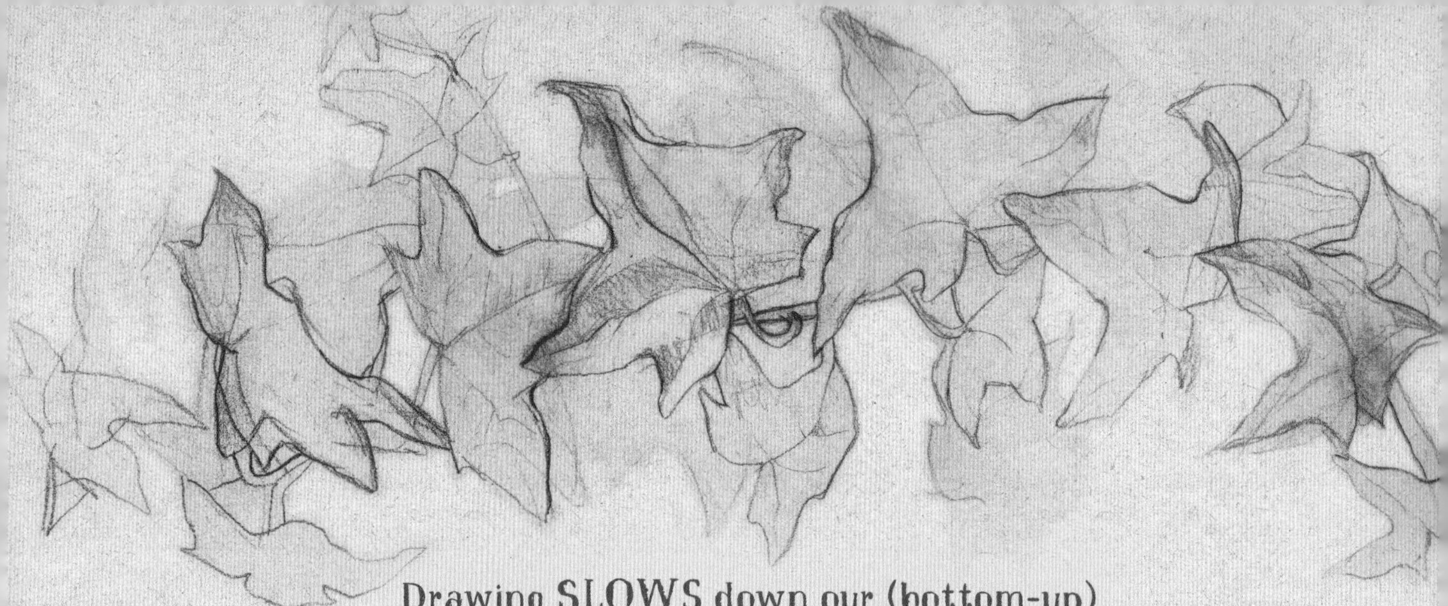

Drawing SLOWS down our (bottom-up) thoughts so we can see them better.

It takes time to draw out thoughts and observations. We have a chance to let more of those "bottom-up" sensations and perceptions, buried memories, and unacknowledged assumptions surface. Nonverbal feelings and thoughts emerge and we see them take shape on the drawing surface. Our attention widens, giving us some respite from the commotion of our daily lives. When we take the time to pay attention, we become more self-aware and potentially more sensitive to others as well.

We can PLAY with our thoughts from the top down.

Drawing provides a reflective space for us to observe, discover, and invent, as we play out real and imaginary scenarios. The meaning of lines and marks can change; parts and wholes can shift. Like spectators at a horror film, we may play with a sense of risk and danger without actually putting ourselves in harm's way. We observe and direct our thoughts for our own cognitive pleasure and in the process develop metacognitive control, enhancing our ability to analyze and strategize about our own thinking. Ordinary or mundane moments become interesting as we observe our hands, eyes, and minds at work on the drawing surface.

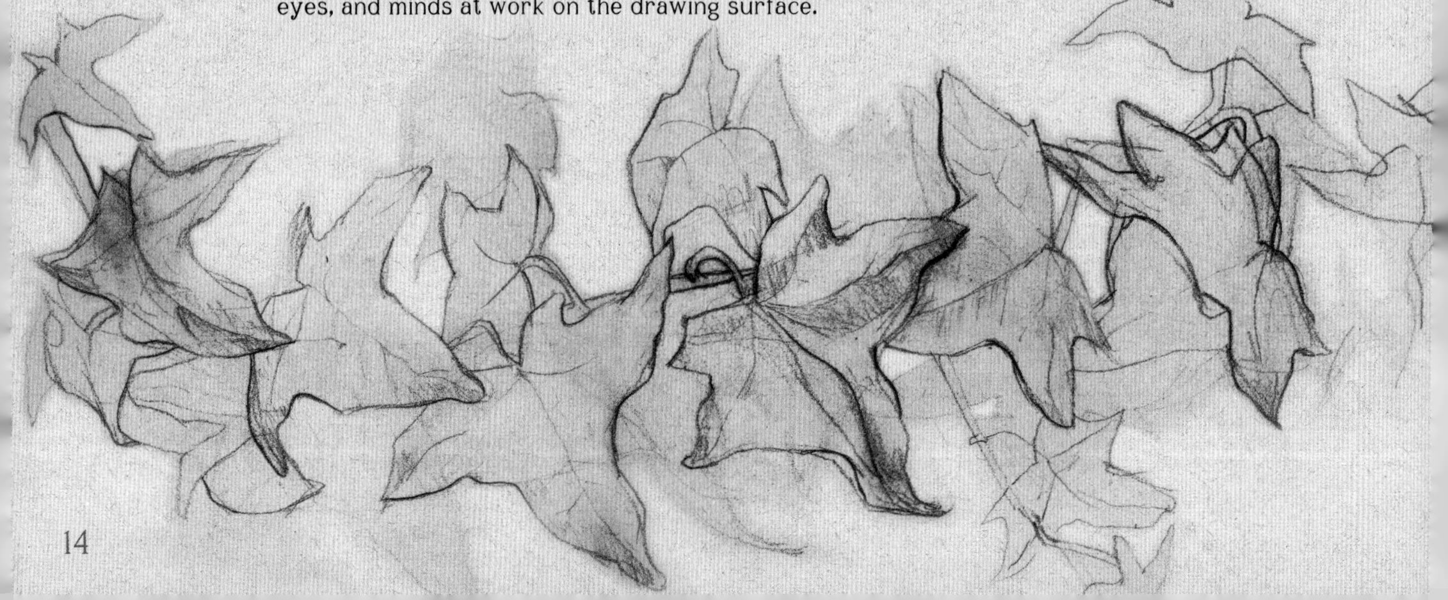

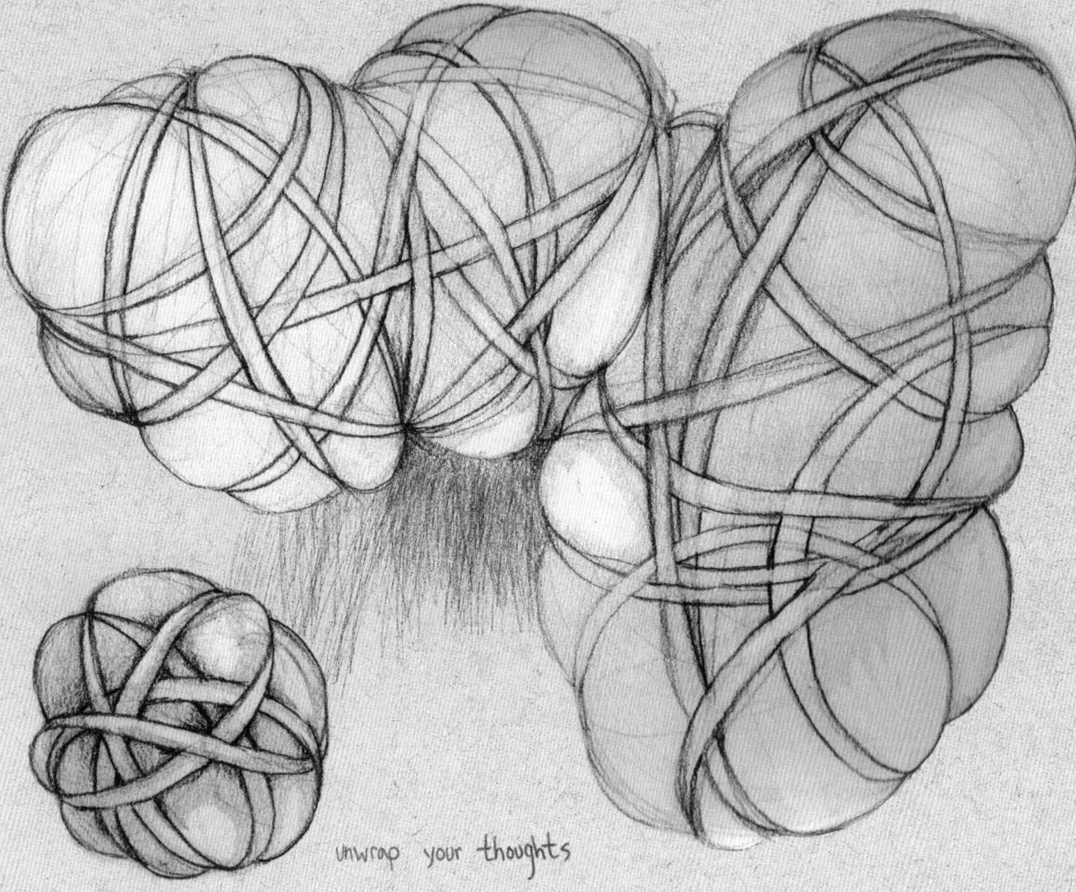
unwrap your thoughts

How to
Take a Line for a Walk

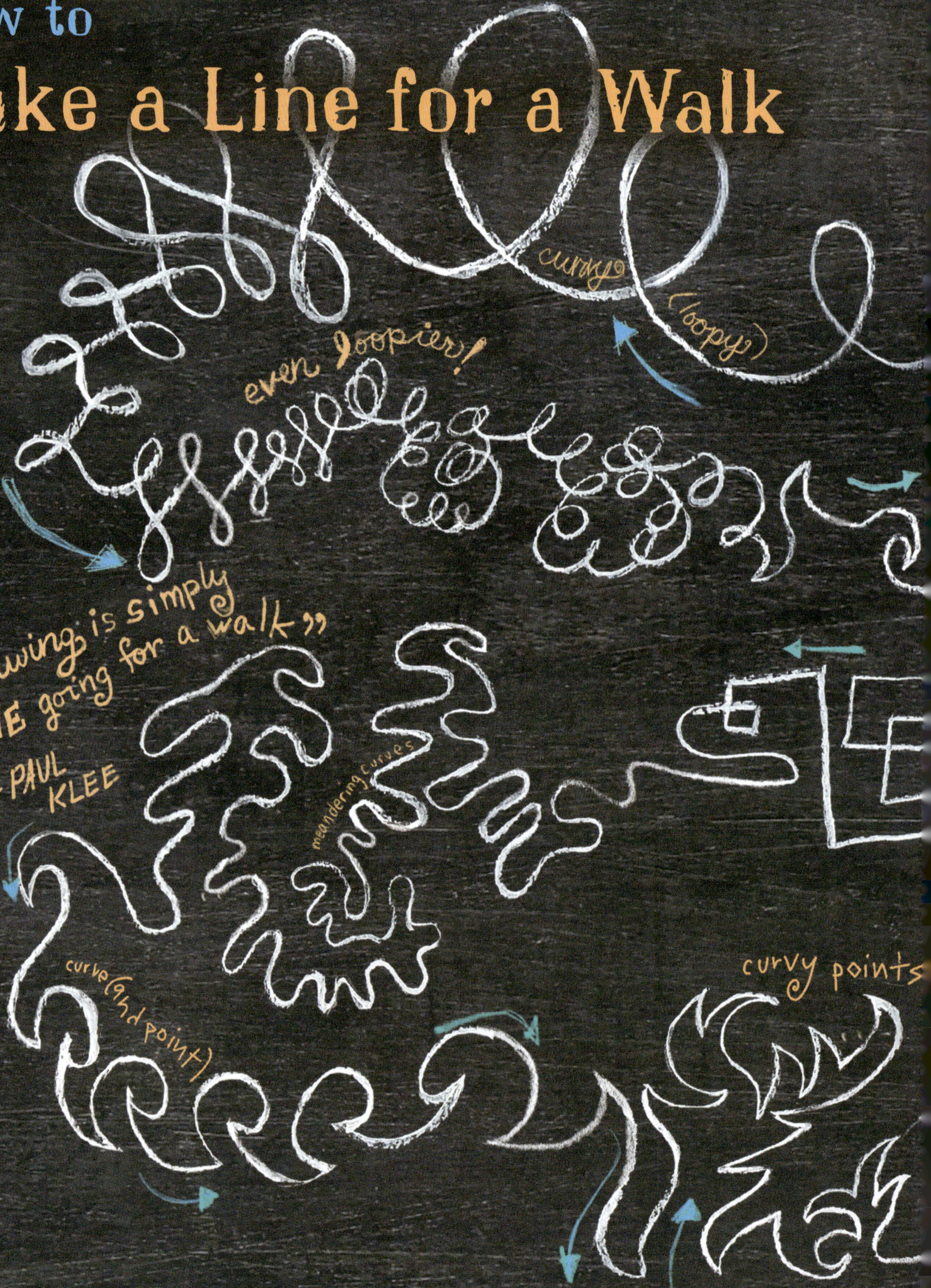

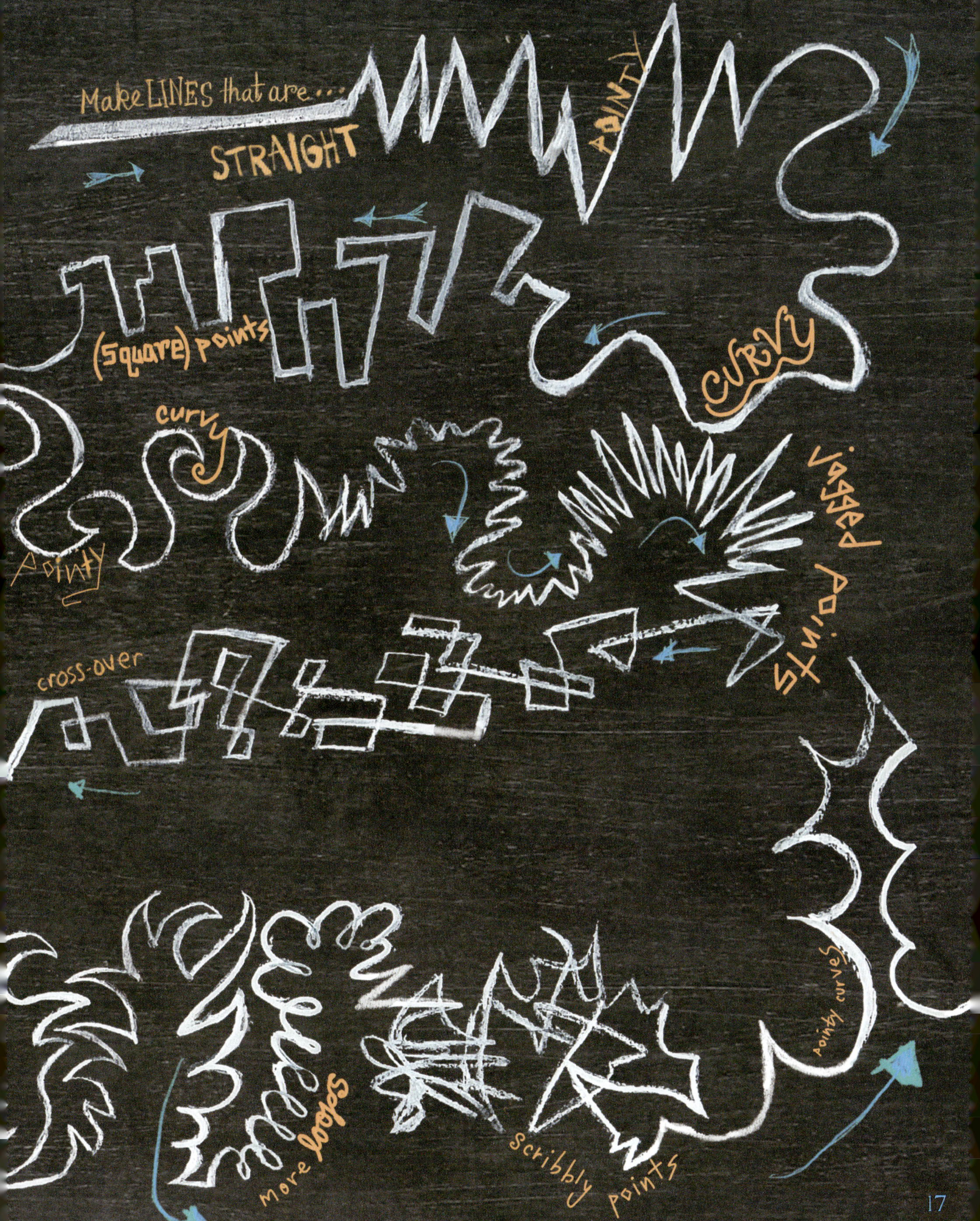

Make LINES that are . . .
STRAIGHT
POINTY
CURVY
(square) points
curvy
pointy
jagged points
cross-over
pointy curves
more loops
scribbly points

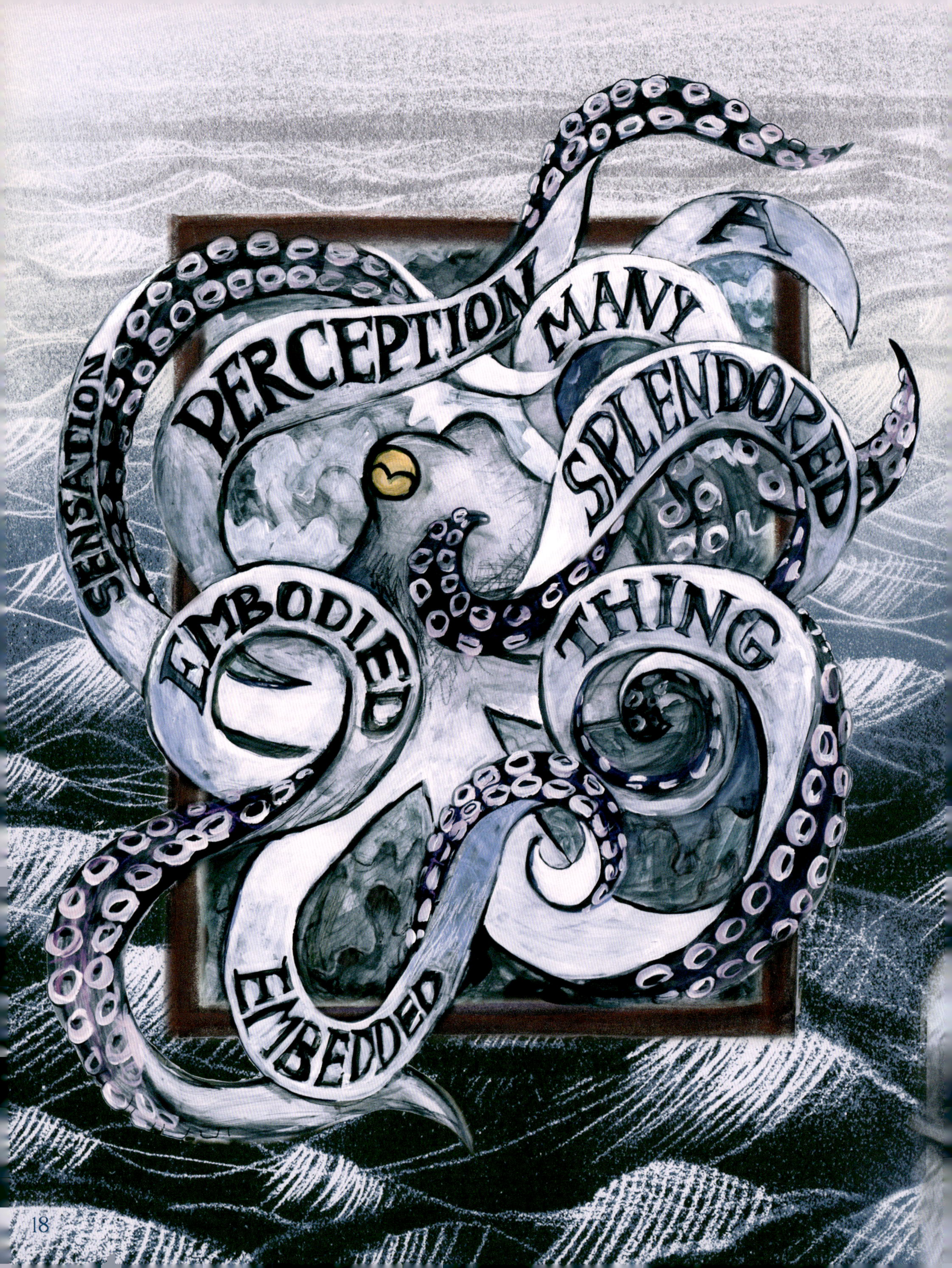
A
PERCEPTION
MANY
SPLENDORED
SENSATION
EMBODIED
THING
EMBEDDED

chapter two

Below the Surface

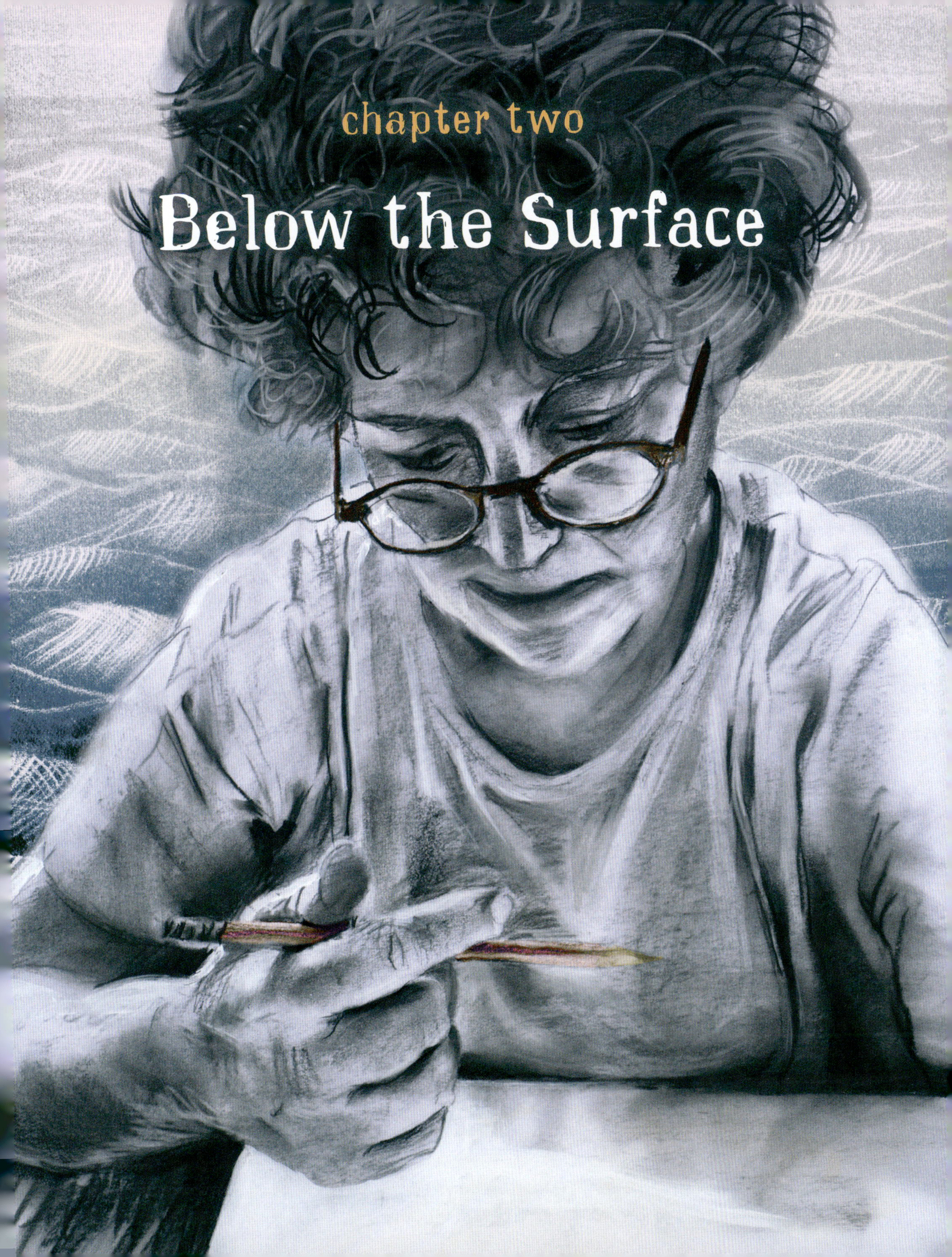

WE ARE LEAST AWARE of what our Minds do best

—Marvin Minsky, pioneer of Artificial Intelligence

Drawing lets us DIVE below the surface of our conscious thoughts, to observe and record sensations, perceptions, and ideas that might otherwise SLIP BY unnoticed.

A feature film or even a single scene might be assembled from countless discrete fragments of sounds and images. Every day, we assemble the impression of a unified reality (the movie of our lives) from many sources of information generated by the body's encounters with the external environment. All manner of entangled individual, cultural, and evolutionary histories influence how we pay attention and interpret our experiences. Drawing allows us to explore their depths and learn more about the perceptual processes that guide our everyday activities. We might notice otherwise fleeting thoughts and actions. We might bring back hidden treasures, re-emerging to experience life with fresh eyes.

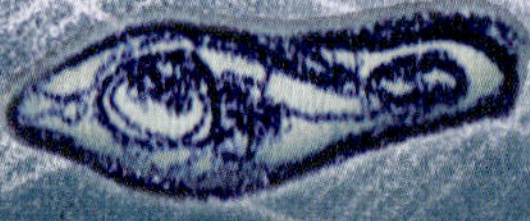

I made these drawings as I watched YouTube videos of amoebas hunting and "eating" paramecium.

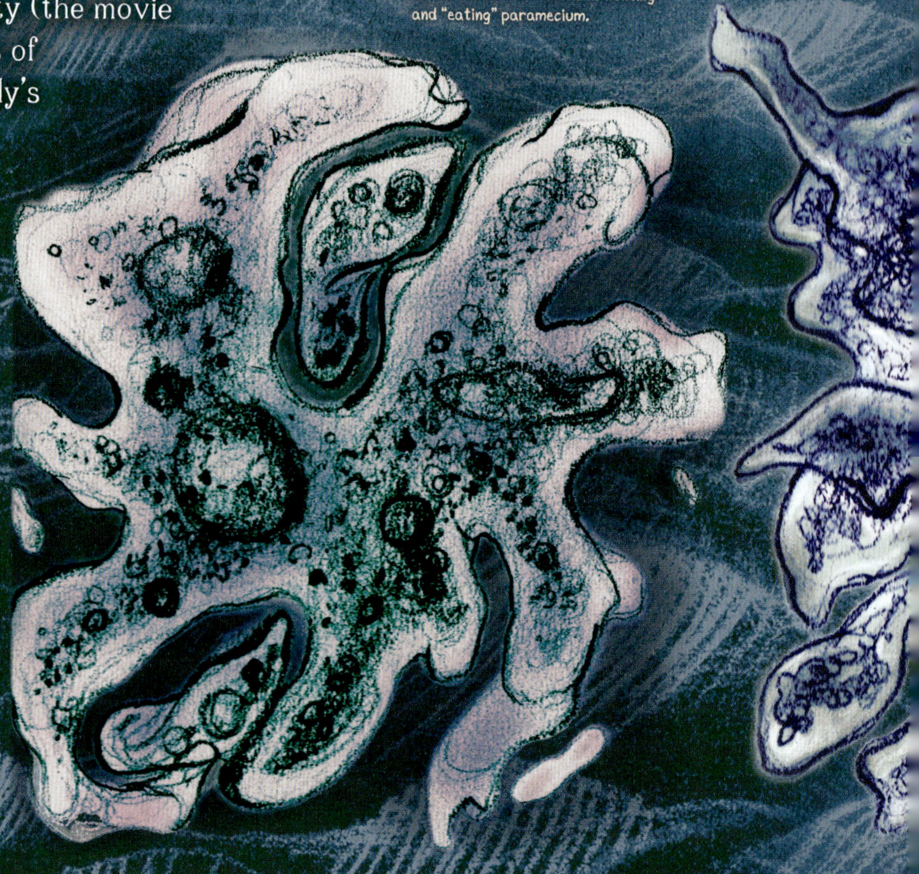

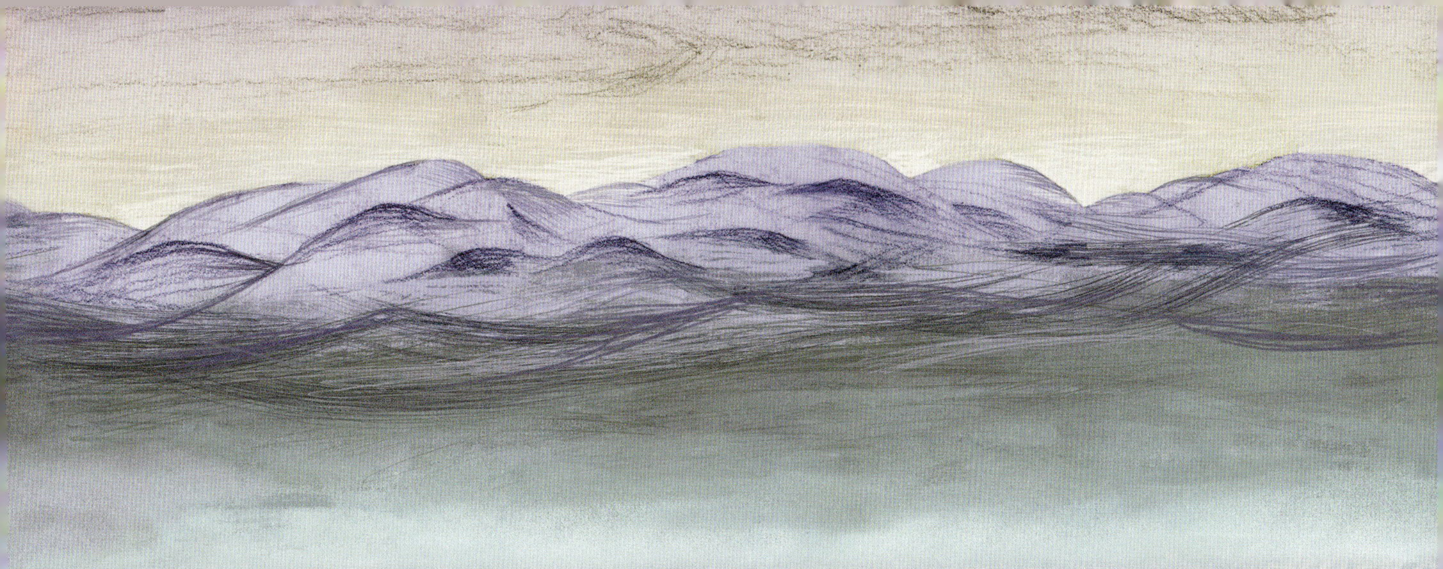

Unaware of the complex processes at work, most of us are lucky enough to get out of bed in the morning without needing to plot our every move. We can walk into the bathroom and brush our teeth without thinking about it, our minds free to consider the weather, anticipate rush-hour traffic, or look forward to a Sunday picnic in the park. Habits and routines allow us to move through the world, unaware of the complex sensory and motor integration between our brains and bodies that makes it possible. Many people have had the experience of arriving at work in their car, a drive they make almost every day, to realize that they have no memory of the steps, stops, and turns they took to get there.

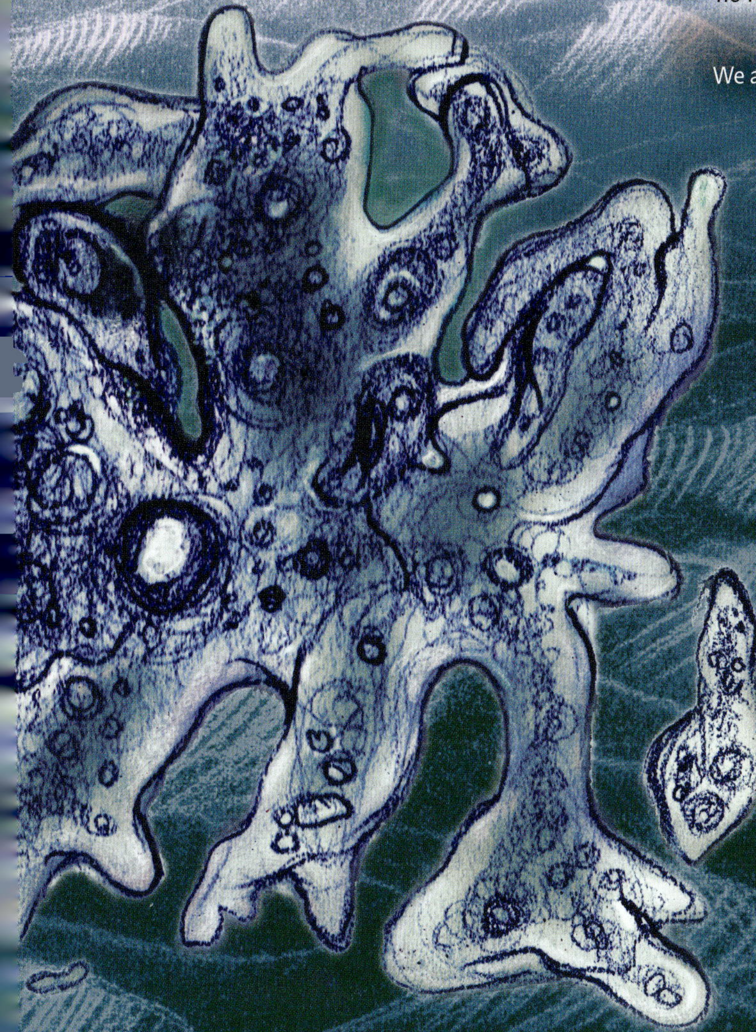

We attend to our perceptions on a NEED-TO-KNOW basis. Our cognitive abilities do not provide a full and complete representation of the world around us at each moment of our lives. Rather, these abilities evolved to help us survive and reproduce in a constantly shifting and uncertain world. We depend on innate reflexes and learned procedures operating under the radar of our conscious minds, which allow us to focus on the task at hand and ignore the rest. We don't bother to attend to the background noise, but somehow notice just enough to respond to the crying baby in the next room or the stranger at the door.

Below the level of conscious awareness, our bodies constantly monitor the external and internal environments for changes, mobilizing to adapt or act if necessary. When I go for a morning run I don't have to turn up a dial to make sure I'm getting the oxygen I need. My breath and heart rate adjust to my level of activity seamlessly without thought or effort. These are basic homeostatic processes, the kind humans have in common with all living things. As with the lowly amoeba, the membrane of separation between us and the world is flexible and porous: we breathe, take in oxygen, and expel carbon dioxide. We turn your head in the direction of an unexpected noise.

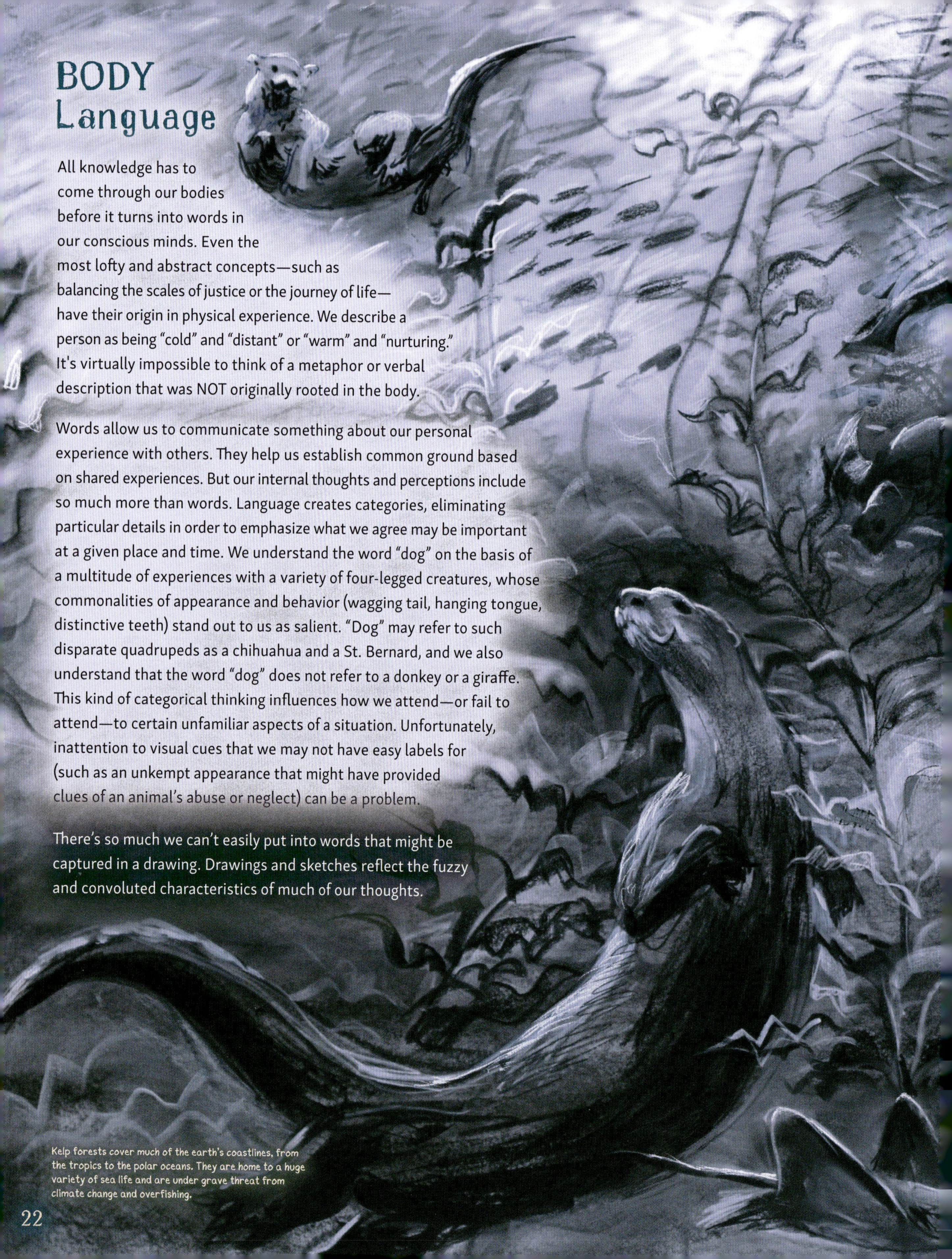

BODY Language

All knowledge has to come through our bodies before it turns into words in our conscious minds. Even the most lofty and abstract concepts—such as balancing the scales of justice or the journey of life—have their origin in physical experience. We describe a person as being "cold" and "distant" or "warm" and "nurturing." It's virtually impossible to think of a metaphor or verbal description that was NOT originally rooted in the body.

Words allow us to communicate something about our personal experience with others. They help us establish common ground based on shared experiences. But our internal thoughts and perceptions include so much more than words. Language creates categories, eliminating particular details in order to emphasize what we agree may be important at a given place and time. We understand the word "dog" on the basis of a multitude of experiences with a variety of four-legged creatures, whose commonalities of appearance and behavior (wagging tail, hanging tongue, distinctive teeth) stand out to us as salient. "Dog" may refer to such disparate quadrupeds as a chihuahua and a St. Bernard, and we also understand that the word "dog" does not refer to a donkey or a giraffe. This kind of categorical thinking influences how we attend—or fail to attend—to certain unfamiliar aspects of a situation. Unfortunately, inattention to visual cues that we may not have easy labels for (such as an unkempt appearance that might have provided clues of an animal's abuse or neglect) can be a problem.

There's so much we can't easily put into words that might be captured in a drawing. Drawings and sketches reflect the fuzzy and convoluted characteristics of much of our thoughts.

Kelp forests cover much of the earth's coastlines, from the tropics to the polar oceans. They are home to a huge variety of sea life and are under grave threat from climate change and overfishing.

We are often BLIND to our own IGNORANCE

Across a range of disciplines, beginners often jump to conclusions. Newbies often grab the first answer that pops into their heads, not knowing other kinds of questions to ask. They might get lucky occasionally, hitting on an unconventional solution experts might miss. They don't know what they don't know. Much more often, people lacking expertise will often overestimate their understanding of a given subject. Their knowledge gaps are unwittingly filled in with assumptions and erroneous predictions. They mistake imagination for knowledge.

What we think we know and can share is called declarative knowledge, transmitted through words and stories. Yet we are often misinformed or just plain wrong. We all (us humans) are prone to systematic cognitive biases. We often overestimate the extent of our understanding of a given subject, a type of error known as "the illusion of explanatory depth." Cognitive psychologists David Dunning and Justin Kruger found that "C" students often thought they would receive "A's" or "B's" on exams, while "A" students anticipated a "B." Known as the Dunning-Kruger effect, the idea is that the less you know, the more you think you know. (This effect may have been exacerbated in recent years by internet "research.") When you know more, you might be more aware of what you don't know. Most people overestimate their understanding of objects and phenomena they encounter and use every day.

We KNOW MORE than we can TELL

At the same time, we may know more than we realize. We absorb knowledge through our accumulated experiences of being in the world. This kind of hidden knowledge can not always be codified or described in words. It is implicit, as opposed to declarative or explicit knowledge. In the 1950s, the scientist Michael Polanyi developed a theory of tacit knowledge to explain how we know things we cannot describe in words. Tacit knowledge is gained through the interactions of our body with our surroundings; some simple examples are knowing how to ride a bicycle or knead bread. Polanyi called attention to the ways that intuition, gut feelings, or hunches often drive the process of scientific discovery and creation of new knowledge across domains. He linked the concept of tacit knowledge to the central idea of Gestalt psychology, that the whole is more than the sum of its parts.

As we draw, we mirror the ways we stitch together a holistic sense of reality in our everyday interactions with the world. We pay attention to configurations of bits and pieces, literally drawing them together. The spaces in between are as important as the marks themselves. Marks indicate boundaries, planes and volumes, figure and ground. They represent movements, breaks, and turning points. In expert hands, the gaps in between marks leave room for inference.

Tacit knowledge seems to recruit different neural systems than verbal thought. Stephen Wiltshire, a British artist with autism, draws vast and detailed panoramas of cities from memory or imagination. Wiltshire's remarkable ability to draw was recognized by the time he was five, though he did not speak until he was nine. Patients who have sustained brain damage that derails their verbal ability can still sometimes remember how to dance or even sing. Drawing can help make us more aware of and able to utilize the variety of ways we come to understand and behave in the world that are independent of words.

I don't think about what my fingers are doing while I type, and this allows me to focus on what I am trying to say. I (and you) can only pay full ATTENTION to one thing at a time. Once I stop typing, I feel the slightly cool temperature and dampness of the air on my skin, and I hear a dog barking in the distance and the echoes of my own fingers tapping on the keyboard. I look up from the screen and see the play of light on the windowsill. And I notice internal sensations: a feeling of satisfaction after a nice meal, the lingering warmth and flavor on my tongue.

The automated procedures, habits, and ROUTINES that we use to walk, talk, and maybe ride a bicycle make it possible to attend to other things. As we move through life the force of habit sets in. This makes daily tasks easier. But it also enables us to sleepwalk through too much of our adult lives.

The fascination a young child experiences watching shifting patterns of sunlight and shadow on the windowsill is still available to us at any given moment—if we just look for it. And drawing can help.

Next time you are strolling through town, look for a parent and young child crossing the street. You may notice the adult looking straight ahead, moving purposefully to the other side. In contrast, the child may be looking all around, skipping, hopping, zig-zagging, swinging a free arm as the parent pulls the other hand forward.

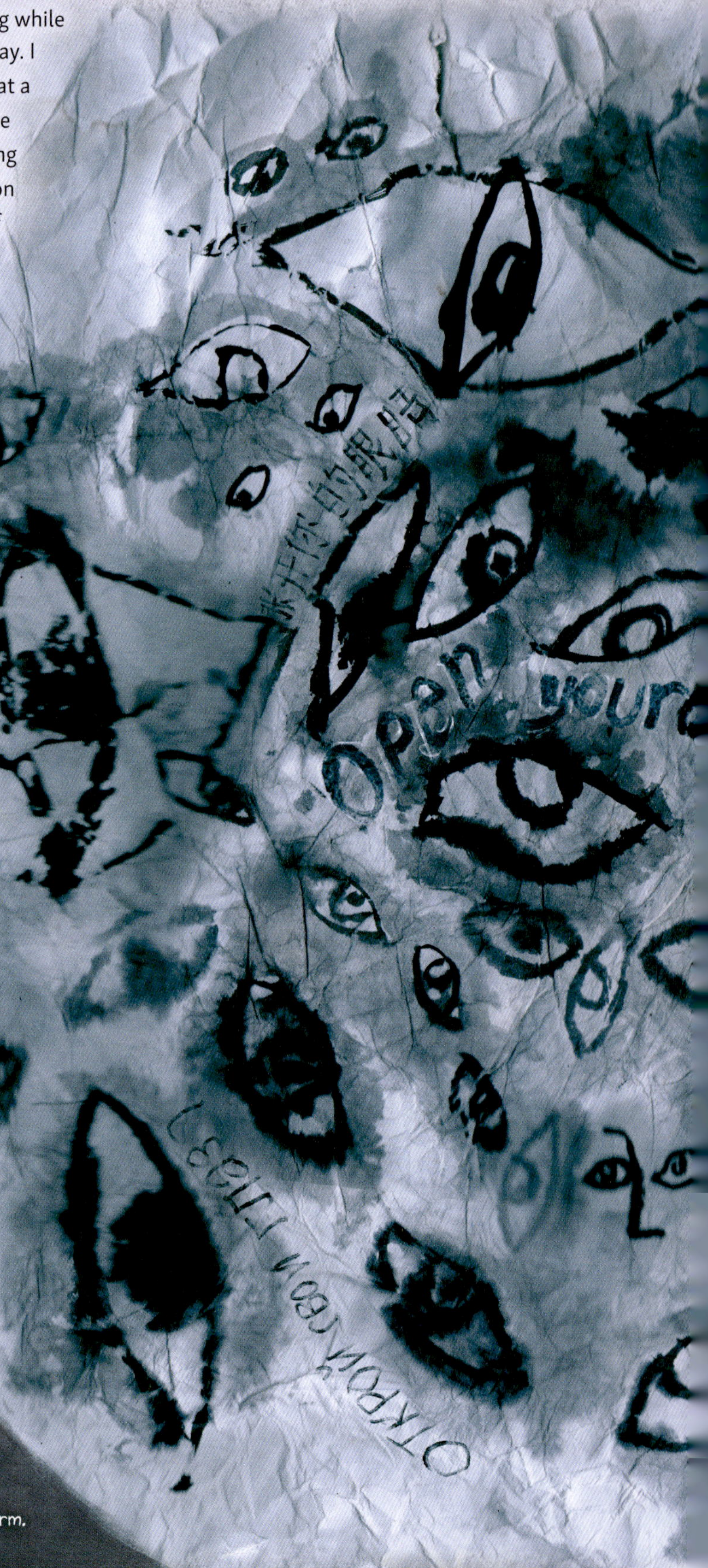

DISCOVER YOUR TOES!

Take off your shoes and socks. Imagine you are seeing your toes for the very first time. Spread them out as wide as you can, and wiggle them around! Pick up your pencil, and try to imagine it resting on the edge of your big toe. Trace the contour on your paper as the form turns inward, letting the line go and picking up again at the edge, working around each toe, until you've reached the outside edge of your pinky toe. Add the toenails, continuing to imagine your pencil tip moving along the actual form. Toes can be pretty peculiar when you take a good look!

Everything is waiting to be (re)discovered

Infants experience a continuous flood of sensations. In order to find their way through this flood and make meaning, they observe and intervene in the environments in which they find themselves, gradually identifying boundaries, in both time and space. A colorful rattle or wood spoon helps them learn what they can do. They are curious and often amazed by the effects of their actions. By learning to identify the natural edges of things, beginnings and endings, they find themselves in a world of discrete beings, objects, and events.

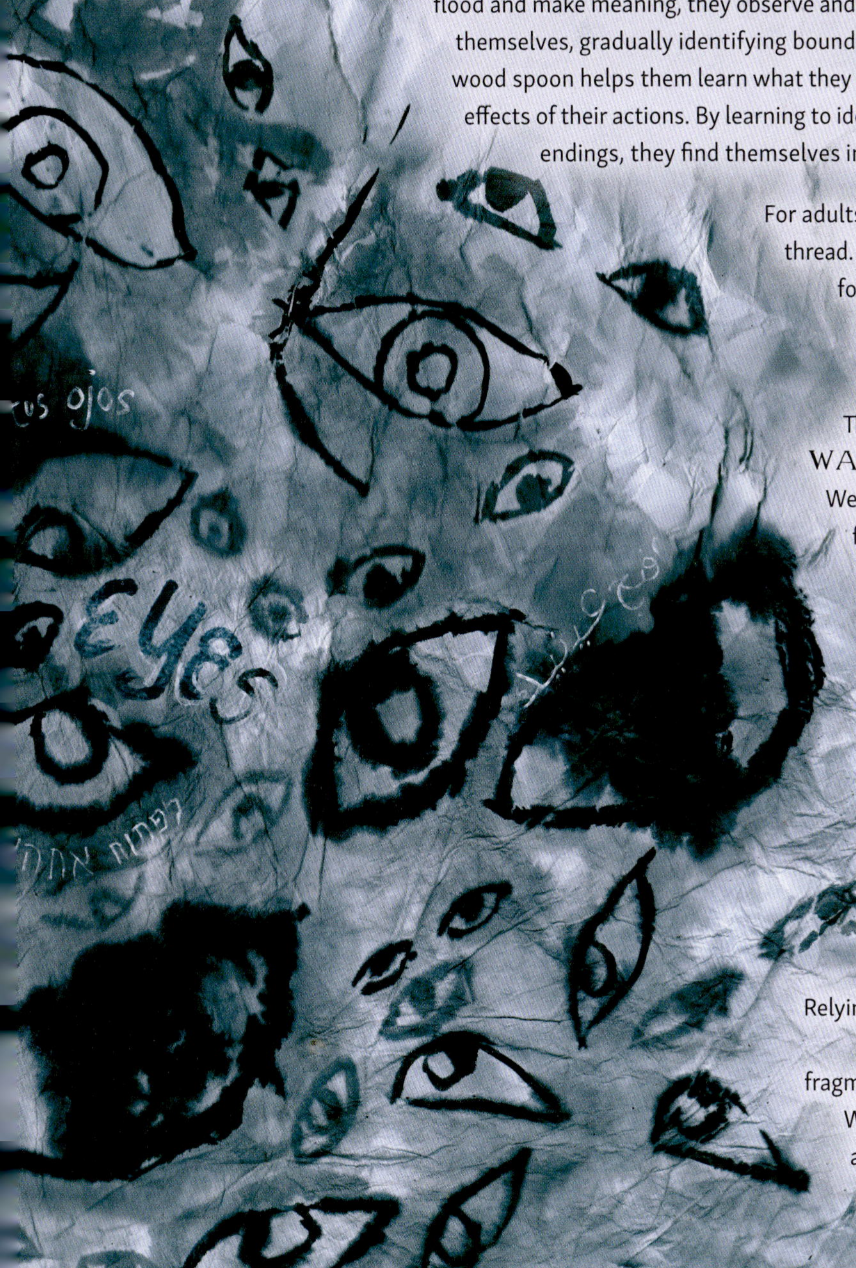

For adults, spools of thread are simply objects for holding thread. For babies, spools can be for stacking and sorting, for chewing on, for rolling, for banging together to make noise. Without prior knowledge, they will naturally explore multiple possibilities.

There was a time when most of us learned how to WALK. It turns out there is no one way to get there. We learn to balance on two feet, to shift our weight from one foot to the other, to feel our way. There is a common musculoskeletal and neural architecture that makes it possible. Eventually most of us get there. Yet our individual ways of walking are as unique and recognizable as our fingerprints. And if we think too much about putting one foot in front of another, we might be stopped dead in our tracks.

We think we see a WHOLE scene at once, but that is not what is actually happening in our eyes and brain. We can only focus on a tiny piece of the visual field at any moment. Relying on prior knowledge and innate predispositions, we go with the most probable interpretation of fragmentary information, revised as new data appears. We are able to discern figure/ground relationships, and model 3D objects from the retinal images they generate based on hypotheses formulated from our lived experiences.

YOUR FIELD OF VISION

Draw a slightly horizontal oval on your paper (roughly the same shape as the drawing of eyes here). Keeping your head stationary, quickly map out your field of vision. Pay attention to the edges and overall shape of the area you can see without moving your head. What do you notice about your eye movements? Our eyes dart from spot to spot in milliseconds and gather together relevant fragments, searching for high-contrast edges, movement, and telling details. All that information is fed through the optic nerve to the primary visual cortex at the back of our brain, then sorted, compared with prior knowledge, and knitted together to form the unified moving picture in our minds we understand as "reality."

PERCEPTION is a MANY-SPLENDORED thing

Vision is one of the primary sources of information about the world for us humans. Neuroscientists estimate that around 40% to over 50% of the cerebral cortex (the surface of the brain) is devoted to visual processing. It is difficult to pin down because aspects of visual cognition are recruited in so many cognitive processes. Making sense of the visual field alone is quite complex. We must learn to integrate separate cues, such as size, position, shape, and color. It's not always easy to figure out what you are looking at, which is why optical illusions can be so effective.

Vision is part of "exteroception," awareness of external stimuli, which includes sound, taste, smell, touch. When you close your eyes, you may become aware of sounds or smells you had not noticed the moment before.

Our internal awareness, "interoception" is the perception of inner homeostatic processes such as breath and heartbeat, hunger, thirst, and emotional awareness. "Proprioception"is the awareness of the position and relation of parts of our bodies in space, and vestibular awareness is our sense of balance that keeps us upright. Kinesthesia, the sense of movement, nociception, the ability to sense pain, and thermoception, our ability to sense differences in temperature, are some other sources of sensory information.

A multitude of tiny acts of attention to these multiple sources of information about what is happening outside and inside your body determines what it feels like to be you, right now, in this place, at this moment.

DRAWING SOUND

With pencils in both hands, close your eyes. What do you hear? Use the pressure of the pencil to indicate volume. Try using simple lines, moving up and down, as if you are tracing sound waves, their amplitude and frequency. Or...try drawing the shapes, patterns, or gestures suggested by the sounds you hear.

"SEE like someone who has JUST been BORN!"

— Paul Cézanne, 1902

DRAWING INTEROCEPTION

Focus on your internal state. Are you hungry, energetic, worried, or content? How does it feel to be you right here and now? Without resorting to recognizable imagery, make an abstract mark, or series of marks, that might convey that feeling. You might want to try it again, using symbols or images to express your feelings.

We can DRAW out the many ways we FEEL OUR WAY through the world

When we draw, we engage more than just our eyes. Our perception of weight, balance, and movement in visual images depends not just on vision, but on understandings derived from many aspects of our bodily experiences. We see, we move our hand, we feel our way across the paper. Just as we ground verbal metaphors in physical experiences, we construct visual metaphors that are grounded in the whole body, not just in our sense of sight. Our perception of weight, balance, and movement in visual images depends on understandings derived from bodily experience.

Our eyes do not work like cameras. Drawing is able to capture the hidden complexities of perception in a way photography cannot. A line or set of marks can relay non-visual attributes, like weight, texture, movement, and sound. For most of us this is metaphorical, but for some people, multiple senses actually mesh. Numbers may have a color, tastes a shape. This condition is called SYNESTHESIA, and is more common among artists than the general public. Wassily Kandinsky, the early twentieth-century Russian-born painter, a pioneer of abstraction famous for his visual depictions of music, is one of many important artists with synesthesia.

The late nineteenth-century French painter Paul Cézanne (often acknowledged as the father of modern art) said, "You must paint the smell of the pine trees." His fractured landscapes and still lifes make visible the process by which our minds integrate small, independent perceptions into a sense of a coherent whole, and thus helped give birth to cubism and twentieth-century modern art. Cézanne's paintings are full of visual ambiguities and contradictions.

In "Cézanne's Doubt," the French philosopher Maurice Merleau-Ponty analyzed the visual ambiguities in Cézanne's paintings in an effort to capture the subjective and sometimes inconsistent processes of perception. Merleau-Ponty's work in phenomenology and existentialism anticipated the current science of embodied cognition. He described the complexities and contradictions that emerge when we focus on the subjective EXPERIENCE of perception rather than the OBJECTS of perception.

I made this drawing watching videos of the diverse, teeming life of coral reefs, which take up less than 0.1% of the Earth's oceans, yet are home to at least 25% of all marine species.

DRAWING ON SYNESTHESIA

Think of two contrasting flavors: hot chili peppers and vanilla ice cream, for example. Even better, if they are available, take an actual taste. Draw the taste and smell (NOT the look) of each. If there is someone else around, see if they can guess which is which.

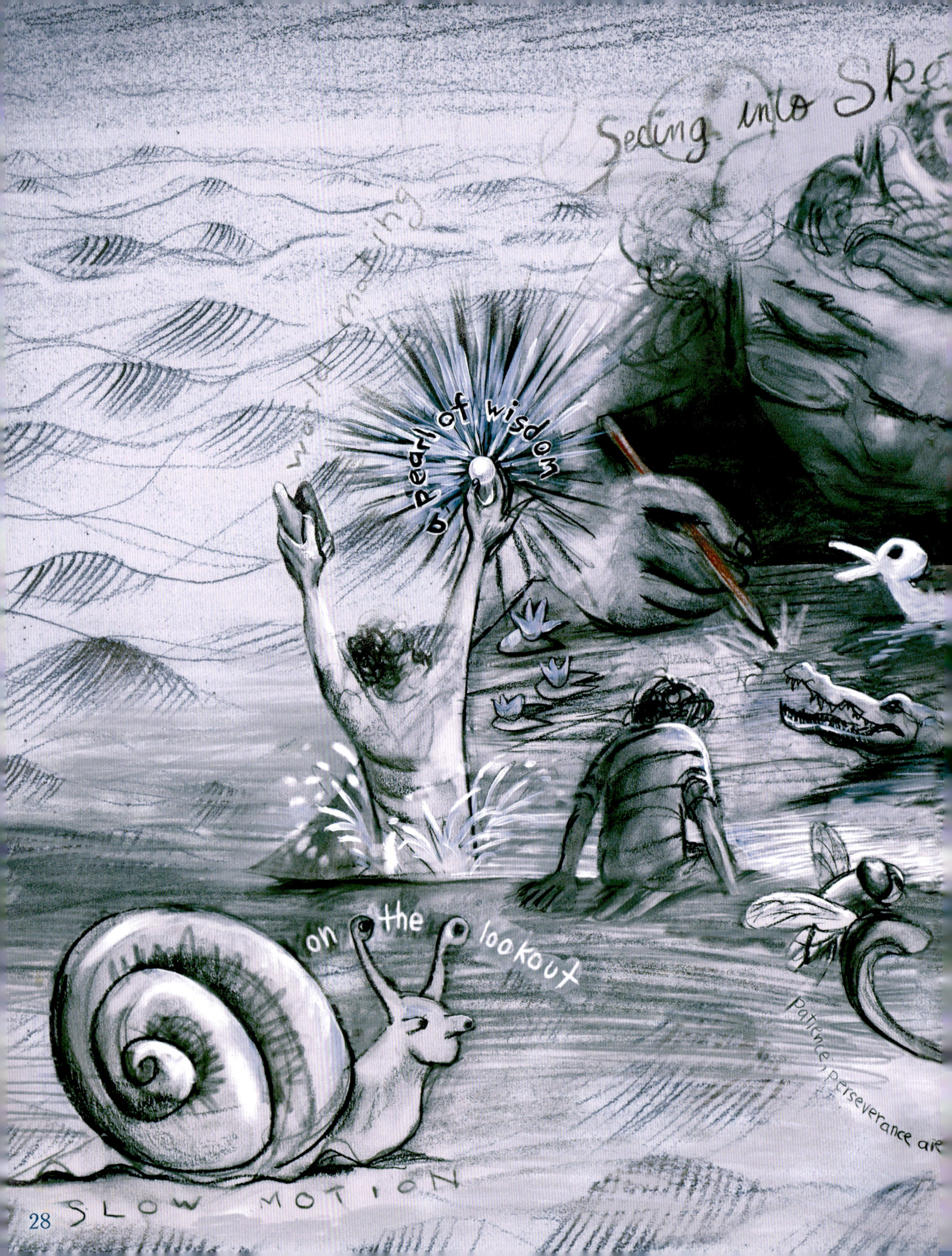
Seeing into Ska
a pearl of wisdom
on the lookout
Patience, perseverance ar
SLOW MOTION

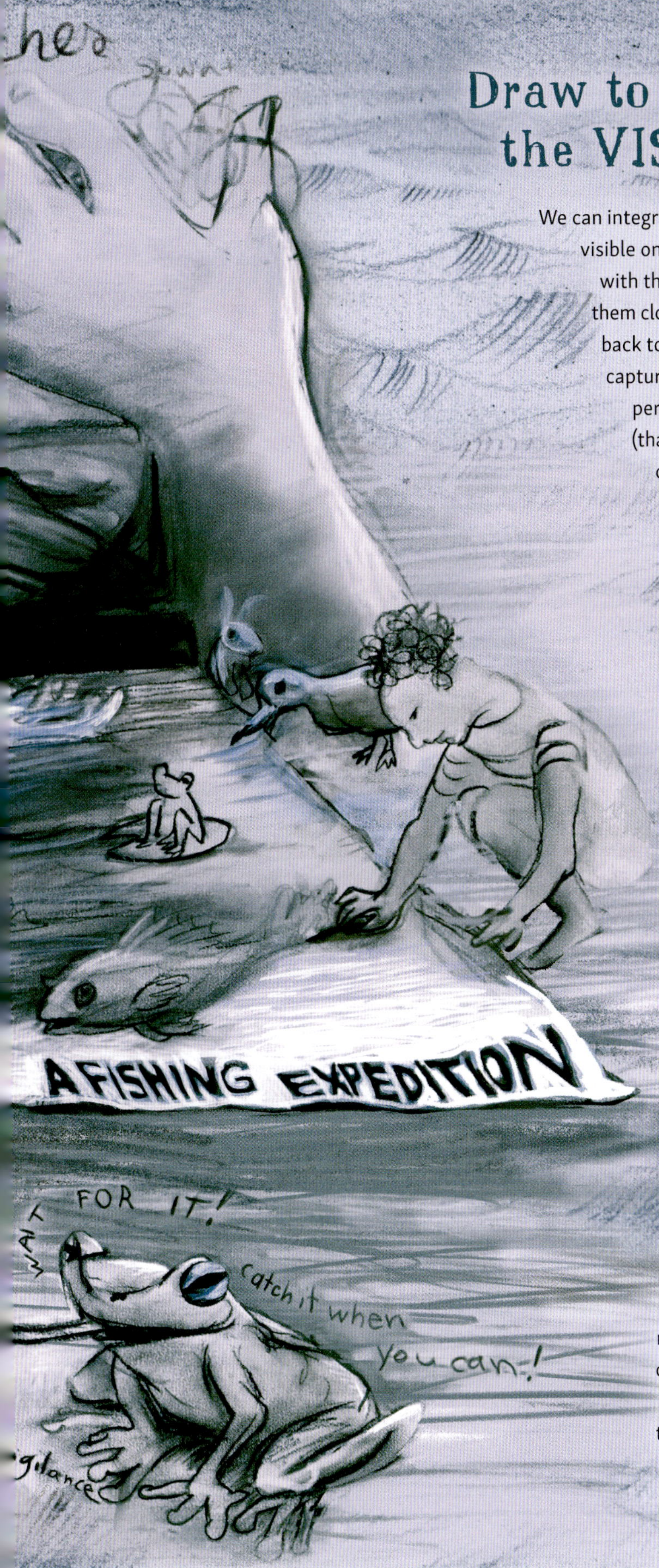

Draw to investigate and record the VISIBLE and INVISIBLE.

We can integrate all kinds of feelings and thoughts when we make them visible on the drawing surface. Indicating our feelings and thoughts with the form and qualities of marks and lines, we can reexamine them closely, pull them apart, and invent new ways of putting them back together again, surprising even ourselves. Drawing helps us capture and PAY ATTENTION to fleeting sensations and perceptions that would otherwise fade away. Both the visible (that patch of sunlight on the wall) and the invisible (a feeling of loneliness or excitement at the sound of a train going by in the distance) may find their way into our drawings.

Draw into the PRESENT moment. Through drawing, we can train ourselves to be in the moment, to sense what is happening inside and outside our own bodies. It takes practice. We need to dive deep into the myriad sensations continually flowing in between our brain, bodies, and the world, bits of flotsam and jetsam usually filtered out of conscious awareness. The filtration system our brain uses during most of our waking moments screens out what we have learned may not be immediately useful or relevant. To fully observe and embrace the present, we can practice putting this filtration system on pause while we draw.

Drawing makes the familiar STRANGE again. The longer we are in the world, the more familiar everything appears. The boundaries between ourselves and rest of the world become fixed. Drawing from observation can reveal how fragmentary and contingent our perceptions actually are. We notice the back and forth, the push and pull of shapes and edges bumping up against each other. We see opportunities to revise and reconfigure form and space. The partial, provisional nature of our sense of reality, the "sketchiness" of much of human thought, visibly emerges beneath our hand as we struggle to make form out of experience. It isn't easy to depict a solid and convincing sense of a consistent, three-dimensional world because that is not actually what we see.

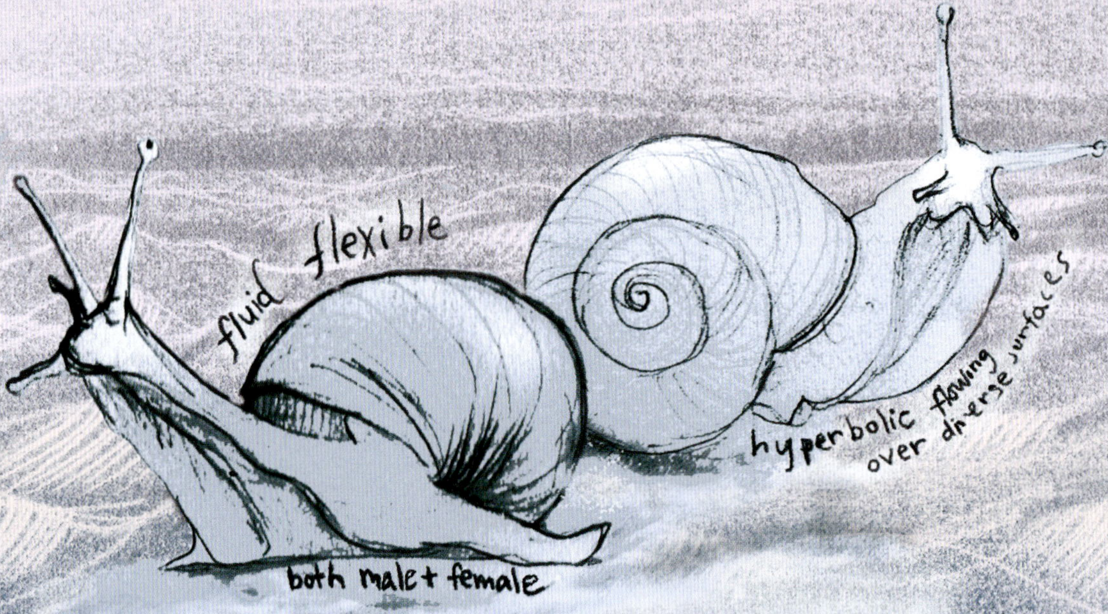

Unlearn. Be Humble. Be INEFFICIENT.

Observe the ebb and flow of internal and external sensations and perceptions. Drawing can help us realize how much there is to learn, moment by moment, about how we experience and come to understand ourselves and the world in which we live.

When I am absorbed in noticing the temperature of the air, the sounds of the crickets chirping, cars driving past, or soft conversations in the next room, I can set aside thoughts of past and future ... notice ... question ... savor ... the people, places, and things around me at this particular time and place.

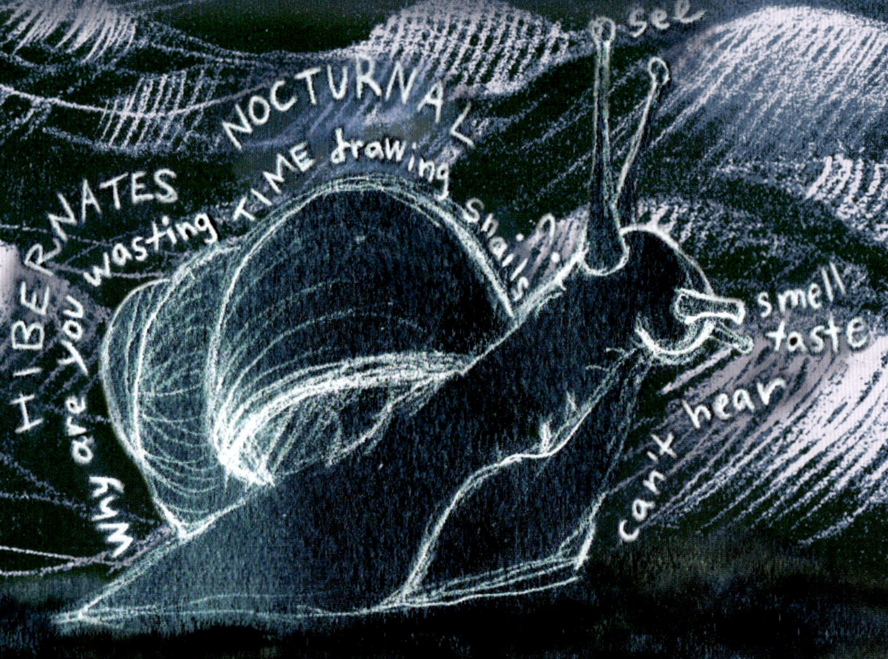

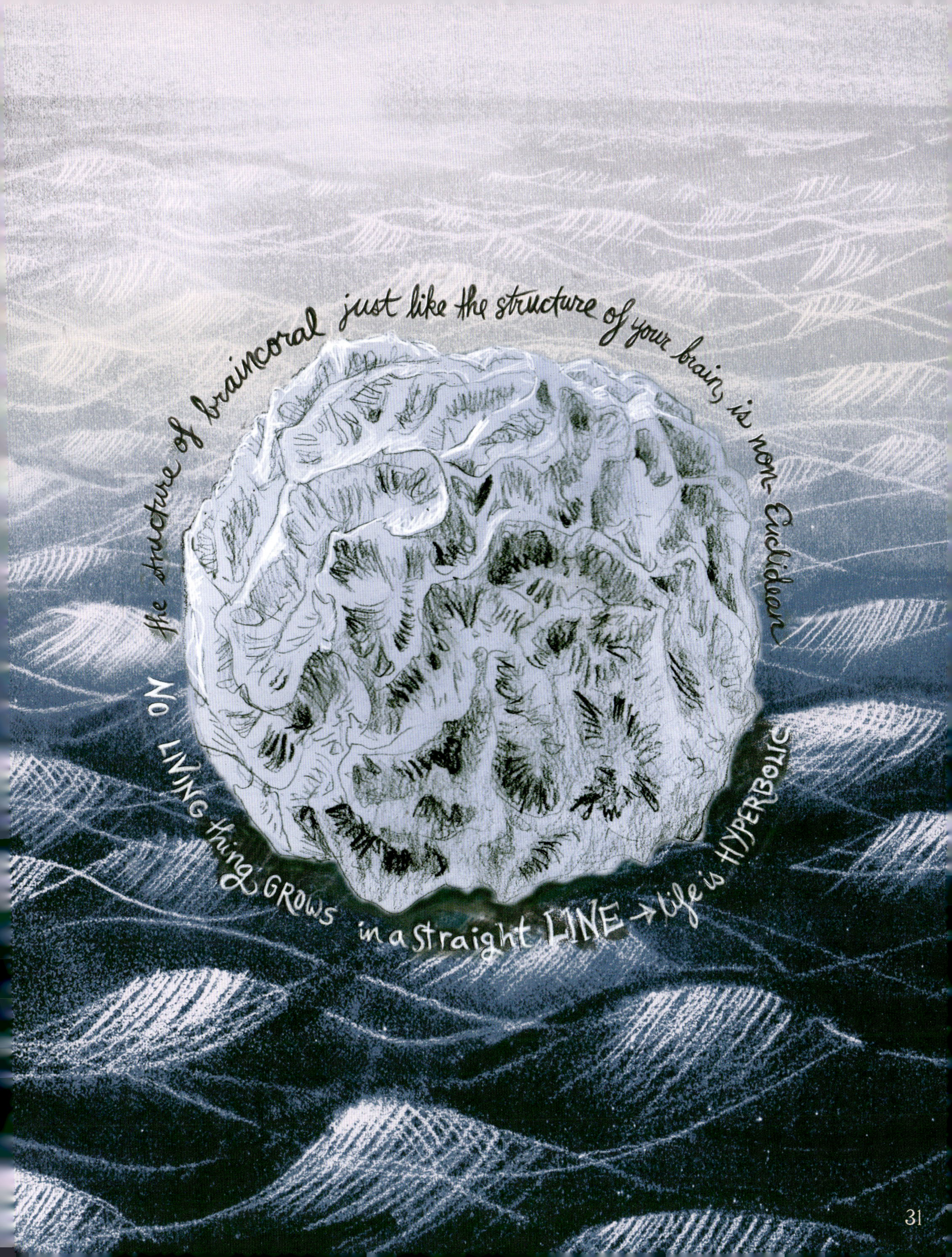
the structure of braincoral just like the structure of your brain, is non-Euclidean
NO LIVING thing GROWS in a straight LINE → life is HYPERBOLIC

How to
Show Feelings

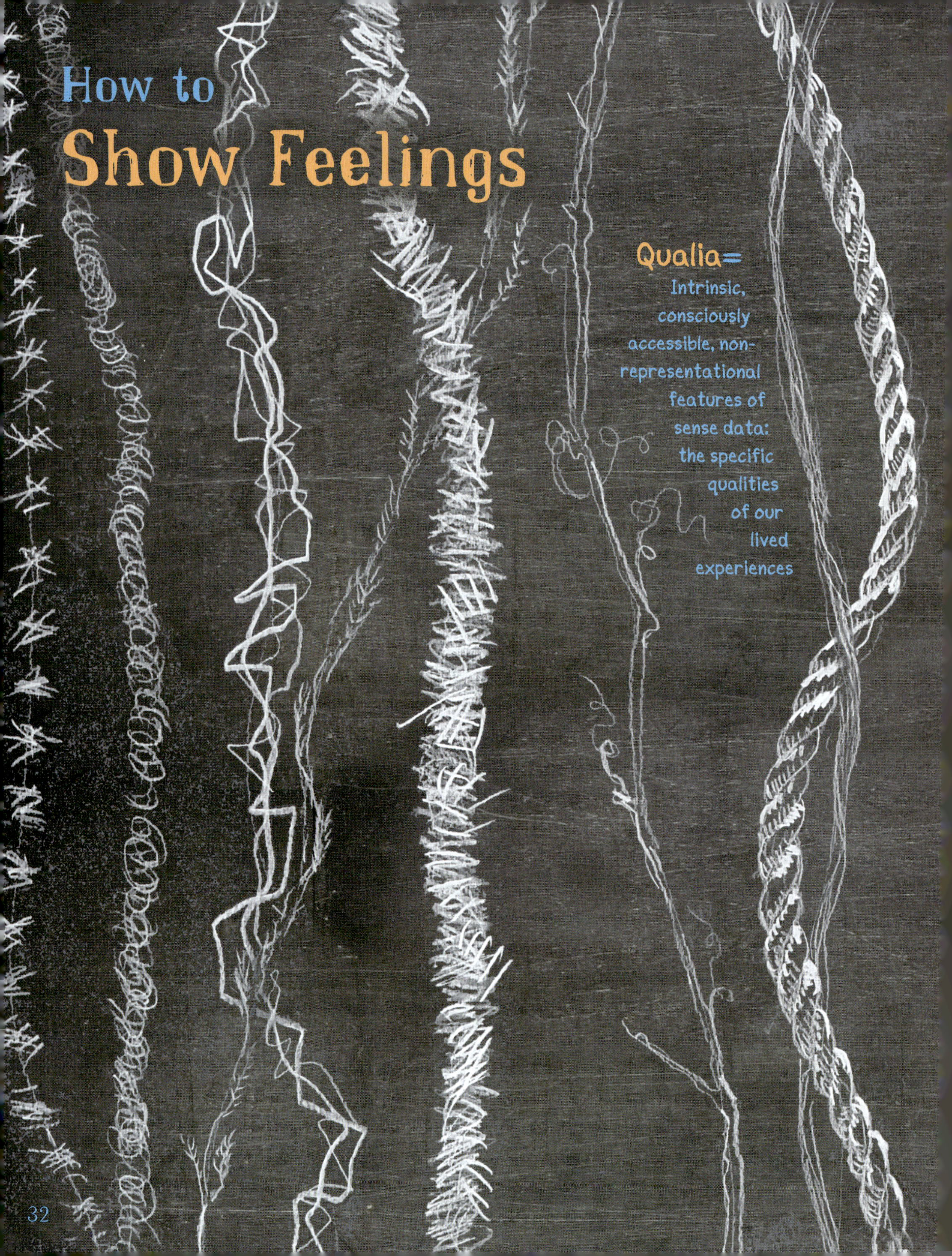

Qualia=
Intrinsic, consciously accessible, non-representational features of sense data: the specific qualities of our lived experiences

Collect objects that are linear in form: twine, branches, yarn, beads, wire, et cetera

notice each one's specific texture and structure

Is it... rough, smooth, bumpy, scratchy, soft, or stiff?

loose, floppy, brittle, fragile, or sturdy?

Make lines that saunter, sashay, limp, amble, meander, plod, lope, scurry

prowl, dash, shuffle, stride, waddle, march, lurch, swagger

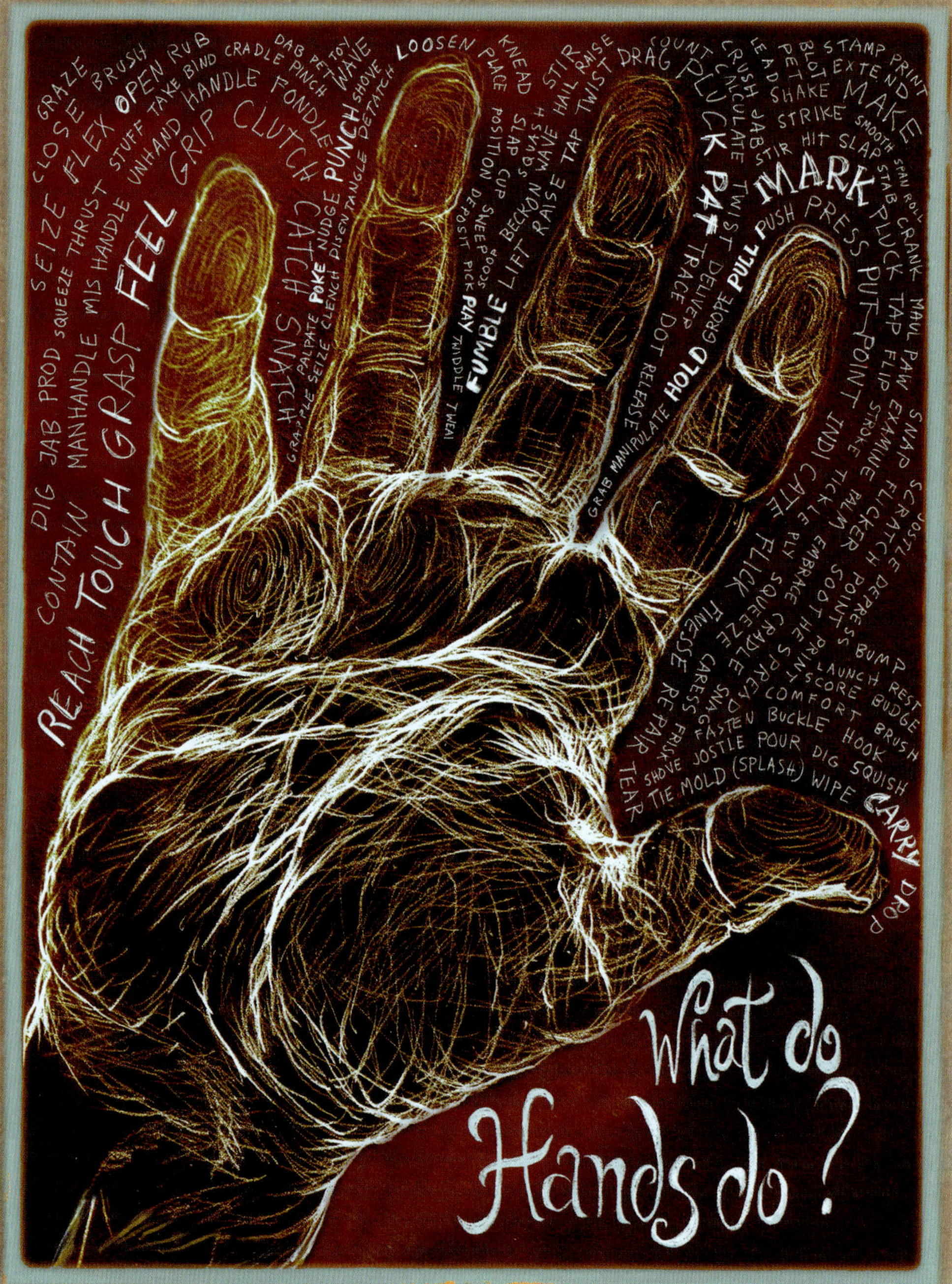
What do Hands do?
REACH TOUCH
GRASP
FEEL
GRIP
CLUTCH
CATCH
SNATCH
PUNCH
POKE
FUMBLE
LIFT
HOLD
PULL PUSH PRESS
MARK
PLUCK PAT
MAKE
CARRY
FLEX OPEN RUB
CONTAIN
MANHANDLE
SEIZE
LOOSEN
KNEAD
COUNT
INDICATE
FLICK

chapter three

The Thinking Hand

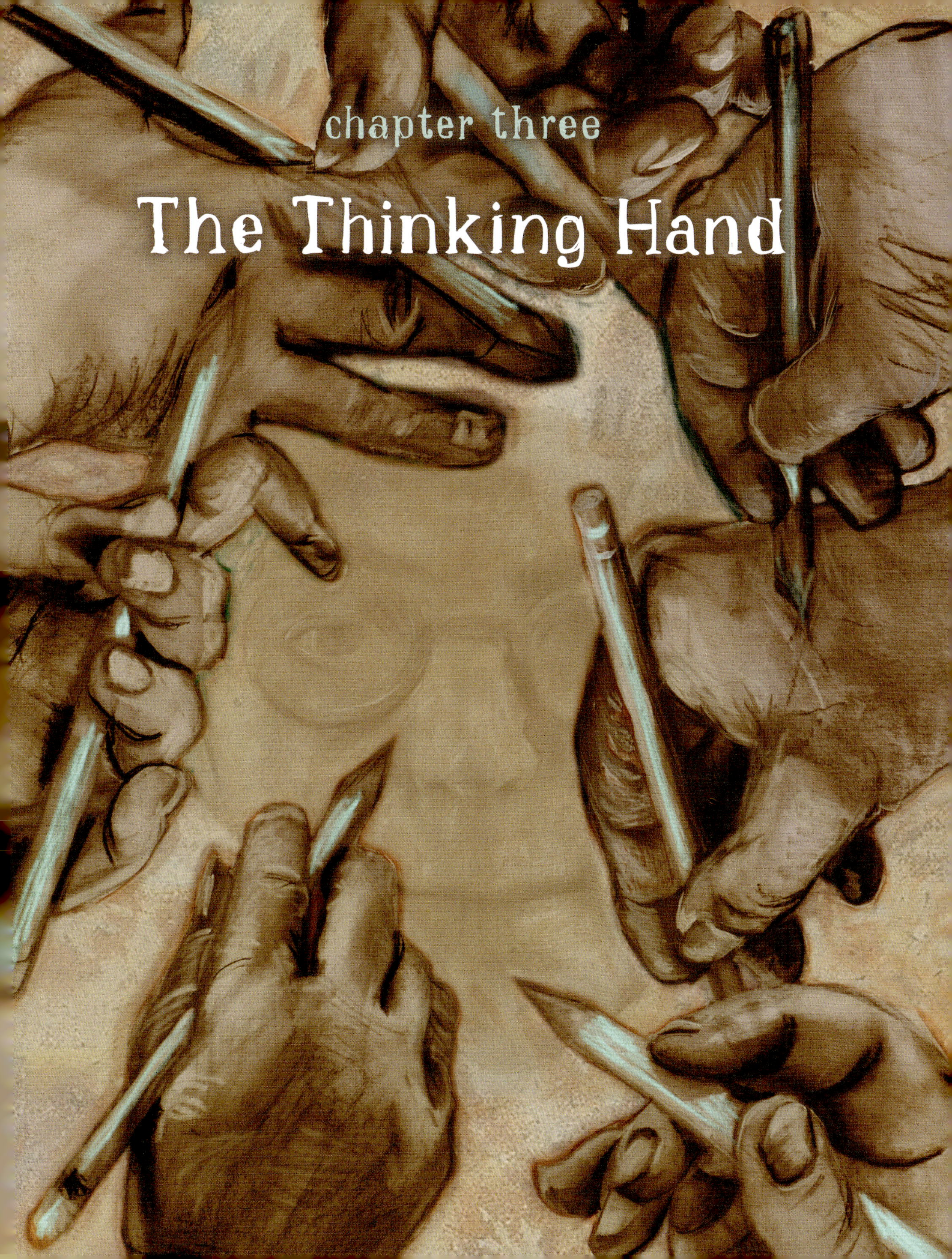

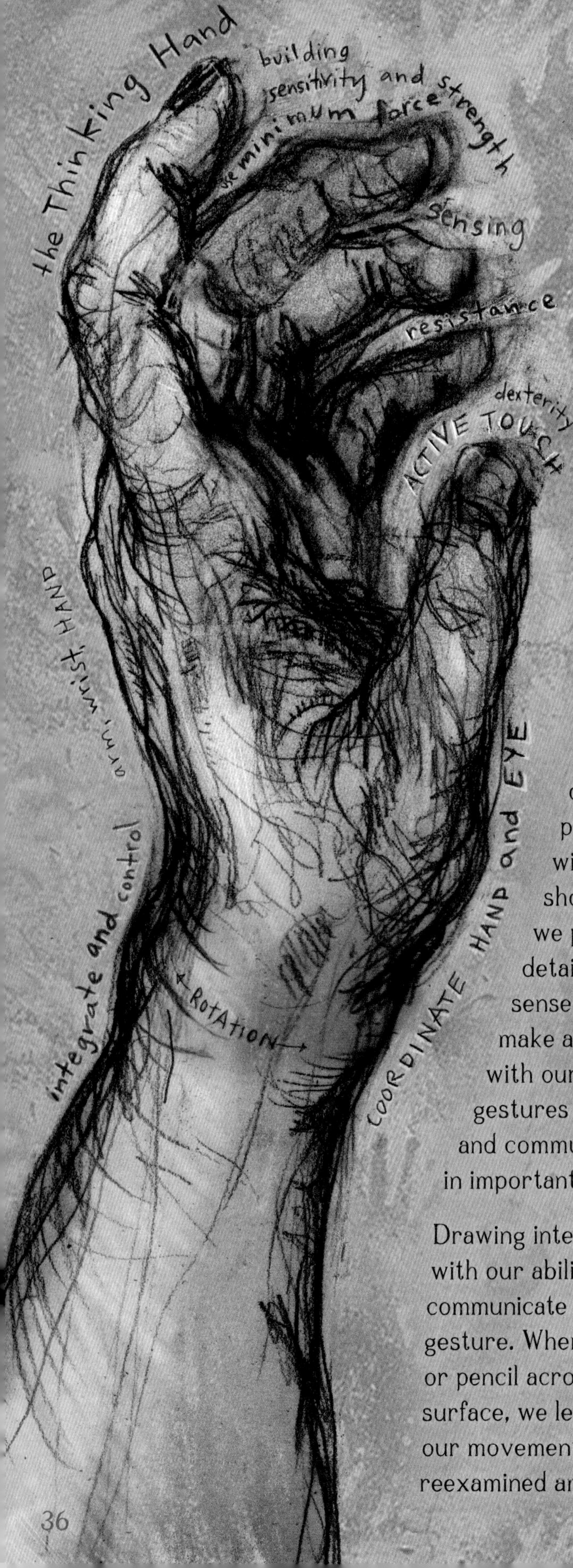

Drawing helps us take advantage of the ways we can use our HANDS to OBSERVE, DISCOVER, and INVENT

Human hands are capable of an astounding range of deliberate and reflexive actions. The movements of our fingers and wrists can be both powerful and precise, especially when they are well-coordinated with movements of our arms and shoulders. At our fingertips, we possess a remarkably detailed and subtle sense of touch. We make and use tools with our hands. Hand gestures help us think and communicate in important ways.

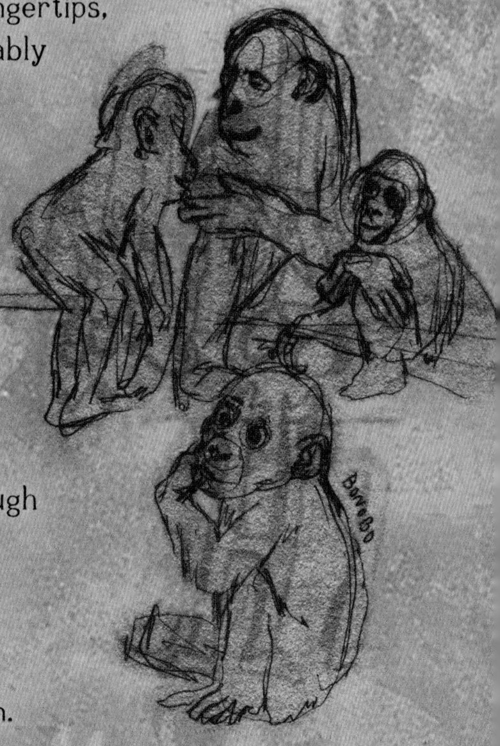

Drawing integrates tool use with our abilities to think and communicate symbolically through gesture. When we move a pen or pencil across the drawing surface, we leave the traces of our movements behind to be reexamined and revised later on.

Down from the Trees

The strong and agile hands of our arboreal primate ancestors evolved to reach, grasp, and hold on as they swung from branch to branch. To live in trees, they needed strong, mobile shoulders and arms. When our ancestors came down to the ground to walk on two feet, they brought their powerful, agile shoulders, arms, and hands with them. Walking on two feet, they no longer needed their hands to hang onto tree limbs and grab fruit. On the ground, hominids could use their hands in new ways. Our ancestors retained variations in the kinds of grips they could use. They had evolved with the ability to delicately pick up tiny objects with thumb and forefinger and pull apart resistant objects with great force.

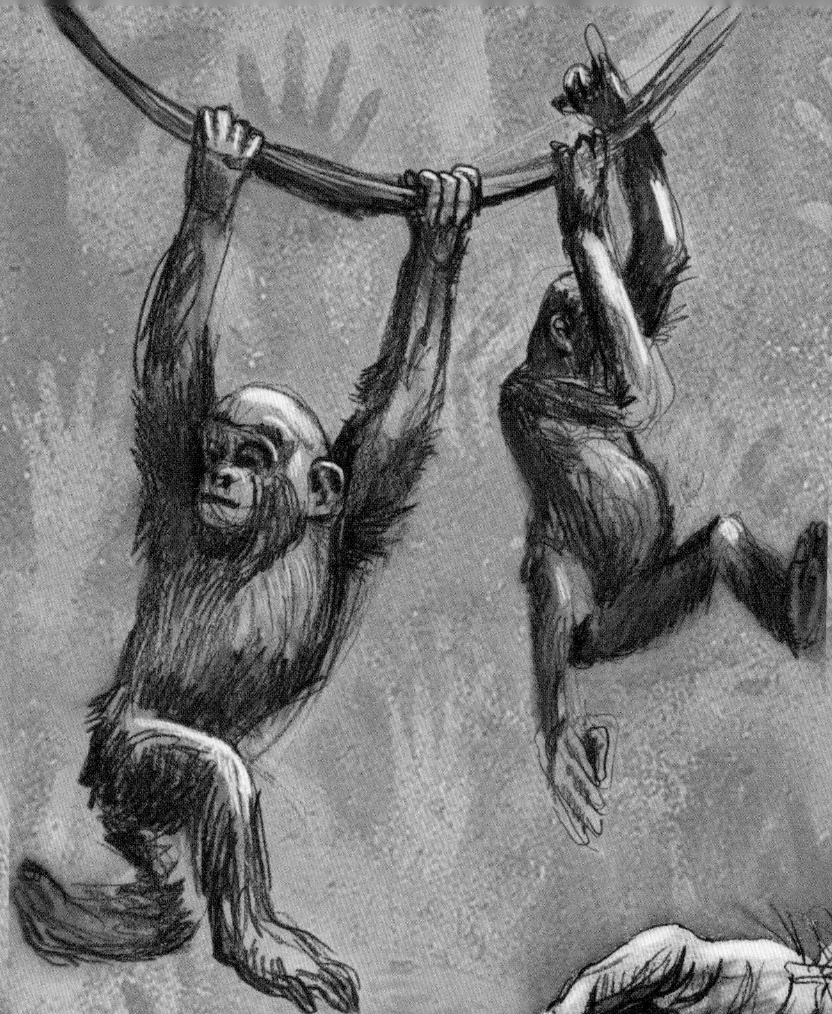

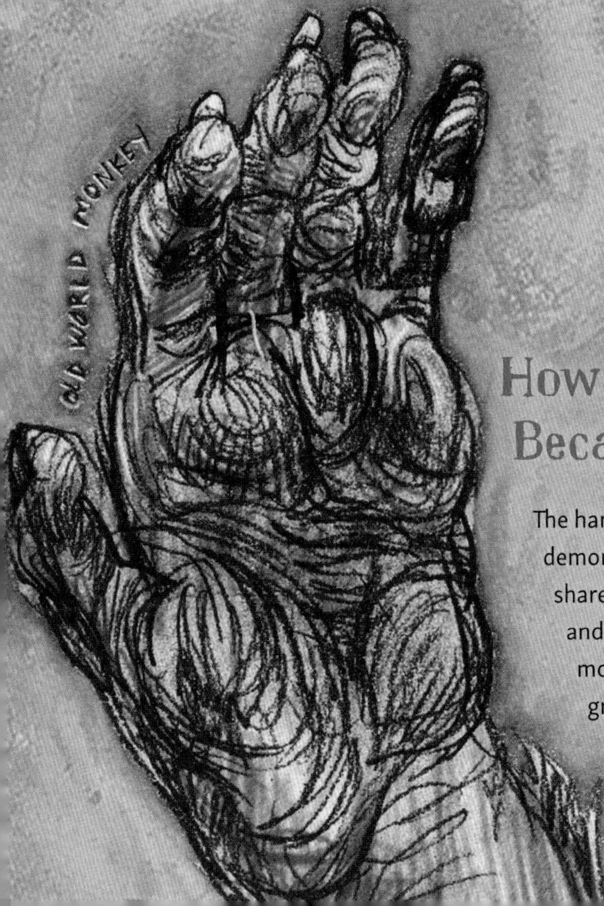

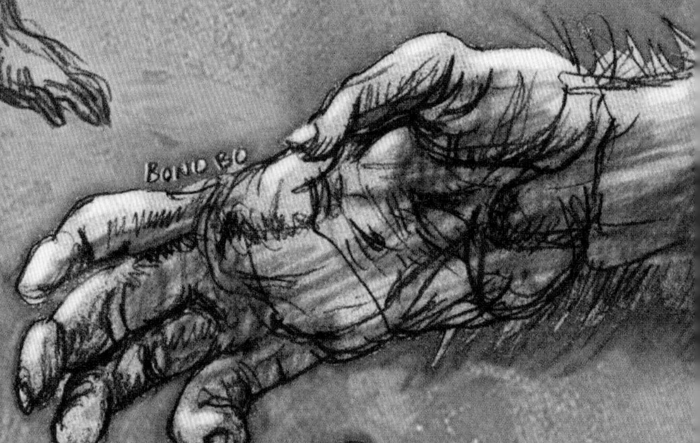

How the Paw Became a Hand

The hands of our closest relatives demonstrate the commonalities we share. Yet our fingers are shorter and our thumbs are longer and more powerful, which gives us greater dexterity and power.

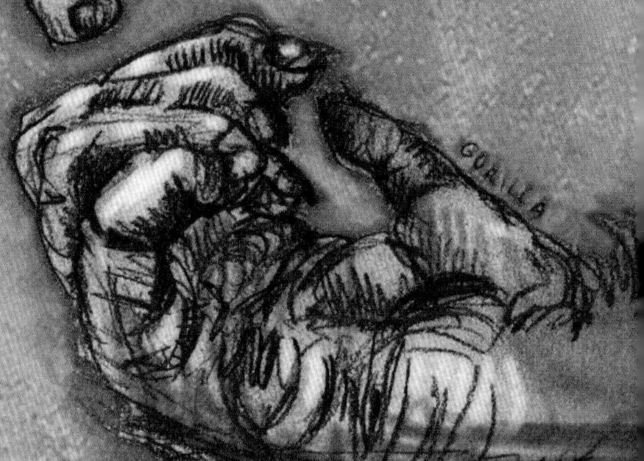

Since descending from the trees, hominid brains, bodies, and hands simultaneously developed greater flexibility. The neurologist Frank Wilson argues that the cognitive capacity of the brain evolved hand in hand (so to speak) with the biomechanical properties of the shoulder, arm, and hand. Our cognitive and manual complexity and adaptability were shaped by the forces of natural selection on our prehominid ancestors.

We establish connection and comfort each other with our hands. Holding hands with a loved one lowers blood pressure and reduces the experience of pain. Even holding a stranger's hand can help alleviate physical and emotional suffering.

Our grasp can be both forceful and delicate. We can chop down trees and perform brain surgery. As with our many other inherited abilities, we learn to use our hands for diverse purposes not dictated by the pressures of natural selection. For example, we play (and build) pianos, pitch baseballs with surgical exactitude, and scale vertical cliffs just for the fun and challenge of it.

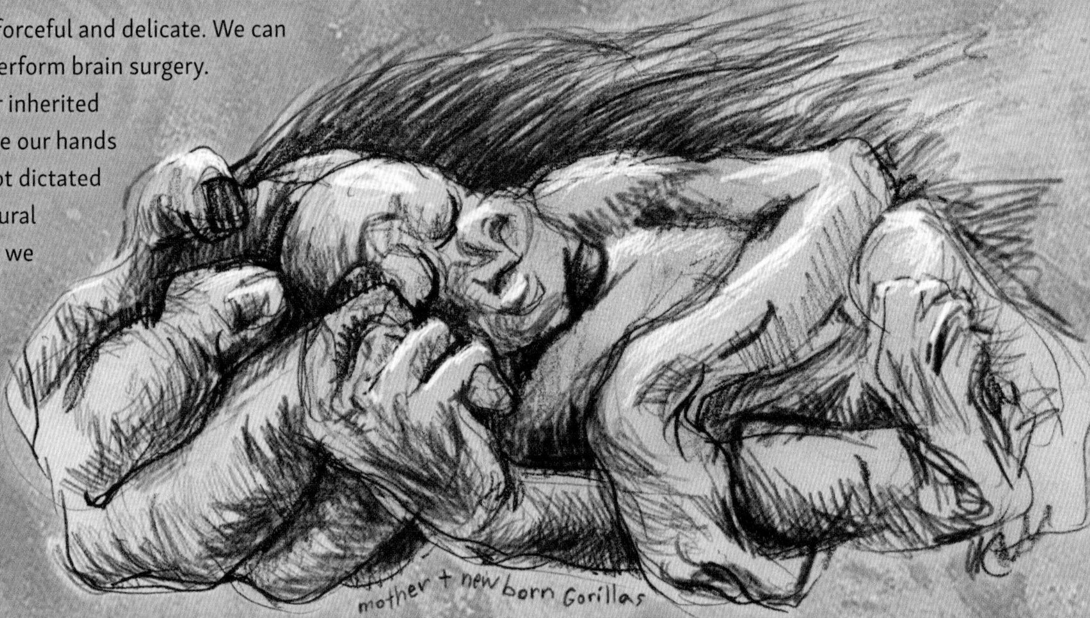

Penfield's Homunculi model the size of each part of the body in proportion to the area of the cerebral cortex that controls it.

These body parts are drawn in proportion to the area of the SENSORY cortex devoted to them.

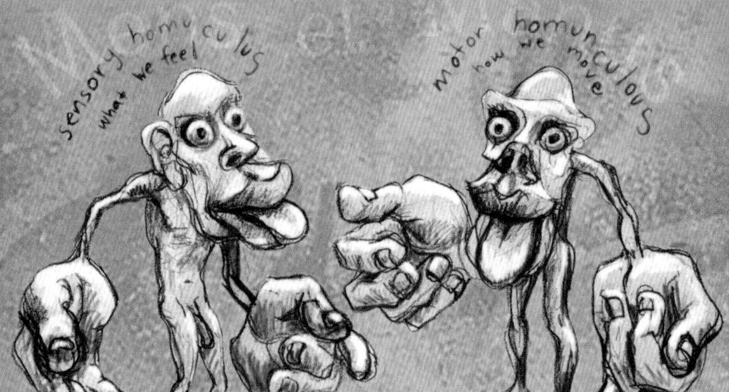

These body parts are drawn in proportion to the area of the MOTOR cortex devoted to them.

Wilder Penfield was an early pioneer of brain surgery to treat epilepsy. While operating, Penfield mapped the cortex using electrical stimulation while the patient was awake. In this way he was able to map the surface areas of the motor and sensory cortices of the brain that correspond to specific areas of the body. He found that the hand, as an organ of both perception and action, takes up a disproportionate share of cortical real estate. Compare the size of the thumb in both figures to the size of their thighs. There are some differences between the sensory homunculous on the left and the motor homonculous on the right, such as the ears. For example, the ears are relatively large on the sensory side, yet almost disappear on the motor homunculous, as ears are responsible for hearing, but most of us are not able to voluntarily wiggle them! In both, however, the hands dominate.

What Do HANDS Do?

A nearby rock may present an opportunity to be thrown, if it is small enough, or sat upon, if it is large enough. The psychologists James and Eleanor Gibson invented ecological theories of perception and development, which called attention to the kinds of opportunities for action certain environments might present to humans or nonhuman animals. The Gibsons called these opportunities "affordances." Human hands seek out affordances to grasp and to hold, to explore and pick apart, sometimes seemingly on their own, without the involvement of our conscious minds. We doodle mindlessly while on the phone. Whole industries of fidget spinners and anti-stress squeeze balls have grown up around some hands' occasional compulsion to find something, anything, to do ...

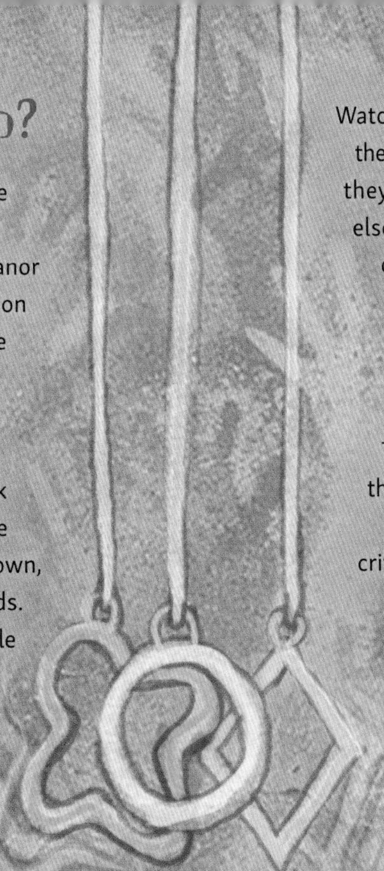

Watch young babies discover their hands. At first they wave them about aimlessly, surprised when they accidentally hit themselves or something else. Eventually they gain some control. Babies discover their hands' abilities to exert force to impact the things around them. As they discover ways to control their own hands, they discover agency, their ability to grasp the objects and beings within their reach. They learn to soothe themselves (by sucking their thumbs or whole fists!) and communicate with others. The discovery of their hands is a critical milestone in babies' physical, cognitive, and social development. They are learning about the opportunities for action, the "affordances," the environment and their own bodies provide. An individual's unique cognitive and motor abilities develop through interactions with the environment and others.

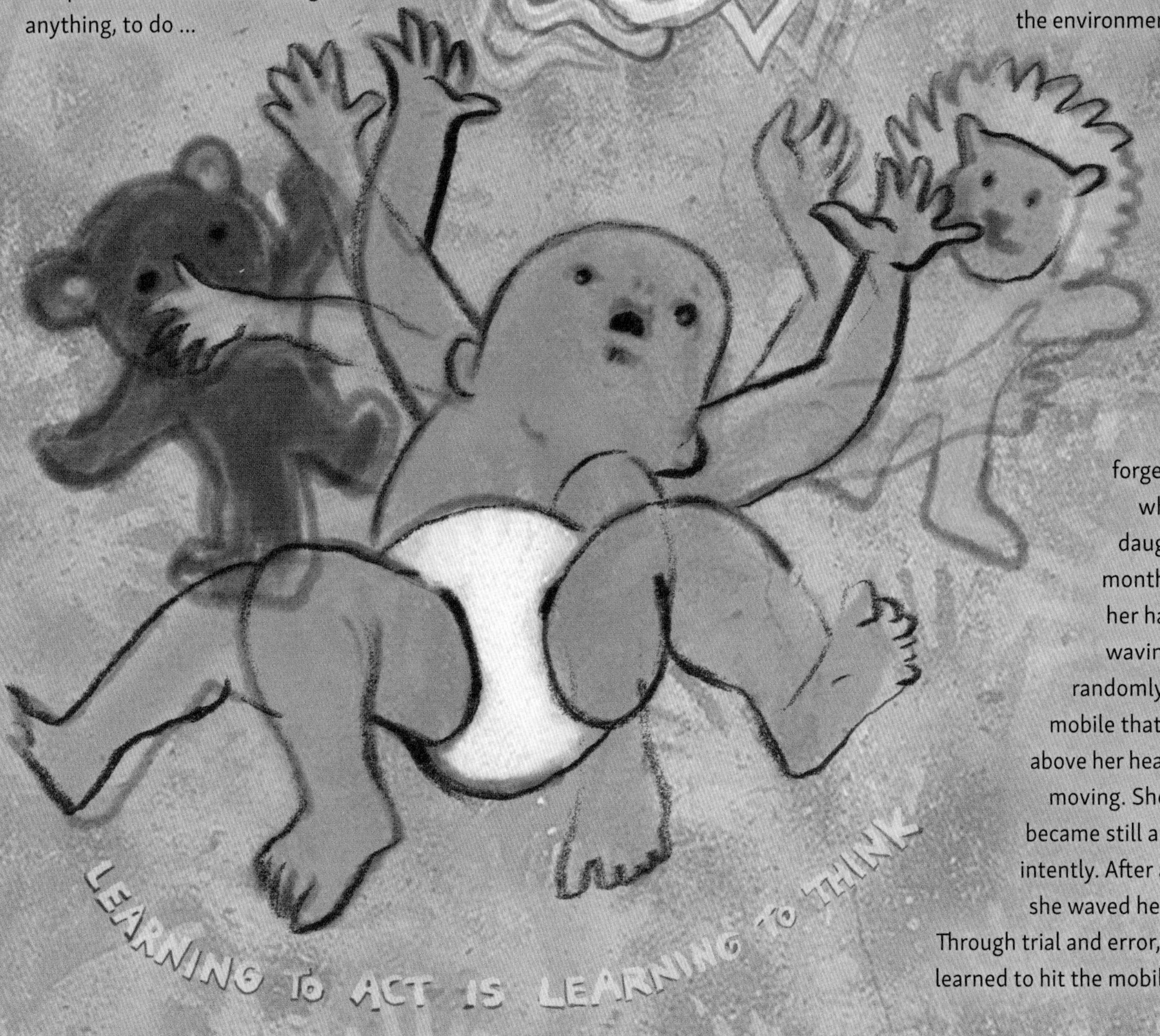

I will never forget the moment when my oldest daughter, at three months, discovered her hands. She was waving them about randomly, and struck a mobile that was dangling above her head that started moving. She immediately became still and stared at it intently. After a few seconds she waved her hands again. Through trial and error, she gradually learned to hit the mobile on purpose.

My Mother's Garden

My mother loved to dig in the dirt. She was locally famous in our suburban community for her prize-winning hybrid roses (dozens, each unique in color, shape, size, and variegation). All July, August, and into September, we feasted on juicy strawberries, fresh corn, tomatoes, and squash, and sometimes pumpkins. She had spent her childhood on her grandmother's farm, and knew what she was doing. As a young child, I liked to sit next to her as she weeded and pruned, planted and harvested. Today, when I dig a hole in my own garden for my neighbor's gift of a trumpet vine, I remember my mother's instruction to feel the qualities and resistance of the earth. I gently break apart the roots, taking just enough dirt out of the hole so that, after I settle it in and press the dirt firmly down around it, the plant is at the proper level with the soil.

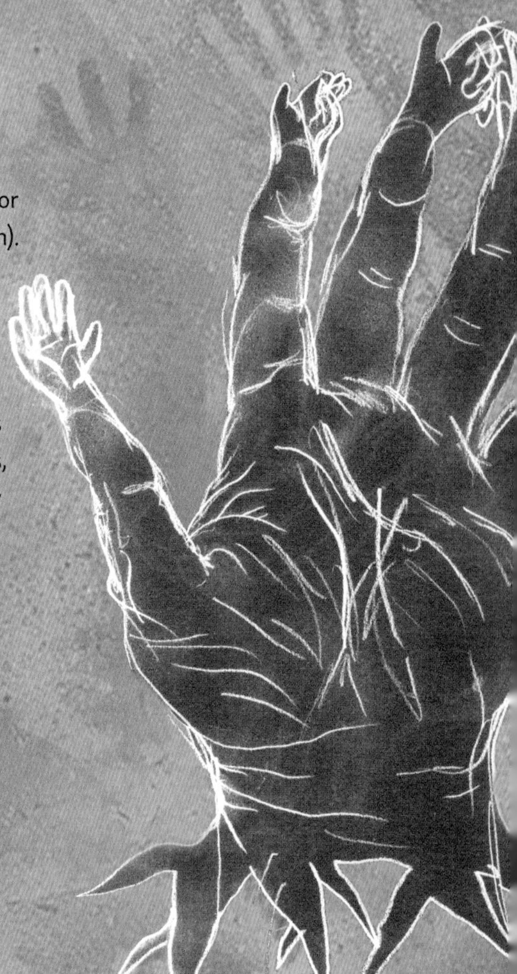

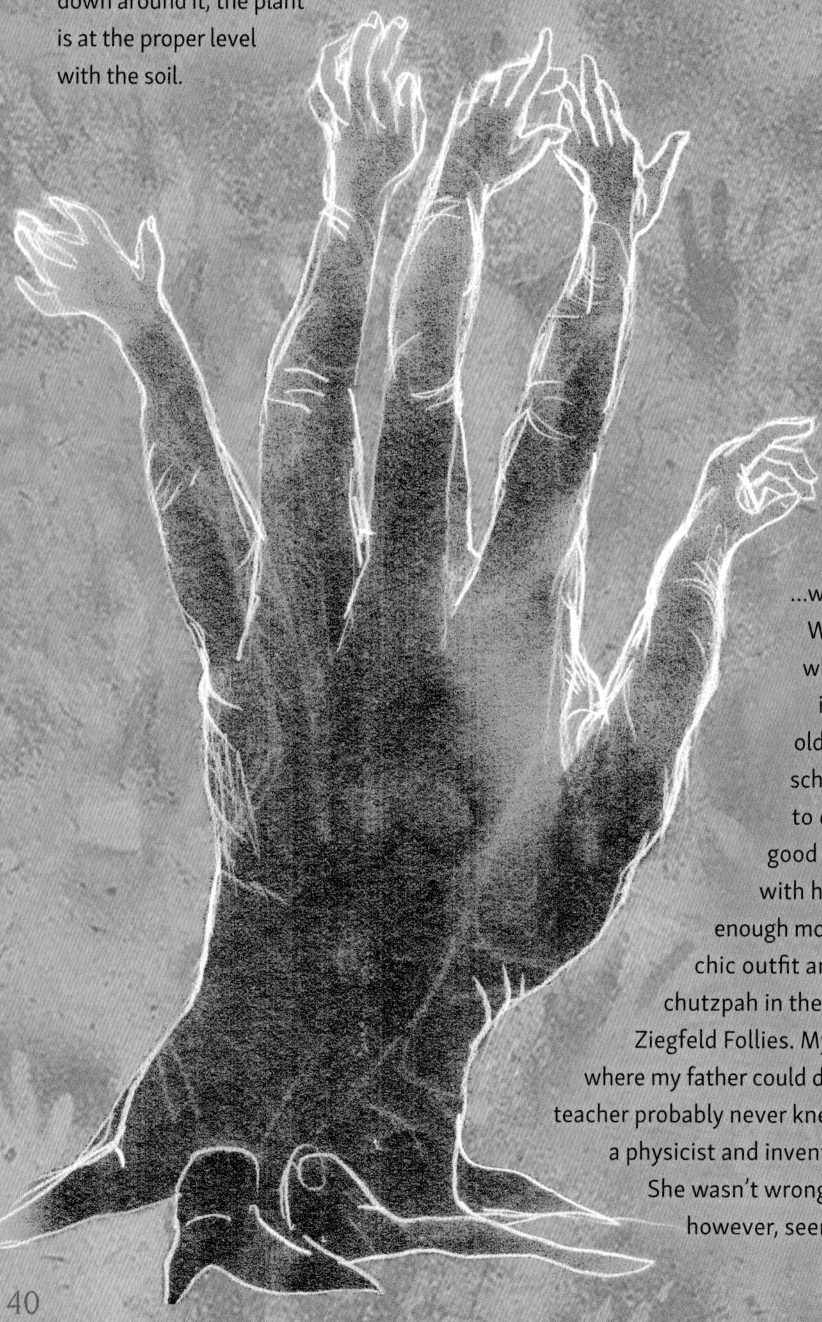

My Father's Hands...

...were broad and powerful, yet patient and meticulous. When I was small he had a workshop in the basement where he made all kinds of furniture, gadgets, and toys, including a dollhouse for me. When he was ten years old, his teacher called his mother (my grandmother) into school to tell her that it might not be worthwhile for him to continue his formal schooling, but that he was very good with his hands. My grandmother was also very good with her hands. As a young immigrant, she managed to put enough money aside from her sweatshop work to sew herself a chic outfit and assembled portfolio of drawings that (with some chutzpah in the mix) earned her a job as a designer with the famous Ziegfeld Follies. My grandmother Rose provided a corner of her kitchen where my father could dissect and reassemble radios. My father's fifth-grade teacher probably never knew that despite some mild dyslexia he grew up to be a physicist and inventor. She thought he would be excellent at carpentry. She wasn't wrong: carpentry became his life-long hobby. His teacher, however, seemed to believe that being intelligent and being good with one's hands were mutually exclusive.

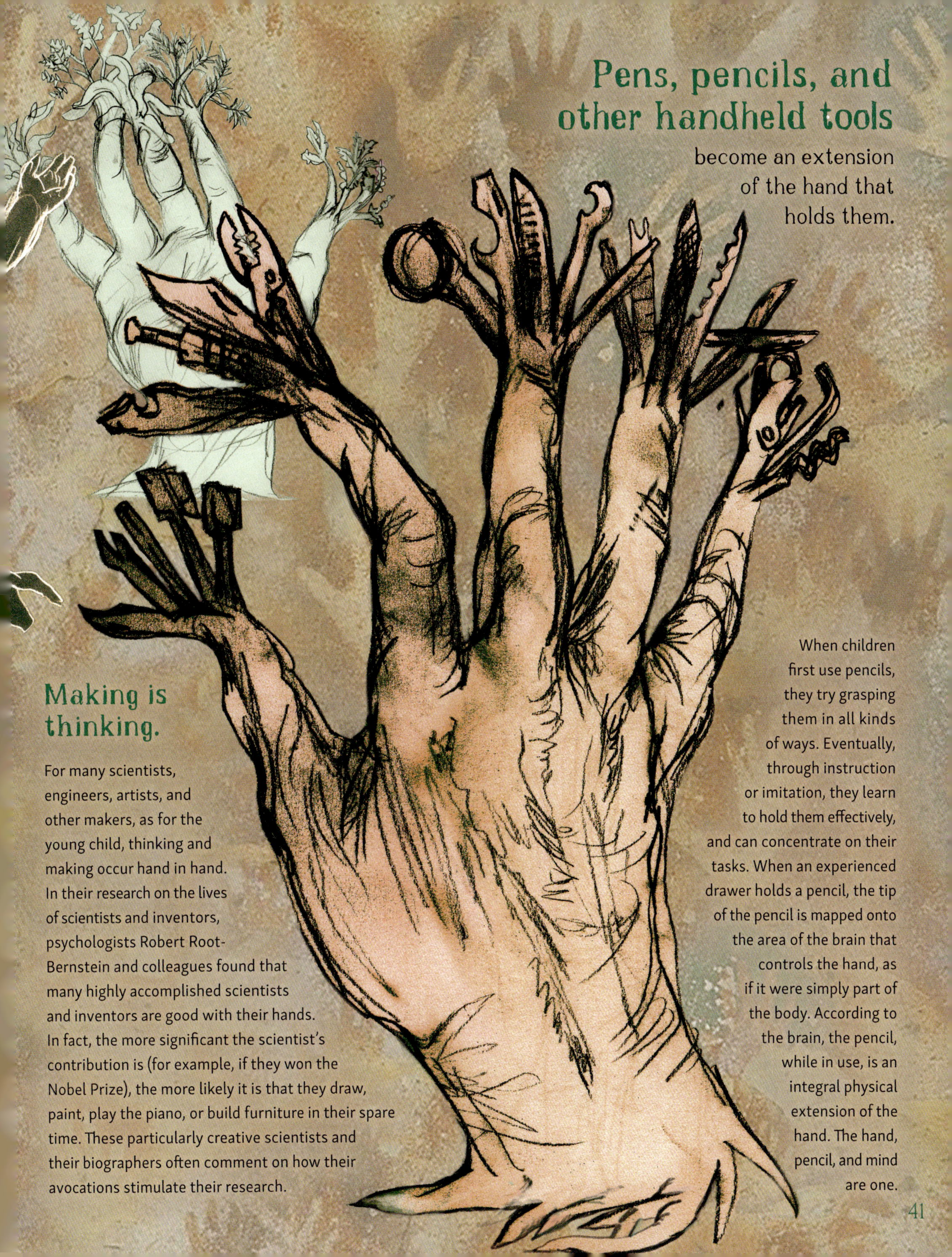

Pens, pencils, and other handheld tools

become an extension of the hand that holds them.

Making is thinking.

For many scientists, engineers, artists, and other makers, as for the young child, thinking and making occur hand in hand. In their research on the lives of scientists and inventors, psychologists Robert Root-Bernstein and colleagues found that many highly accomplished scientists and inventors are good with their hands. In fact, the more significant the scientist's contribution is (for example, if they won the Nobel Prize), the more likely it is that they draw, paint, play the piano, or build furniture in their spare time. These particularly creative scientists and their biographers often comment on how their avocations stimulate their research.

When children first use pencils, they try grasping them in all kinds of ways. Eventually, through instruction or imitation, they learn to hold them effectively, and can concentrate on their tasks. When an experienced drawer holds a pencil, the tip of the pencil is mapped onto the area of the brain that controls the hand, as if it were simply part of the body. According to the brain, the pencil, while in use, is an integral physical extension of the hand. The hand, pencil, and mind are one.

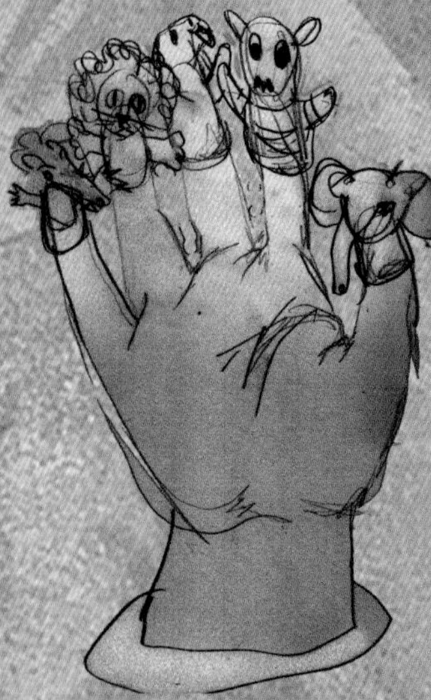

Hands-on Learning

We hold knowledge in our hands as well as our heads. Friedrich Froebel understood this when he invented the kindergarten in Germany in 1837. He designed a sequence of objects, or "gifts," wooden blocks and other objects that children manipulated in order to learn. "Froebel's Gifts" are models for modern educational manipulatives as teachers today still find students often learn best through hands-on activities.

Educational "Sloyd," or handicraft, a compulsory subject in many Scandinavian schools, is a combination of wood, metal, and textile work. It started in Finland in 1865 and became integrated into elementary education not for vocational training, but because it was viewed as essential to the mental, emotional, and social education of children. Today Sloyd is compulsory in Finish, Danish, Swedish, and Norwegian schools, and is seen as essential for all young people's cognitive development regardless of their future career paths.

As an art educator I have personally witnessed what a difference hands-on activities can make in young people's grasp of otherwise difficult and abstract concepts. This is especially true for students facing the greatest challenges. Several years ago, I helped design and implement an experimental project integrating high-quality, standards-based instruction in the visual arts, math, and literacy in New York City public schools located in high-poverty communities. Students learned new ways to think about and explore academic subjects through hands-on art-making activities. They scored higher on standardized tests, especially in math. They also developed a greater appreciation for the relationships between different subjects, As one fourth-grade student explained, "I never realized before how art was not just making things, but about learning and understanding stuff, not just about art, but science and social studies and math and ELA … how everything is connected."

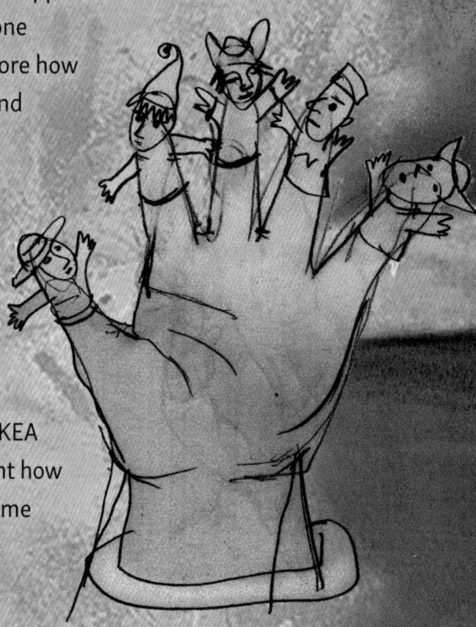

Studies by psychologist Dan Ariely and his colleagues have shown that when people build things with their own hands, they tend to value them more highly than when they receive the same product already assembled. In a paper entitled "The IKEA Effect: When Labor Leads to Love," researchers recount how people, asked to fold origami cranes and frogs, became so attached to them that they valued their novice creations more highly than those made by experts.

Manual crafts are too often sidelined, and understood as mere vocational training for those who struggle with traditional academic schooling. Table saws and hand tools from shop classrooms showed up in great numbers on eBay in the 1990s as schools repurposed these classrooms as computer labs (with the changing job market in mind).

In my own experience, teaching art in elementary school classrooms in the 2000s, I watched children's basic manual skills with scissors and glue decline year by year. It is telling that many high-tech professionals in Silicon Valley, the same individuals who have made the ubiquitous digital devices that seem to control our lives, keep those same devices out of the hands of their own children, giving them clay, crayons, and paper instead.

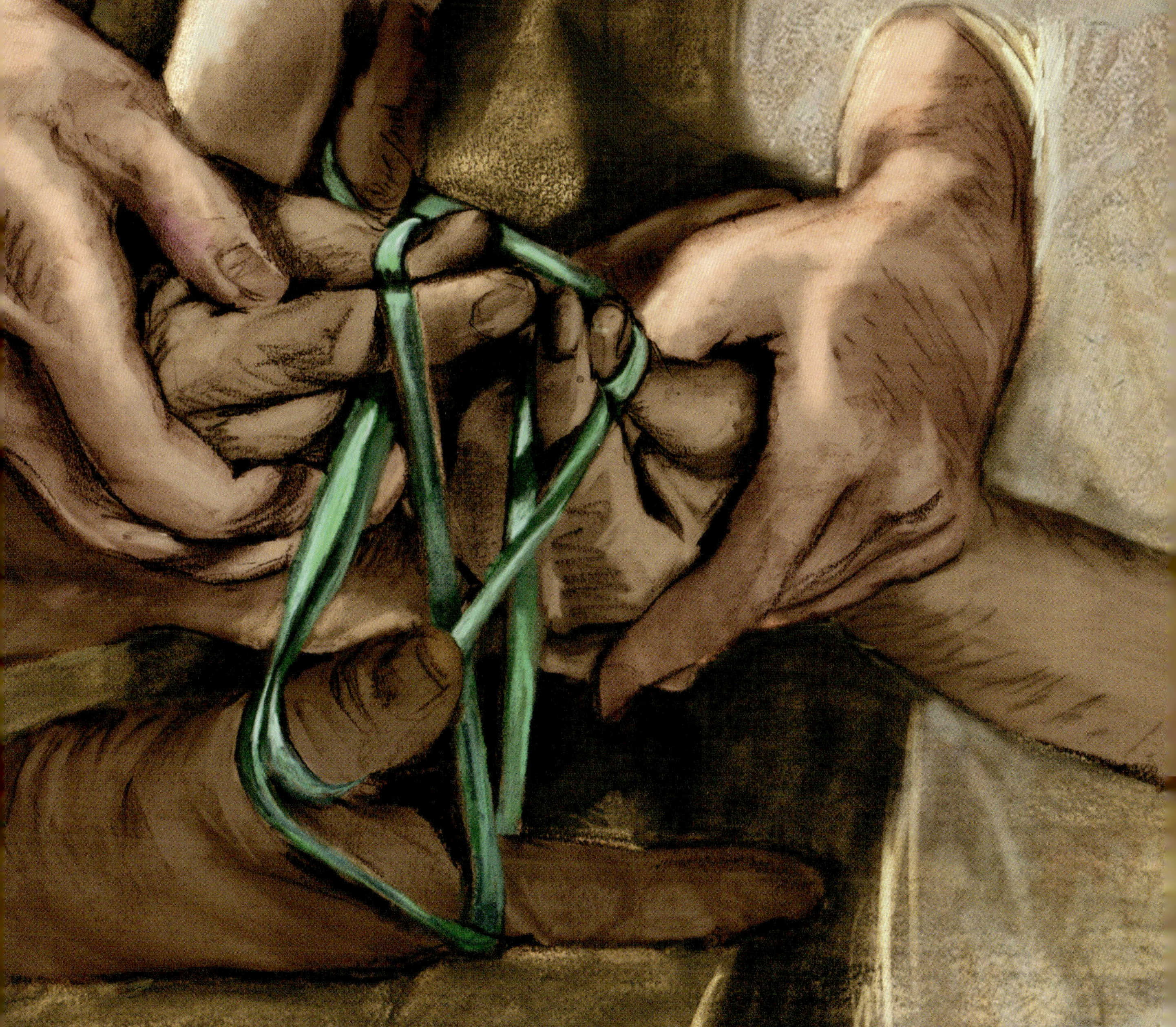

The Hand Speaks

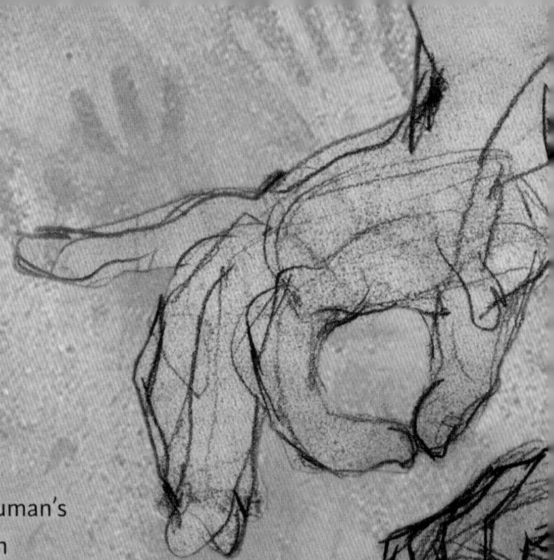

Any good comedian or storyteller knows how to use their hands to engage their audience. Gesture as a mode of communication precedes words, in evolution and in individual human development. Social animals, such as wolves and lions, communicate with each other in complex ways through gesture, sometimes in ways even we can understand.

A typically developing human infant learns to look in the direction of another human's pointing finger between six and nine months of age. Soon after, usually between nine and twelve months, babies begin to clap, wave and point themselves, in order to communicate with others. Babies point to what they want and reach toward a caregiver to be held and carried well before they ask for what they want by name or learn to walk. Long before they say, "Pick me up," they reach their arms out toward their parent, who cannot doubt the meaning of the gesture.

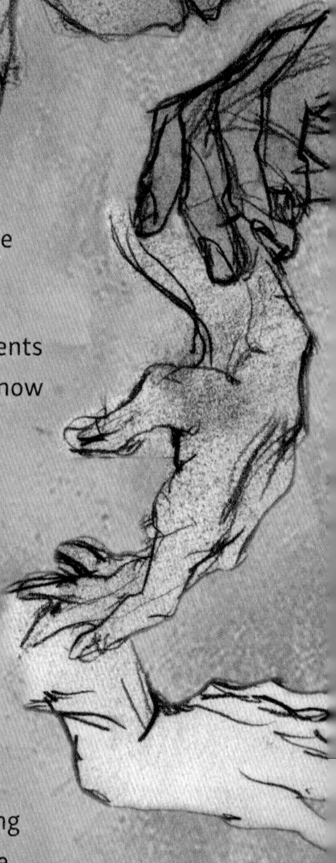

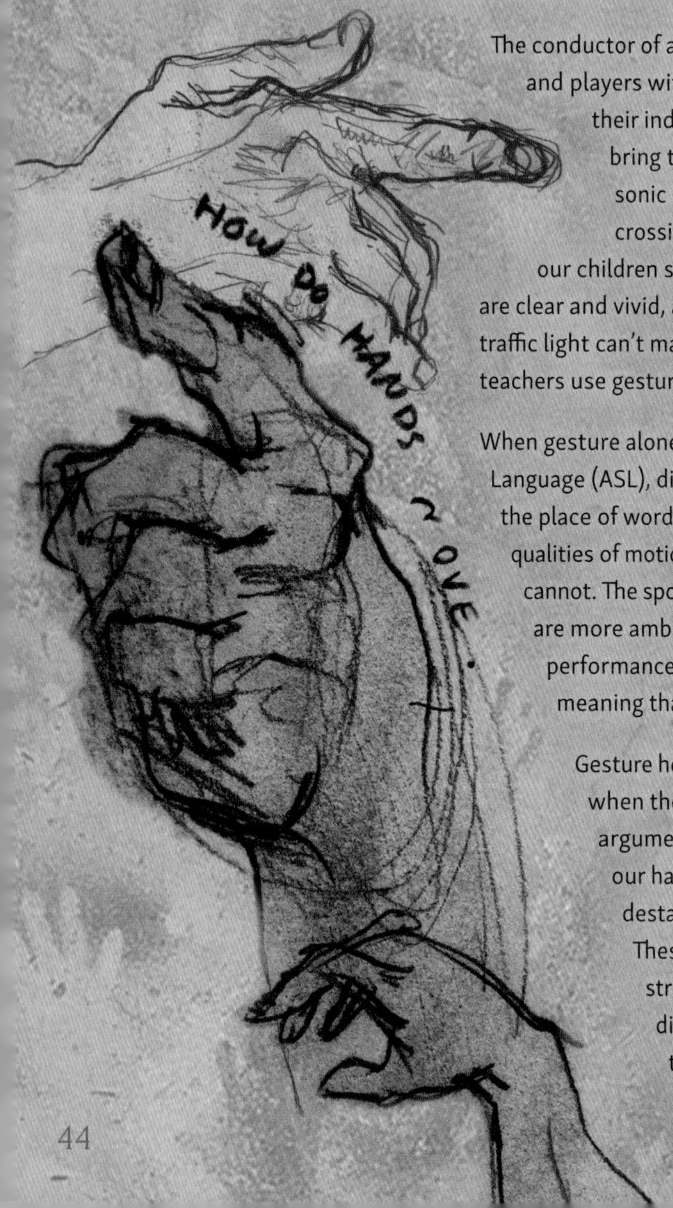

The conductor of an orchestra coordinates all the many instruments and players with a well-known set of gestures. The players know their individual parts, but rely on the conductor to bring them in at the right time to create a holistic sonic experience for the audience. We trust the crossing guard at the busy intersection to keep our children safe on their way to school: his gestures are clear and vivid, and carry an authority that a mere traffic light can't match. Students learn better when their teachers use gesture to augment their instruction.

When gesture alone is used to communicate, as in American Sign Language (ASL), discrete motions denote specific concepts, taking the place of words and phrases in spoken language. Even so, the qualities of motions, their speed and grace, can be expressive in ways that words cannot. The spontaneous, improvised gestures that accompany spoken language are more ambiguous and fluid than those used in the context of orchestral performance, traffic control, or ASL. They provide an alternative stream of meaning that sometimes, but not always, matches what is being said.

Gesture helps us THINK. Even people who are blind from birth will gesture when they talk. When we try to answer a difficult question or make an argument, we have a much more difficult time if we are asked to sit on our hands. We may change the way we think just by moving our hands, destabilizing thought in a way that makes conceptual progress possible. These kinds of spontaneous gestures, which externalize thinking in a less structured form than words, can assist learners to "feel" their way through difficult problems or concepts. Regardless of any response from others, the gesture itself helps to form new understandings for the learner; hands sometimes know what words may not yet be able to articulate.

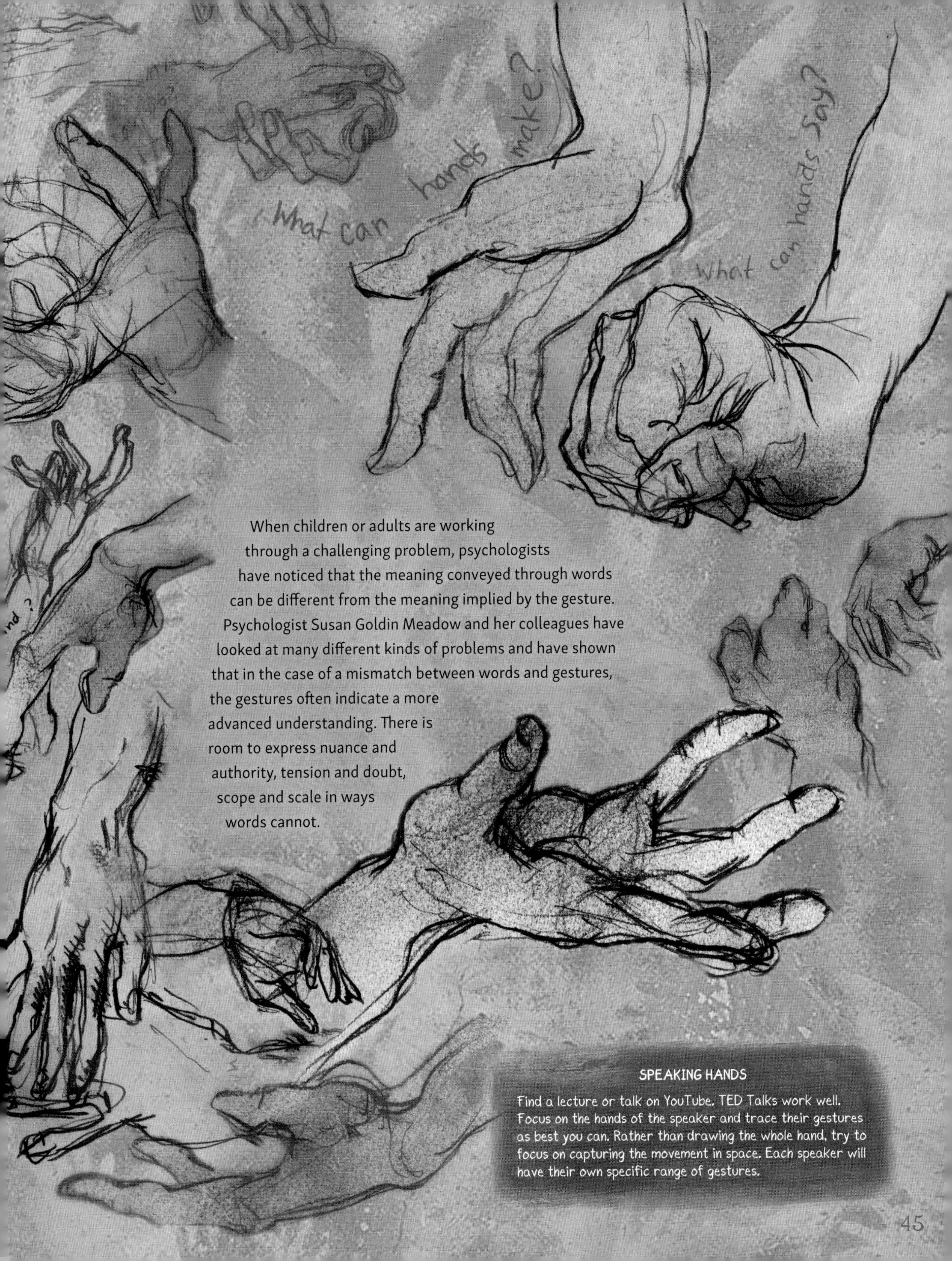

When children or adults are working through a challenging problem, psychologists have noticed that the meaning conveyed through words can be different from the meaning implied by the gesture. Psychologist Susan Goldin Meadow and her colleagues have looked at many different kinds of problems and have shown that in the case of a mismatch between words and gestures, the gestures often indicate a more advanced understanding. There is room to express nuance and authority, tension and doubt, scope and scale in ways words cannot.

SPEAKING HANDS

Find a lecture or talk on YouTube. TED Talks work well. Focus on the hands of the speaker and trace their gestures as best you can. Rather than drawing the whole hand, try to focus on capturing the movement in space. Each speaker will have their own specific range of gestures.

Thinking with a Pencil

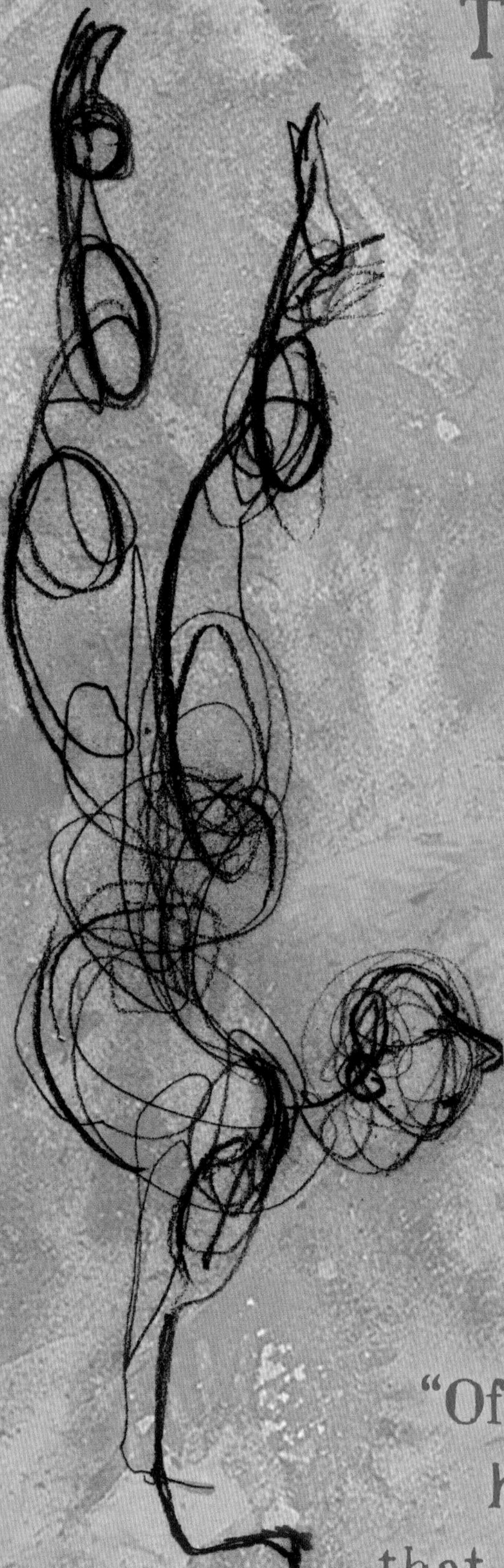

Drawings, like words and gestures, may represent things in the world. Sometimes gesture (and gestural) drawings can describe more specific information than words can. For example, there are a limited number of words to describe the height of an object (words like tall, short, medium), but one can use a hand gesture to describe the height of a thing by placing the hand at one of an infinite number of possible positions. Drawings can contain all kinds of information that can be difficult or even impossible to verbalize.

Gesture studies have recently emerged as significant field within psychological research but "gesture studies" in art and design have been around for centuries. Rough sketches can capture the continuous and unplanned qualities of the spontaneous hand gestures that accompany speech. In art, gesture studies are a specific type of rough sketch with a long history in the quick sketches and preparatory drawings used to explore ideas and solve problems for larger works.

Traditionally artists have paid a great deal of attention to capturing gesture: those "first thoughts" make their work vivid and alive. In a figurative gesture drawing the artist mimics the movements of the figures with the movement of the hand. Kimon Nicolaides was an influential drawing teacher at the Art Students' League of New York in the 1920s and '30s whose book *The Natural Way to Draw* is still widely used today. He emphasized gesture in his figure drawing classes. He encouraged his students to loosen up and freely make marks and lines in response to an observed model. "Often students do them well and are quite surprised at the results, which are far beyond any knowledge they have. The reason is that by working quickly they accidentally find the gesture. The gesture is a feeler which reaches out and guides them to knowledge." He noticed that somehow his students were able to capture more than they were actively conscious of noticing. This happens frequently when drawing quickly. The experienced drawer learns that hands and eyes working together can see much more than eyes alone. This may be why hand gestures and gestural sketches can exhibit more advanced understandings than words alone.

"Of all the hand-held tools that have been invented, the sort that makes traces on a surface is especially noteworthy—the stylus...

We can also use the sensitivity we all hold at our fingertips when we draw. Nicolaides taught his students "to bring into play your sense of touch and to coordinate it with your sense of sight for the purpose of drawing." He asked them to feel that the tip of their pencil was actually touching the subject of their drawing. This is called "contour drawing," and requires a high degree of hand-eye synchronization. Normally our eyes tend to dart around as we scan a scene, in restless bursts of activity known as saccades. It takes a conscious effort and deliberate practice to slow down eye and hand so they move together.

Nicolaides explained, "Imagine that your pencil point is touching the model instead of the paper. Without taking your eyes off the model, wait until you are convinced that the pencil is touching that point on the model upon which your eyes are fastened." He exhorted his students to move slowly and sensitively, not letting the eye get ahead of the hand. It's not an easy instruction to understand and follow; it goes against our ordinary ways of seeing. I found this out one day as a college student teaching a Nicolaides-inspired drawing class at a local adult education center. A middle-aged man stood up and exclaimed that it was all "poppycock" or some equivalent, and went downstairs to complain to the manager. The perception of edges is central to the process of visual perception, yet operates so far under the level of commonplace consciousness, it takes much concentration and practice to truly "see" the edge as it wraps around the form.

"Drawing is both an action and a form of perception, finely-tuned for detail by the coupling of the movements of the eye with those of the hand. One draws for perception, not from perception," writes artist and researcher Angela Brew. She argues that observational drawing is a perceptual process that engages both the eye and hand simultaneously, rather than a translation from visual perception by the eye to the motor action of the hand. Her practice-based research and pedagogical methods allow her to experiment with engaging the hand in coordination with the eye to facilitate perception.

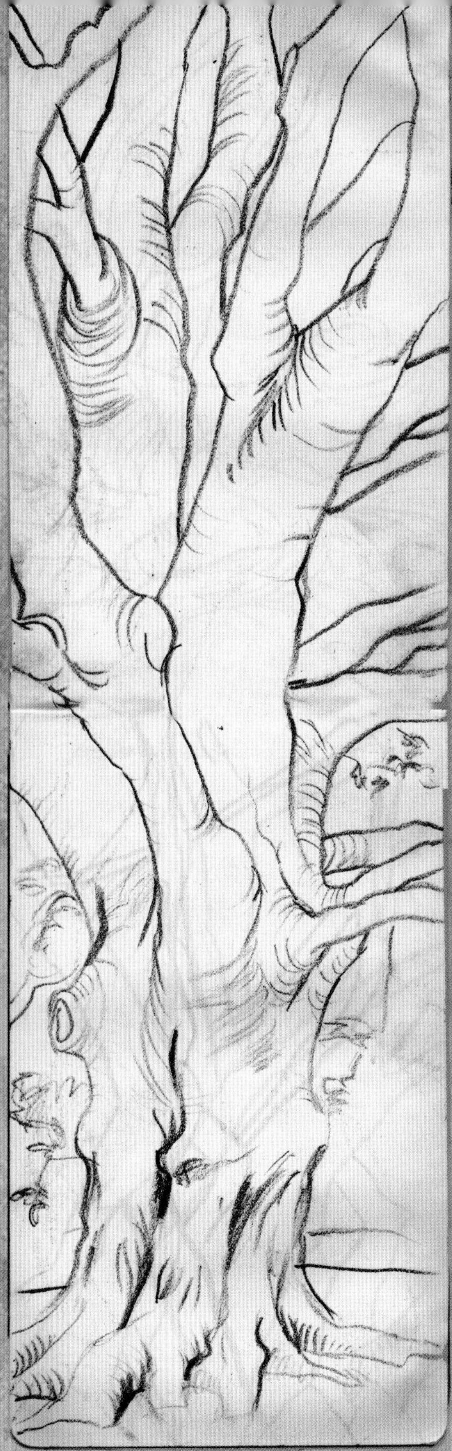

CONTOUR DRAWING
as taught by Angela Brew

Put the index finger of your nondominant hand on your ear and the point of your pencil on the paper. Move your pencil in unison with the finger touching your ear as you slowly trace its curves and spirals. Allow your pencil line to get darker and lighter as you cross over the forms.

...brush, pen, pencil, crayon, or marker. The movement of the tool over the surface is both felt and seen."

— J.J. Gibson, cofounder with E.J. Gibson of Ecological Psychology

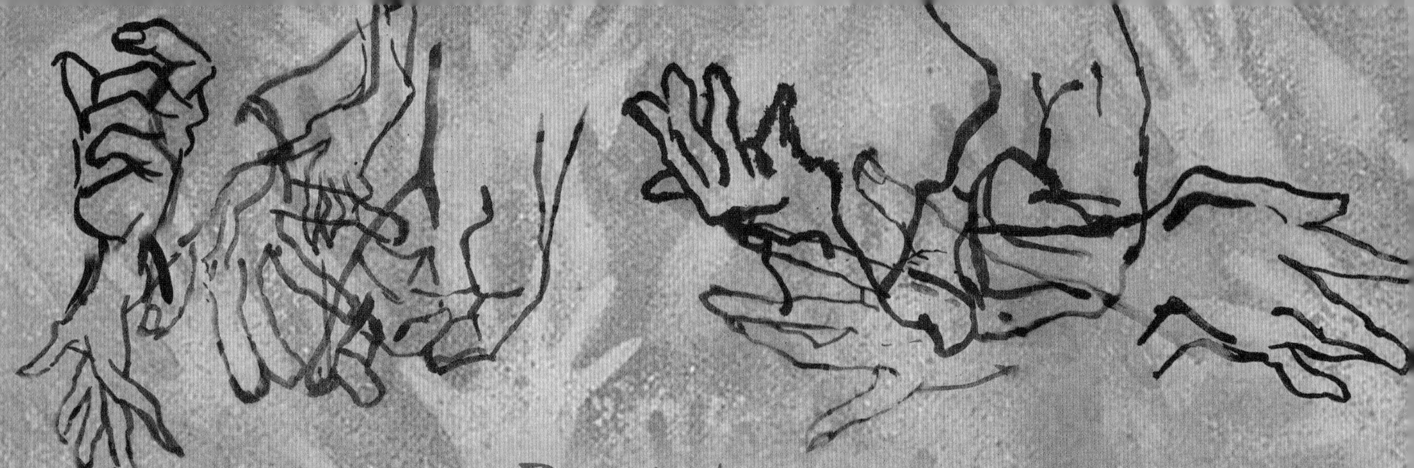

Resistance

Young children draw scribbles at first. Their hands trace marks and lines across smooth or rough surfaces, giving otherwise fleeting gestures material presence. They learn what happens when they press down hard and the minimum force they need to make a visible mark. The material resistance they encounter helps them learn to control their hands and fingers. Each tool leaves a different kind of trace. With crayon or marker or stick in the sand, the varying qualities of the marks teach children about what their hands can do.

As adults we still encounter many forms of RESISTANCE when we draw. Pencil and paper don't always cooperate. Hand-eye coordination does not come easily. There is stuff out there that will not conform to the ideas in our minds. As a young artist, the smooth, elegant lines I admired in the drawings of others seemed unattainable and—honestly—they still do. My own lines are often clumsy and awkward, full of false starts and hesitations. I have learned to tolerate the frustration of falling short of my own ideals. Physical materials have their own intrinsic qualities, not always in sync with my wishes. I learn from their unique qualities.

A change in tools can be liberating. A pencil provides infinite nuances of width and value, yet pen and brush (and brush pens!) are currently my favorite tools for informal sketching. I like the loose and imprecise yet expressive line I can't help but make. Marks that start out one way become something else. Thinking through and with materials opens up new possibilities.

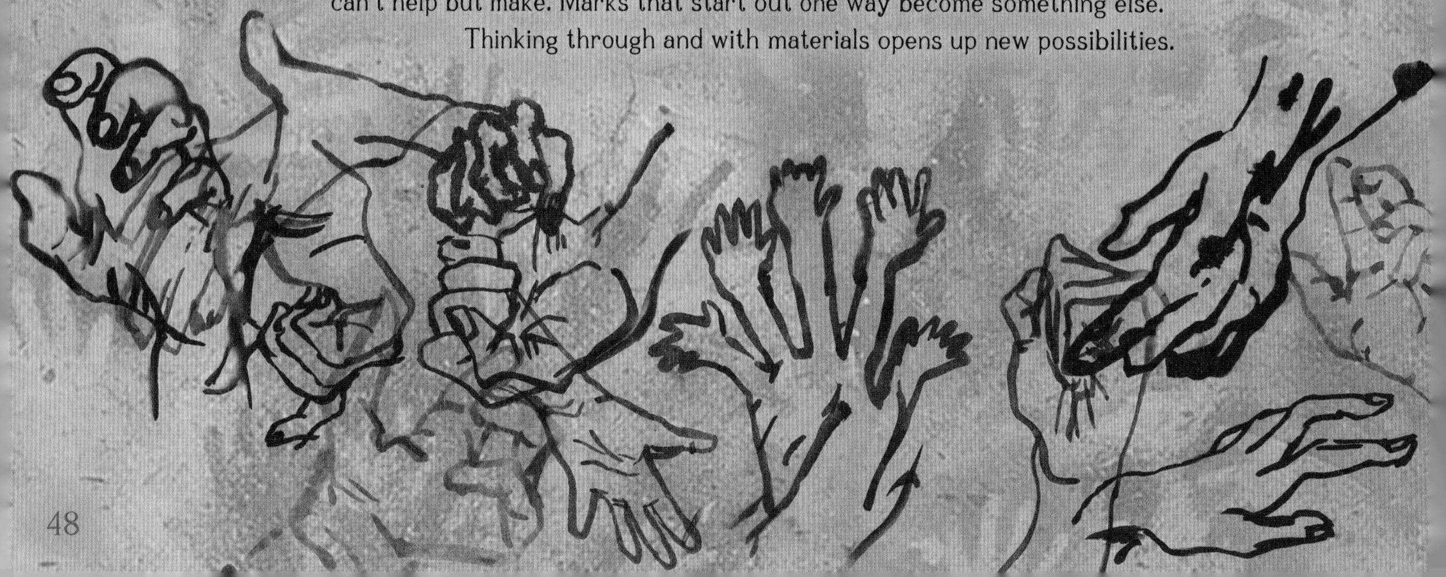

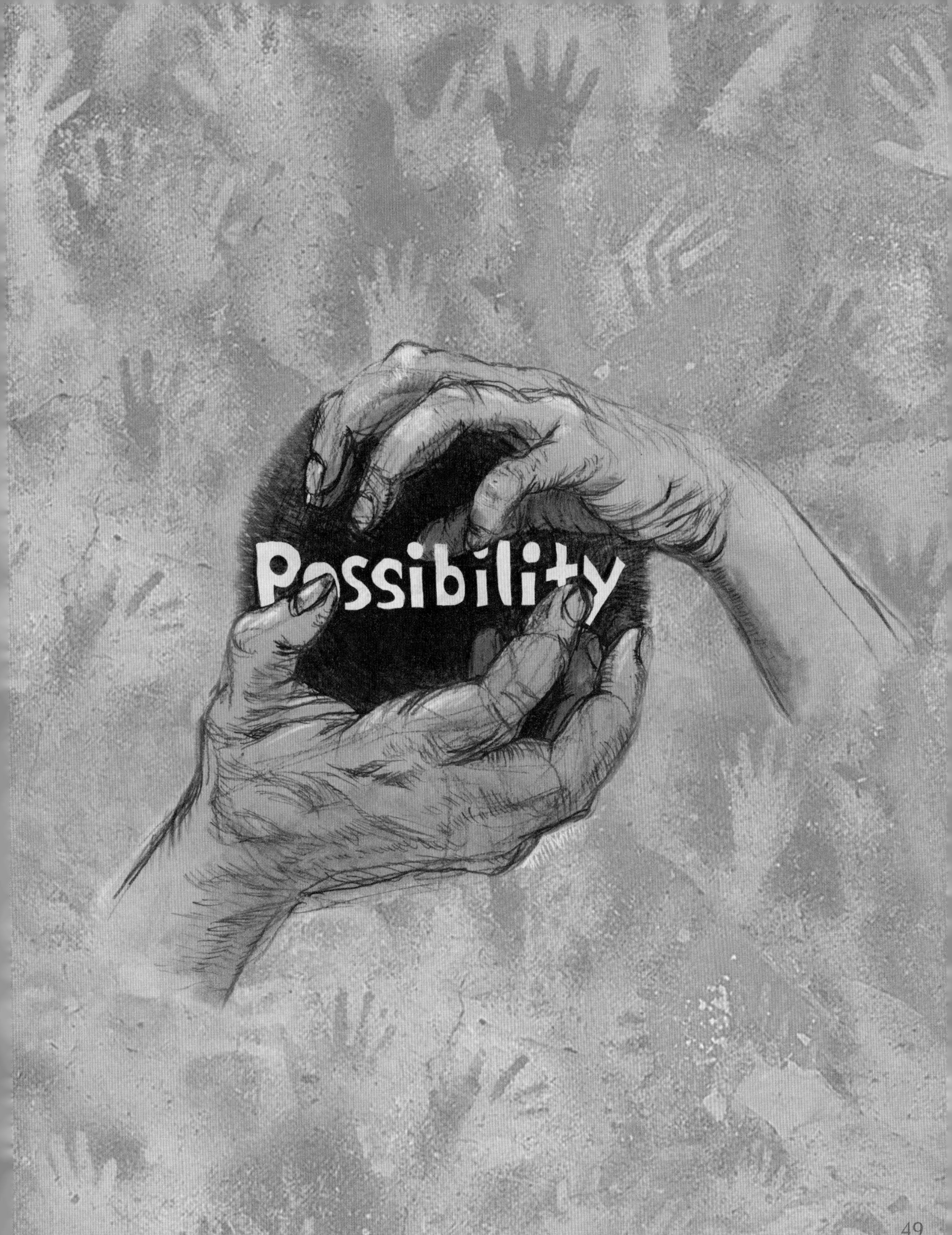
Possibility

How to
See Shapes

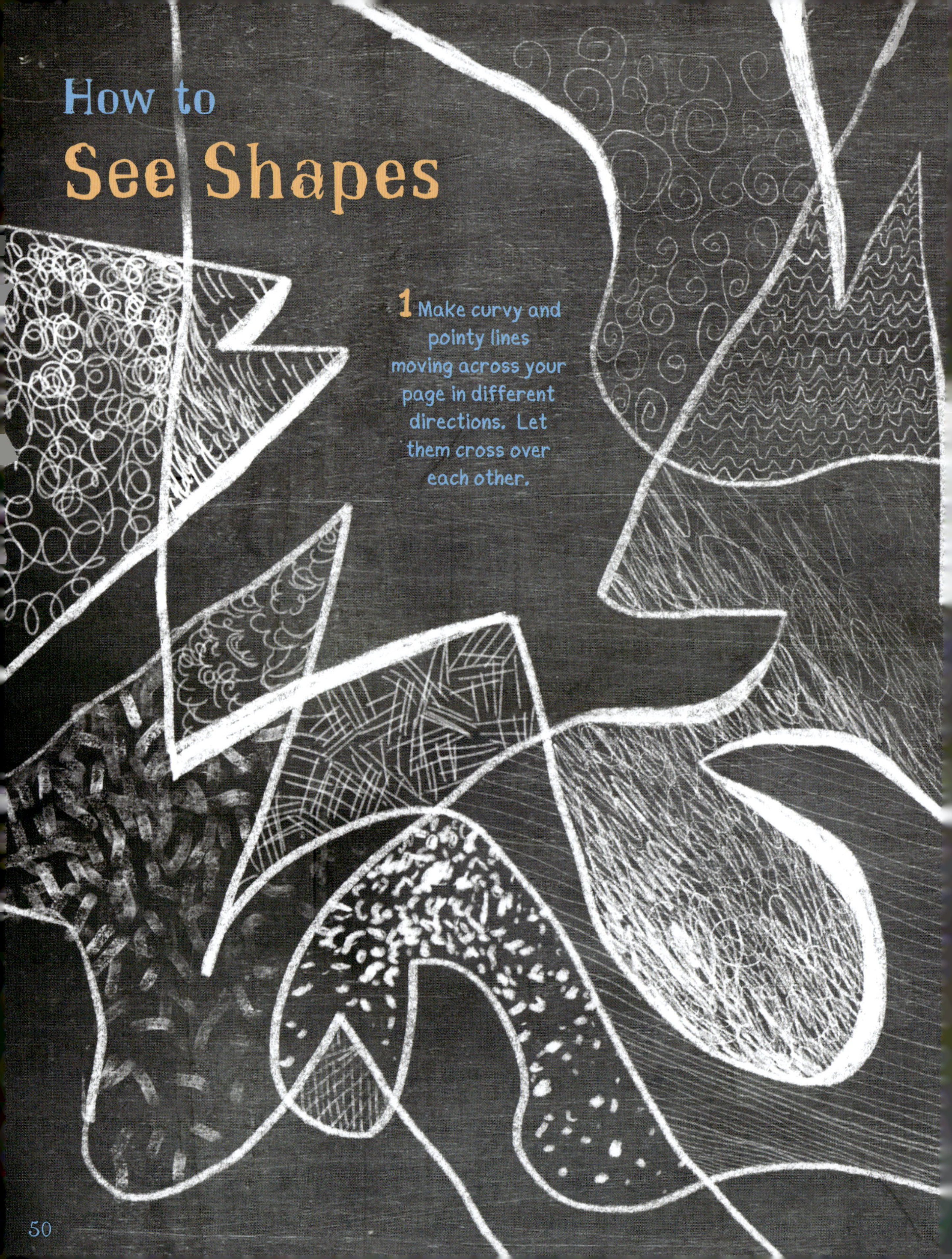

1 Make curvy and pointy lines moving across your page in different directions. Let them cross over each other.

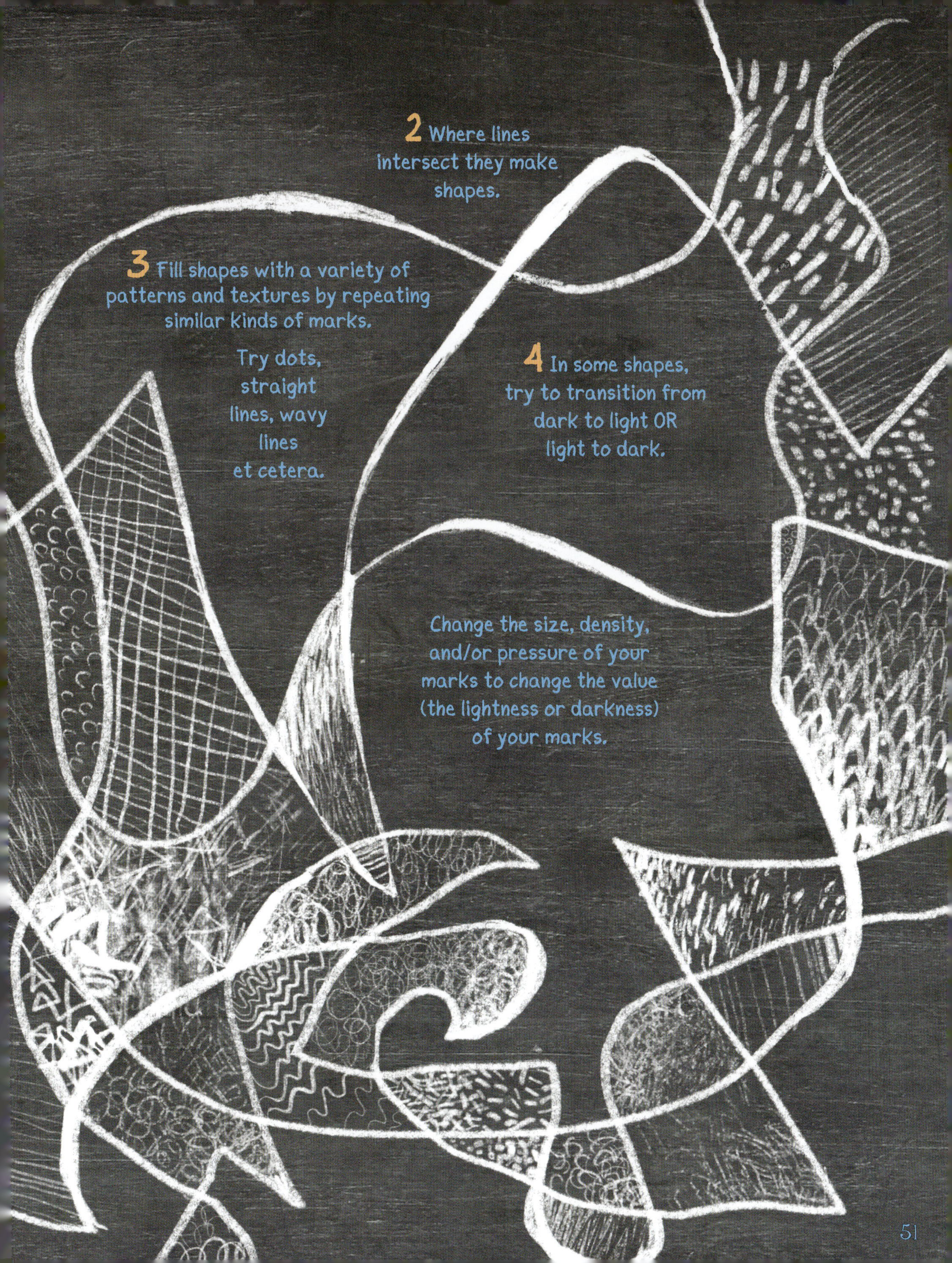

2 Where lines intersect they make shapes.

3 Fill shapes with a variety of patterns and textures by repeating similar kinds of marks.

Try dots, straight lines, wavy lines et cetera.

4 In some shapes, try to transition from dark to light OR light to dark.

Change the size, density, and/or pressure of your marks to change the value (the lightness or darkness) of your marks.

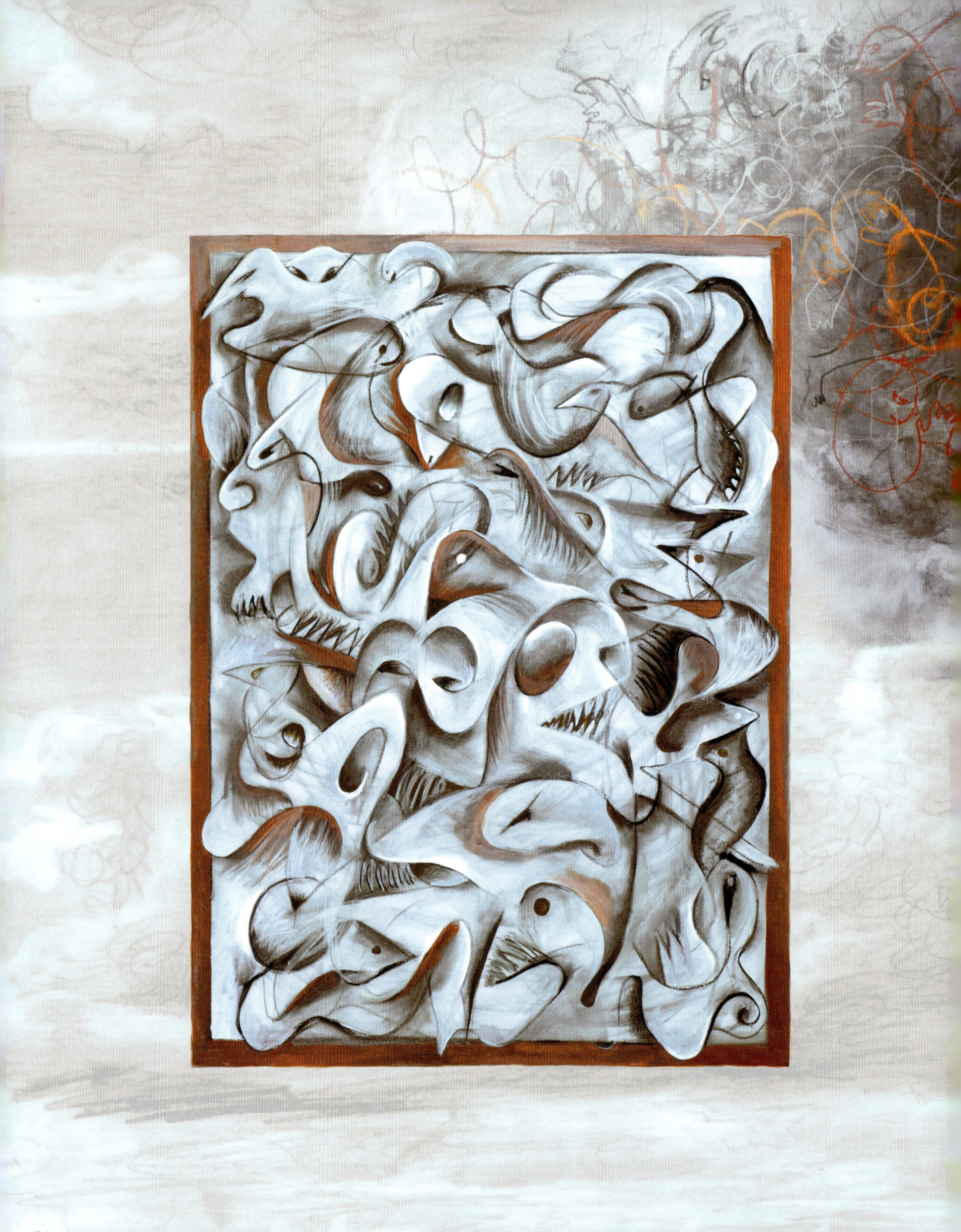

chapter four

Imaginary Friends

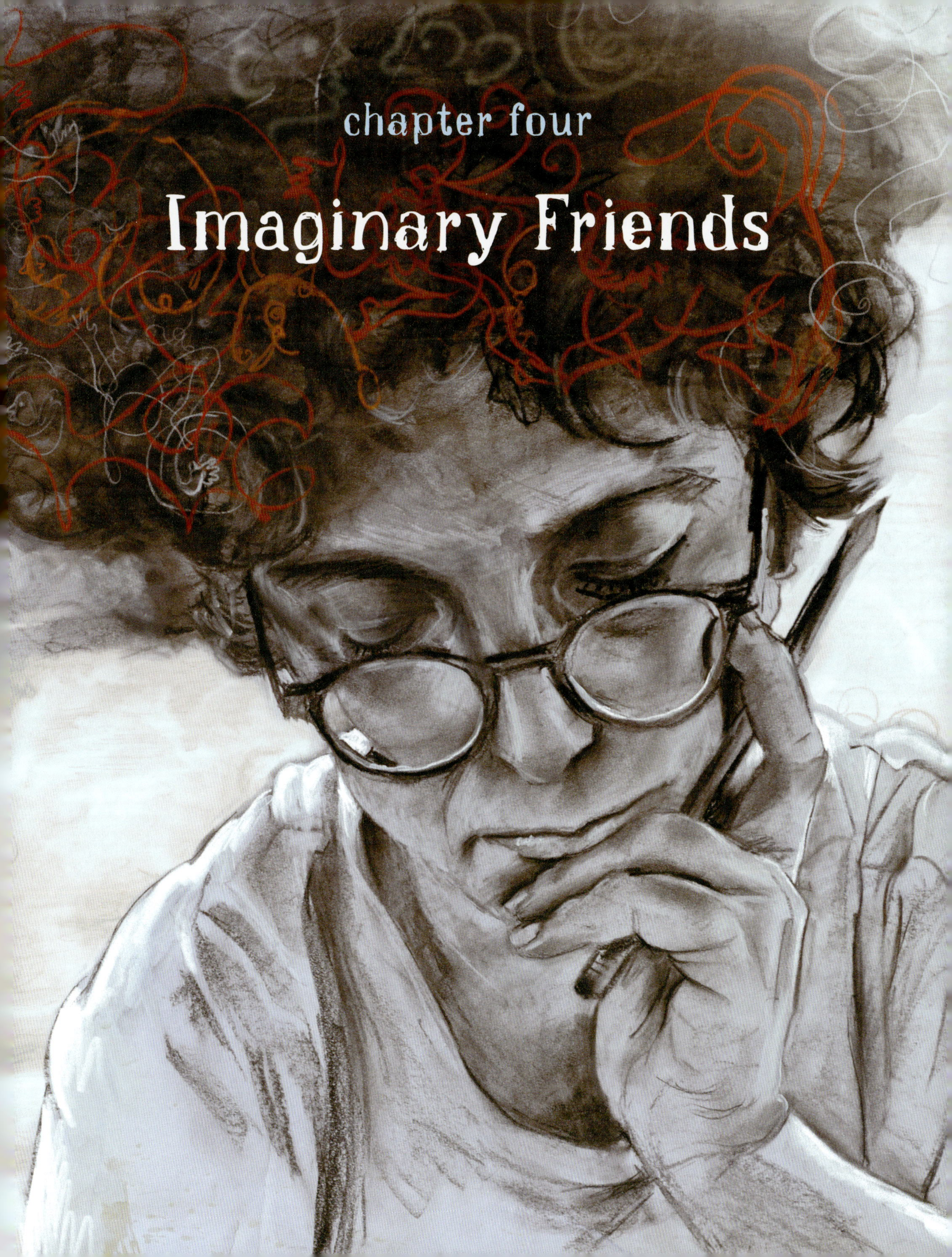

Drawing helps us harness the tendency of the human MIND to PERCEIVE order, pattern, MEANING, and agency in seemingly RANDOM events.

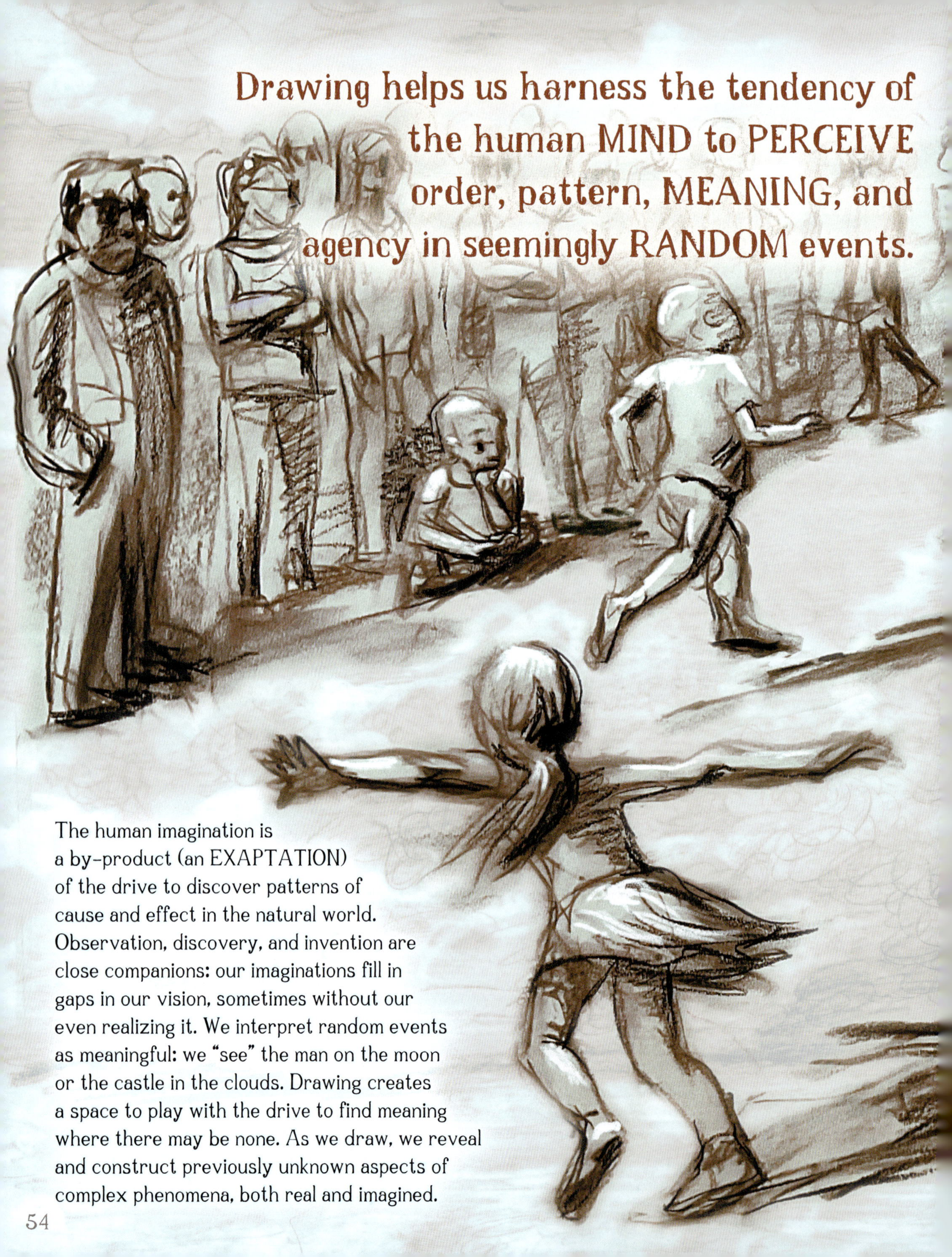

The human imagination is a by-product (an EXAPTATION) of the drive to discover patterns of cause and effect in the natural world. Observation, discovery, and invention are close companions: our imaginations fill in gaps in our vision, sometimes without our even realizing it. We interpret random events as meaningful: we “see” the man on the moon or the castle in the clouds. Drawing creates a space to play with the drive to find meaning where there may be none. As we draw, we reveal and construct previously unknown aspects of complex phenomena, both real and imagined.

Why are children often more imaginative than adults?

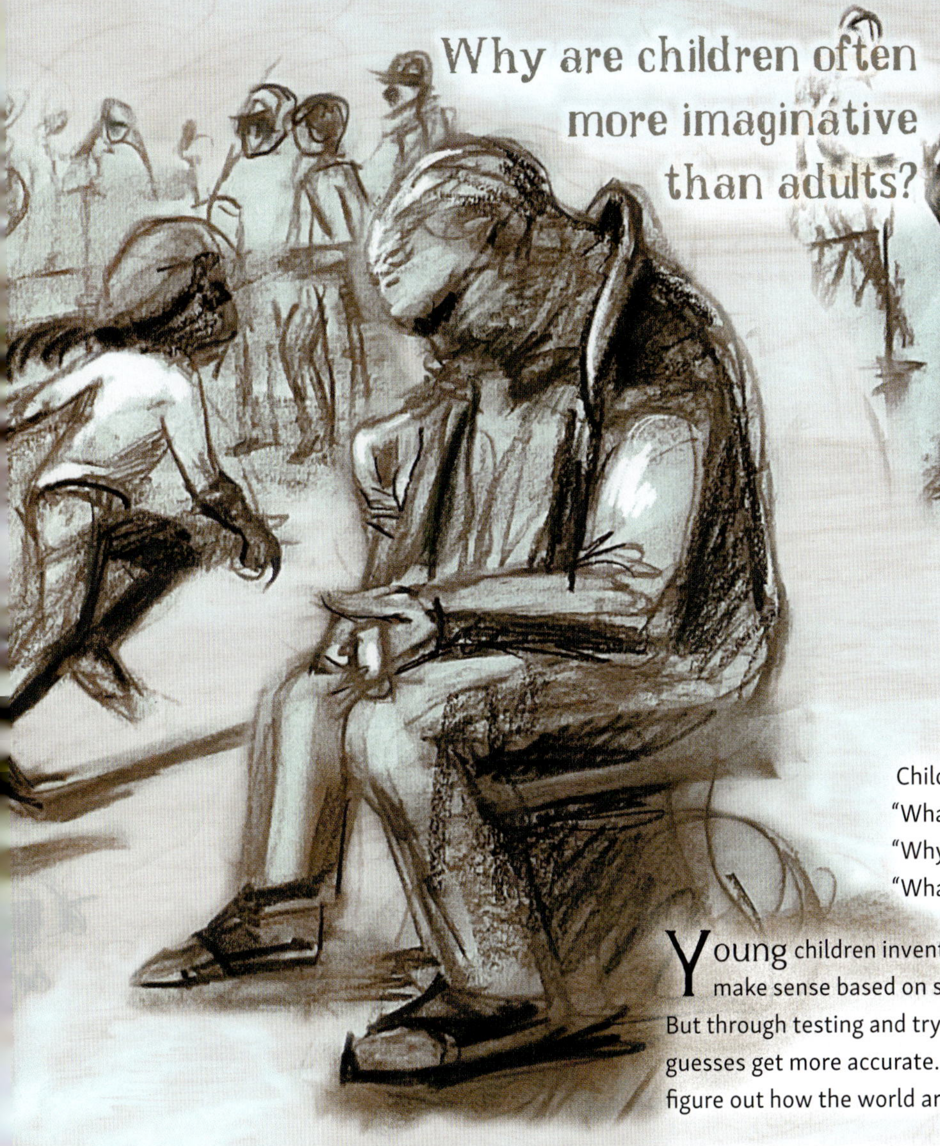

Answer: They know they don't know. They guess, observe and experiment. They guess again.

Answer: Their imagination helps them figure things out.

Answer: They just got here. They are not yet a hurry to get somewhere else! (Anyone trying to rush a young child off to preschool or kindergarten will know what I mean!)

Children ask BIG questions.
"What is the wind for?"
"Why is the sky blue?"
"What if I could fly?"

Young children invent answers that may be wrong but seem to make sense based on superficial observations and comparisons. But through testing and trying things out, trial and error, their guesses get more accurate. They use pretend play to help them figure out how the world around them actually works.

Developmental psychologist Alison Gopnik spent decades observing babies, children, and adults in her lab. She invented the metaphor of the lantern vs. the spotlight to describe the difference in awareness between adults and young children. Adults tend to focus their attention, like a bright spotlight, on what they already know and understand. Young children do not understand a lot of what is happening around them, but they pay attention to much more. The "lantern" of their awareness illuminates a much broader area of possibility. In the adult's mind, the relationships between forms and functions become fixed. Spoons are used for eating or preparing food. Unless there is a young child around, it's easy to forget that they can also be used for banging on the table to make noise.

The lens of prior assumptions and expectations focuses the "spotlight" of adult consciousness. When we draw, we can it turn off and see again in the broad "lantern light" of young children. Drawing can reveal a novel and surprising world, ripe for discovery.

"Every child is an artist. The problem is how to remain an artist once we grow up."
— Pablo Picasso

Counterfactuals = hypothetical, alternative "facts" that both children and adults use to build models of the world "as if" or "if only" things were different.

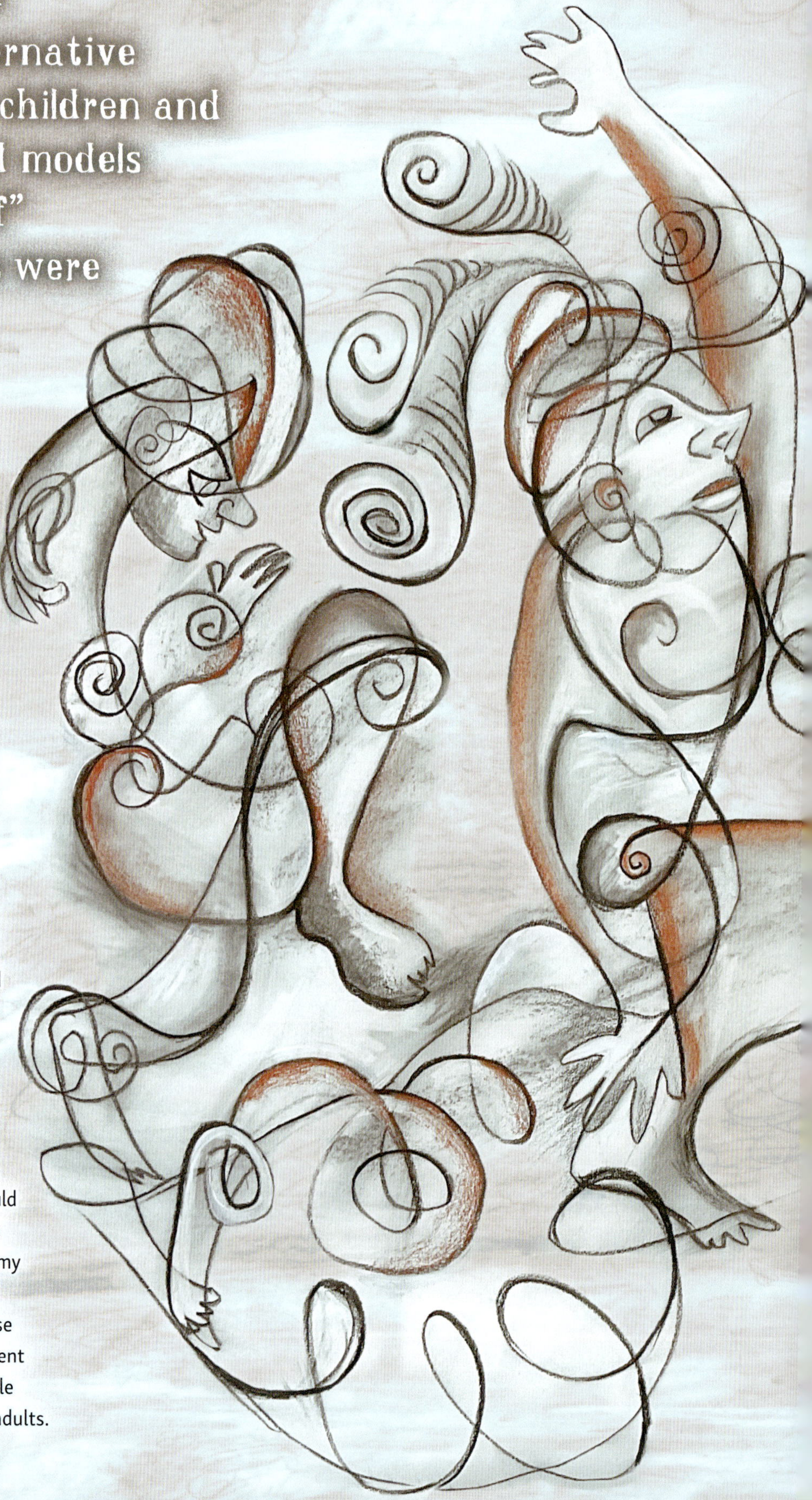

Children are continually engaged in a process of discovery. They are learning to understand and interact with people and things, trying to make sense of what is going on in their immediate surroundings. Children enlist their imaginations, ask "what if," invent COUNTERFACTUALS to help build their understanding of themselves, others, and the wider world. They create imaginary friends and worlds to play with possibilities.

When I was a child, I believed that a community of fairies lived under my mother's rhododendron bushes. There were nice ones and not-so-nice ones. I would watch as they sometimes battled for power among themselves. They seemed to be connected with the natural world and occasionally I would ask them to make the sun shine, or for rain, or for the wind to blow. I knew I had invented them, but I had no ultimate power over them. They would come and go, grant my wishes or ignore them, as they pleased. One day I asked my mother, "Are they real?" My mom said, "They are real in your mind if you choose to believe in them." (Early encouragement like this is common in the lives of people who go on to pursue creative work as adults.

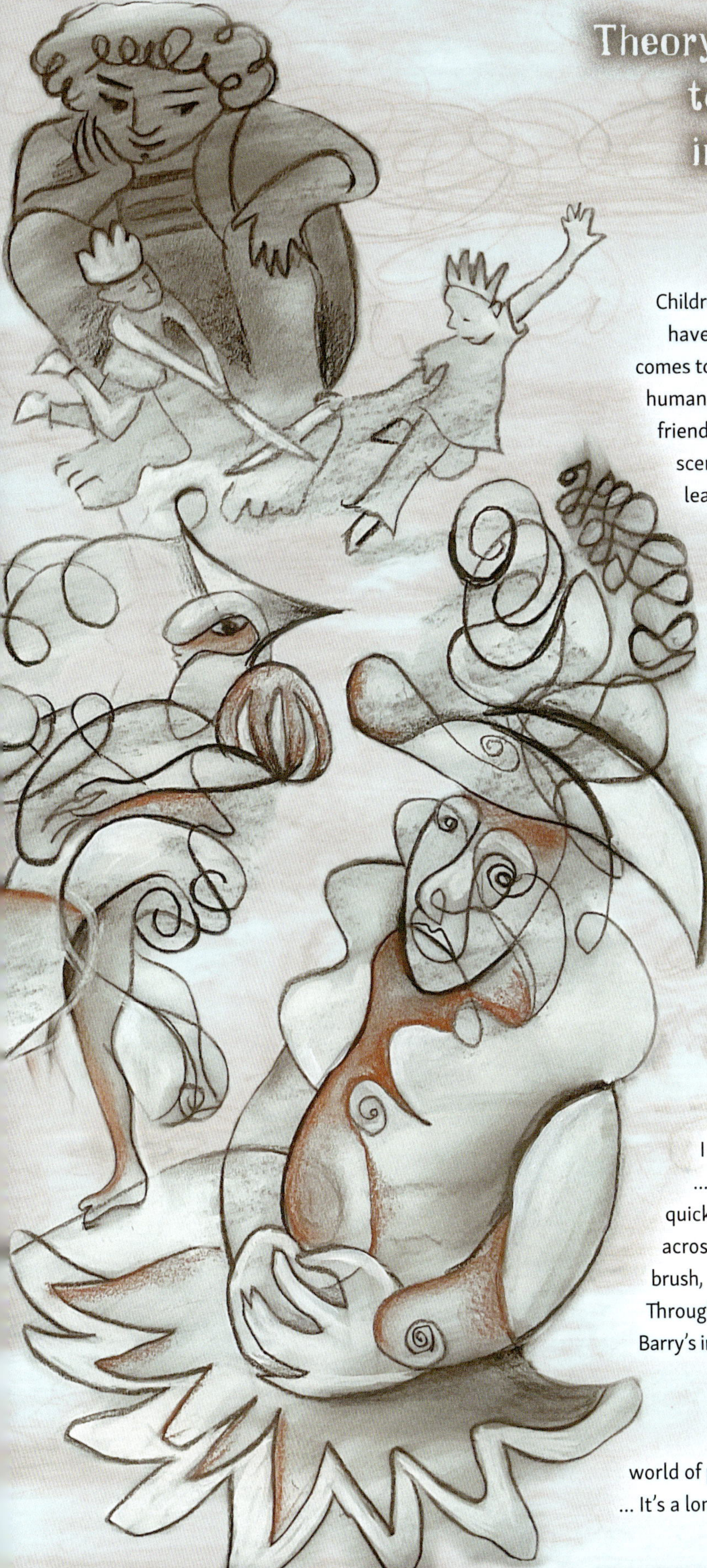

Theory of mind = the capacity to imagine someone else's inner life: their thoughts, beliefs, and intentions

Children with a rich fantasy life may be more empathetic and have a more developed THEORY of MIND when it comes to understanding the motivations and intentions of real humans. Pretend play and interactions with their imaginary friends can help them think through how a variety of actual scenarios might play out. Through make-believe, children learn to see patterns and make sense of the real world.

Once established, imaginary friends can seem to take on a life of their own, despite the child's understanding that it is "just pretend." The developmental psychologist Marjorie Taylor tells the story of a mother's frustration when her daughter's imaginary pony failed to show up for the birthday party. There was nothing that could be done. The pony was just not in the mood for a party. My own daughter, at thirteen, recalled the imaginary world she created as a young child: "I would set up a situation and then just watch what happened. It wasn't up to me."

Adult artists and writers who regularly traffic in imaginary worlds sometimes talk about their invented characters as if they, like children's imaginary friends, had minds of their own. The graphic novelist Lynda Barry says, "It is funny to think of the characters in my comics as being mine. I didn't plan their arrival. I didn't know they were coming ... I don't know why I drew them again at first, but they quickly took over my comic strip. When I moved my brush across the paperwall, they were there. When I stopped my brush, I'd lose the signal, and I couldn't get it back by thinking." Through direct engagement with materials in the real world, Barry's imaginary world comes to life. The painter Phillip Guston once said, "When I leave the studio and get back to the house and think about what I did, then I like to think that I've left a world of people in the studio. A world of people. In fact they are more real than the world I see ... It's a long, long preparation for a few moments of innocence."

> "You may say this is a visionary world, but it has ITS OWN WAY, and is, while you look at it, just the SAME as the real world."
> — Gong Xian

A place to wander and to live. Drawing can create a complex, detailed imaginary world that can be a place of escape and solace, but also where things might happen that would be catastrophic in real life. Once it is made visible on the drawing surface, an imaginary world can invite exploration and discovery, "just the same as the real world." It is a place to wander, both for the maker and the viewer.

One of my favorite artists of all time is the seventeenth-century Chinese painter Gong Xian. He lived during a time of great sociopolitical upheaval and uncertainty. The blank spaces in his eccentric, invented landscapes are as palpable and alive as the layered darks. It is a rich, complex, and personal world, full of dark corners and ambiguous, pregnant empty spaces. The white of the paper or silk becomes a place for the imagination to fill.

In ink or graphite, marks take on meanings beyond their material qualities. In the hand of a master, paper and ink evoke a virtual reality that feels perhaps even more vivid than the one we experience every day. Gong Xian describes the kind of heightened experience he is after as "the place where people can be fascinated is not only the land of wine!"

That paper and ink can be experienced "just the same" as actual things and places in the world is built into the way we process visual and spatial information. Imagination, perception, and memory rely on the same neural substrates. Functional brain imaging reveals that we use the same parts of our brain to make sense out of what we are seeing now as when we remember or imagine a scene not currently in front of us.

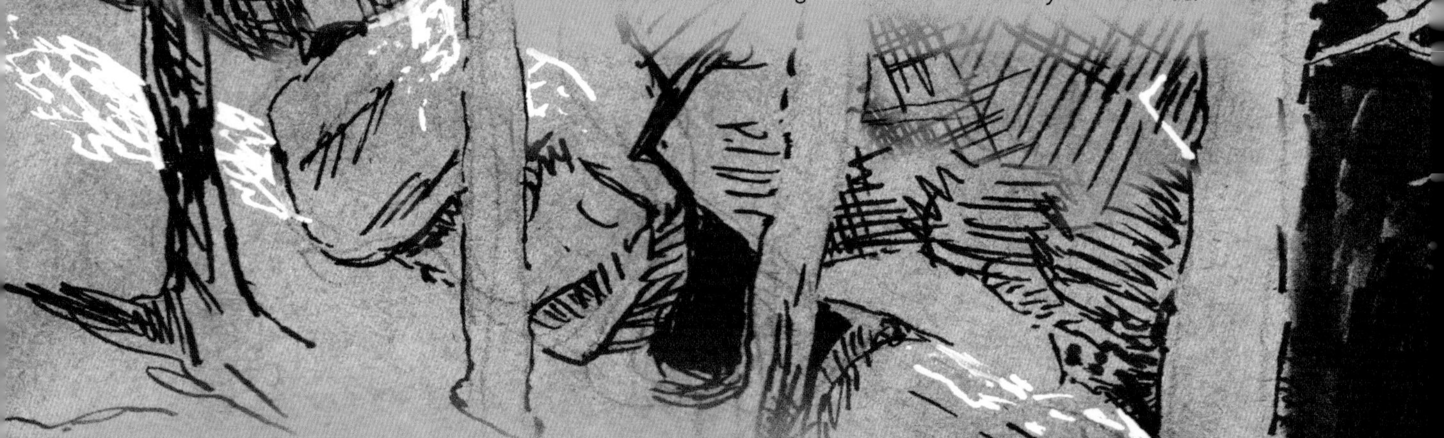

The brain fills the GAPS in our knowledge WITHOUT our knowledge.

The same secondary visual areas of the brain are active in processing retinal information, reconstructing images from memory, inventing mental models, and executing an action in the real world. When we imagine or try to remember, however, we have to work a little harder. EEGs show a greater degree of activation during visualization tasks than in direct perception. Each time we remember something, we are actually reconstructing the experience. (Did we really see a bear, just a few yards away last time we went hiking? Or was it more like 50 yards ...) Errors creep into our accounts. It can become impossible to disentangle accurate memories from our confabulations.

"There are those [paintings] through which you might TRAVEL, those in which you may SIGHTSEE, those through which you may WANDER and those in which you may LIVE. Any paintings attaining these effects are to be considered excellent, but those suitable for traveling and sightseeing are not as successful in achievement as those suitable for wandering and living."

— Guo Xi, Song Master

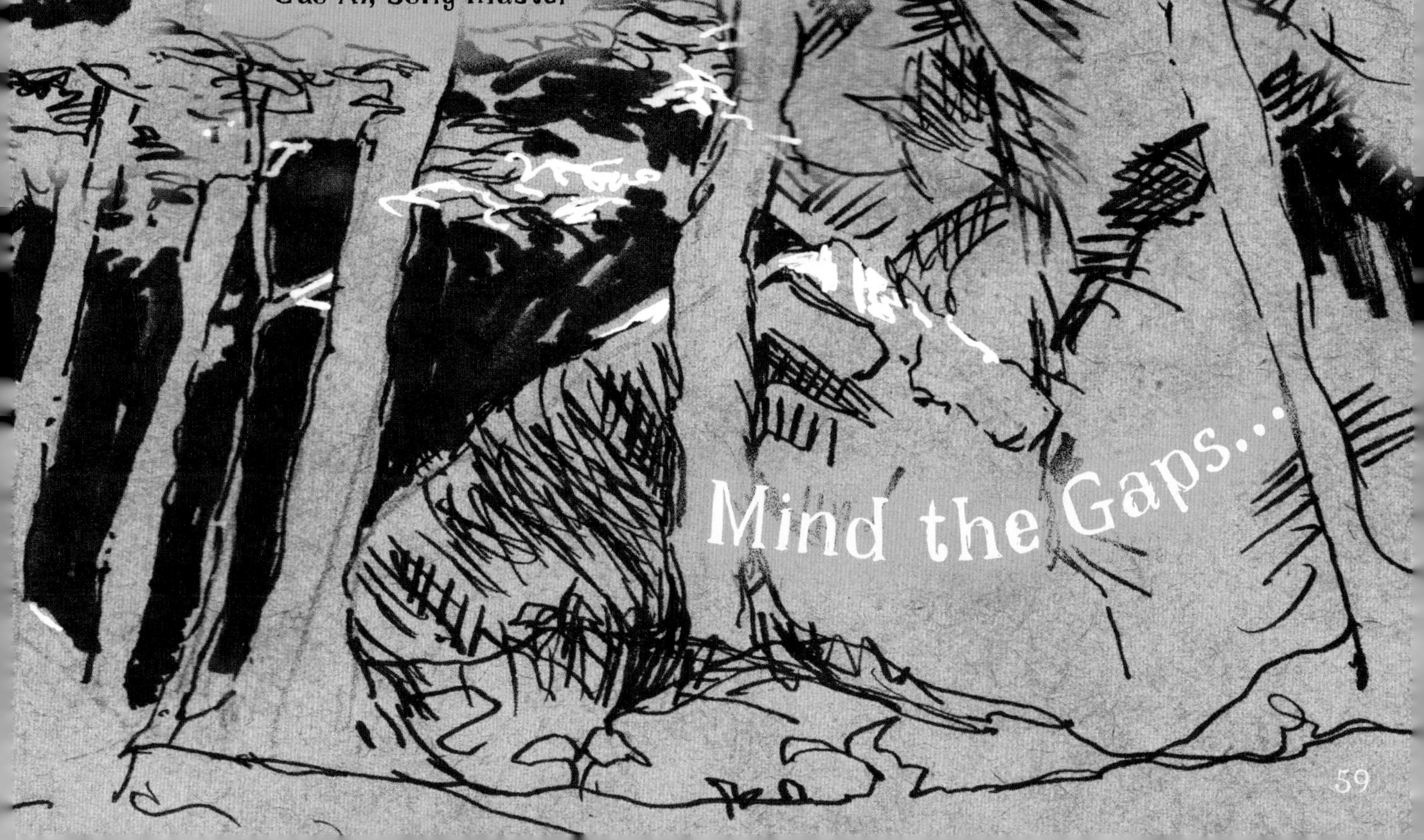

Mind the Gaps…

We search for PATTERNS, CAUSE and EFFECT, agency and intentionality, to make sense of experience and figure out how to act. The imperative to distinguish between danger and opportunity pushes us to make hypotheses based on incomplete or ambiguous data. We make educated guesses and invent systems to explain what we don't understand and predict what might happen next. Comparing present experience to prior knowledge, we often build theories based on scant evidence. Our existing understanding of how things work in the world is stretched and sometimes twisted to accommodate new information.

Apophenia = the perception of a connection between or meaningful pattern among unrelated or random phenomena.

We tend to notice that which CONFIRMS what we already think we know and discount or ignore the pieces that don't fit: BIAS creeps in. Once we construct theories and beliefs about the world, we tend to identify with them, cling to and defend them, valuing them at times even more than our lives. Evidence to the contrary sometimes only deepens our commitment to false beliefs. Wild conspiracy theories, like the imaginary friends of our childhoods, can take on lives of their own.

We might have learned lessons and internalized stereotypes that we apply inappropriately. Just because your last romantic partner cheated on you doesn't mean the next one will. Relying too heavily on history weighs down the present and closes off possibilities for the future. There is a growing awareness of the huge human costs of implicit as well as explicit bias in education and criminal justice. Psychological research has been marred by "observer-expectancy" and "volunteer bias," the ways in which researchers tend to find the results they want and in which volunteer subjects are self-selected and not representative of the general population. Medical research that focuses only on male cardiac patients, for example, means doctors miss different warning signs of heart disease in women, and female cardiac patients have been shown to have worse outcomes when they are treated by male doctors. Insufficient or biased training data can cause artificial intelligence to fail, since the training data must go through a human-mediated selection process, making predictions based on past prejudices. Facial recognition surveillance systems are being put into place across the US even though they may misidentify Black and Asian faces at a rate of 10 to 100% greater than White faces.

"Stop sometimes and look into the stains of walls, or the ashes of a fire, or clouds, or mud or like places, in which, if you consider them well, you may find a really marvelous idea ... the composition of battles of animals and men, various compositions of landscapes and monstrous things, such as devils and similar things, which may bring you honor, because by indistinct things the mind is stimulated to new inventions."
— Leonardo da Vinci

DOODLE BIRDS 1

Make a scribble. Then make at least four more, as many as you have room for. Take a close look at that first one. Add a dot (an eye), a triangle (a beak), a couple of lines for legs, and a few more for each foot. Try again with the other scribbles. Make each little bird as unique as possible.

Do the exercise over again, adding other odd bits to create dinosaurs or monsters or aliens from outer space.

Pareidolia = the illusion of a clear, recognizable image in indistinct, ambiguous stimuli.

Throughout humankind's time on earth, we've always looked for SIGNS and WONDERS that might reveal our destiny. Astrology. Palmistry. Numerology. The nineteenth-century study of bumps on the head that was supposed to reveal mental traits, known as phrenology, once seemed as solid and believable as the claims of neuroscience today.

When tragedy or true love strikes, people say, "It was meant to be." The idea that it might just be something that happened is too unsettling. Randomness is scary. We crave causes and explanations and invent them when they are hidden or inaccessible.

Why do some see a Man in the Moon? Others see a rabbit, a goddess, or a chariot. When we don't know for sure, we project stories or images we have learned from others onto the external world. We project meaning and intention where there may be none, seeing into smoke and clouds and tea leaves. We can have difficulty telling the difference between what is out there and what we may have conjured in our minds.

Yet, if you understand how your mind works, you can learn to deliberately use the tendency to find meaning in random events for good. Engage in metacognition (thinking about thinking), relaxing (top-down) cognitive control to access the default mode network. Free your imagination. If you are able, look up at the sky right now. Are there clouds? If so, what can you find in them?

DOODLE BIRDS 2

Take a page of the doodle birds, monsters or aliens you made in the previous exercise. Turn it upside down. Copy elements from what you see, but transform the marks you made before into a landscape, cityscape, or interior scene.

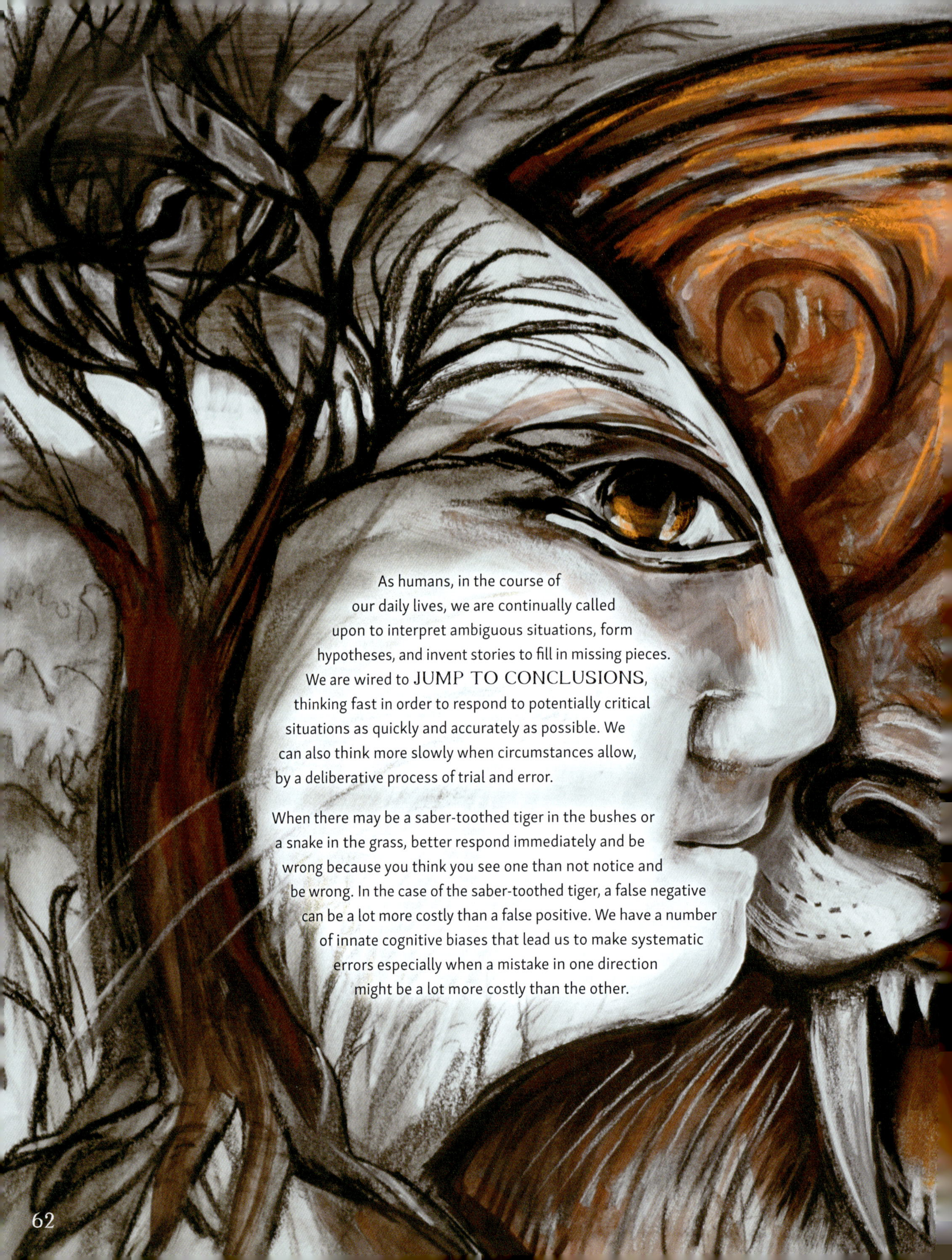

As humans, in the course of our daily lives, we are continually called upon to interpret ambiguous situations, form hypotheses, and invent stories to fill in missing pieces. We are wired to JUMP TO CONCLUSIONS, thinking fast in order to respond to potentially critical situations as quickly and accurately as possible. We can also think more slowly when circumstances allow, by a deliberative process of trial and error.

When there may be a saber-toothed tiger in the bushes or a snake in the grass, better respond immediately and be wrong because you think you see one than not notice and be wrong. In the case of the saber-toothed tiger, a false negative can be a lot more costly than a false positive. We have a number of innate cognitive biases that lead us to make systematic errors especially when a mistake in one direction might be a lot more costly than the other.

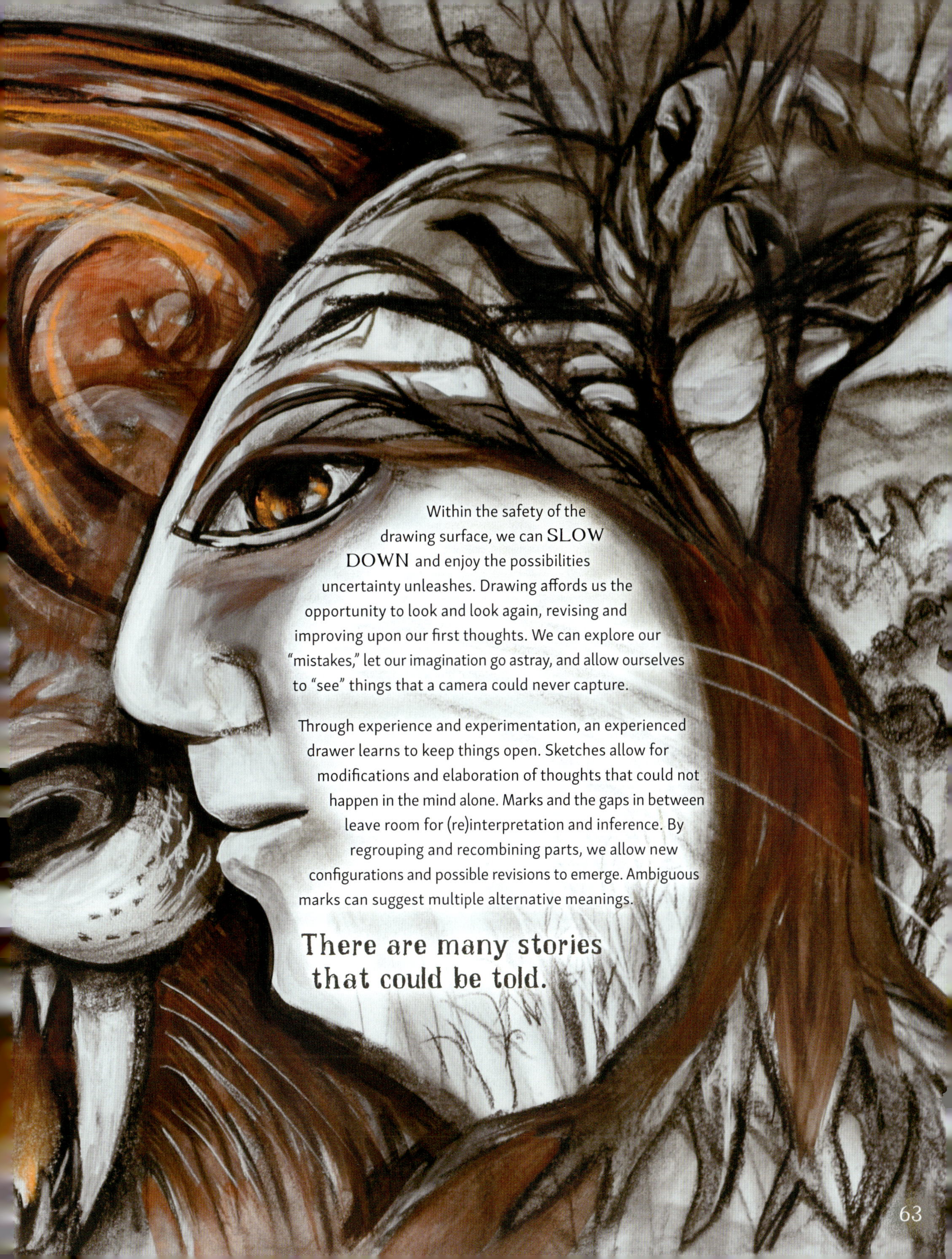

Within the safety of the drawing surface, we can SLOW DOWN and enjoy the possibilities uncertainty unleashes. Drawing affords us the opportunity to look and look again, revising and improving upon our first thoughts. We can explore our "mistakes," let our imagination go astray, and allow ourselves to "see" things that a camera could never capture.

Through experience and experimentation, an experienced drawer learns to keep things open. Sketches allow for modifications and elaboration of thoughts that could not happen in the mind alone. Marks and the gaps in between leave room for (re)interpretation and inference. By regrouping and recombining parts, we allow new configurations and possible revisions to emerge. Ambiguous marks can suggest multiple alternative meanings.

There are many stories that could be told.

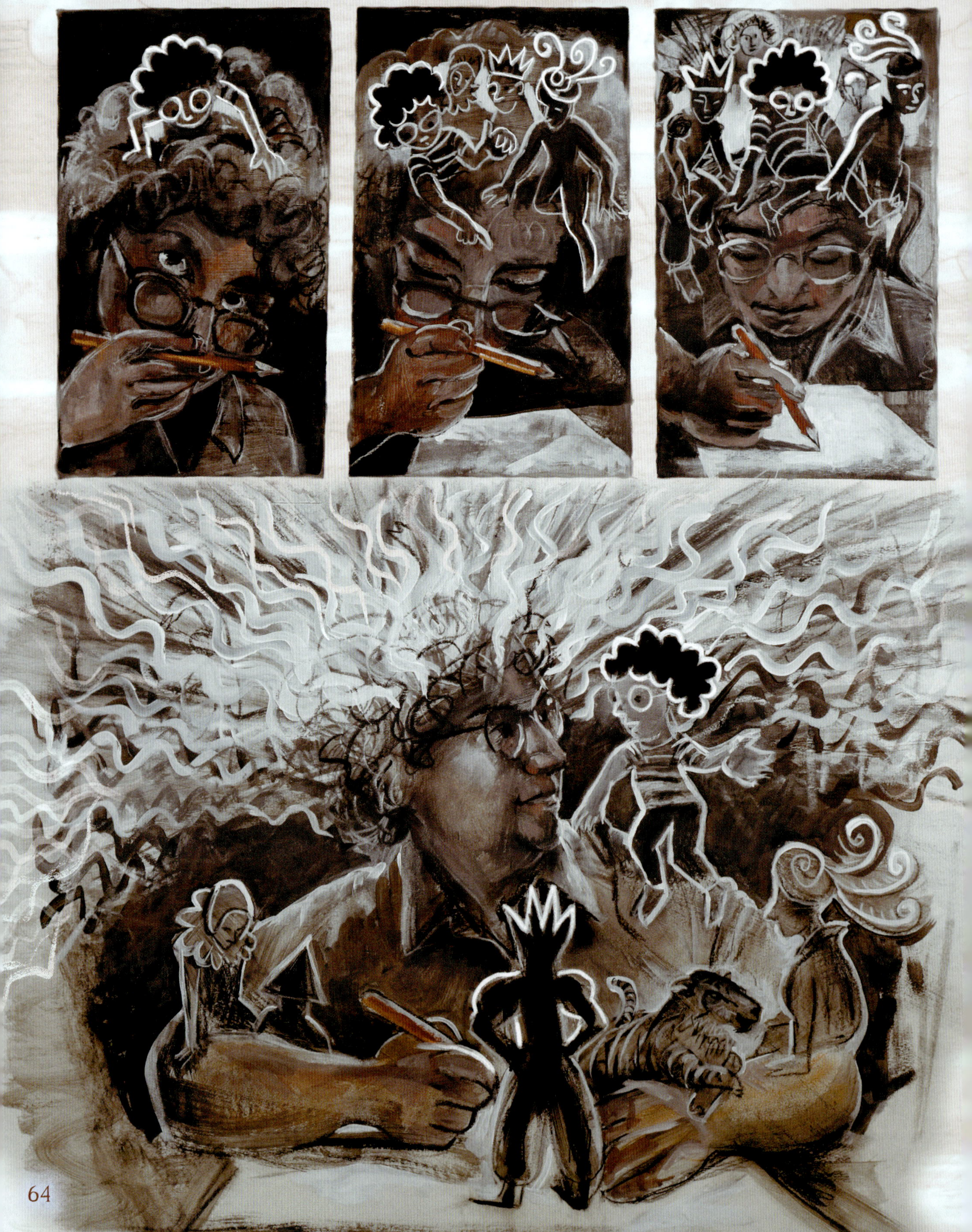

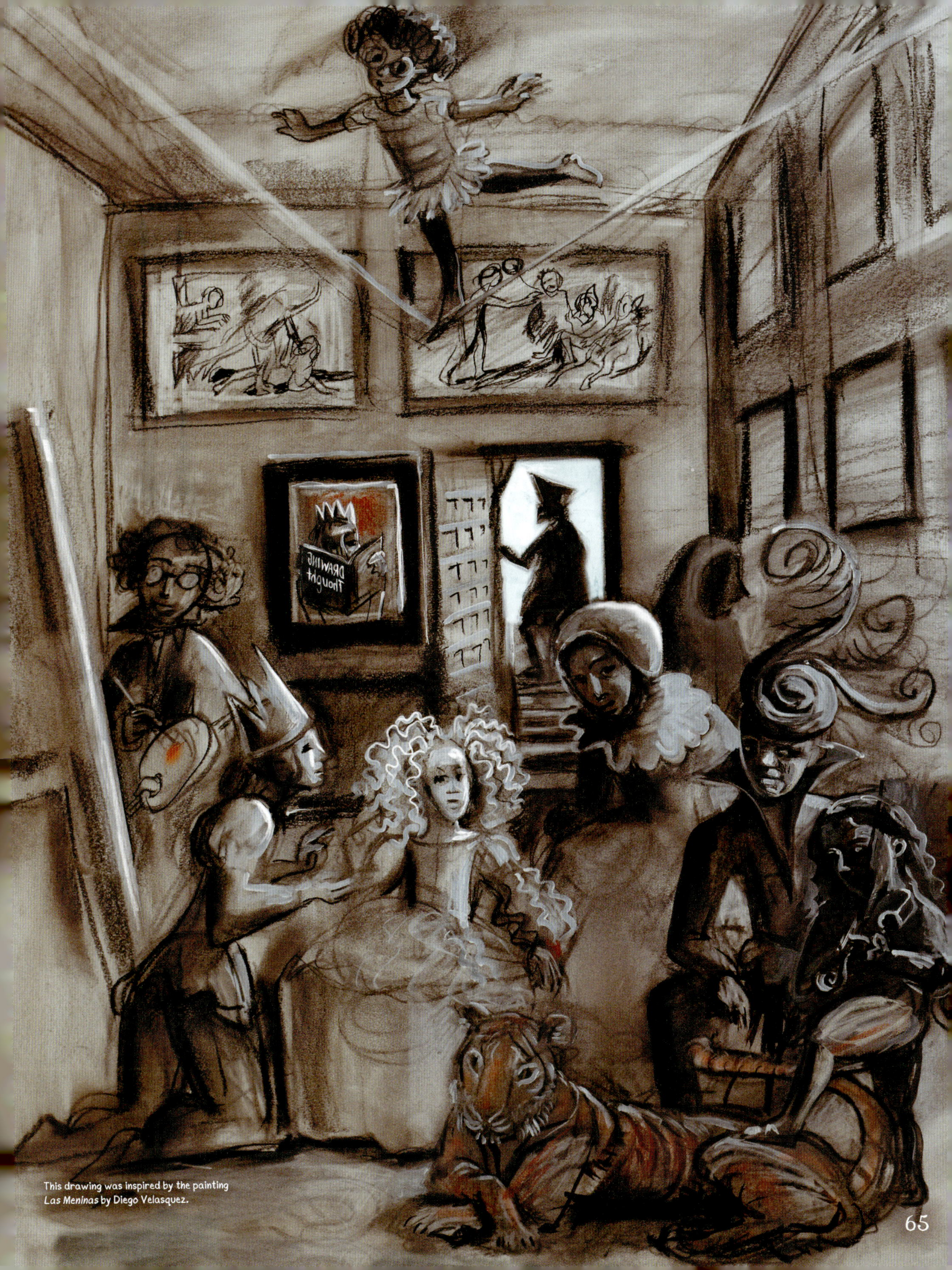

This drawing was inspired by the painting *Las Meninas* by Diego Velasquez.

"LOOK at things as if they could be OTHERWISE...

I came into the world, as you did, at a specific time and place. From that first moment, I accumulated a unique set of life experiences that shape my sense of reality, which is different from yours. We each have our own individual points of view, and as we look out toward the horizon of possibility, we all see something different.

Yet we can all try to imagine how things could be otherwise. We are able to recover that delicious freedom of children at play, asking themselves, "What if?" What lies beyond the horizon? What fantastic and fabulous forms do we see in the clouds overhead?

Drawing helps us get to know our own particular perspectives better. We become more aware of the limits of what we see from where we sit. We can envision alternatives. Looking down roads not yet taken, we may picture what adventures might await, where the process of drawing itself can take us. We can follow a suggestion, a squiggle, shadow, or smudge, and see where it leads...

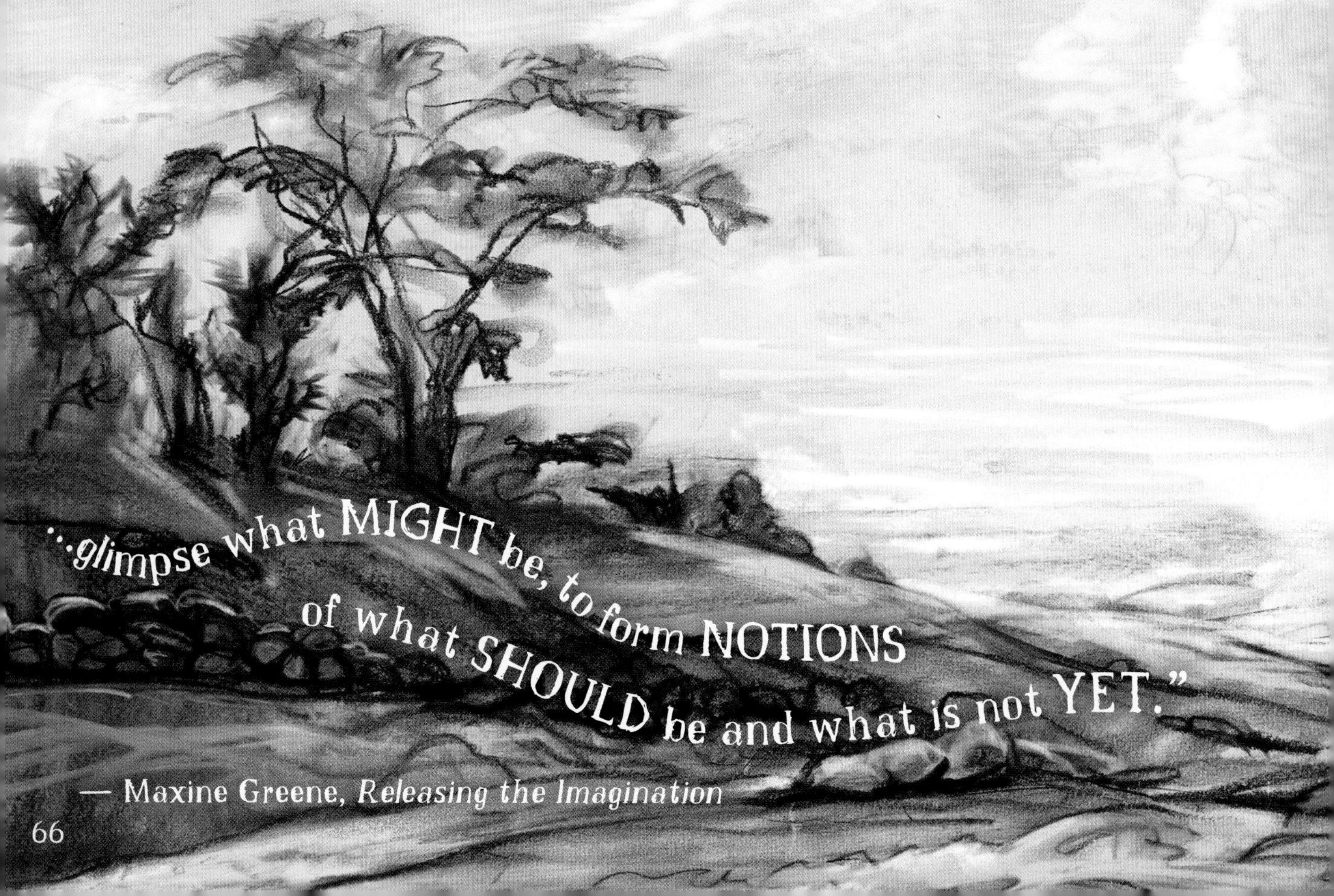

...glimpse what MIGHT be, to form NOTIONS of what SHOULD be and what is not YET."

— Maxine Greene, *Releasing the Imagination*

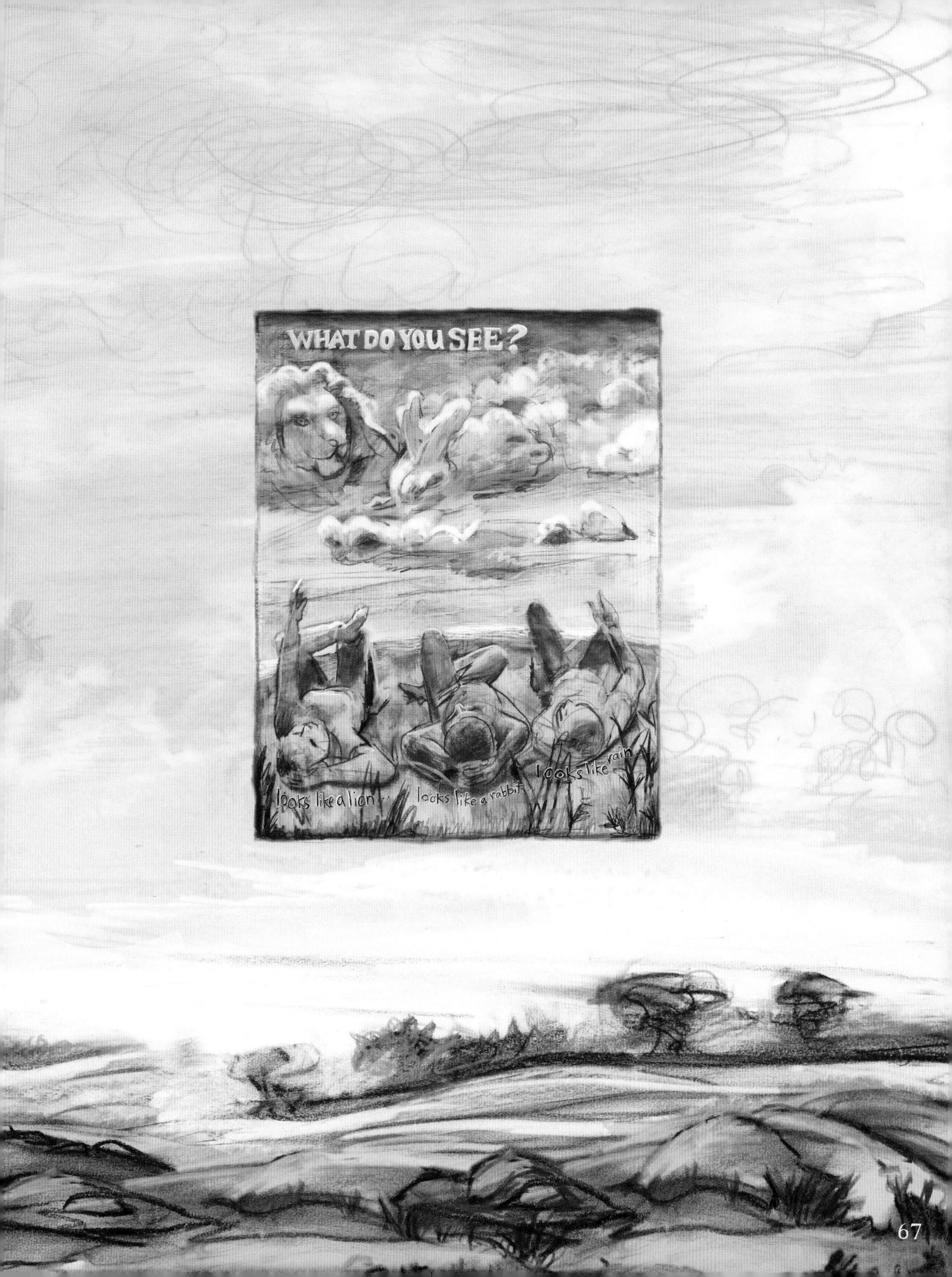
WHAT DO YOU SEE?
looks like a lion...
looks like a rabbit.
looks like rain

How to
Overlap Shapes

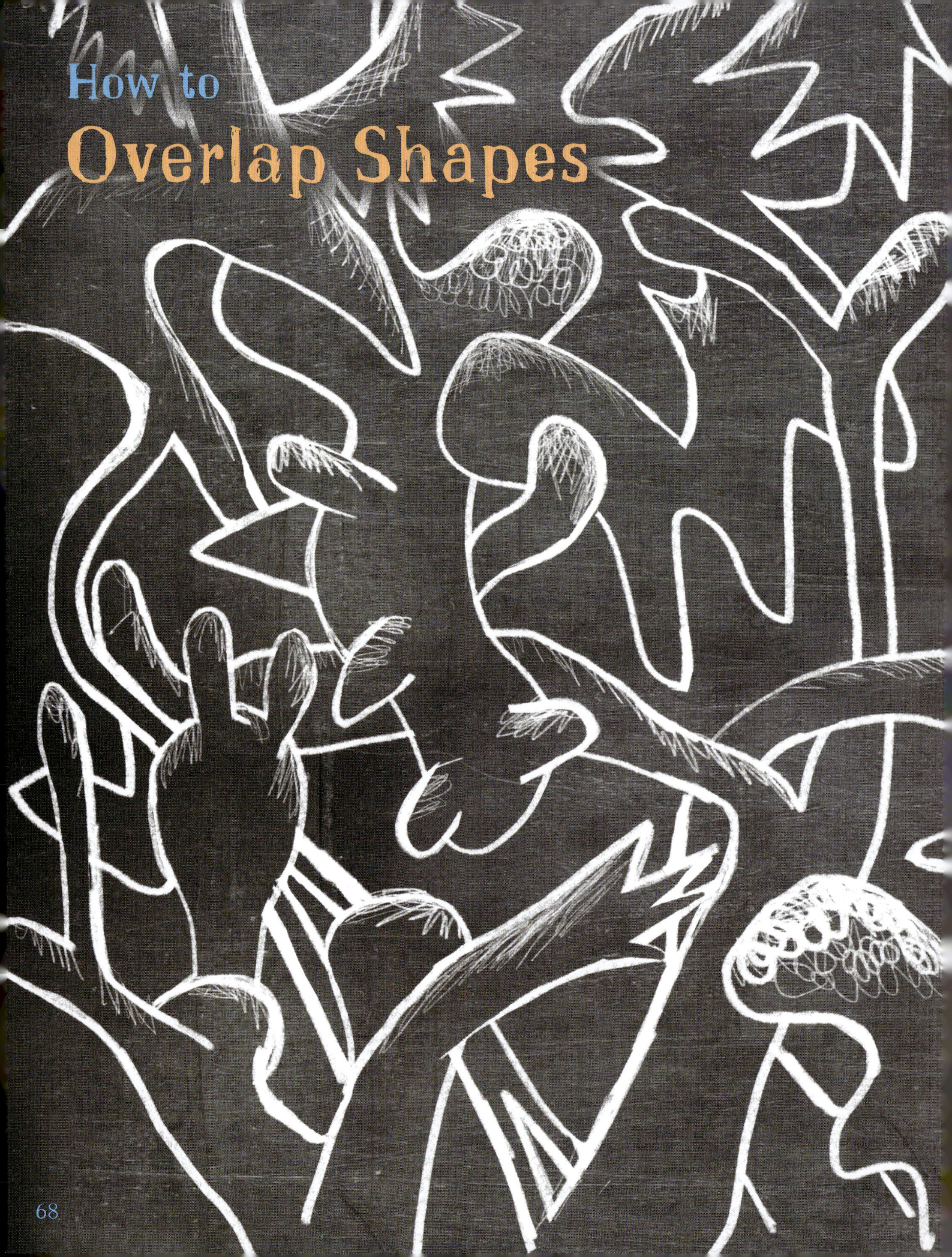

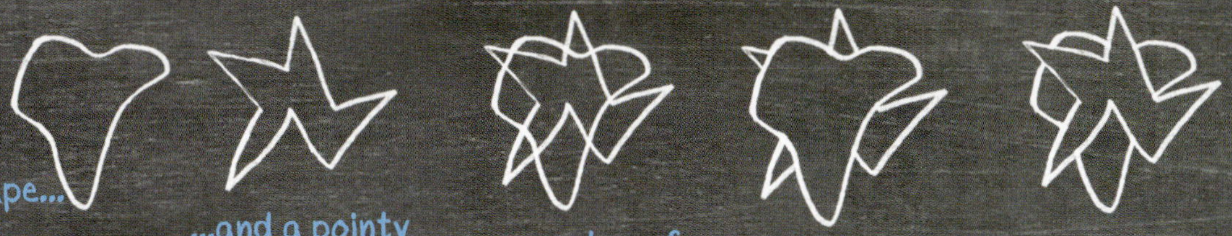

1 Draw a curvy shape...

...and a pointy shape...

...on top of each other.

2 Decide which one is in front, and erase hidden parts of the other shape.

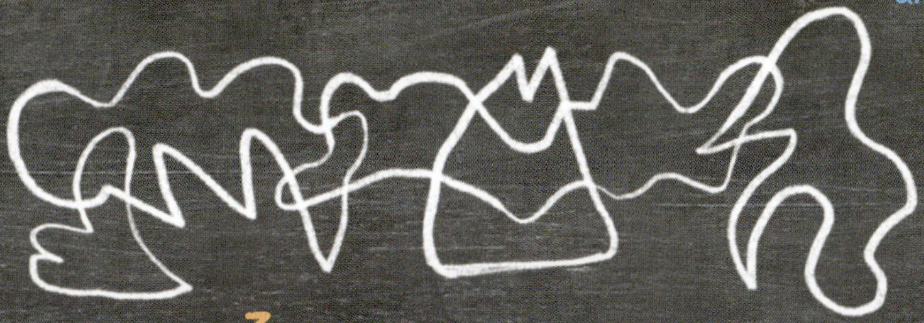

3 Draw a bunch of overlapping shapes.

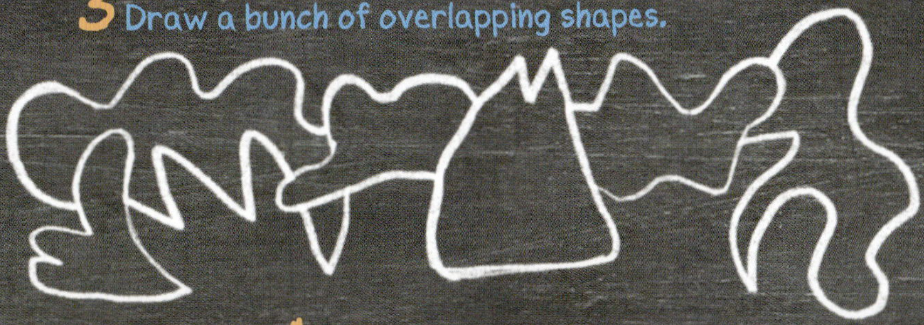

4 Decide what is in front and erase hidden parts.

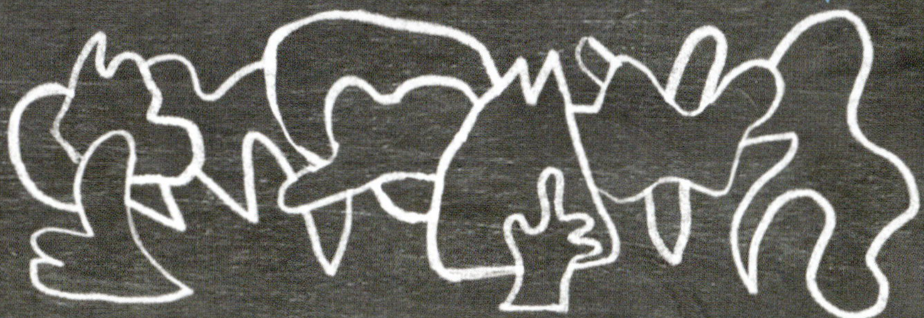

Add more bits and pieces.

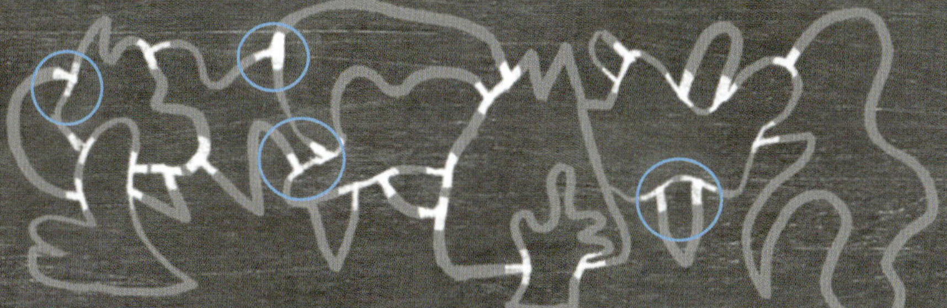

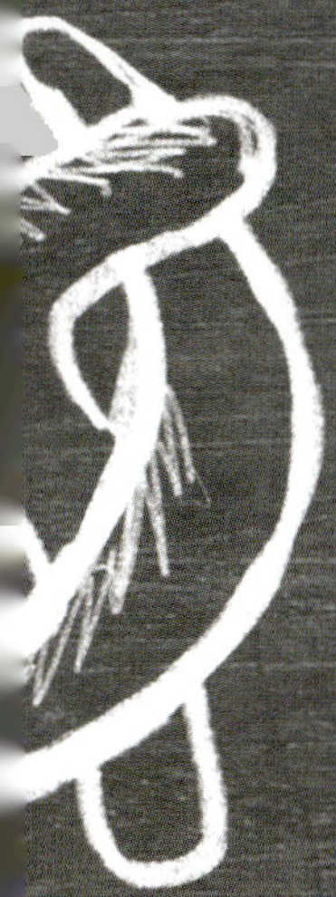

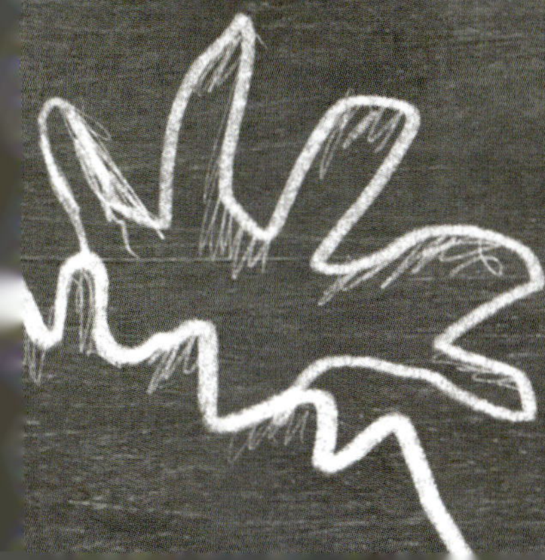

Pay special attention to "Y" and "T" joints.

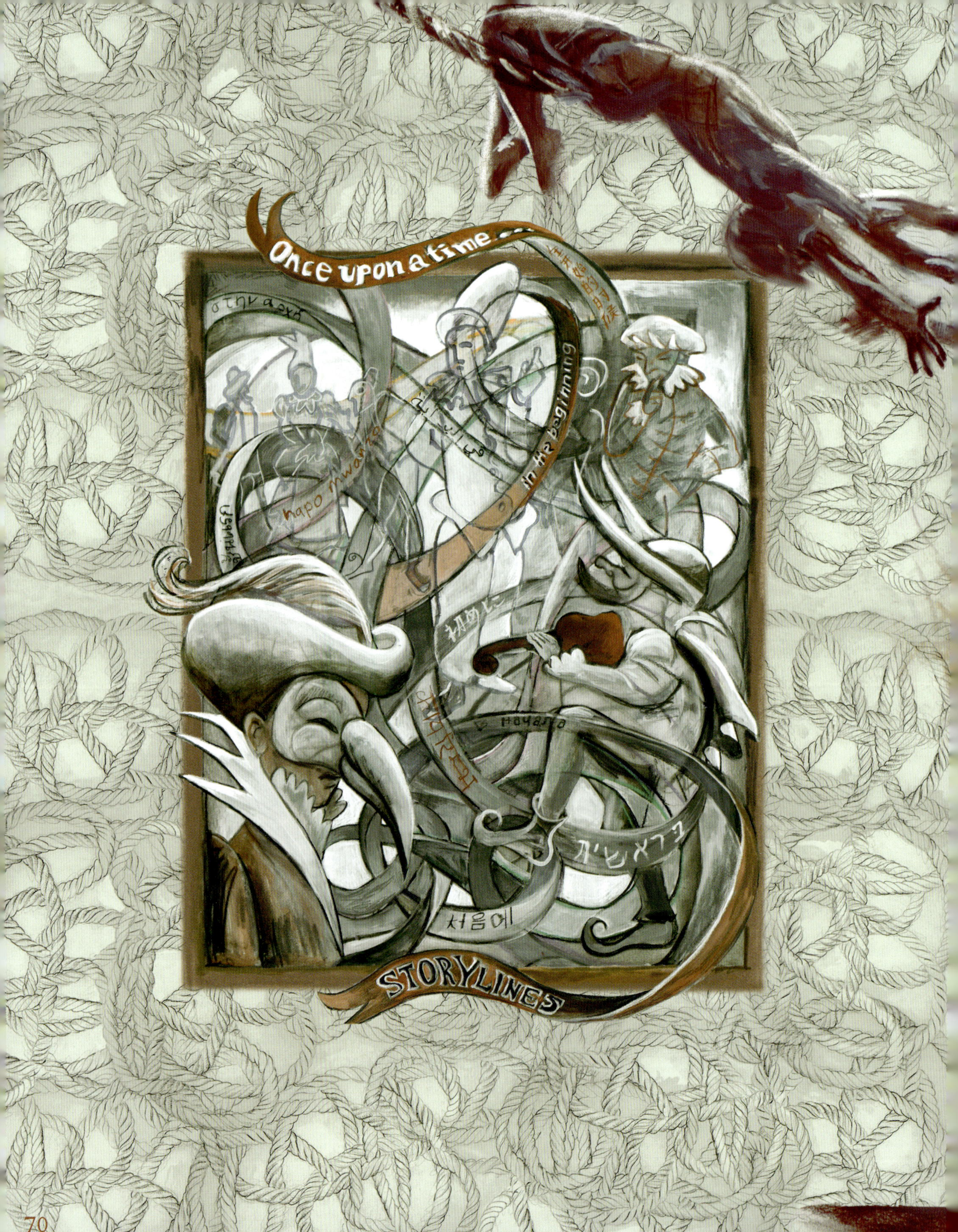
Once upon a time ...
In the beginning
hapo mwanzo
στην αρχή
начало
בראשית
STORYLINES

chapter five

Drawn Together

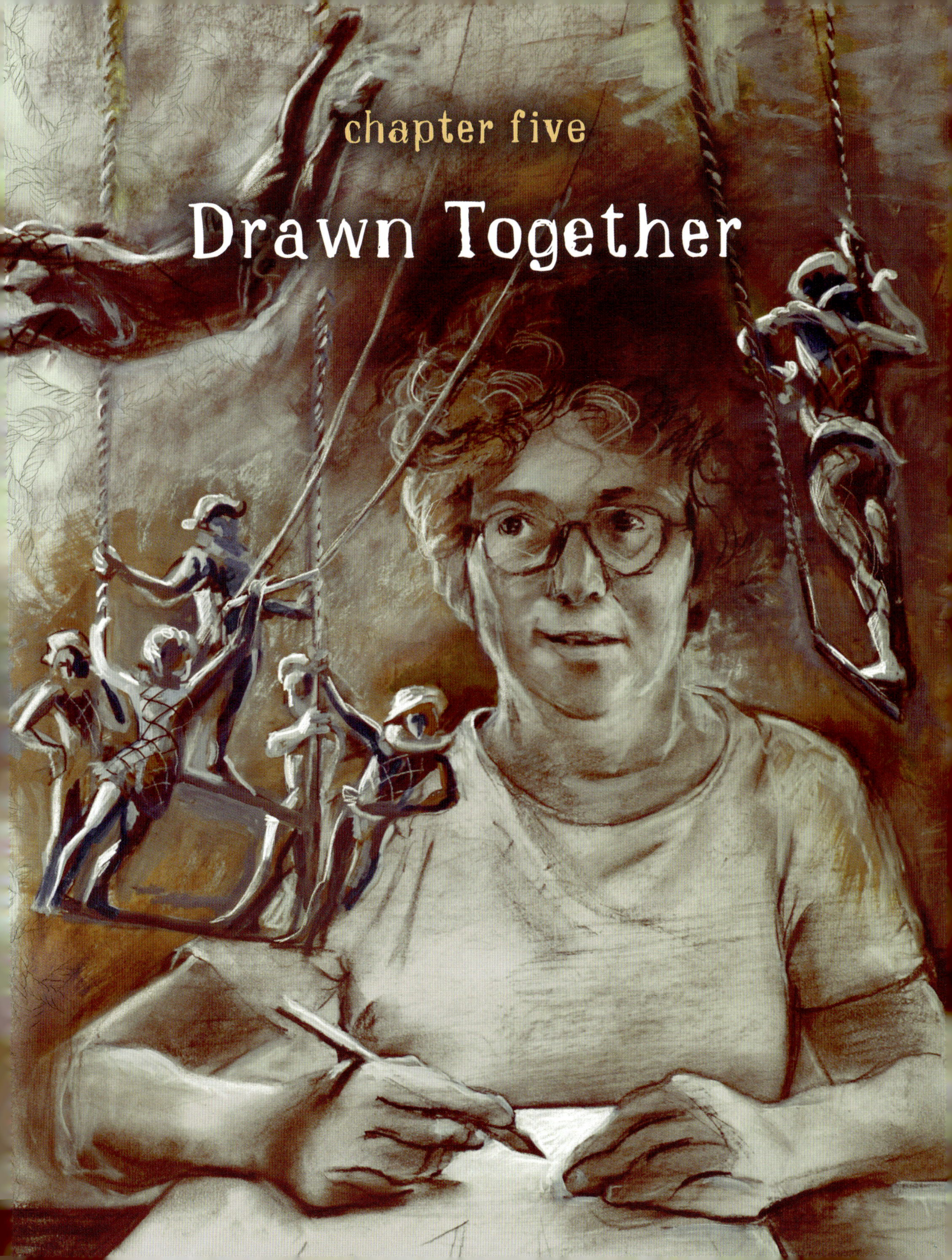

We share stories and find CONNECTIONS between ourselves and others. We rely on the knowledge and know-how of those who have preceded us. We picture a FUTURE we might all share.

When we draw, we CONNECT one mark to another, one part to another, and one thought to another. We observe relationships between things in the world and set up corresponding relationships on the drawing surface. We may draw connections between our ideas, experiences, other people's stories, and bits and pieces from the larger culture in which we live. In drawing and in life, the WHOLE is greater than the sum of its parts. A drawing encodes individual and shared perceptions and experiences. It's a record of what we have seen and felt, to be viewed by our future selves and others.

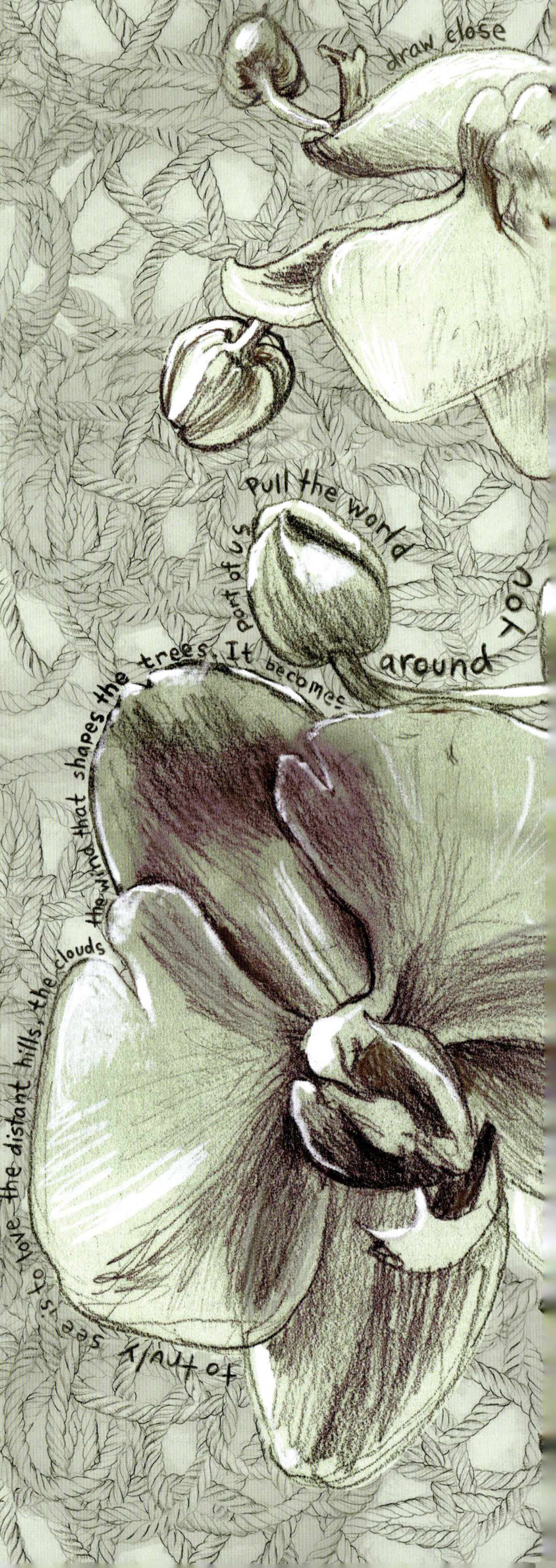

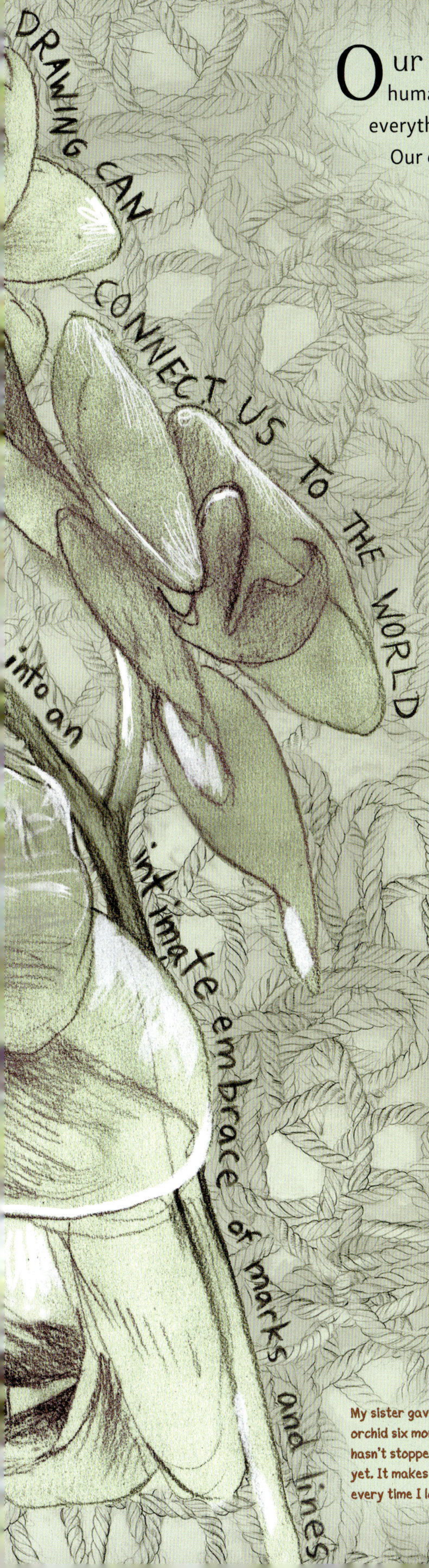

Our ability to work together to achieve common goals facilitated the spread of the human race across the planet. In the face of global pandemics and ecological disasters, everything we can do to cultivate and nurture human ingenuity and cooperation matters. Our continued existence and perhaps all life on earth depends on how well we are able to think and work together to imagine and build a future world we all want to live in. Drawing together, metaphorically but also literally, could play a part.

Drawing can provide a feeling of connection even when we are alone. It can fill a time of solitude with quiet pleasure. When we draw, we imaginatively project ourselves into the world of the drawing, to record what we see, the images and stories that emerge from our minds, or even abstract collections of marks and lines. Drawing helps us connect with others through our imagination, when we are not together in real life. During the long lockdowns of the COVID-19 pandemic, drawing helped people cope with social isolation.

Forced isolation is painful because social relationships are so essential to individual survival. Prisoners who are held in solitary confinement are far more likely than the overall prison population to experience severe psychological harm, and almost seven times more likely to commit acts of self-harm and suicide. Some episodes of psychological depression may be a feature, not a bug, of our sociality: an adaptation that leads us to take a step back from others when we experience dysfunction in our social relationships. This could explain why evidence-based talk therapies, such as cognitive behavioral therapy, can be at least as effective over time as psychotropic medications (and sometimes more effective) as a treatment for depression. Talk therapy can support a healing process of self-reflection to help us resolve troubling social concerns.

Becoming more aware and mindful of our own internal worlds can positively impact our communication with others. Drawing provides an arena for introspection, where we can learn about ourselves and reach out to share thoughts and feelings with others.

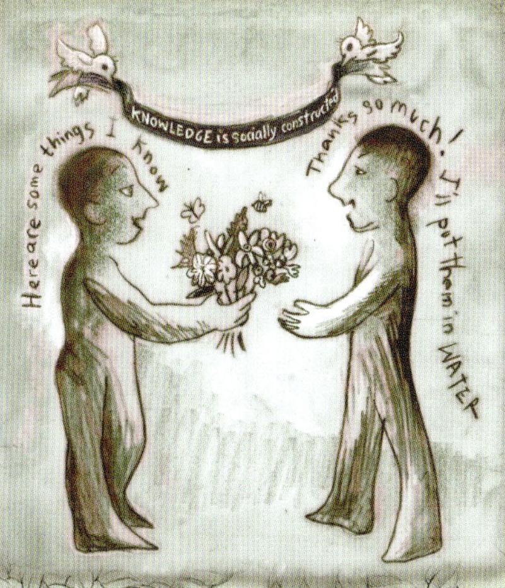

My sister gave me this orchid six months ago. It hasn't stopped blooming yet. It makes me happy every time I look at it.

Drawn to Faces

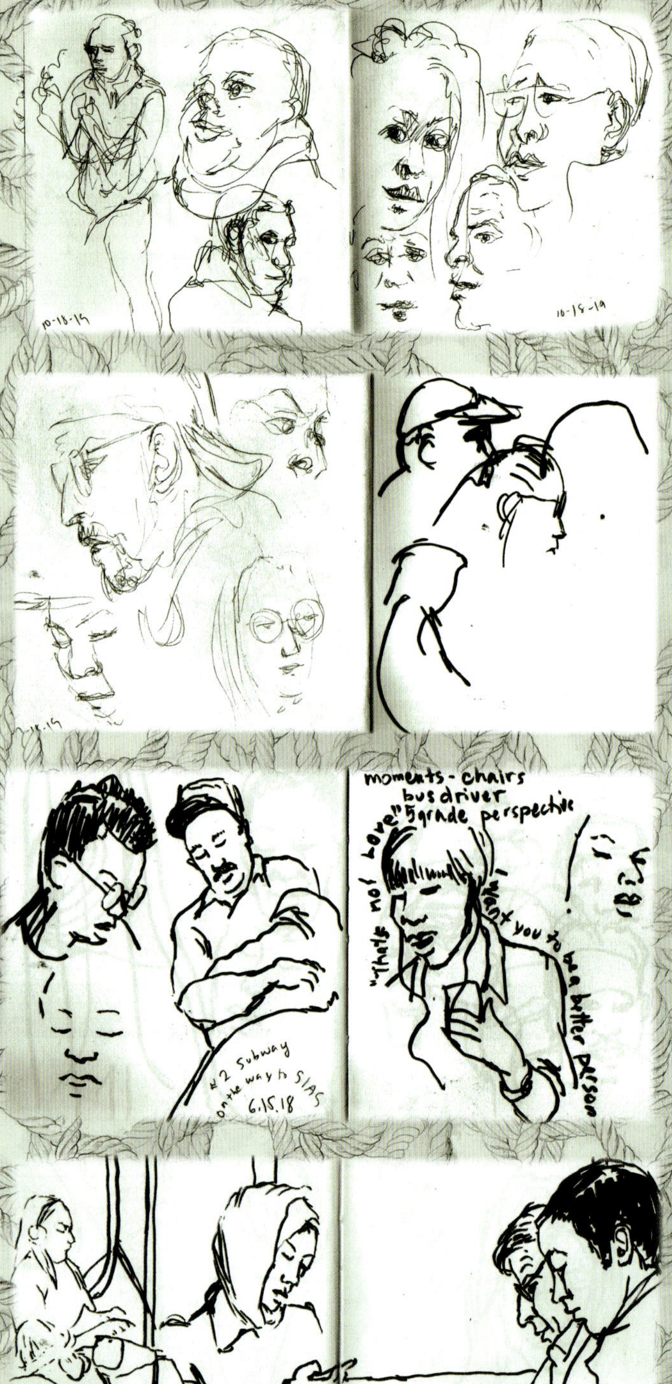

Most humans are fascinated by other people's faces. Newborns will fixate on a configuration of shapes that is face-like and focus on their parents' faces with surprising intensity. The "fusiform face area" is one of the few parts of the brain that is specialized for a specific function: it helps us recognize small details that identify familiar faces, part of a network that can be trained to recognize subtle differences in similar objects, such as birds or Chinese characters. But most of us need no training to recognize either faces or facial expressions, at least among people who look like us.

We are not so adept at recognizing people who don't look like us or like people we know well. There is a well-documented "own-race bias." This is a huge problem in the workplace, in the criminal justice system, and across society. When we are feeling positive emotions, such as joy and humor, however, research suggests that we may get better at recognizing faces across racial differences.

We scan the surface of faces for a slight downturn or lift of the upper lip, a widening or narrowing of the eyes. Micro-movements in facial features might communicate, or even betray, another's emotional state.

We are so predisposed to see faces and facial expressions that we see them in all kinds of places. Take a moment right now, and look around. Can you find something in your immediate environment that reminds you of a face? Does it seem to have a personality or expression?

FOUND FACES

Take some random objects from your desk or junk drawer. Paper clips, rubber bands, thumbtacks, pushpins ... whatever small items may be at hand. Arrange them to make a face. Draw it. Does it seem excited or frustrated? Melancholy or joyful? Friend or foe? Change the position of objects to change the expression, and draw again.

It's difficult to look at an electrical outlet and not see a face. We see faces in mountains, in buildings, in a crumpled piece of cloth. Graphic and industrial designers use our innate attraction to faces to create appealing logos and products.

I love to ride the New York City subway because I see the diverse faces of my fellow passengers. A world of strangers opens up, as I notice what makes each individual unique. I no longer feel surrounded by strangers, but by specific humans, each carrying their own histories, worries, burdens, and joys. As I trace a nose or jaw, the cut or flow of hair, I feel a momentary surge of affection for someone I will never see again. I especially love to draw in the subways when traveling. Suddenly, in Paris or Singapore, I no longer feel like a stranger. These people are my people too.

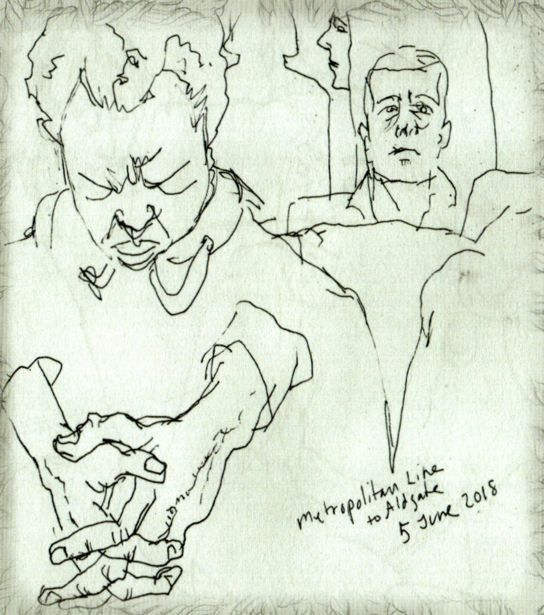

"But that face facing me, in its expression—in its mortality—summons me, demands me, requires me: as if the invisible death faced by the face of the other—pure alterity, separate, somehow, from any whole—were my business' ... the other is my neighbor." — Emmanuel Levinas, from *Alterity and Transcendence*

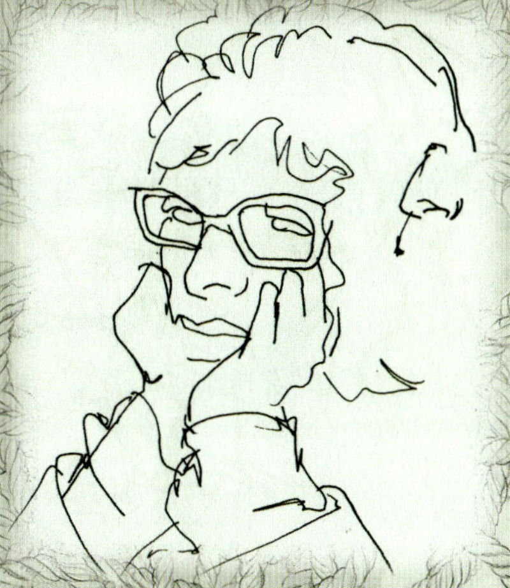

SKETCH IN PUBLIC

Find a crowd, in a park, a food court, a playground, or some other public place. Draw with a pen. Focus on your subject and try not to look at your paper. Have a couple of portraits going at once, so if someone notices you drawing them and it feels uncomfortable you can quickly switch to someone else ... or ask permission! People might ask you for your drawings of them. It's nice if you don't mind but you needn't feel obligated.

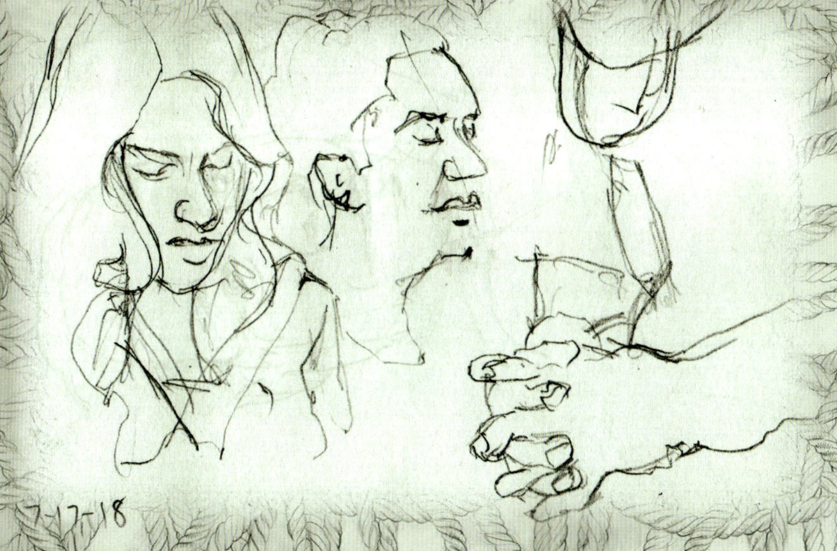

"The EYES are the windows to the SOUL,"

goes the saying. We look in each other's eyes for insight into each other's minds. I look where you are looking. Your gaze may clue me into a hidden intention that helps me predict what you might do next. You can try to fake a smile, but if the expression in your eyes doesn't match the expression of your mouth, I might call your bluff. The muscles around the mouth can be easily controlled voluntarily, the muscles around the eyes less so.

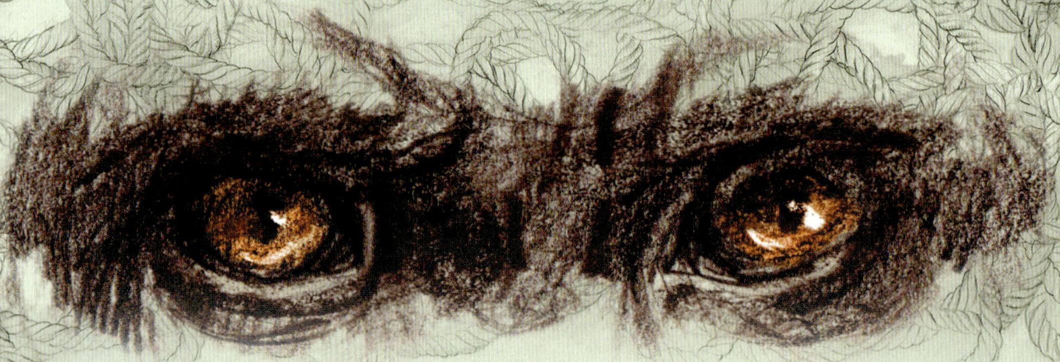

We look each other in the eye to signal willingness to engage and avert our eyes to signal avoidance or submission. Professional poker players often wear sunglasses to hide their own thoughts while they scan for "tells" from others. Psychologists track eye movements and study pupil dilation to gain insight into mental processes.

Developmental and comparative psychologist Michael Tomasello and colleagues study young chimps, bonobos, orangutans, and humans. They have found that from a very young age, humans attend to one another's gaze whereas our closest cousins do not. Tomasello suggests this is evidence of the larger importance of shared intentionality among humans.

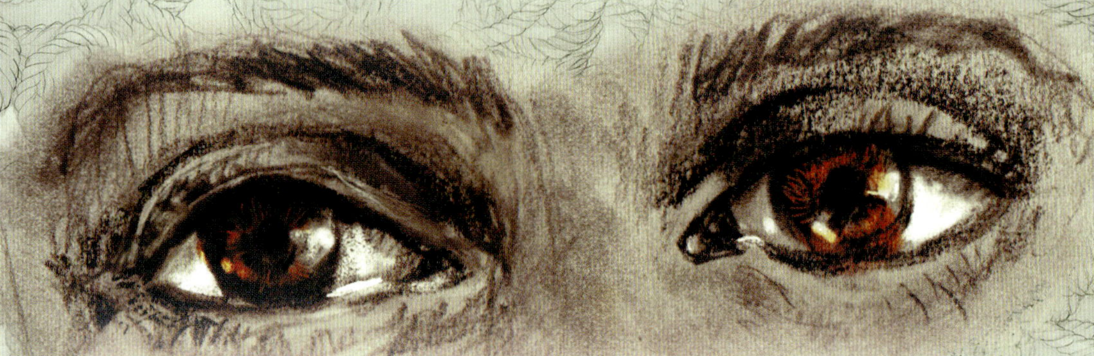

The whites of our eyes (known as the "sclera") are much more visible in humans than in other animals. The exceptions are the dogs we have specifically bred to be our almost human companions. The white sclera in humans emphasizes our gaze in the way the black sclera of gorillas' or chimpanzees' eyes do not. The contrast between the sclera and iris, along with the almond shape of the eye opening, allows me to see what you are looking at. The direction of your gaze is one of the many clues that help me understand your perspective on a situation.

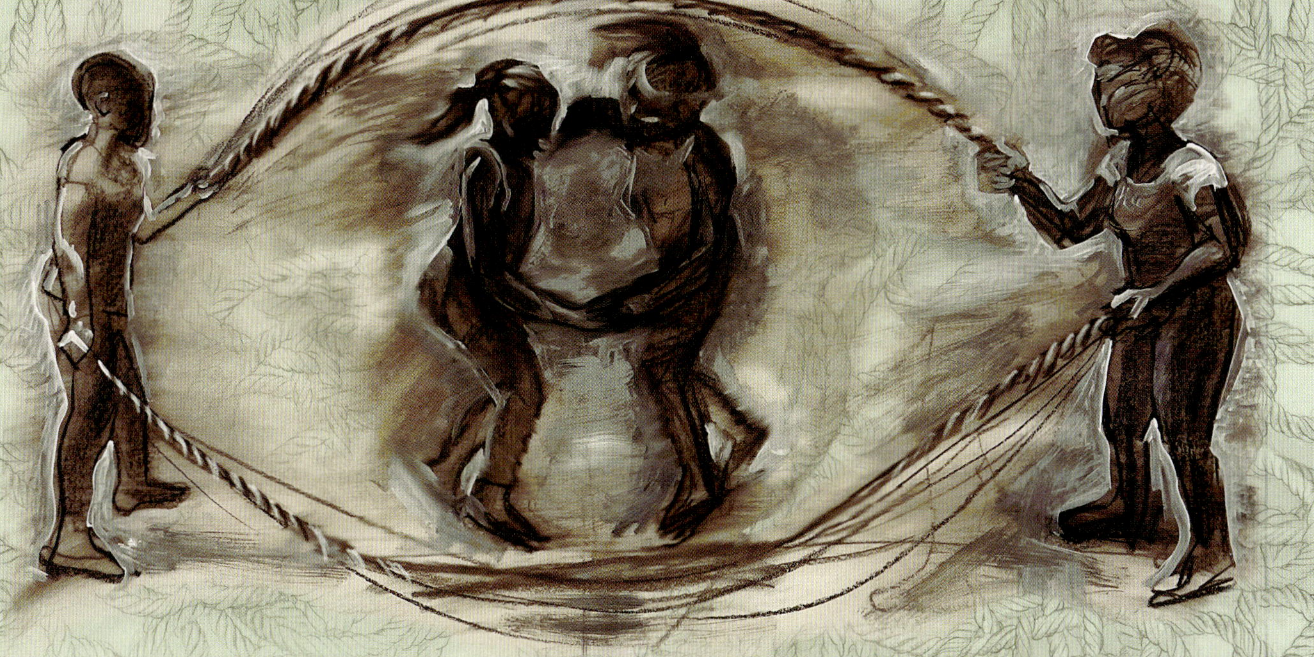

teamwork

Other mammals cooperate to achieve a common goal, and even seem to demonstrate empathy and altruistic behaviors. Rats, for example, will share a special treat, like chocolate, with a cage mate and work to free them if they are trapped.

Tomasello has spent many years comparing young humans with other young primates, and has noted many similar behaviors. Humans and chimpanzees will cooperate for a common purpose, such as obtaining food. But in Tomasello's studies, a young chimpanzee (unlike a rat), if given the opportunity, will take all the food for himself. Human children, given the same opportunity, will share with their partners. Unlike young chipmanzees, they seem to be concerned with fairness.

Young chimps and many other animals seem to play together for fun. Yet competition, rather than cooperation, is often the motivating factor among most young primates. Humans collaborate for fun. Play among young humans involves much negotiation around issues of sharing and taking turns. Unlike our chimp cousins, we enjoy communication, sharing, and teamwork for its own sake, even when there are no immediate rewards.

synchrony

When others smile, yawn, or cough we often do too, without thinking about it or knowing why. The ideas that float through our minds are more influenced by others than we realize. We cross our arms or legs in the same way as the person we are talking to without noticing it. We unconsciously synchronize our behavior, which helps us mentally connect with others. We tend to feel most comfortable with and befriend people who seem to respond to situations in similar ways. Common cultural backgrounds and past experiences predispose us to (but don't determine) common responses.

It might initially feel more difficult to work with others with backgrounds and experiences that are different from your own, which lead them to think and respond differently you do. Diverse teams of people are often more creative and productive, however, than more homogeneous teams. The creativity effect is enhanced when group members actively embrace their differences. I have observed the creative impact of diversity myself in collaborative drawing workshops over many years. Quite often, the more diverse the group, in terms of age, cultural background, and level of drawing expertise, the more exciting the final drawing will be.

DRAW TOGETHER!

Get a group of people standing together around a table, with a piece of paper as big as the table. The floor can work too! Broad colored markers encourage big, bold lines. One way to get started is to have each person "make their mark," drawing something that represents them or how they are feeling/what they are thinking about at the moment (it can be abstract.) The next step is to rotate positions, and start drawing connections between the individual drawings. These connections can be based on similar colors or shapes, or they can be thematic, related to the symbols or other kinds of images that may have popped up. Keep rotating around the drawing and making connections until everything is connected to everything else.

MIRRO

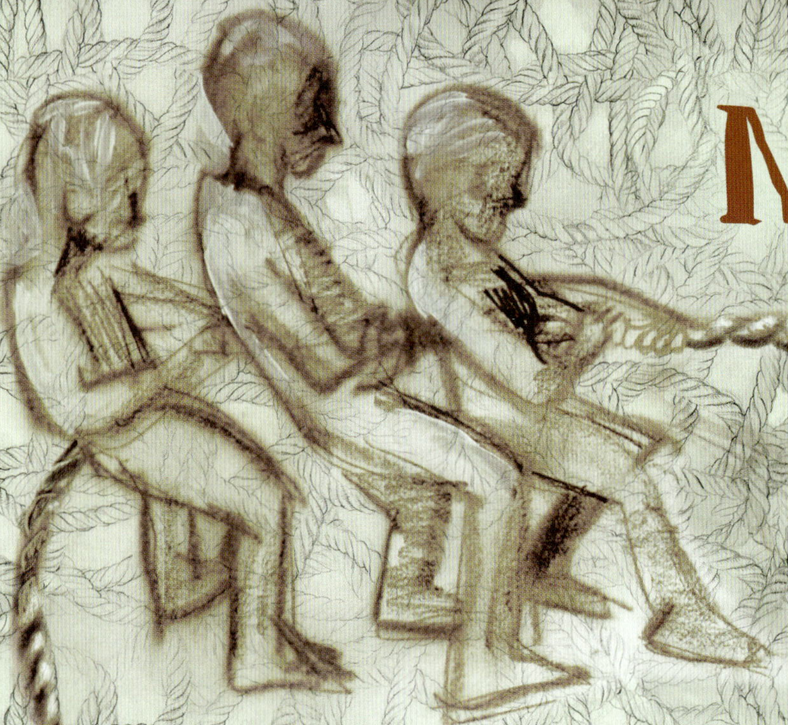

When we mirror the body language of the person we are talking to, they tend to pay more attention to our words. When we see someone echoing our body language, even unconsciously, we may feel understood, and thus more open to what they have to say.

To understand other people's actions, we mentally simulate their behaviors. In the 1990s, in Parma, Italy, researchers investigated the neural basis of hand movements such as grasping. They noticed that when macaque monkeys saw other monkeys or even a human researcher reach for a banana, a pattern of neurons fired in their brain as if they were reaching for that same banana, though their body remained still. These specialized motor neurons, which respond whether the subject is performing an action or simply observing it, have come to be called mirror neurons.

We have multiple perceptual systems that help us understand and communicate with one another. It has been theorized that mirror neurons are at the foundation of our ability to communicate with others. If someone tells you they feel your pain, they may literally feel it. This neurological activation is strongest when we have had similar experiences to those we are observing. The mirror neurons of spectators at Wimbledon will be more active if they actually play tennis themselves. We also seem to infer the feelings of others through the mental simulation of facial expression activated through the mirror system.

RING

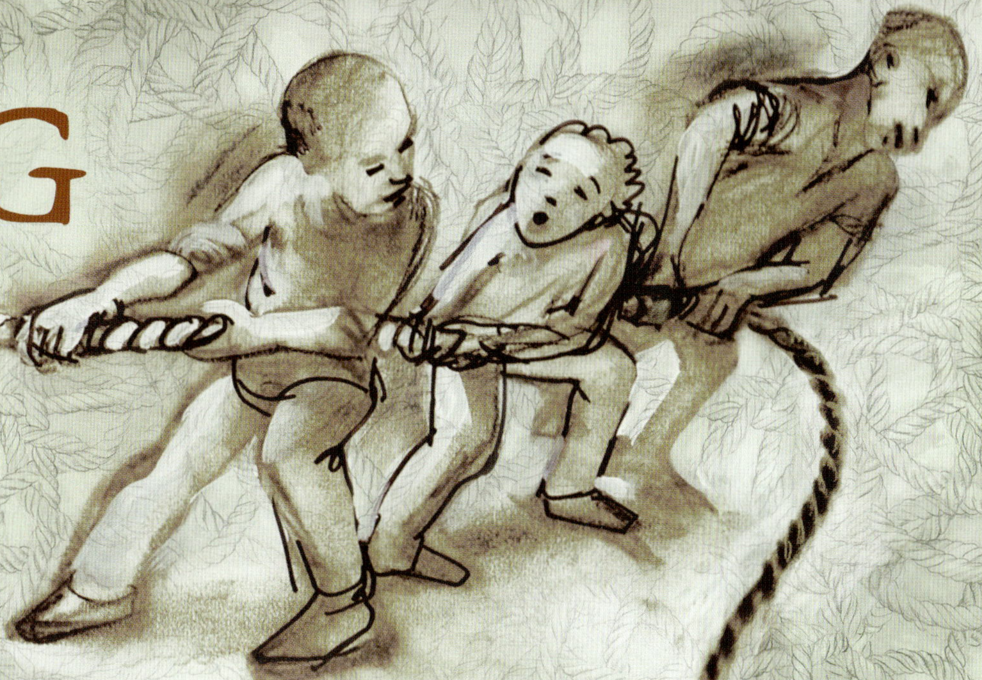

We attend to other people's body language and gestures to get insight into their motivations and intentions. When we look at a drawing, we can appreciate the marks as movements or actions taken by the drawer because we ourselves have made similar kinds of marks. The universality of drawing as an activity makes it easy to relate to. We follow along. Mirror neurons may play an important role in the understanding and appreciation of works of art, according to art historian David Freedberg and neuroscientist Vittorio Gallese. They have proposed that we literally "feel" the movement of the brush or pen, when we observe its trace.

Sixty years before Giacomo Rizzolatti and his team discovered mirror neurons, Kimon Nicolaides was teaching his legendary figure drawing class at the Art Students League in New York City. Nicolaides intuited from his experience teaching drawing that we come to understand the world through imaginatively projecting ourselves into what we see. He said, "You should draw, not what the thing looks like, not even what it is, but what it is doing. Feel how the figure lifts or droops ... A drawing of prize fighters should show the push, from foot to fist, behind their blows that makes them hurt."

Art students, like the macaque monkeys, understand the actions of others by mentally simulating their actions. Nicolaides said, "It is necessary to participate in what the model is doing, to identify yourself with it. Without a sympathetic emotional reaction in the artist there can be no real, no penetrating understanding."

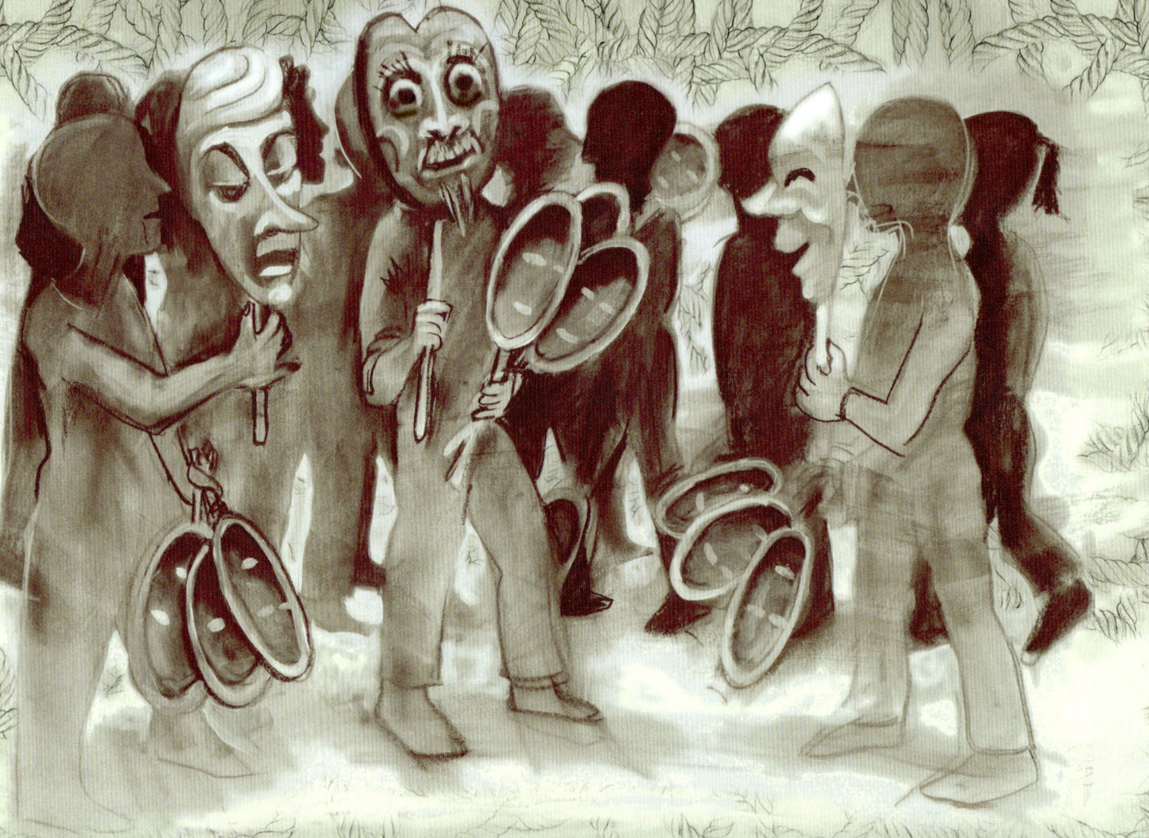

A suggestion, please...

We play out our lives as the central character alongside a cast of thousands, many of whom are extras in our life stories, just as we may be the extras in theirs. We perform roles that have been handed to us and some we have chosen for ourselves: parent or child, sister, brother, partner, companion and friend, leader, witness or disciple. We may wear many hats in a lifetime, a year or a day.

We improvise: we must make judgments and decisions based on incomplete information. The stories other people tell us help us fill in missing pieces we cannot complete alone.

Improvisational comedians often ask for a suggestion from the audience to get a story going. For example, someone might give a pair of comedians the suggestion "popcorn." Popcorn reminds one performer of butter, which reminds him of a cow, so he starts the scene saying "time to milk the cows." Popcorn reminds his partner of watching films, and she comes into the scene as a movie star. But as her partner has already established that they are on a farm, she has to figure out a way to make it work. She says: "Working with you has given me so much material for my next picture, 'How Now Brown Cow!'" One word conjured up two disparate ideas, that they can now blend into one scene neither person would have come up with on their own.

The painter Phillip Guston shocked the art world in 1967 when he turned away from abstract art to narrative work. His daughter, Musa Mayer, found scribbled notes in a drawer that said: "I wanted to tell Stories." In an interview he explained, "When the 1960s came along, I was feeling split, schizophrenic. The war, what was happening in America, the brutality of the world. What kind of man am I, sitting at home reading magazines, going into a frustrated fury about everything—and then going into my studio to adjust a red to a blue.

"I thought there must be some way I could do something about it. I knew ahead of me a road was laying. A very crude, inchoate road. I wanted to be complete again, as I was when I was a kid. ... [I] wanted to be whole between what I thought and what I felt."

Musa Mayer continues, "He had rediscovered the, "pleasures of narrative." He told a writer, "You're painting a shoe; you start painting the sole, and it turns into a moon; you start painting the moon, and it turns into a piece of bread." These late works of Phillip Guston are still controversial over fifty years later. Some include a painter in a Klansman hood smoking a cigarette at his easel. Guston said, "These are self-portraits." His daughter writes, "With the painter, we are invited to examine our own complicity, 'What would it be like to be evil?' my father mused. 'To plan, to plot.'"

Tell Me a Story...

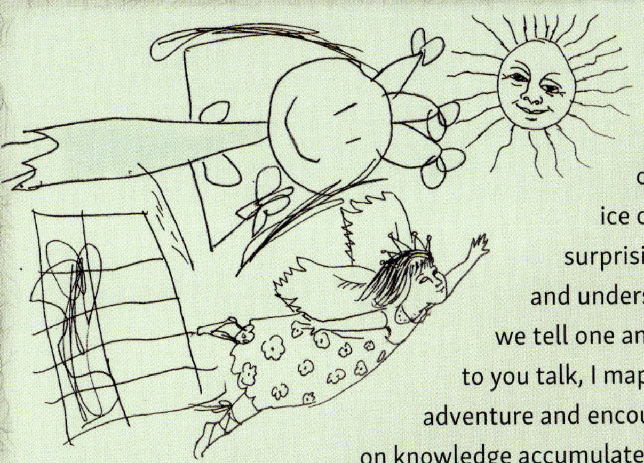

... asks a child ... and then they tell you theirs. From an adult's point of view, the fact that the puppy licked their face that morning or an ice cream cone fell on the ground may not be particularly fascinating or surprising. But as we listen, we can share in the child's joy or disappointment and understand just a little bit better what really matters to them. The stories we tell one another help us figure out how to get along and live together. As I listen to you talk, I map my own experiences and other stories I've heard onto your tales of adventure and encounters with others. Through stories we cultivate common ground based on knowledge accumulated over many lives, not just our own. Social bonds forged through shared stories allow us to build collective systems of meaning and beliefs.

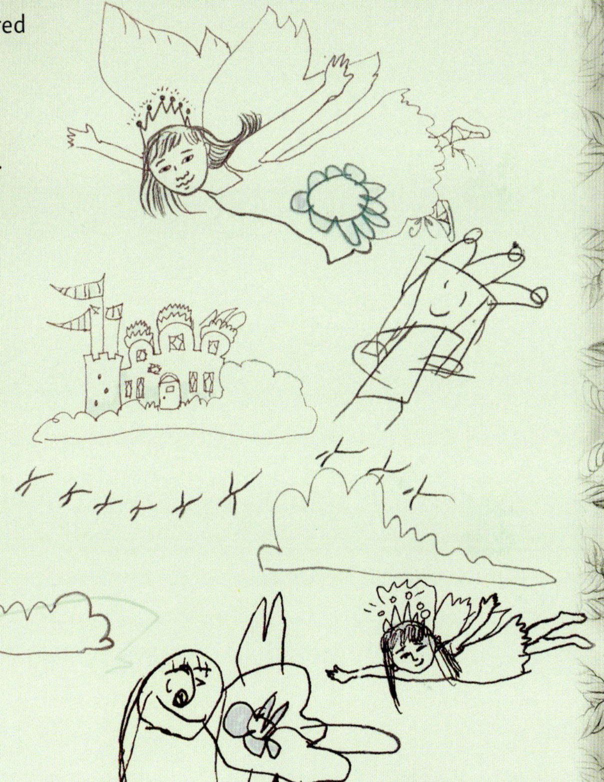

Drawings, like our stories, can weave together socially constructed knowledge, images, values, and beliefs with our own lived experiences. When we draw, we not only draw out our own perceptions and ideas, but draw in those of the larger culture in which we live. We gather tangled webs of meaning and inference that make the work comprehensible to ourselves and others.

Cognitive psychologists Jennifer Drake and Ellen Winner find that children who are exceptionally gifted drawers are really good at absorbing culturally specific drawing conventions. They write, "It is a mistake ... to see Western-style realism as the prime sign of artistic talent, when this style is but one of the many possible representational conventions that artistically gifted children master so early and so independently." The gifted children Drake and Winner describe are good at drawing what they see and imagine BECAUSE (at least in part) they are good at learning how other people in their world draw from observation and imagination.

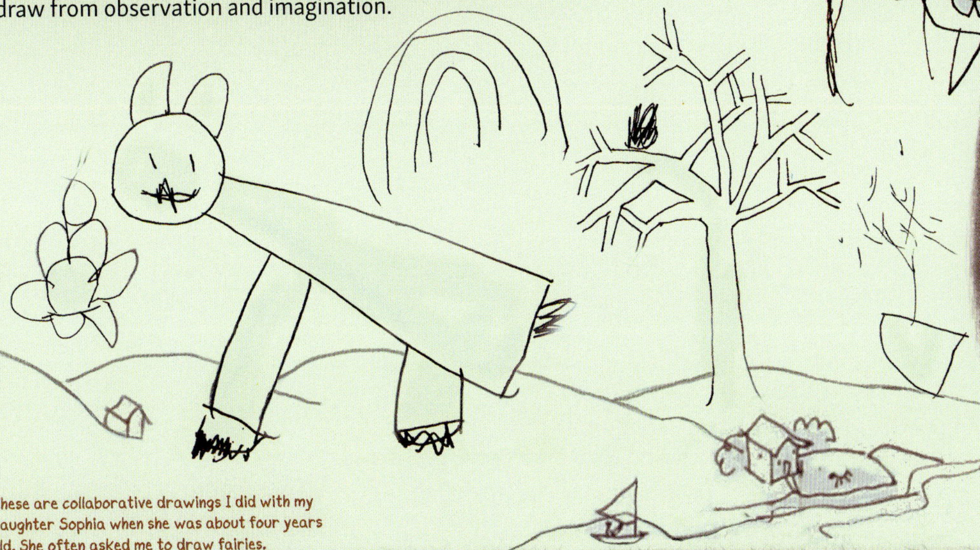

These are collaborative drawings I did with my daughter Sophia when she was about four years old. She often asked me to draw fairies.

DRAW WITH A CHILD

If there is a young child in your life, get the biggest piece of paper around and start filling it together. Take turns copying parts of each other's drawings. Ask the child for suggestions.

Tricks of the Trade

When I was a child, I adored my oldest sister (still do). She loved to draw, and so did I. For years, my mother saved a still-life drawing my sister had made at fourteen, along with my four-year-old version of it. I can vividly remember sitting next to her, doing my best to copy the details I admired in hers. In fifth grade, I devoured every single How to Draw book in our school library. Then, at about sixteen, I discovered life drawing and I was hooked. It wasn't easy to draw from live models but I found I could get better by studying other people's drawings. I was lucky enough at seventeen, to study with the great master of human anatomy, Robert Beverly Hale, at the Art Students League in New York City (where Kimon Nicolaides had taught in the 1930s).

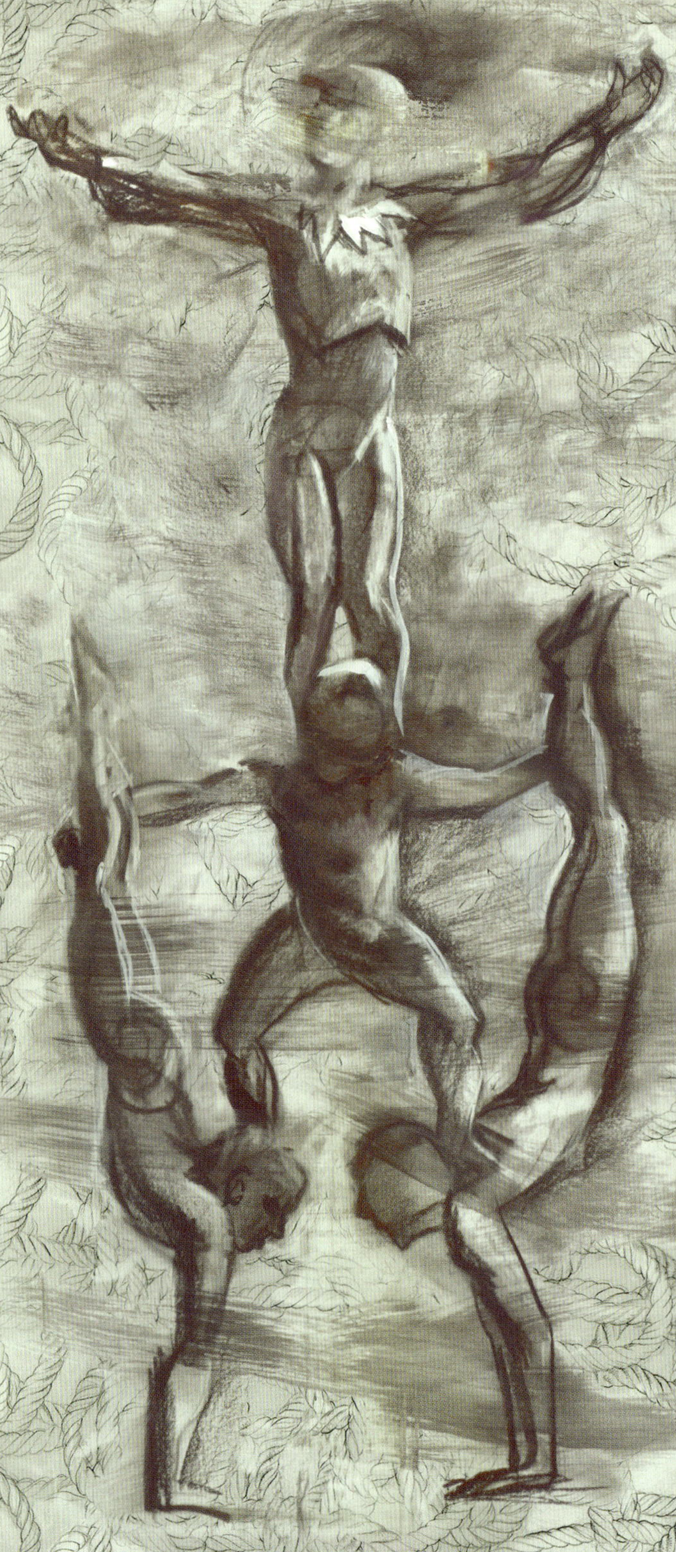

Hale taught us how to locate important anatomical landmarks, muscles, and bones in the live model and the drawings of the old masters. We learned to construct our drawings with that knowledge in mind. One of Hale's favorites (and mine) was the sternocleidomastoid muscle that spirals down up from the back of the ear to the V at the base of the neck. I have never seen a neck in the same way again. I began to look for common structural features in the various sizes, shapes, and ages of male and female bodies posing for us in class. Years later, teaching figure drawing myself, I saw how a few of these tricks of the trade could help young artists flourish in both skill and confidence.

Lately, I've been working on drawing landscapes. It's not a subject I've devoted much time to in the past, so I've gone back to the masters. The Chinese seventeenth-century drawing instruction book, *The Mustard Seed Garden Manual*, offers copious examples and variations gleaned from the ancients, along with words of advice. I've been studying trees according to the *Mustard Seed Garden's* images and principles. As I walk in the woods, the twisting and turning of individual trees and specific types of foliage reveal themselves with new clarity to my now slightly more educated eyes.

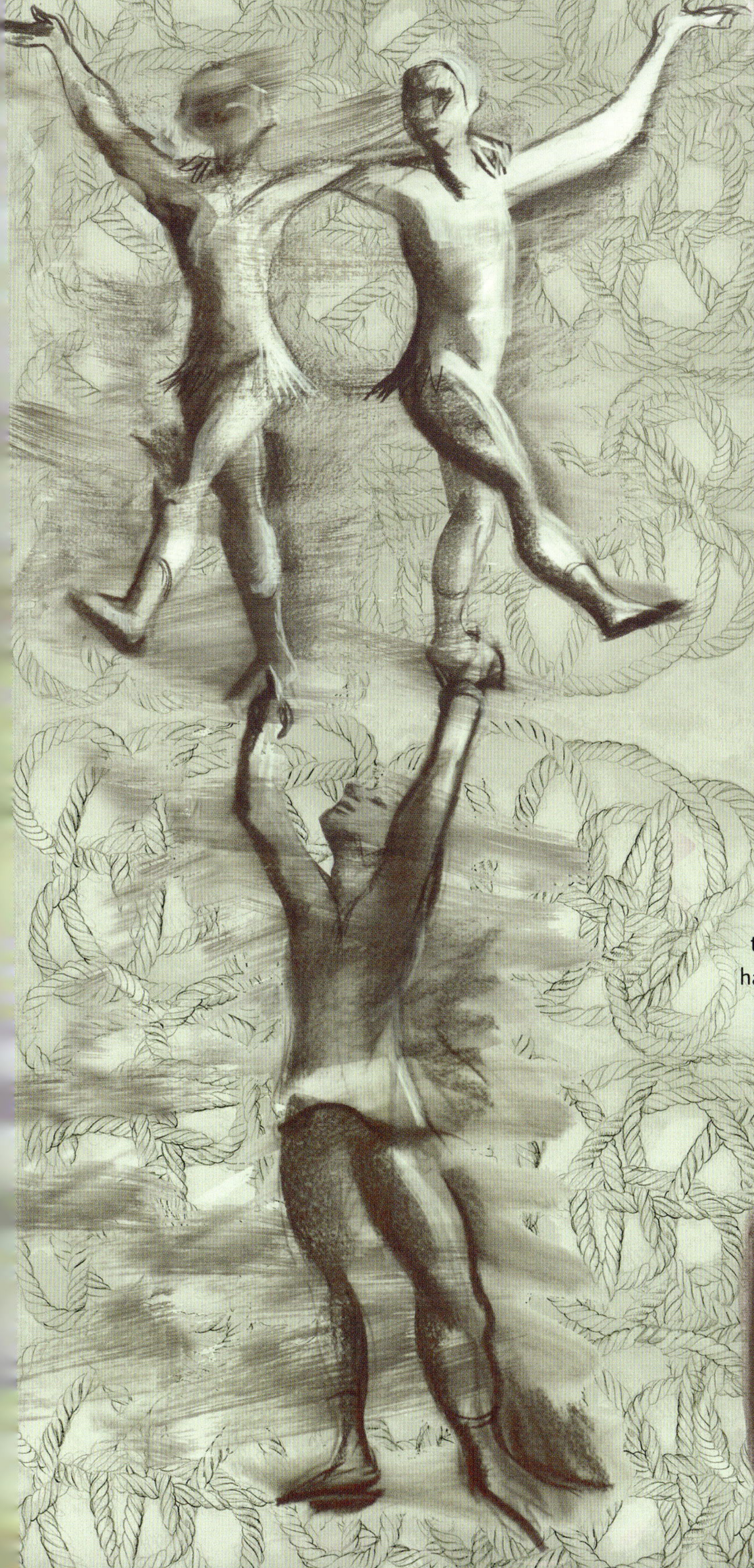

Skilled drawers often learn "how to see," because they have learned from others what to look for. Working from observation or imagination, they can pick out just the key details, landmarks, or defining features they need to represent the being, object, or scene in front of them. Bottom-up visual system processes are mediated by top-down attentional strategies that filter out extraneous detail. These top-down strategies are tricks of the trade, passed down through generations of practitioners.

Just as young children learn how to talk, walk, and many other essential skills by mimicking those around them, artists in Europe, China, and around the world have learned to draw by copying works they admire.

A common thread running through psychological research on observational drawing is the finding that artists have learned not only "how to see," they have learned what to look for. Artists are able to pick out salient details from complex scenes, and record just the information needed to represent their subject. They know what to look for because they have internalized visual formulas developed by other artists over the centuries.

STAND ON THE SHOULDERS OF GIANTS

Find a master drawing that you particularly admire. Print out a copy and glue it down to a larger sheet of paper. Extend the lines and shapes, imitating the style of the original as best you can.

Next, copy a master drawing that you admire. Add and subtract parts to make it your own. For instance, add a background that isn't in the original. Try to make it look as unified as possible, as if it were done by one person.

"When the INTENSITY of LOOKING reaches a certain degree, one becomes aware of an equally intense energy COMING TOWARDS ONE, through the appearance of whatever it is one is scrutinizing... The ENCOUNTER of these TWO ENERGIES, their DIALOGUE, does not have the form of question and answer. It is a ferocious and inarticulated dialogue. To sustain it requires faith. It is like burrowing in the dark, a burrowing under the apparent... Sometimes when the dialogue is SWIFT, almost instantaneous, it is like something THROWN and CAUGHT."

— John Berger

The Drawing Dialogue

People who draw a lot often describe it as "a way to have a conversation with myself." Drawing is fundamentally nonverbal, in that it relies on visual and spatial thinking, rather than verbal reasoning. But there is a back and forth between action and reflection in the process that can feel like call and response, as if the drawing had a mind of its own.

Drawers often explain their drawing in anthropomorphic terms, saying that the drawing "wants" or "needs" something. A drawer may notice and respond slowly and deliberately to light, quick marks that were made spontaneously at first. Immersion in the drawing process allows for a flood of unanticipated perceptions, feelings, and thoughts (from the bottom up) that can then be examined, analyzed, and evaluated (from the top down). Raw experience is received and processed into new insights and understandings, and the traces of action in the form of marks and lines on the drawing surface serve to constrain and invite further actions.

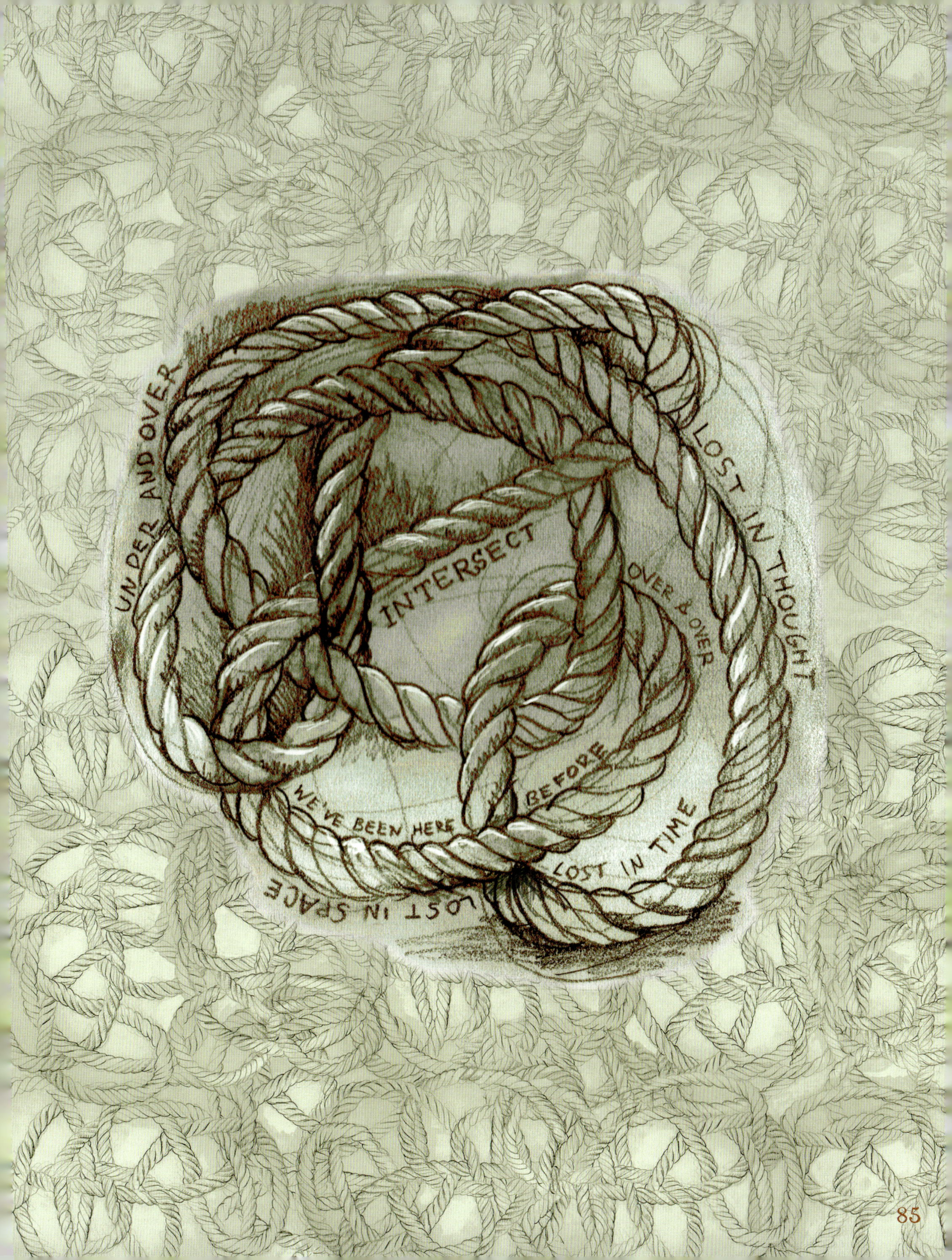

UNDER AND OVER
LOST IN THOUGHT
INTERSECT
OVER & OVER
WE'VE BEEN HERE
BEFORE
LOST IN TIME
LOST IN SPACE

How to

Imagine a Place

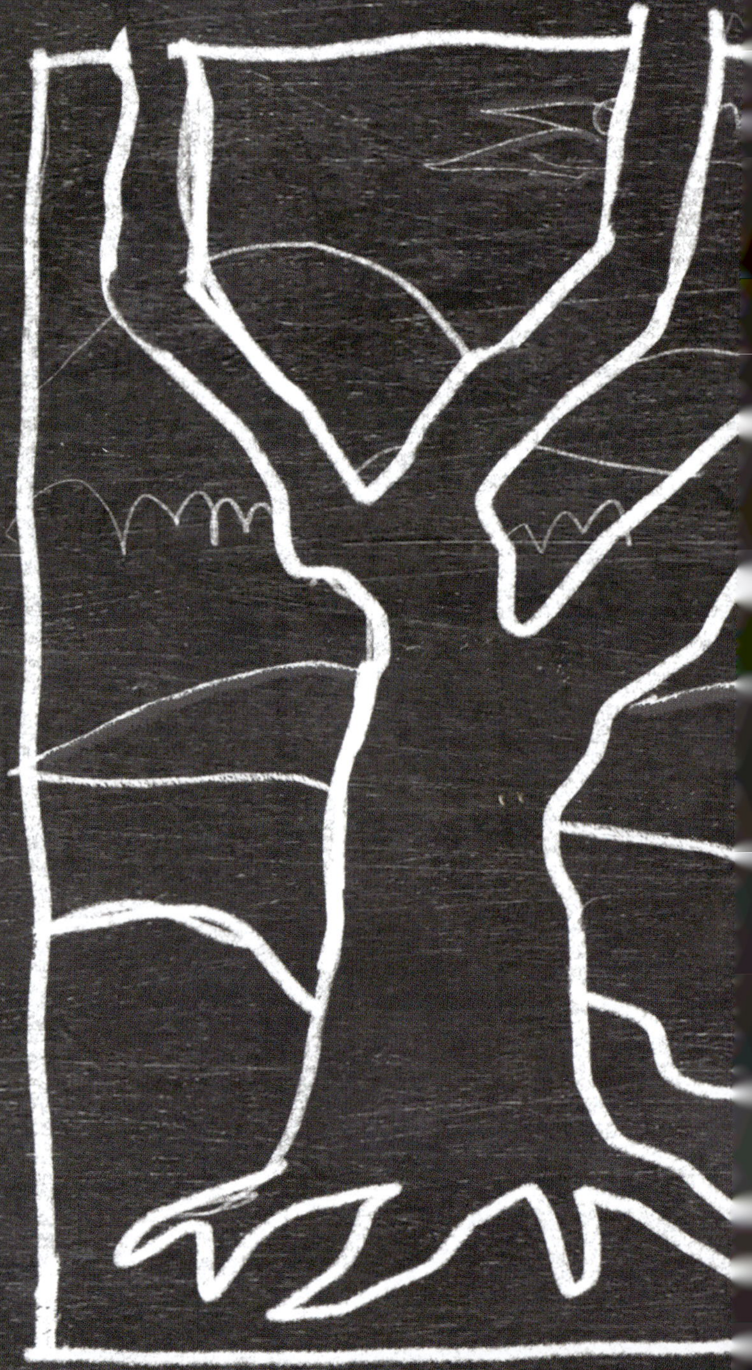

Background

1 elements appear smallest in relation to their actual size
2 elements are fuzzy, low contrast, detail not visible
3 elements are higher on page/closer to the horizon line

Middle ground

1 elements bigger in relation to background elements, smaller than foreground elements
2 more detail and contrast than background, less detail and contrast than foreground
3 elements overlap background elements and are rooted lower on the page

Foreground

1 elements start lowest on page, and overlap elements in middle ground and background
2 elements shown with greatest detail and/or contrast
3 elements large in comparison with the actual sizes of middle ground and background elements

Organizing pictorial elements in foreground, middle ground, and background layers creates the illusion that the drawing surface is a window onto another world.

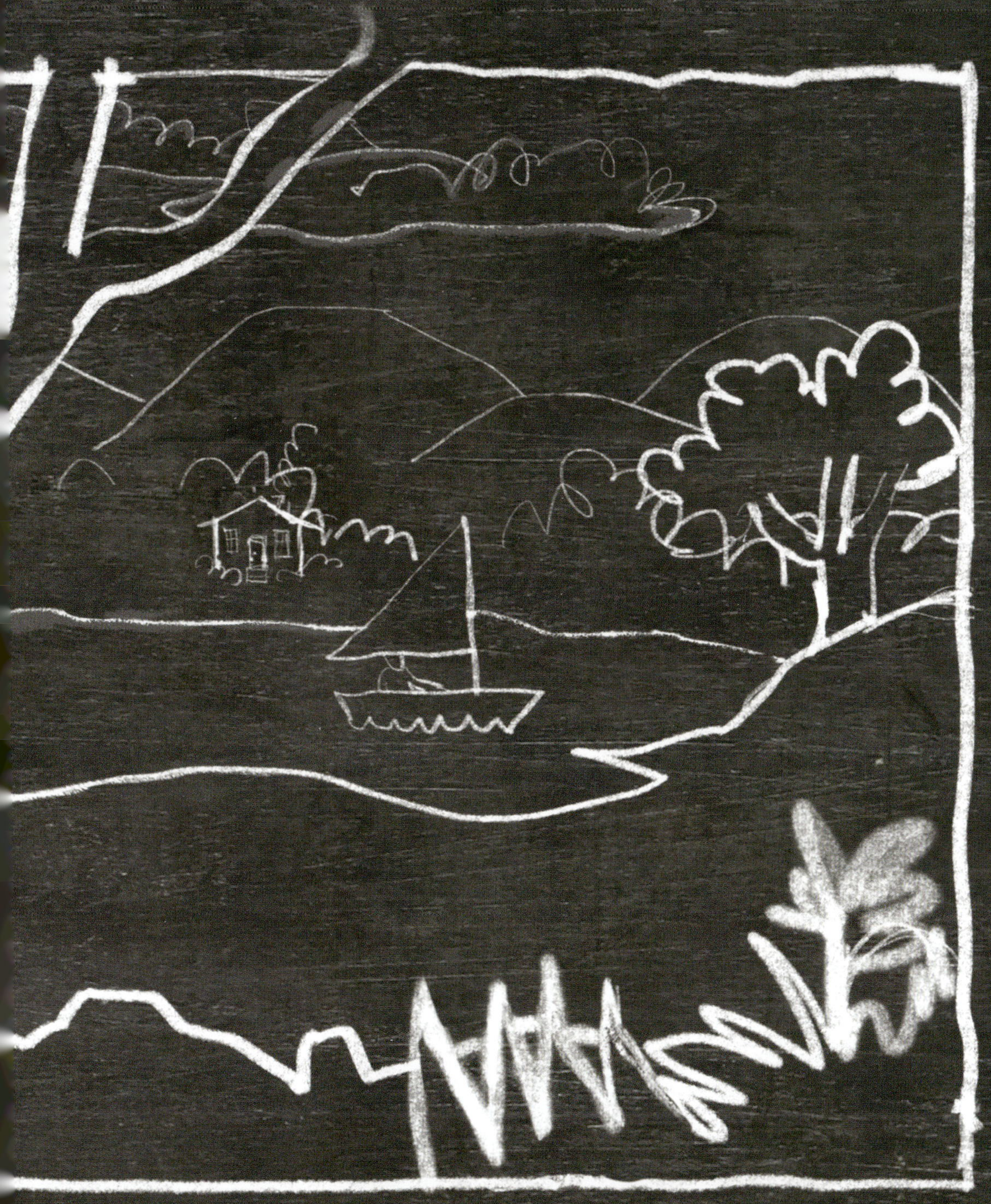

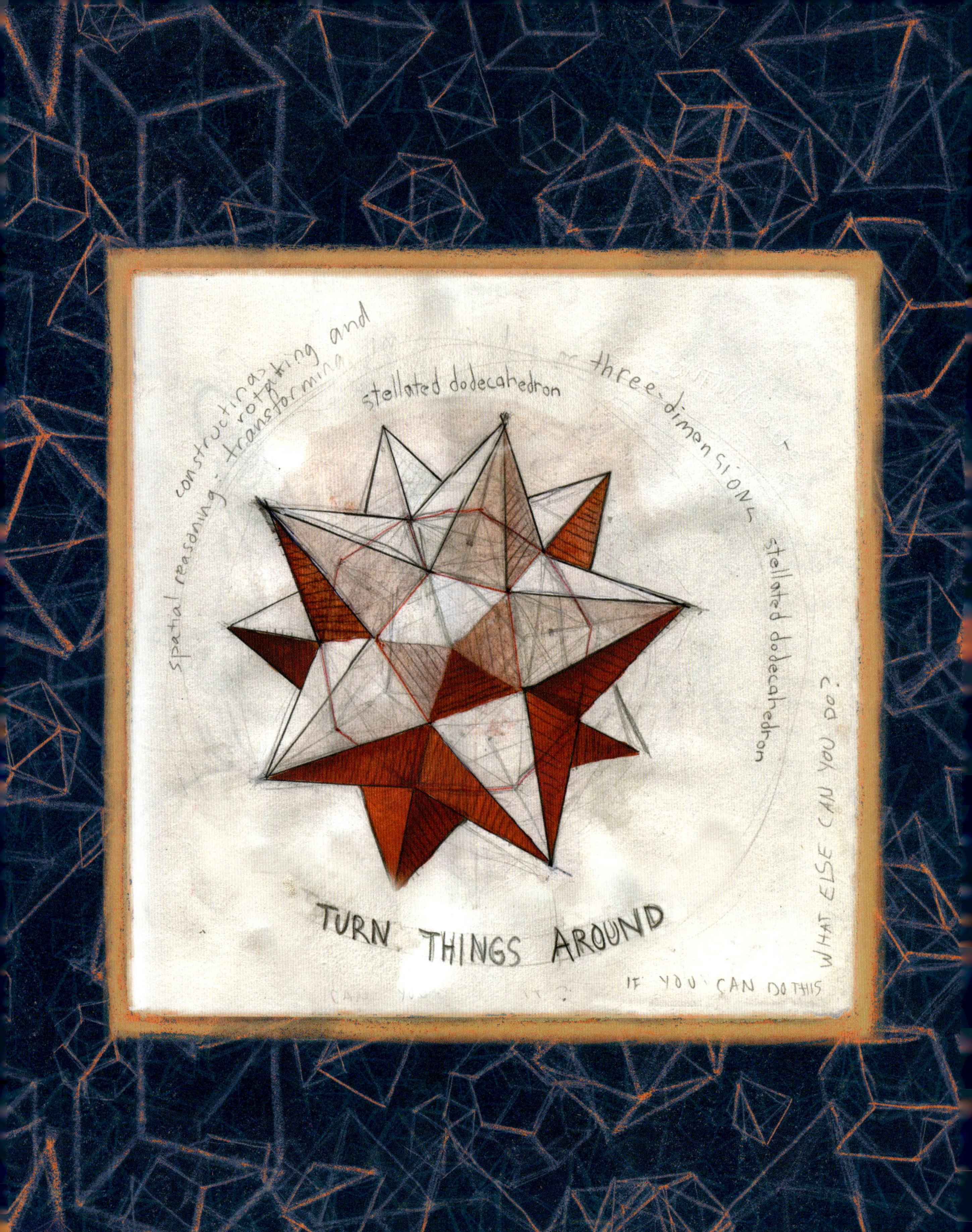
spatial reasoning - constructing rotating and transforming
stellated dodecahedron
three-dimensional
stellated dodecahedron
TURN THINGS AROUND
IF YOU CAN DO THIS
WHAT ELSE CAN YOU DO?

chapter six

Thinking Space

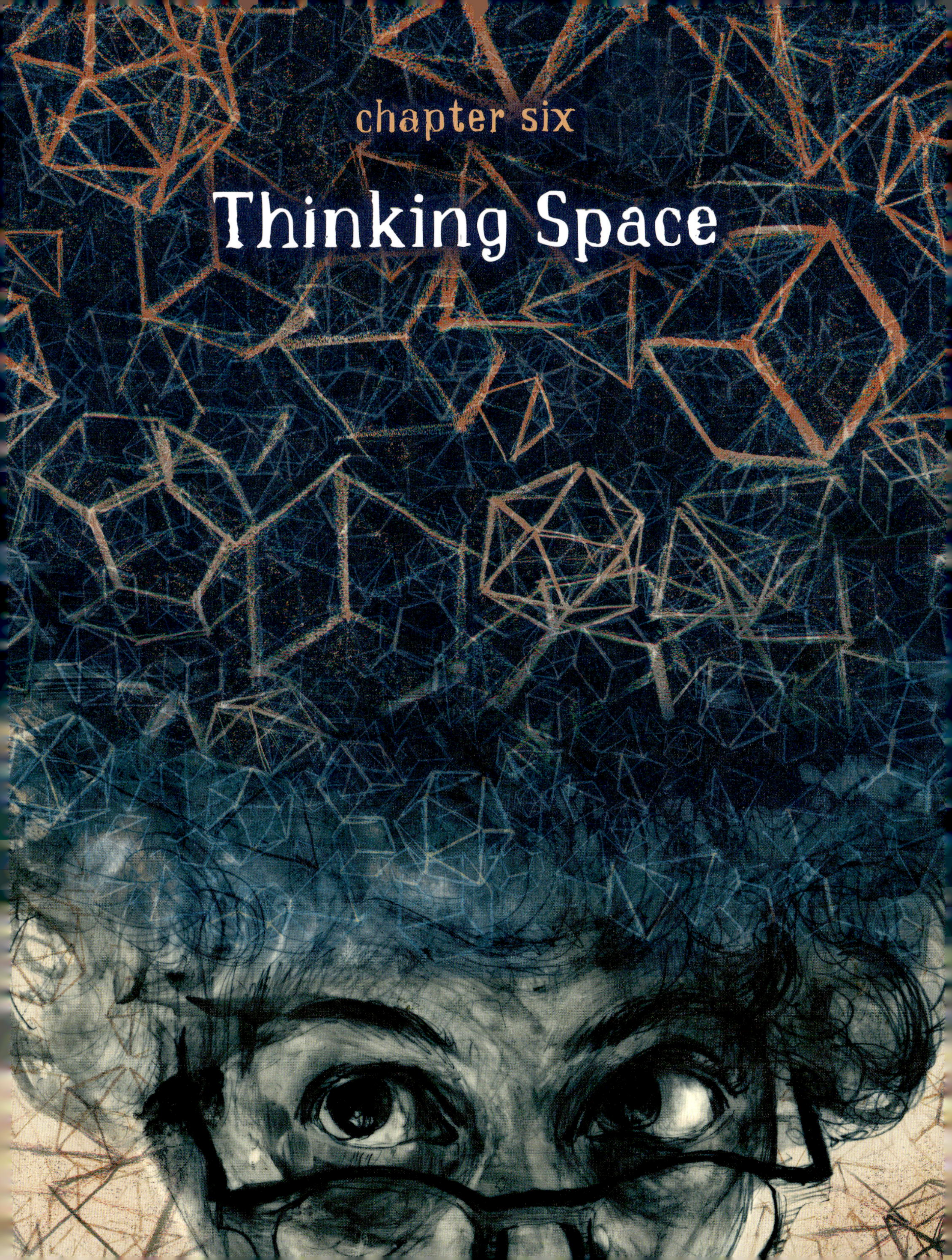

The blank page can be a physical extension of our minds. We DRAW out two- and three-dimensional models of REAL and INVENTED objects, actors, and scenes, pull them apart, and put them back together in new ways.

We sometimes say we need to "turn things over in our minds" when we feel the need to analyze a subject thoroughly. We want to get "on top" of a situation, "cover" a topic, "uncover" the facts, or put something "to the side." Spatial analogies permeate our thinking so completely that we usually don't notice them.

SPATIAL reasoning is the ability to retain, retrieve, generate, and transform visual images in the mind. ANALOGIES compare two phenomena as a way to understand one (the target) by identifying common features it shares with another, more familiar phenomenon (the source).

Both spatial and analogic reasoning rely on our ability to perceive deep structural relationships beneath superficial appearances.

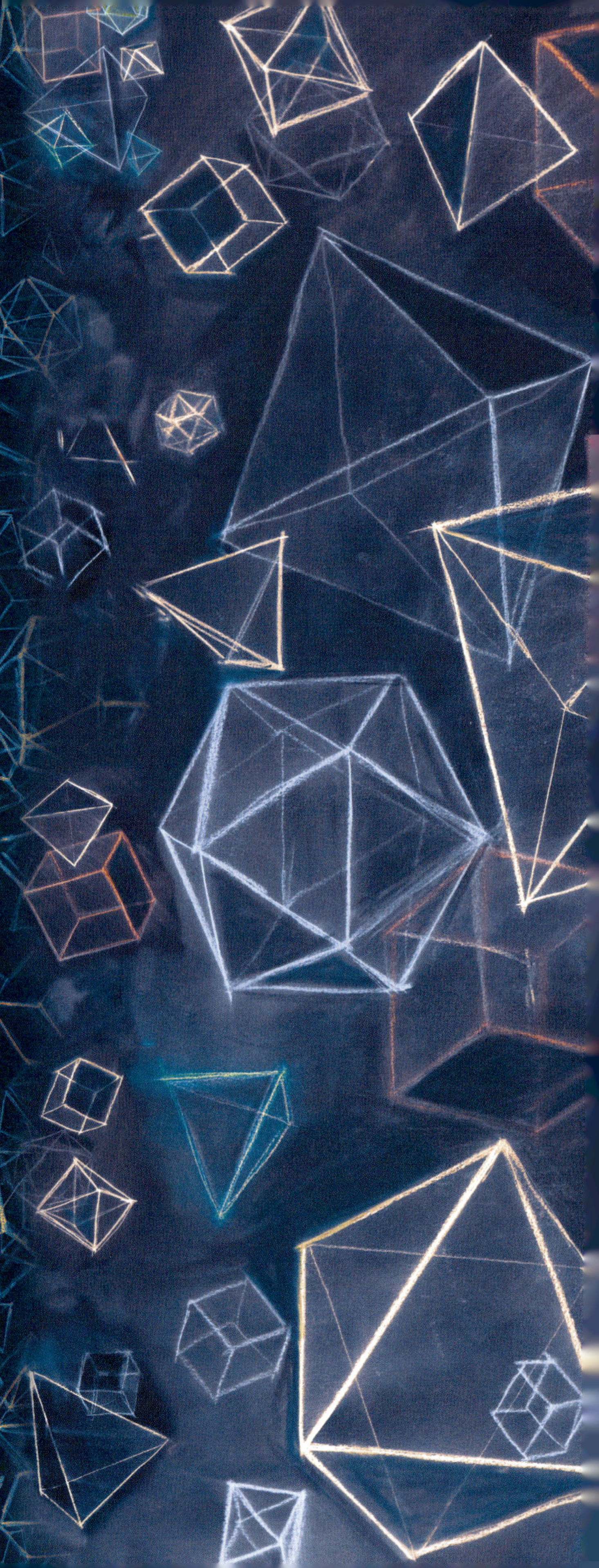

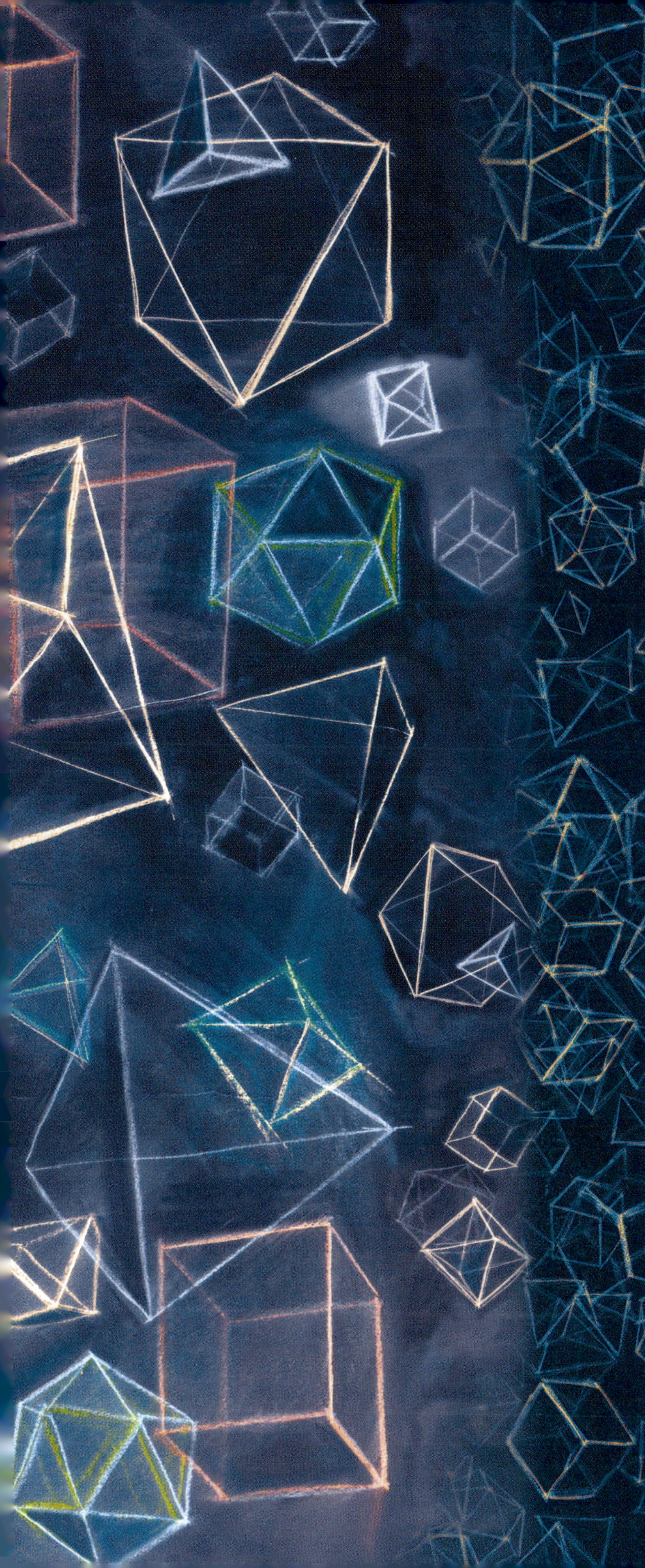

You use spatial reasoning when you try to shop efficiently at the supermarket, wrap a birthday present, pack the car for a long trip, or park the car once you get there. You also use it to imagine (and sketch out) a new layout of the furniture in your living room before you try actually picking up that heavy sofa. A sculptor might imagine the form of the final work in a hunk of marble before starting to chip away at it. A surgeon uses spatial reasoning to plan a repair to a torn knee ligament, explain his plan to the patient on a whiteboard, and actually make the repair. High performance in spatial reasoning is crucial in most science, technology, engineering, and math (STEM) fields as well as in art and design fields. It can be learned and taught, and is linked with innovation and creativity across disciplines.

REASONING can be defined as the "ability to go beyond the information given." SPATIAL reasoning includes the ability to integrate different views of a single object and to imagine it from a variety of viewpoints. It also includes understanding spatial relationships between objects and between multiple arrangements of items within a larger spatial context. The ability to imagine yourself in someone else's shoes, seeing the world from their perspective, requires spatial reasoning. Perspective taking then allows us to FIND ANALOGIES between our experiences and theirs.

Drawing is all about the relationships and movement of FORMS in SPACE. We make marks in two dimensions on the drawing surface and play with them in the virtual three-dimensional world of the drawing. We use spatial reasoning when we work to figure out the relative position and direction of shapes and forms in this imaginary space.

My father, Arthur Kantrowitz, knew a thing or two about space. In the 1950s he developed a way for rockets to reenter the Earth's atmosphere from outer space without burning up. A decade later, his invention helped send men to the Moon and come back safely to Earth. (His invention also made intercontinental ballistic missiles possible: the double-edged sword of science and technology.) As a young child, I sat on his lap while he smoked his pipe and told me about the outer space metropolis that would someday be my home. It didn't seem that appealing.

I wondered where the big weeping willow trees that grew by the pond behind our house would be in my dad's vision of the future. It sounded like a giant indoor shopping mall, but I got the idea.

Dream BIG

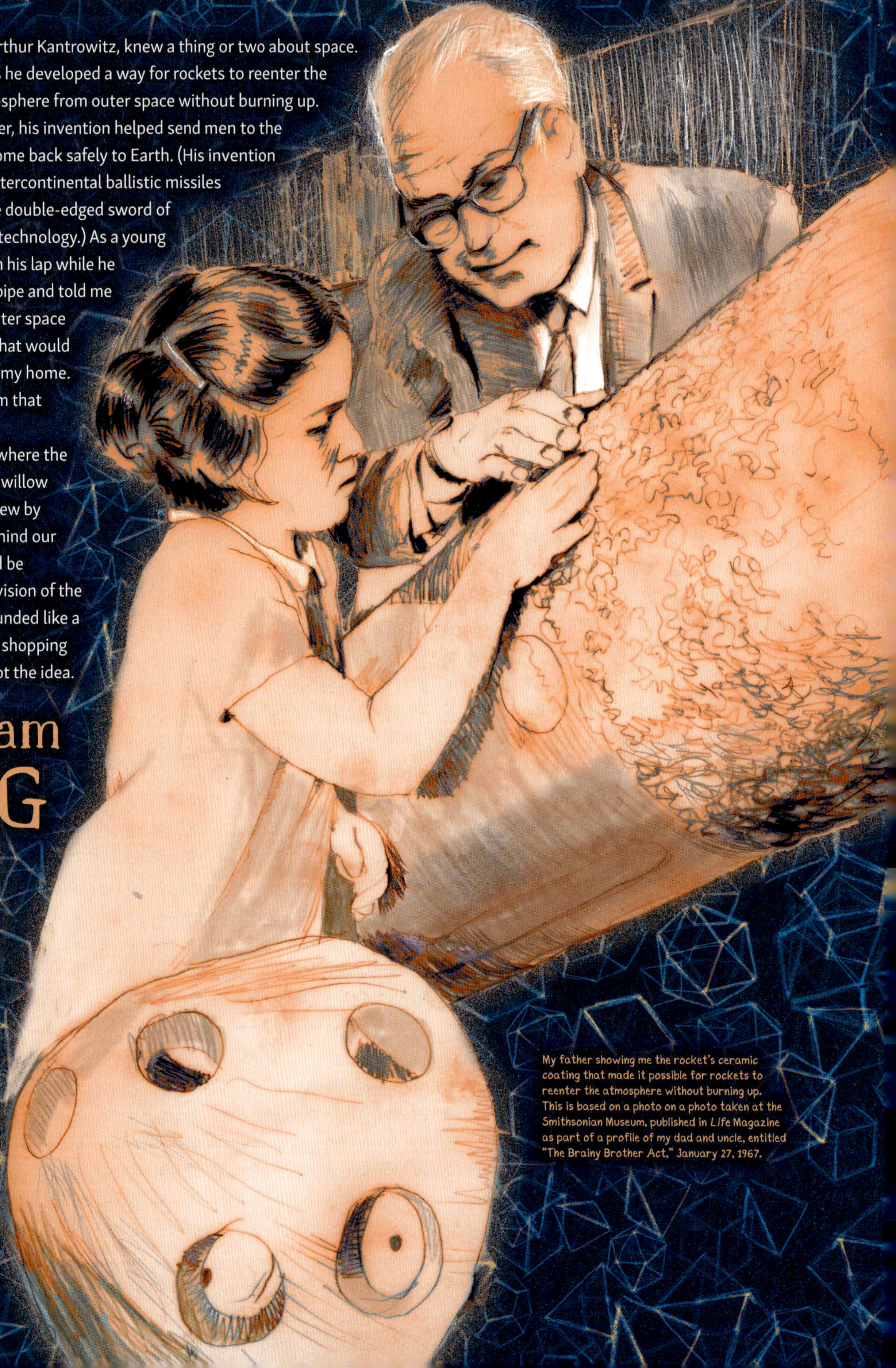

My father showing me the rocket's ceramic coating that made it possible for rockets to reenter the atmosphere without burning up. This is based on a photo on a photo taken at the Smithsonian Museum, published in *Life* Magazine as part of a profile of my dad and uncle, entitled "The Brainy Brother Act," January 27, 1967.

Exploring Space

My father connected the fields of fluid mechanics and aerodynamics through his research into the physical properties of turbulence. He understood similarities in complex processes and structures underlying diverse phenomena. This enabled him to make important contributions in fields as disparate as rocket science, cardiac care, and high-powered lasers. In partnership with my uncle Adrian, a cardiac surgeon and heart transplant pioneer, my dad invented the interaortic balloon pump, a device that gave people who suffered heart attacks a second chance at life and used in ICUs for decades around the world.

Turbulence is a complex, emergent phenomenon that we can see in the eddies that form around river rocks, the swirls we create when we stir cream into our coffee, the trails of airplanes flying through clouds, or the molecular clouds that give birth to stars. Physical structures and their underlying processes can be found in very different phenomena: frost forms through diffusion-limited aggregation, and so do cities and towns. Individual entities, such as ice crystals or house-building humans, moving randomly, bump into others like themselves and stick together, creating branching structures.

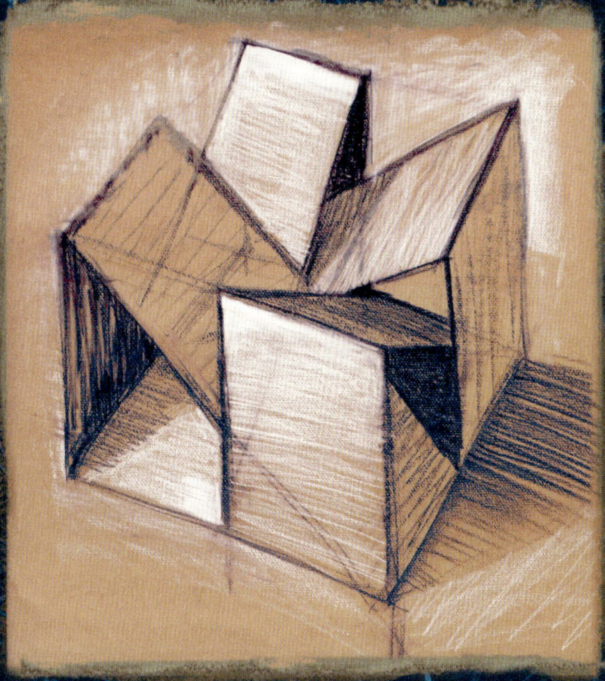

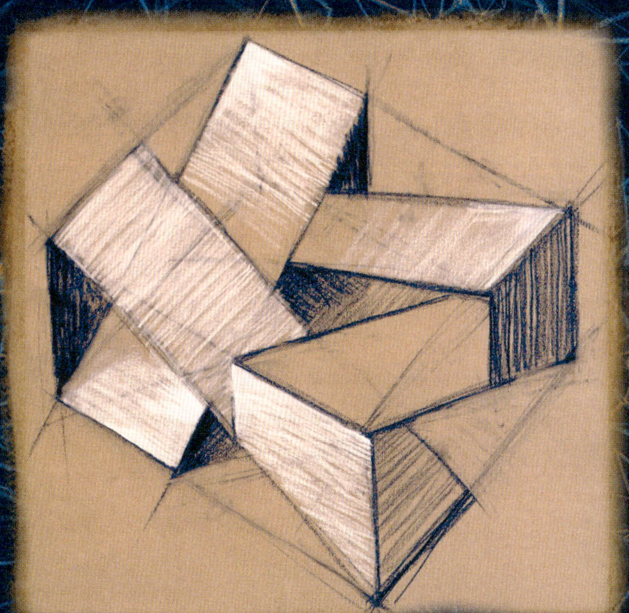

The In-between Spaces

I learned from my father to look for the gaps and intersections in knowledge at the edges between established disciplines (such as rocket science and cardiac care). In these spaces, we might find that things that seem on the surface to be very dissimilar actually have important structural relationships in common. Trans-disciplinary research that focuses on in-between spaces can bring fresh approaches to difficult problems. Experts from different domains of knowledge working together can bring fresh perspectives to each other's disciplines, and in so doing, may discover new solutions to old problems.

DRAW THE GAPS

Find two objects you can place in front of you. The objects can be as simple as a mug and a coffee pot; objects with handles work well. Don't draw the objects themselves. Focus on the shape of the space between the objects as accurately as you can. If there are other spaces, such as the space inside a handle, draw that too. Ignore any details on the objects themselves. This is sometimes called "negative space" but I think of it as "in between" or "relational space." What you are really looking at is the character of the relationship between two objects.

A young child I know once saw a green crab walking along the beach. He said "Hey look! A walking pickle!" He was making sense of a new experience by finding similarities with a familiar one, as we all do. He made an analogy. It takes some background knowledge to go beyond superficial appearances (it's round and green and not too big ... maybe it's a pickle?) You might first need to know that things that walk around on legs are usually animals and not fermented food products. With a little more knowledge, you might note its coastal habitat and its exoskeleton with the aforementioned roundish carapace and conclude that it is a crustacean, indeed a crab, probably male since one claw is much bigger than the other. To go deeper you might use your smart phone to identify the species of crab, especially if you plan on eating it. There are a small number of toxic crabs that can kill you!

What is this like?

Analogies based on structure and function are more useful than superficial analogies based on coincidental similarities. (It's round and green!) Unfortunately, deeper analogies are more difficult to construct. In a highly cited study, cognitive psychologists Mary Glick and Keith Holyoak investigated analogical reasoning. Participants first learned about a successful military capture of a fortress: Rather than approaching the fortress in one big group, the army split up into small groups and attacked from multiple directions at once. Participants were then asked how medical doctors might eliminate a tumor. They learned a single beam of radiation strong enough to destroy the tumor would also destroy healthy tissue. If researchers suggested participants should try making an analogy, most participants got the correct answer: aim a safe level of radiation at the tumor from multiple directions at once. Very few participants figured it out on their own without the hint.

The transfer of knowledge from one context to another is notoriously difficult to achieve. To make deep analogies, we need to pay attention to underlying spatial structures and configurations. This helps us bridge different contexts, such as military strategy and cancer therapy, that appear on the surface to be unrelated.

Openness and fluency of analogical thought seem to be gained through experience. Experts find new meanings through greater access to alternative associations or frames of reference. In many domains, experts use their prior knowledge to identify structures and processes, whereas novices focus on local features and details.

I used to paint family portraits for a living. I learned early on that I could get the correct shape of the mouth, but if the space between the mouth and the nose was too big, it wouldn't look right. The in-between spaces had to be accurate. If I located the individual facial features in proper relationship to one another, I would have a likeness right away, long before I started to define the shape of the mouth.

When we draw, we need to pay attention to the relationships between parts and wholes, uncovering and representing spatial relationships rather than just focusing on isolated, superficial features.

A SURFACE analogy is based on similarities in extraneous details.

A DEEP analogy is based on similarities in underlying processes and structures.

Educator and researcher Michelle Darlington Fava designed and implemented a cross-disciplinary drawing program focused on guiding sixteen-year-old students to learn to make deep analogies. She used a collection of natural objects, such as seashells, crystals, and birds' nests, to stimulate their imagination and develop their analogical reasoning skills. She initially asked them to draw these objects, while asking them what they could infer about their formation by examining the objects' structures. She then asked, "What is this like?" Students first identified superficial similarities. Once time-lapse footage of the growth patterns of similar objects was presented, students were able to get beyond incidental details and identify deeper, structural analogies. They learned to pay attention to underlying relationships and processes.

Science education researchers Robert Goldstone and Uri Wilensky used analogical reasoning to significantly improve students' ability to transfer prior knowledge and understanding to new situations. They created interactive computer graphic models of complex natural processes. They eliminated nonessential details to reveal the deep structures and processes underlying superficially different phenomena. In this way, they enabled students to reason more like experts. The researchers identified intrinsic complex system principles that naturally cross domains, such as positive feedback loops (affecting microphone and speaker sound production, wealth accumulation, and journal citations). A whole system has organizational properties that cannot be deduced from a consideration of the parts in isolation.

"Analogy is the fuel and fire of thinking."

— Douglas Hofstadter and Emmanuel Sander, *Surfaces and Essences*

Drawing Schemas

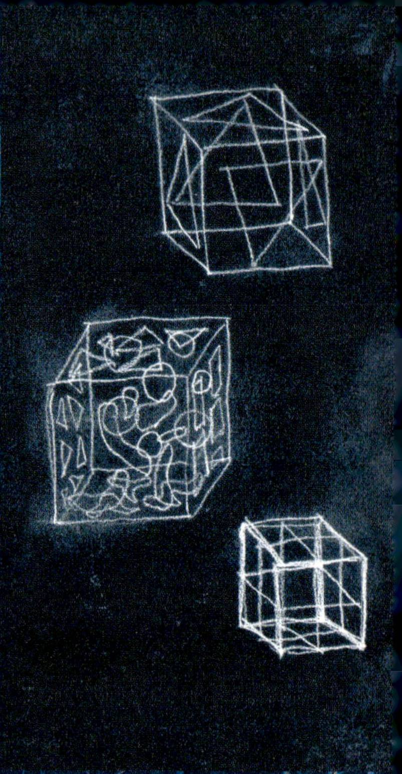

Drawing can provide opportunities to exercise a variety of visuospatial reasoning abilities. As we draw, we relate one mark to the next. We notice and respond to spatial relationships as they emerge. Specific kinds of drawing activities can help us develop abilities to perceive and manipulate spatial configurations. Practicing drawing teaches you to deliberately switch attention from details to larger structures and back again, from parts to wholes. Art educator and researcher Nancy Smith and the Drawing Study Group found a key milestone in the development of children's abilities to draw from observation is the ability to manage relationships between parts and wholes. Focusing in on details can be valuable: it's important to recognize quickly the small details that distinguish an edible plant from a deadly one. But without metacognitive awareness (which may be cultivated through drawing), it's easy to get lost in the details without realizing it.

MULTIPLE PERSPECTIVES

Take a simple object you may have handy, such as a handheld pencil sharpener or tape dispenser. Draw it from the front, side, and top. Try drawing it from other angles, taking care to notice how shapes transform as you change your viewpoint.

Schema = a visual convention or formula

CUBED!

Draw a cube in an oblique projection view (parallel lines stay parallel, one face of the cube is parallel with the picture plane; see illustration above). Now imagine there is a pattern drawn on a receding side. Try to draw that pattern, maintaining the sense of perspective. Repeat on all six sides. Then draw another cube and try it again!

Learning to draw convincing representations of 3D form on a 2D surface helps develop spatial reasoning. "Draw it so they can build it," says Kim Sloane of Pratt Institute in New York City. Pratt is particularly known for its architecture and design programs. Its challenging first-year drawing class meets all day once a week for a full year. The curriculum emphasizes constructive drawing techniques. Class time is split between observational drawing and visualization; in both kinds of drawing, the ability to create convincing three-dimensional forms on a flat surface is paramount. As a visiting instructor at Pratt for two years, I gained a lot of practical knowledge about developing spatial reasoning through drawing.

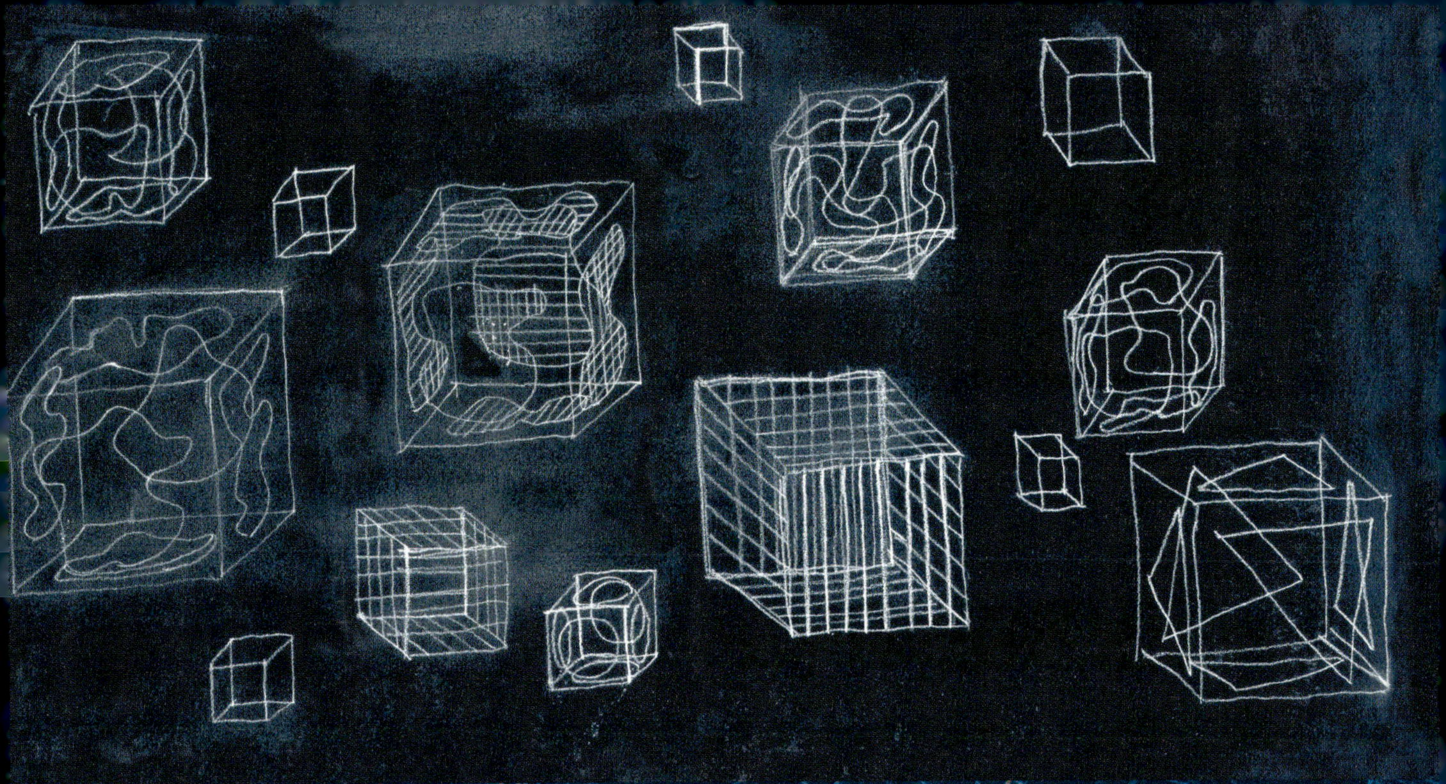

Pratt students start by learning orthographic projection: parallel lines stay parallel. Engineers use orthographic projections to convey their plans clearly to builders. Students draw simple forms and toys, like Lego blocks and toy cars. Linear perspective is an alternative drawing system they learn once they master orthographic projections: that's when things get interesting. With linear perspective, the drawing is constructed from a specific point of view. Things appear smaller as they get farther away. Parallel lines do not stay parallel; they converge at a vanishing point on the horizon line. This can be very challenging for some to master, because students have to learn to override auto-corrections our brains make to compensate for the limitations of a single point of view. A camera captures a scene from a single viewpoint. If we close one eye, we can see like a camera, but that's not how our brains normally process visual information. When we know similar objects are the same size, even when one is farther away, we will naturally draw the one that is farther away bigger than it appears until we learn to do it differently.

SPACE BOX

Draw a box, keeping parallel lines parallel. This drawing system is called "orthographic projection," and is used by engineers and architects. Keep the essential geometry and symmetry of the box, and carve out pieces of the cube's walls to create views into internal spaces.

TRAPEZOID PLAY

Fill a page with a series of trapezoids, parallelograms, and triangles. Avoid making right angles. Shade some shapes in and notices how this begins to create the illusion of three-dimensional space on the flat drawing surface.

Drawing is always a negotiation between what we see and what we know. Technical know-how can replace innate cognitive biases and naive schemas with a more flexible approach.

Drawers can be taught to recognize the deeper spatial structures and relationships underlying surface details. Mastering linear perspective helps the drawer to convey a point of view and create a convincing, coherent three-dimensional world. A basic knowledge of the human skeleton and muscle structure, along with an understanding of gesture, helps students recognize the "bony landmarks" in a live model and imagine the potential for movement.

Kim Sloane uses analogic reasoning in his drawing classes at Pratt. He asks his students how the model's skull, ribcage, or pelvis is like an "atomic ball of string." They learn to construct the figure from balls of string, slinkys, boxes, or toilet paper rolls. After they practice each of these schemas separately, he asks them to put them together: "to best express the different parts of the form: its appearance, volume, direction, or relation to other parts. Entirely new structures are in this way developed for each drawing and each pose."

Drawing strategies

In a recent study of 682 art students by psychologist Rebecca Chamberlain and colleagues, students who were strategic about practicing and using a variety of drawing techniques made works that were rated most highly by others as well as themselves. Drawings by students who spent a lot of time practicing but did not pick up new methods and techniques were not rated highly by either themselves or others. Another study by Chamberlain and colleagues compared Pratt first-year art students to non-art students. They found that art students demonstrated more mental flexibility when presented with complex visual stimuli than non-art students. This greater flexibility increased over the course of their first year. It seemed to be a top-down advantage; their bottom-up perceptual responses were not better than those of the non-art students and did not improve. Chamberlain explains, "There is no fundamental change in the way the visual system works (when and how we see color, edges etc.) but in how we can allocate our attention to different aspects of our visual experience."

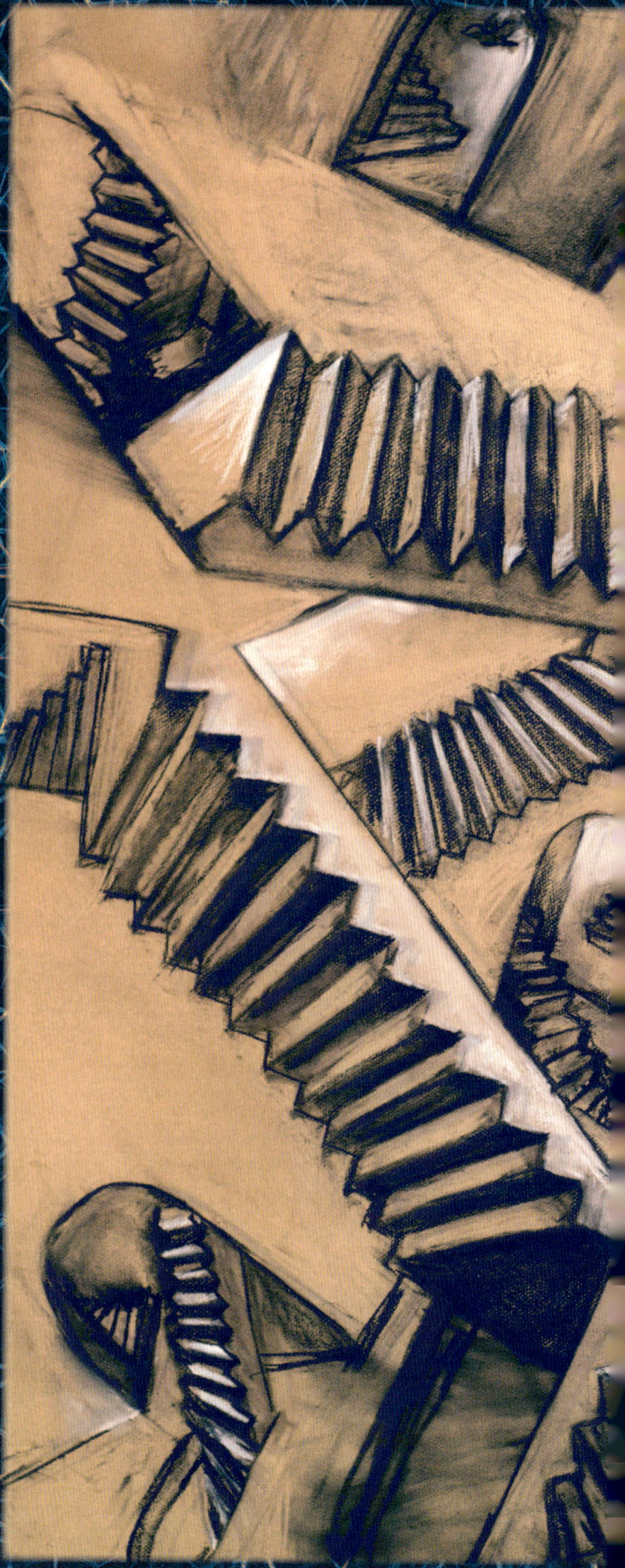

Artists' perceptual advantages

Cognitive psychologist Aaron Kozbelt, a co-author on the Pratt study, has conducted a series of studies with colleagues on artists' perceptual and creative advantages in drawing. He has found that artists have a higher level of perceptual skill than non-artists based on their knowledge of visual schemata. Their advantages seem to be higher level, top down, and strategic, rather than lower level and bottom up.

Kozbelt and colleagues found that novices tend to focus on the simple outline of a form, whereas artists will look for and emphasize specific 3D spatial cues, such as "Y" and "T" junctions (which indicate that one form is in front of another), whether or not these junctions were part of the outline or found inside the form.

Skilled drawers look at their subjects more closely and more often than novices when they are drawing from observation. They are also better at deliberately switching attention from a local to more holistic focus.

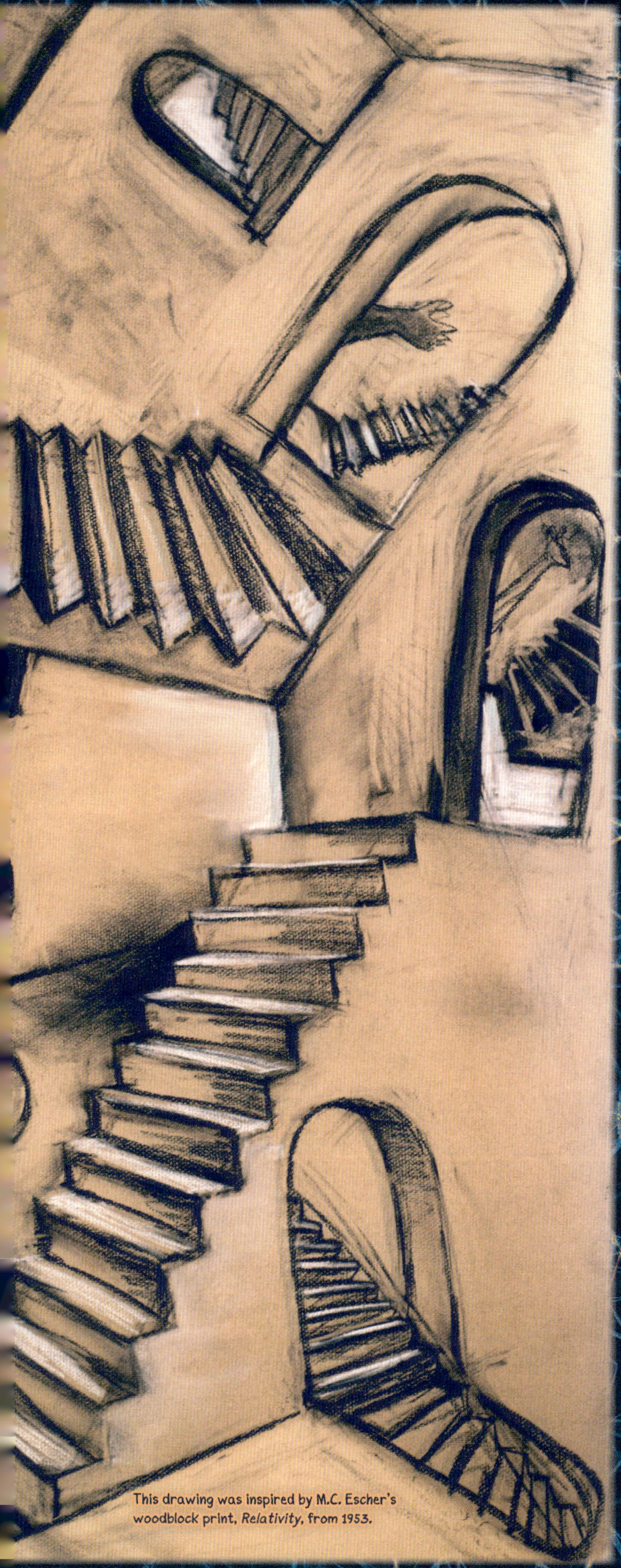

This drawing was inspired by M.C. Escher's woodblock print, *Relativity*, from 1953.

We see and draw with both sides of our brains

Contrary to a popular neuromyth, the right side of the brain is not responsible for human creativity. Neuroscientists have found no right- or left-brain dominance in individuals. There is, however, neuroimaging research that shows that drawing helps to coordinate widely dispersed neural circuits across the whole brain. Both lower-level (perceptual) and higher-level visuospatial sense-making areas are engaged when we draw.

Betty Edwards's best-selling introduction to observational drawing, *Drawing on the Right Side of the Brain*, teaches the beginner to focus on spatial relations, in-between shapes, and spaces. This is not necessarily "right-brained" but is a way to defamiliarize a subject, which helps a learner abandon naive schemas (this is an eye, that is a mouth) and observe more carefully and closely.

The two visual streams hypothesis

Neuroscientists identify two anatomically distinct neural pathways that serve visuospatial perception: the dorsal (where or how) pathway and ventral (what) pathways. The "where" or action pathway is used for navigating spatial relations. When it is damaged, we have difficulty finding our way around. The "what" pathway includes regions like the fusiform face area and other areas involved with object perception and recognition, through the identification of color, texture, shape, and form.

The "what" pathway helps us identify people and objects, independent of their position relative to ourselves. The "where" pathway is "egocentric," in that it helps us judge the dynamic position of our bodies in relation to the environment. When drawing a particular object or scene, it takes a conscious effort, as well as an educated eye, to shift attention to take into account how point of view affects what we are seeing.

There is evidence that drawing might help integrate What and Where pathways. As we develop awareness of and skill in using a variety of perceptual strategies and drawing techniques we build our visuospatial intelligence.

Visuospatial intelligence is linked to creativity in art, design, and STEM-related fields. A longitudinal study tracked 563 academically talented boys from age thirteen into their forties. Creativity was measured by measured by the number of patents held as well as refereed papers in academic journals. Superior spatial ability, as identified by performance on mental rotation and transformation tasks at age thirteen, was linked with superior creative achievement and new knowledge creation later in life.

Spatial reasoning is important in so many real-life contexts. Yet these skills are not generally taught in schools in any kind of systematic way, or at best, sidelined in art class and gym class. Perhaps not coincidentally, in large studies, researchers have found that professional educators tend to score lowest on spatial intelligence tests relative to people in other occupations, such as business, art and design, law, and STEM with similar levels of education. Researchers have also found that spatial skills can be taught through a variety of hands-on tasks (including drawing).

Once acquired, spatial skills can be TRANSFERRED and ´used by learners in new contexts.

Drawing has been studied as an effective way to learn across STEM fields. In their comprehensive review of research on drawing to learn in STEM education, Wu and Rau organize the ways drawing facilitates learning on cognitive and socio-cultural dimensions. They identify the development of spatial cognition as one of the chief cognitive benefits of the use of drawing in STEM education.

Erin Riley's lesson, adapted below, is designed to help develop spatial reasoning. An important component of her lesson is the interweaving of 2D and 3D experiences for her students. A link to Erin's full lesson is in the NOTES.

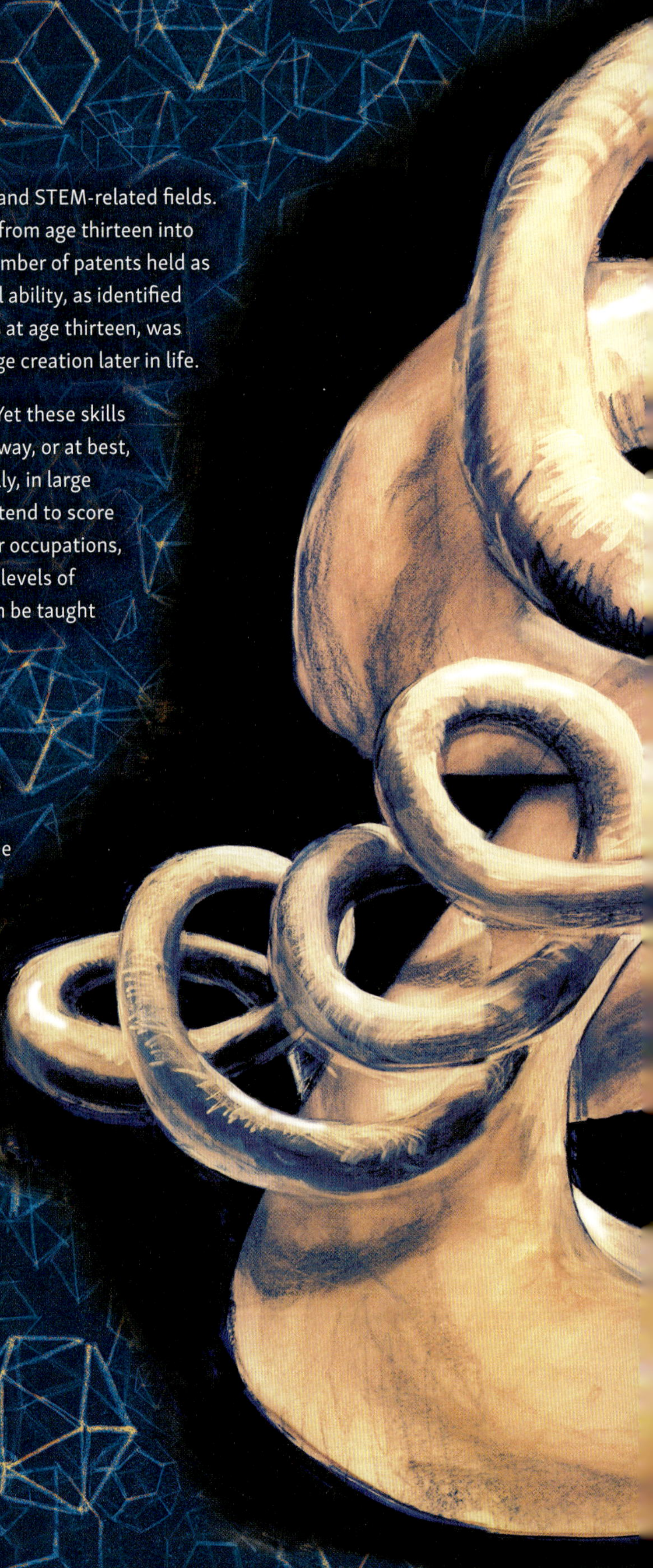

"DRAW LIKE AN ENGINEER"
adapted from Erin Riley

Lego blocks and a partner are needed

1. Build a small four-sided structure with Lego blocks.
2. Draw a floor plan and side elevations of all four sides. In addition, make an isometric drawing based on the Lego structure. Then take your Legos apart and hand the loose Legos and your drawings to your partner.
3. Hand off your drawings to a partner and see if they can recreate your structure.

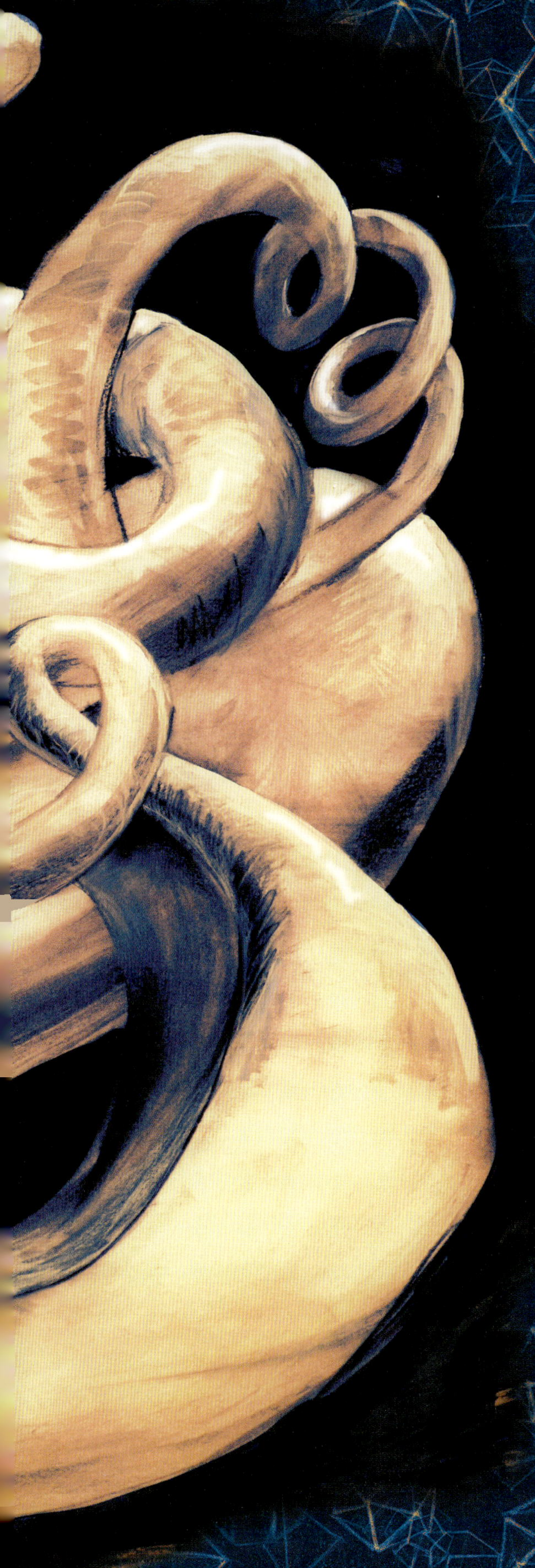

More ways to think about space when you draw...

Observe

When trying to depict a particular object or scene, it's easy to focus on information coming from the "what" visual stream: the little bits and pieces we use to identify particular objects. We can forget about how all the bits fit together. Try to pay attention to the puzzle pieces and in-between shapes (sometimes called "negative spaces"). Hold your pencil in front of you, using your thumb to measure relative size and angle of the forms in front of you.

Discover

Learn to trust the process. You don't need to figure it all out at once. Keep your marks light and ambiguous at first, to allow shapes and forms to emerge in your drawings. Generate multiple possibilities, variations, and interpretations. Looking again and again, revising and reconfiguring shapes and forms, can bring to light relationships, solutions, or visual metaphors you wouldn't have imagined if you hadn't drawn them out.

Invent

Practice by drawing the building blocks: cubes, spheres, cylinders, cones, and pyramids. Then start combining them in different ways. Decide how one form comes in front of another and be consistent. Consider scale and proportion. Try to draw your structures clearly enough so that someone else might be able to build it.

Reaching out with your pencil or pen into virtual space helps you practice creating and transforming mental models in your mind.

“To make a mark or trace a single line upon a surface immediately transforms that surface, energizes its neutrality…

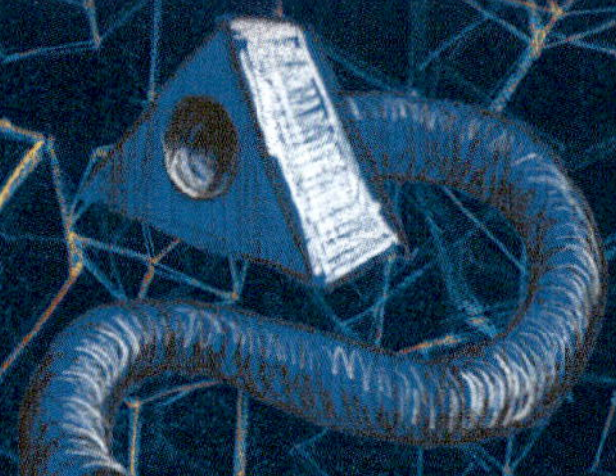
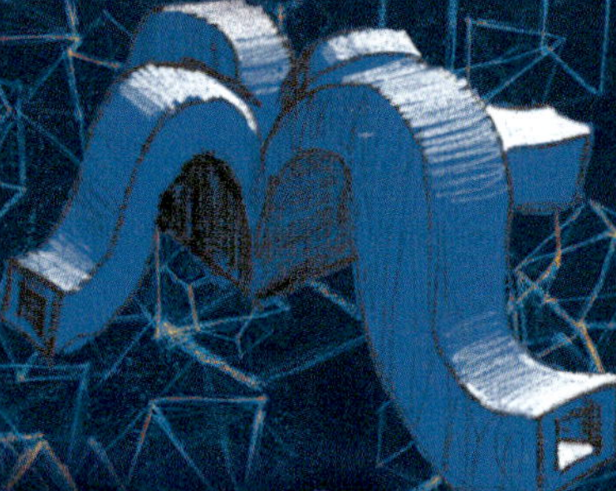
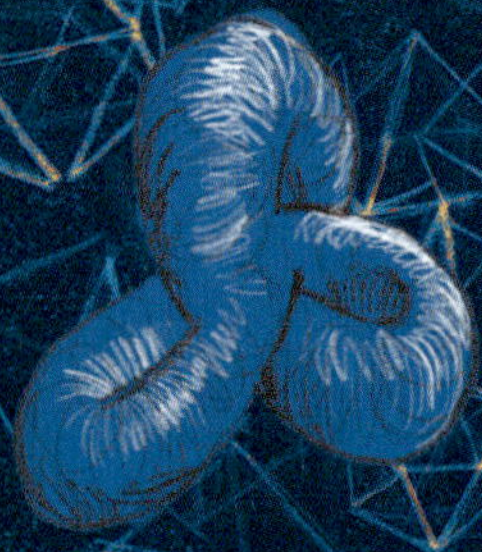
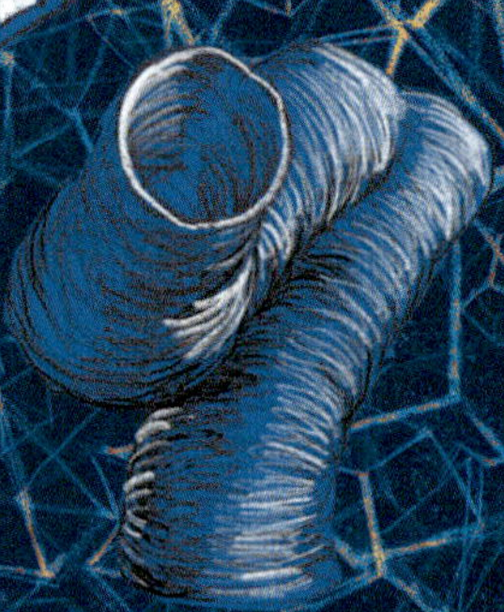

When we use the blank page as a “thinking space,” it becomes an arena to explore a virtual world where we can invent and transform characters, objects, and scenes. An anonymous participant in a workshop I led on reverse-engineering a piece of origami with drawing wrote on their drawing:

> *“Reconstruct the feeling of the direction in space—touching stuff. Drawing gives you the space to have a cognitive event … interacting with how things feel. Instruction needs multiple perspectives at once so much thinking doesn’t happen in language—resist!”*

Think of the drawing surface as an experimental laboratory for the mind.

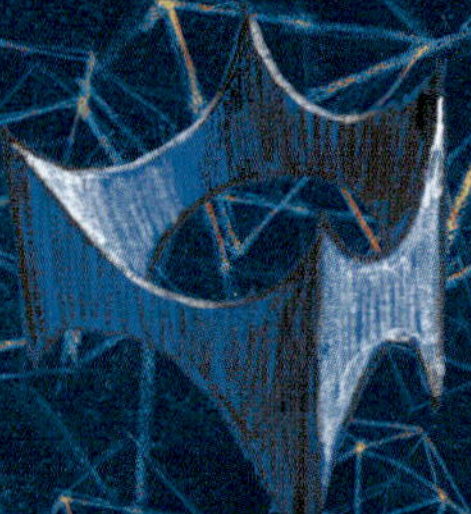
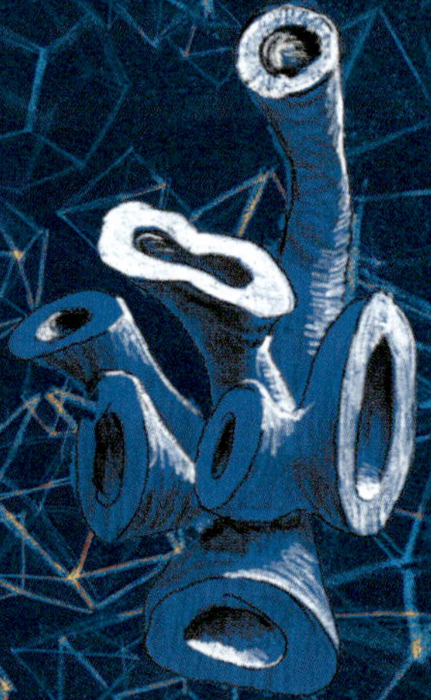
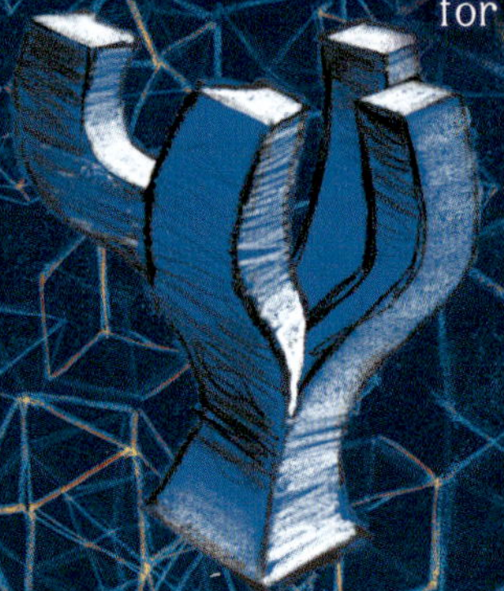
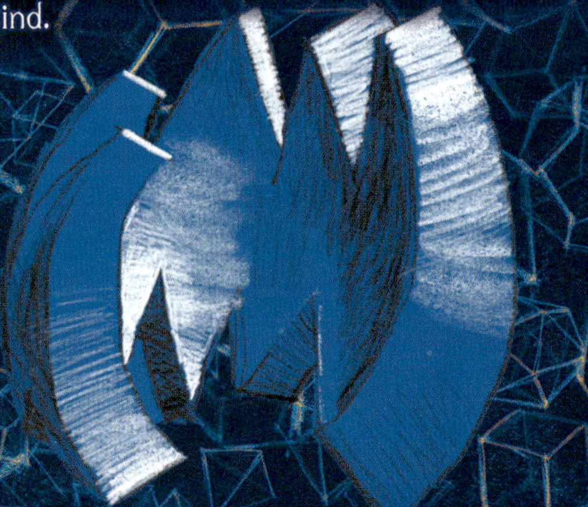

Inspired by François Blanciak, *SITELESS*

…the graphic imposition turns the actual flatness of the ground into virtual space, translates its material reality into the fiction of imagination.”

— David Rosand, *Drawing Acts*

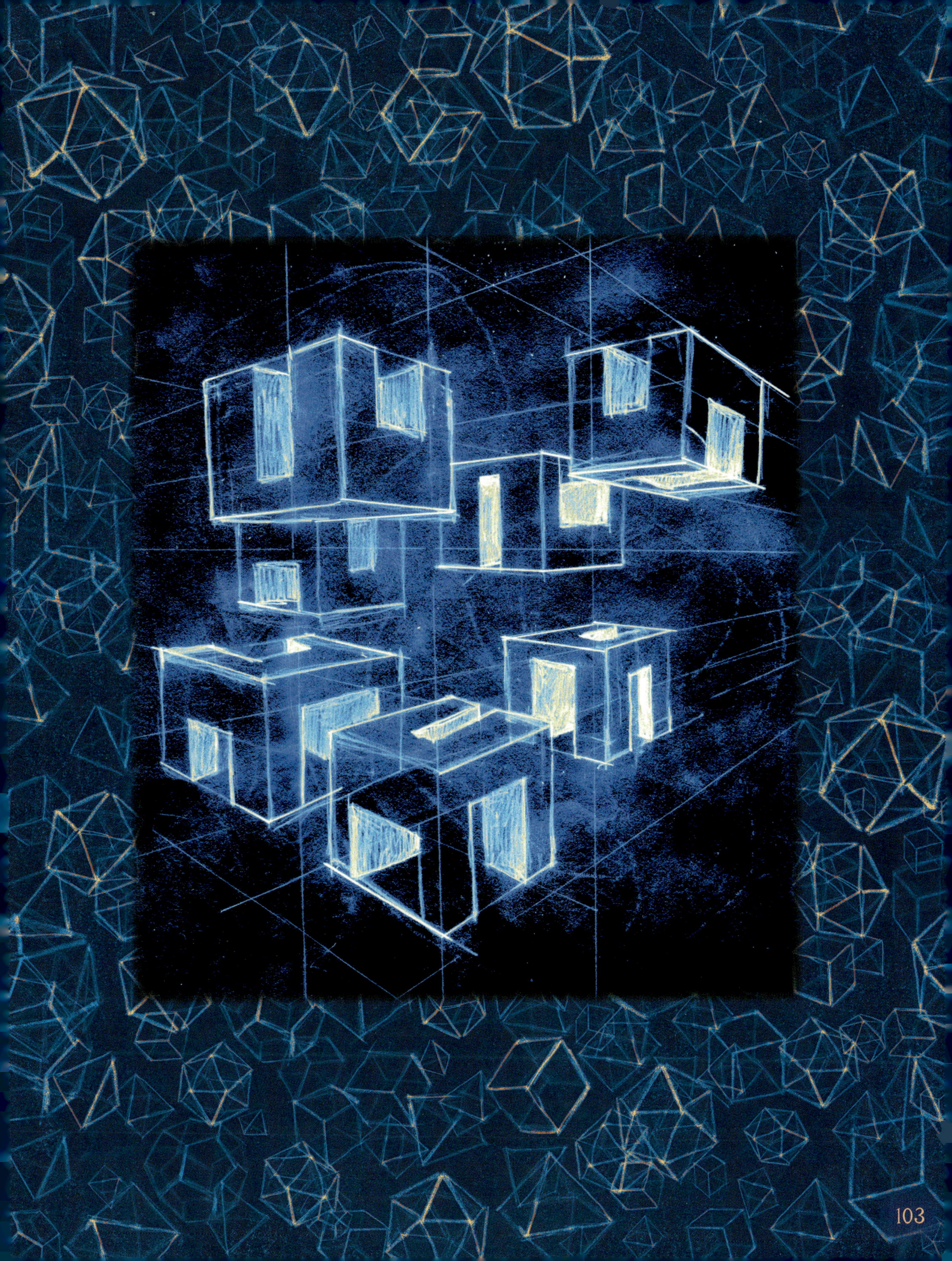

How to
Make Space

When parallel lines stay parallel, the viewer's position in relation to the object or scene is not specified. It is as if we are seeing the shape from an infinite distance. There is no defined point of view.

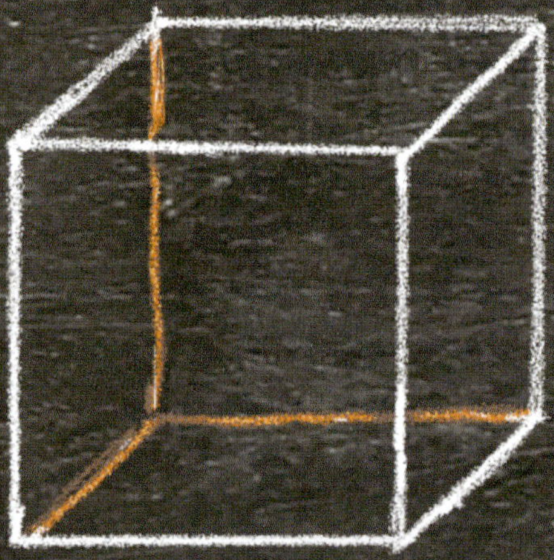

Oblique projection = At least one plane is at an angle, tilted away from the viewer.

Orthographic projection = Three axes are tilted away from the viewer.

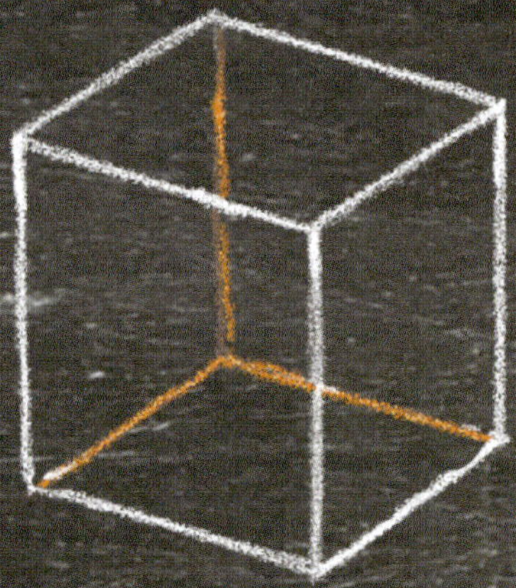

Isometric projection = Three axes are EQUALLY tilted away from the viewer.

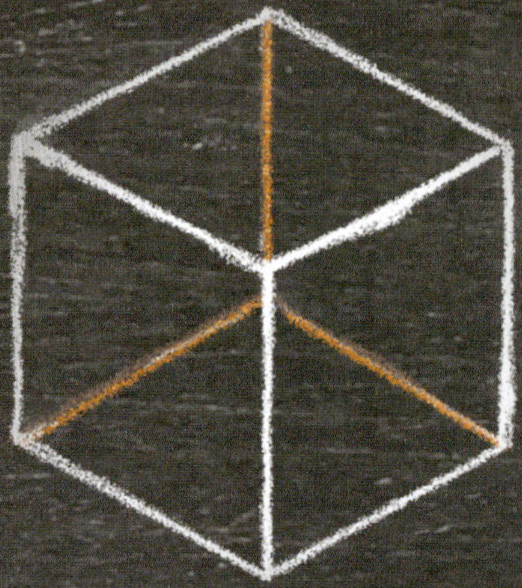

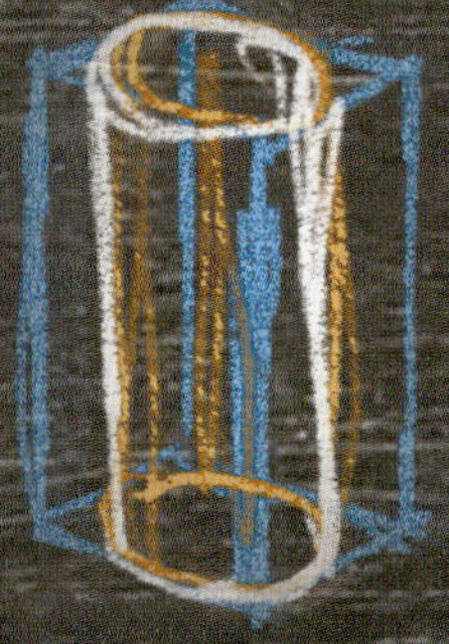

You can inscribe a variety of three-dimensional forms inside a cube or rectangular prism. Practice drawing different combinations of cylinders to develop skill at drawing circular forms in space.

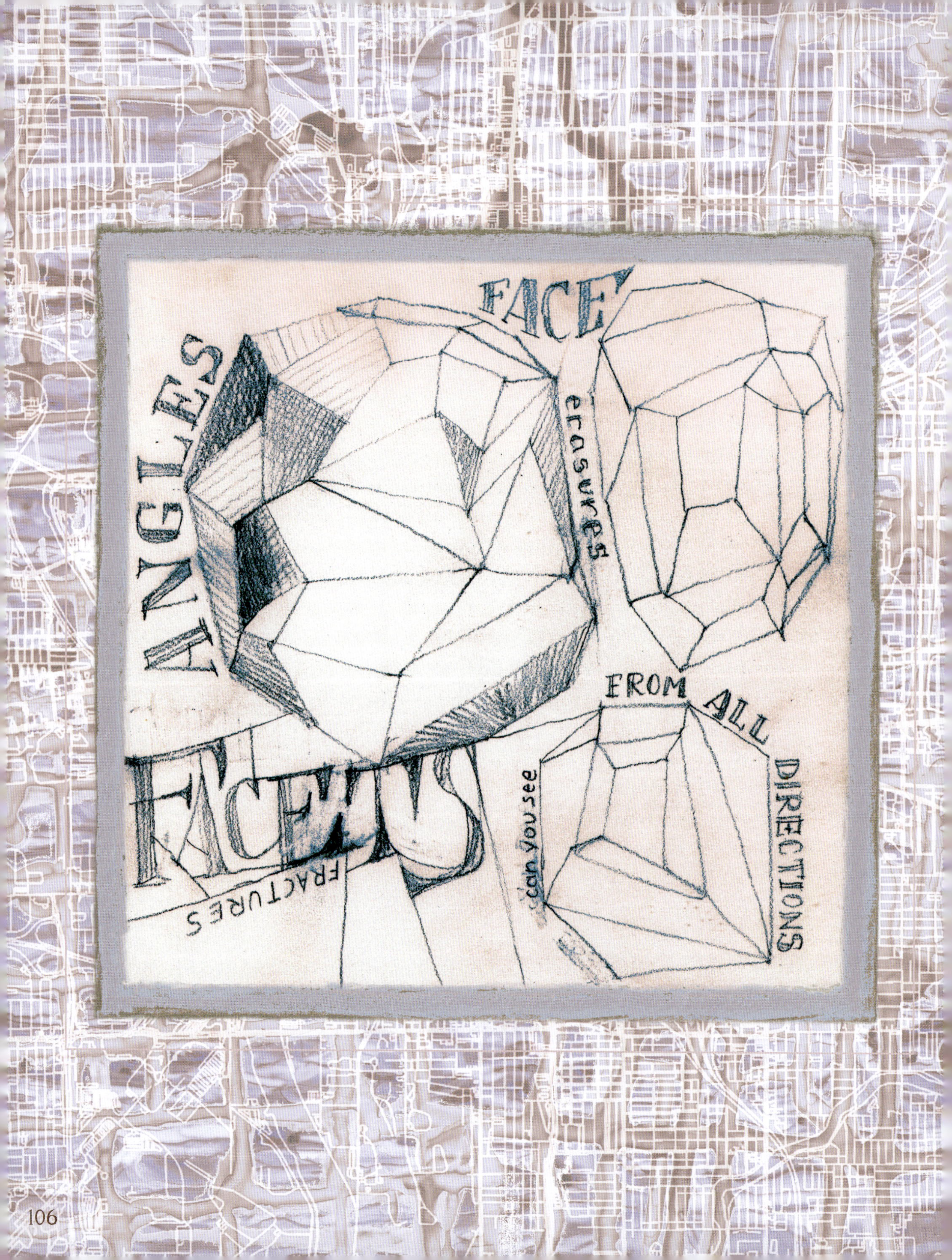
FACE
ANGLES
erasures
FROM ALL DIRECTIONS
can you see
FACETS
FRACTURES

chapter seven

A Tool of Thought

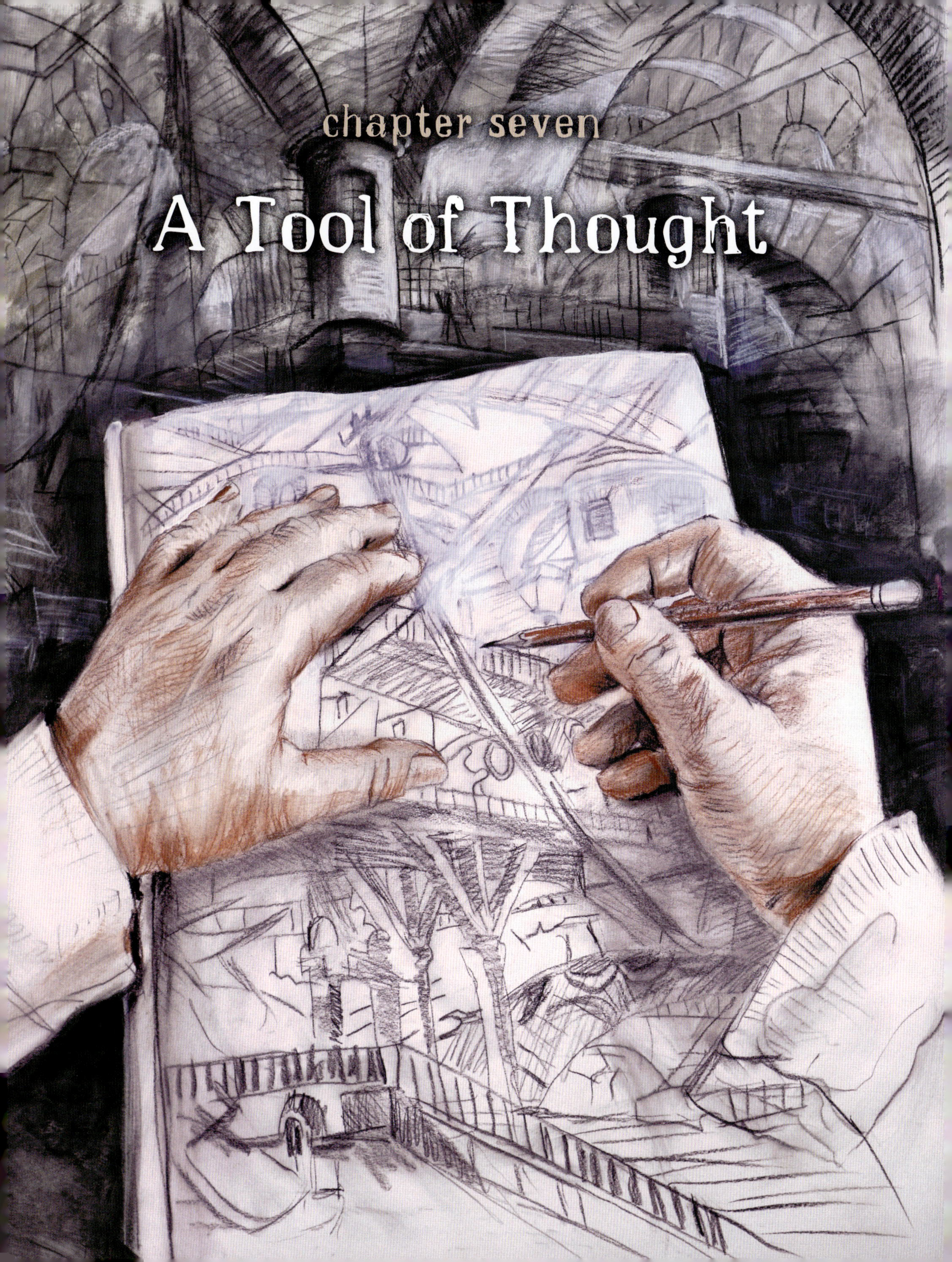

Learn from EXPERTS who use drawing as a TOOL of THOUGHT in many disciplines

All kinds of experts draw as part of their professional practice. They sketch to generate and explore new ideas and observations for themselves. They communicate with colleagues through diagrams, maps, plans, blueprints, and other forms of schematic representations. Scientists and engineers, makers and builders in many fields, often make sketches to collect observations, test concepts, and develop mental models. Rough sketches and detailed plans drawn by an expert surgeon or carpenter may not look like an artist's drawings. Experts might indicate features or use graphic conventions and symbols that require prior knowledge to decode. Yet, like artists and designers, they use drawing as a tool to think through and grapple with complex issues and concepts that might not be as easily explored in words.

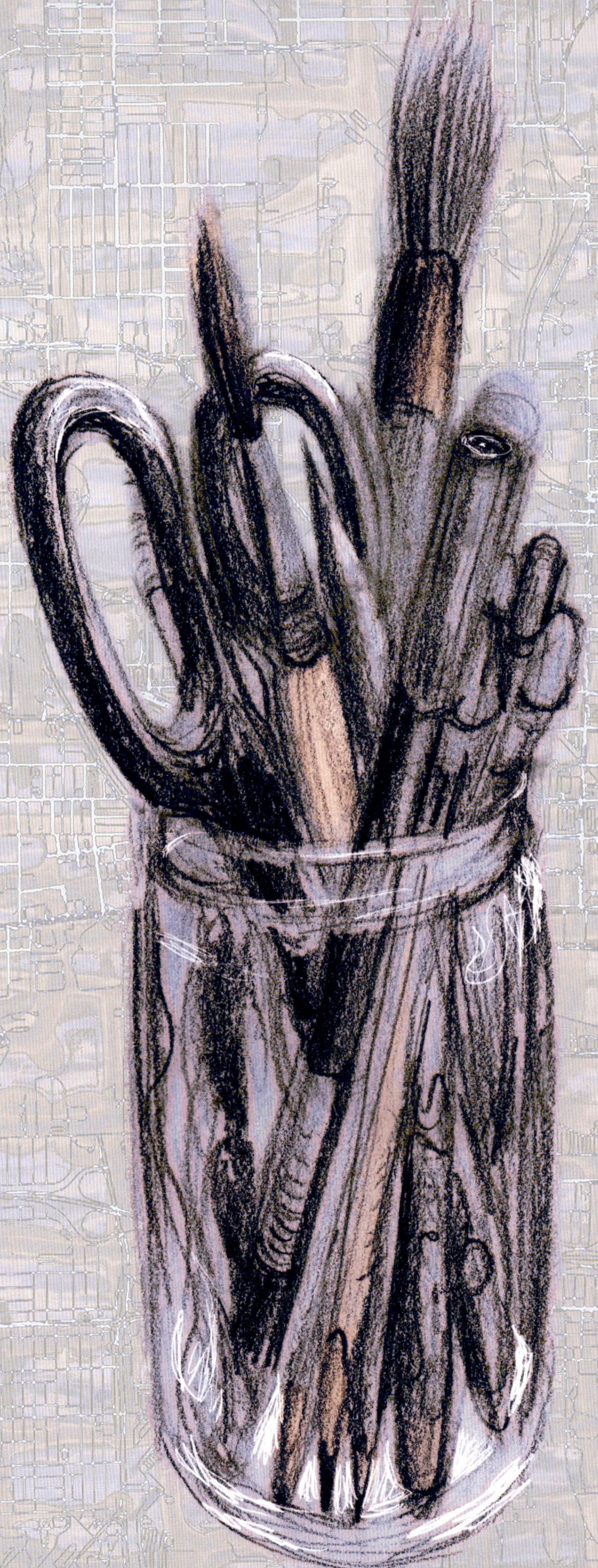

The first tools early humans made were handaxes, found all over the world. Hitting two rocks together created a sharp edge, which was much more effective than the original rock for cutting and chopping.

There is a long history of hypotheses regarding the relationship of tool making, gesture, and the invention of language, going back to Darwin. The "technological pedagogy" hypothesis proposes that increasing sophistication of handaxes during the Lower Paleolithic period is evidence that more sophisticated means of communication were available. Cognitive neuroscientists have discovered common neural substrates and systems (such as Broca's area) for tool use and language production. Advances in handaxes may have coevolved with the development of language as a tool of thought.

The tools we use evolve over time to serve changing needs, opportunities, and sometimes purposes other than their original intent. Around 10,000 years ago, people discovered that some kinds of earth could be baked to make vessels to store food and water. Potters wheels were invented to make those clay vessels more efficiently, probably around 4,000 to 3,000 years ago in Mesopotamia and China, possibly hundreds or even thousands of years before someone thought to use wheels for transportation. Wheelbarrows and chariots seem to have first appeared in Ancient Greece, between the sixth and fourth centuries BCE. A few millennia later, bicycles and then automobiles were invented. Tools evolve over time, sometimes incrementally, sometimes by leaps and bounds.

Tools like handaxes and bicycles help with an immediate physical task like opening shellfish or getting from here to there. LANGUAGE is a TOOL of THOUGHT, enabling us to reason, remember, and communicate with one another. Humans have invented physical tools of thought. A map or a calendar, a clock or a compass, help one orient and organize oneself in time and space. Mathematical notation systems, computer programing languages, and other symbol systems are other examples of tools of thought.

New tools often borrow conventions of their predecessors. Our smartphones have become mega-tools of thought and action. Most of our phones' homescreens have an icon that looks something like a camera, which we "open up" when we want to take a photo. The icon itself is a tool of thought that we can click and drag as needed. Your homescreen most likely includes icons for maps, calendars, and perhaps even a compass. Everyone's smartphone contains many common "tools of thought," including drawing apps!

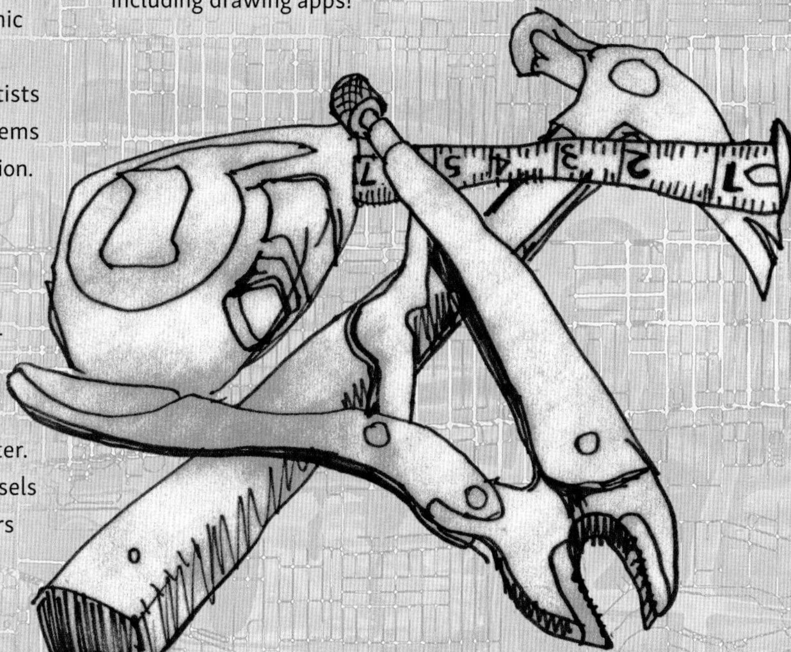

Drawing encompasses a broad set of representational practices that have evolved over time in different places and cultures, for many different purposes. When we look at drawings (such as paleolithic cave drawings) without understanding the context in which they were made, we can only guess at the intentions of the maker. Drawings and sketches leverage innate characteristics of visuospatial reasoning (relative position and scale, for example). Sometimes drawings include recognizable representations of things in the world (e.g., an antelope or buffalo) and sometimes use culturally specific symbol systems and designs that may be difficult for the uninitiated to decode.

Living with uncertainty (as we found out during the COVID-19 pandemic) can be difficult. It can feel comforting to imagine we understand what's going on, even when we don't, but unwarranted certainty can often be problematic and sometimes quite dangerous.

Uncertainty

Drawing can both reveal and leverage uncertainty to help build new knowledge. In one study, researchers found that when managers were asked to sketch out their understanding of digital technology after explaining it verbally, they became much more aware of what they didn't understand. Drawing revealed the gaps in their understanding more effectively than verbal language.

Science educator Eliza Bobek asked seventh-graders to either draw or write an explanation of a chemical reaction they had just learned a bout. In a post-test, those who drew learned the material more thoroughly. Students who scored lower on spatial reasoning measures benefited the most from drawing out their explanations. For the seventh-graders, like the managers in the previous study, drawing revealed gaps in their understanding that were not as evident in the written explanations. The drawing process then supported the drawers' use of spatial reasoning to fill in some of those gaps and make inferences based on prior knowledge.

DO YOU KNOW HOW A BICYCLE WORKS?

1. Write down everything you think you know.
2. Try to draw it from memory.
3. Look up a picture of an actual bicycle. If you are like most people, chances are you made some mistakes, which are likely to be more obvious in the drawing than in your verbal description.

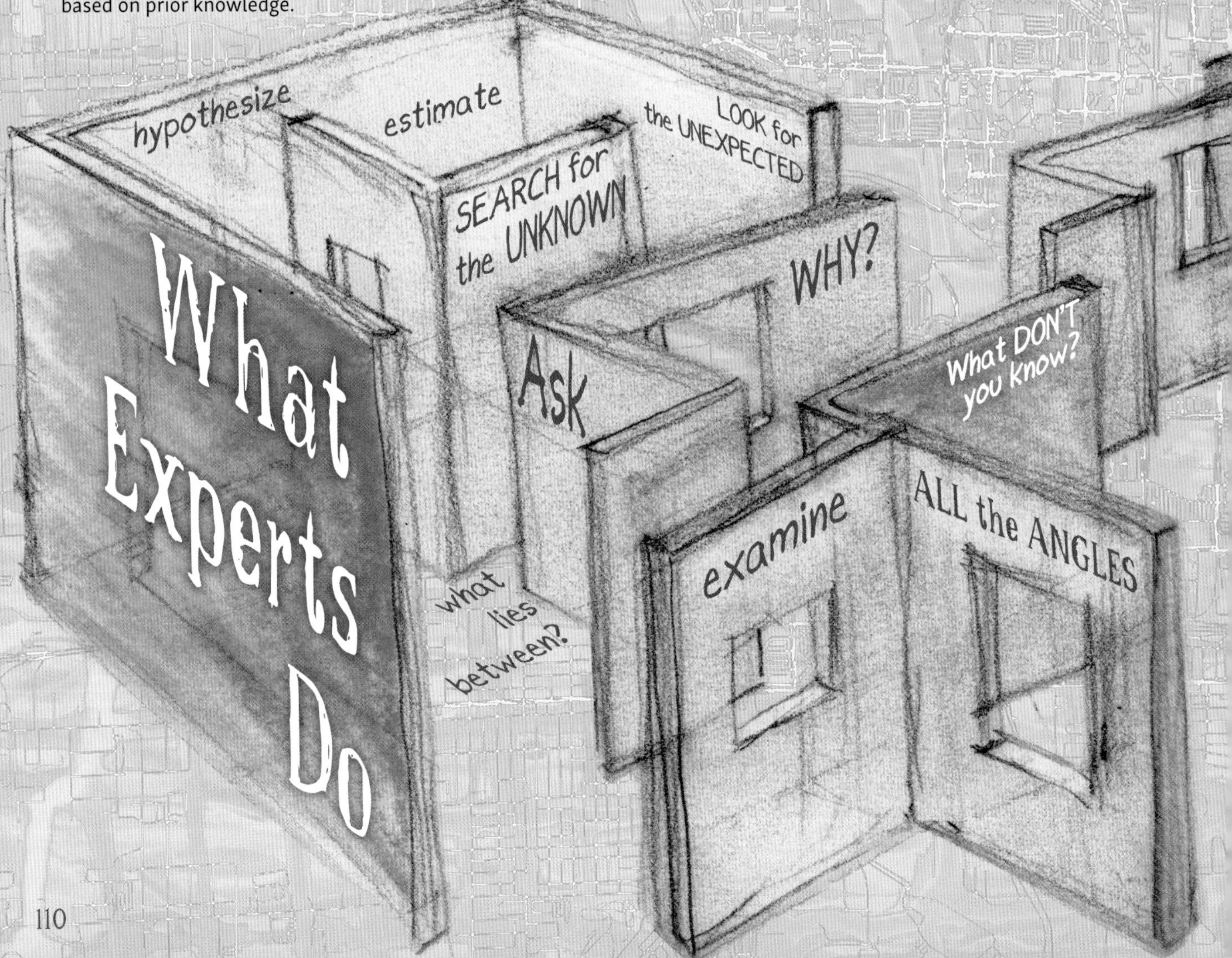

Drawing offers an arena to perceive incompleteness, make inferences, and ask questions. Experts in many fields sketch to test initial thoughts and cycle through iterations to correct and improve their ideas.

There are specific and often multiple sets of graphic conventions in every discipline where drawing is part of professional practice. Surgeons sketch to visualize procedures and communicate with medical students and patients. Architects sketch to generate ideas and make detailed, digital drawings that are accurate enough to communicate with the builders, electricians, and plumbers who will turn their ideas into reality.

Constructive Perception

Experts' exploratory sketches in many disciplines have certain common features. They are often fuzzy at first, making it easier for something unplanned to emerge. Novices jump in, prematurely rushing to finish. Experts slow down and take the time to question their first thoughts, looking for subtle and unintended features that help them recognize errors and generate new ideas.

Experts use the ambiguities in their sketches to suggest alternatives. Cognitive psychologists Matsaki Suwa and Barbara Tversky compared experts in industrial design and architecture with students and office workers. Suwa and Tversky observed that experts demonstrated a greater ability to reorganize their perceptions and make new associations. Suwa and Tversky call this expert skill "constructive perception." For example, an architect uses constructive perception to imagine how people might move through a space by indicating the direction of movement on a sketched floor plan. It's a metacognitive skill, a way of thinking about thinking, that can be taught and learned within the context of a specific discipline or domain of knowledge.

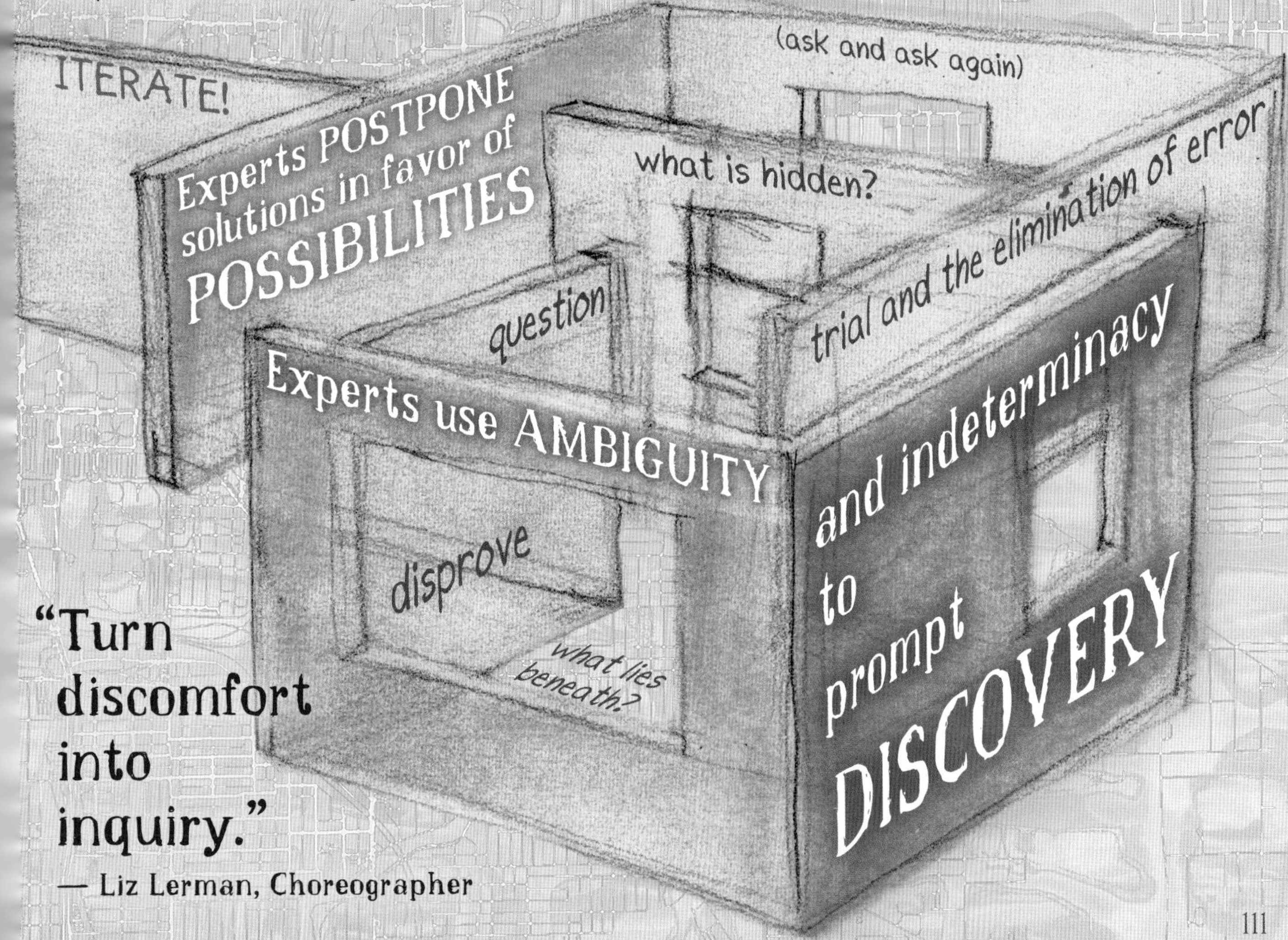

"Turn discomfort into inquiry."
— Liz Lerman, Choreographer

More than TALENT

Some people are born with innate advantages over the rest of us. The average US male is 5'9". Basketball player turned politician Bill Bradley is 6'5" (only the third-tallest member of his 1965 legendary team at Princeton). He still holds the all-time Ivy League record for most points scored and all-time highest scoring average.

Starting out, height in basketball clearly helps, but it does not predetermine excellence. There are exceptions. At 5'3", Tyrone "Muggsy" Bogues, the shortest player in NBA history, "was regularly among the NBA leaders in assists, steals and assist-to-turnover ratio." (It is notable that with assists and steals he found his ecological niche as a short player. He did not lead in skills requiring height, such as dunks.)

A range of innate traits influence what activities any individual has the potential to excel at, yet are useless without opportunities to discover and develop these gifts. Because expertise is usually quite specialized in specific domains, what is called talent often results from extensive and targeted practice as much as, and sometimes more than, native abilities (which, presumably, would be less specific to particular tasks). For example, elite chess players' excellent memories for configurations of chess pieces is lost as soon as the pieces are rearranged in random, rather than in functionally significant (and therefore learned) patterns.

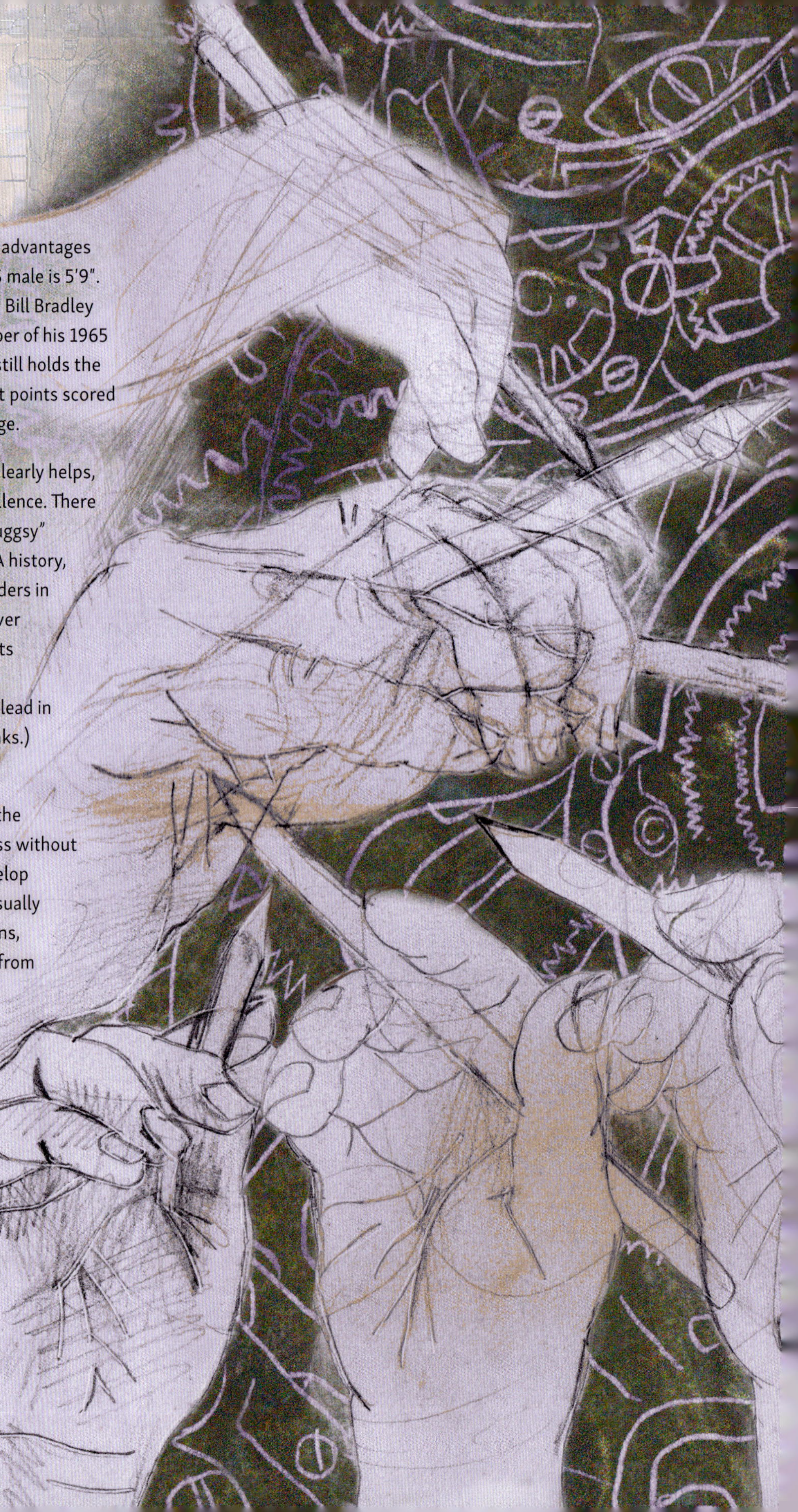

The Role of Deliberate Practice

Perfect pitch was long thought of as a rare gift that very few individuals, like Mozart, had at birth. It was then discovered that perfect pitch was more prevalent among Asians who spoke tonal languages (in which the tone or pitch of the word is used to distinguish meaning). Is there a genetic advantage? No, it turns out the English-speaking children of Asian immigrants are no more likely to have perfect pitch than the children of European-descended parents. It's the early exposure to tonal language—or very early musical training in Mozart's case, perhaps—that seems key.

Sustained, deliberate, effortful, and well-designed practice underlies excellence in music, chess, figure skating, wrestling, golf, medicine, perception, memory, reading, and many other domains, including drawing. Although each discipline has its unique characteristics and competencies, mastery takes time and effort, and this is as true for drawing as for most other skillful pursuits. Maybe many more than 10,000 hours, sometimes fewer. But just putting in a lot of time doesn't cut it. Practice needs to be purposeful and strategic. When high achievers hit a plateau or get stuck, they don't just keep doing the same thing. They analyze exactly what is holding them back, and hyperfocus on that one aspect until they hit on a method that starts them moving ahead again. When they get stuck they find a new tool or tactic that allows them to progress.

I wanted to draw a lot of hands from my imagination for this book, and I wasn't really pleased with my ability to do so. After drawing my own hands over and over and not really getting any better at it, I took some time out to refresh my memory of the bones and muscles, seeking out resources to further my understanding. This knowledge sharpened my observation of actual hands, the anatomical details that reveal gesture and position. I developed new schemas that I can use to draw hands more easily from my imagination, without having to rely on reference.

Automaticity

Experts in any domain improve their performance by developing automaticity in subroutines through practice. The automation process turns declarative knowledge that is top down, requiring conscious direction, into procedural knowledge from the bottom up, which no longer requires cognitive effort (like riding a bicycle). Mastery can be understood as the procedural fluency that frees a Rembrandt or a Hokousai to spontaneously express the unique qualities of their subject without worrying about the details. The more you can do without conscious attention, the more free you are to attend to the unique and significant aspects of the task at hand. Imagine a truly creative cook, who is able to chop, dice, grate and mince at lightning speed and almost without looking, so that their attention is completely free to experiment with nuances of taste and texture. In any domain there are trained practitioners with conventional skills who lack the resources needed to create something unique or respond effectively to unforeseen obstacles. Technical expertise is easier to achieve than creative expertise. A solid foundation makes truly creative contributions to one's discipline possible.

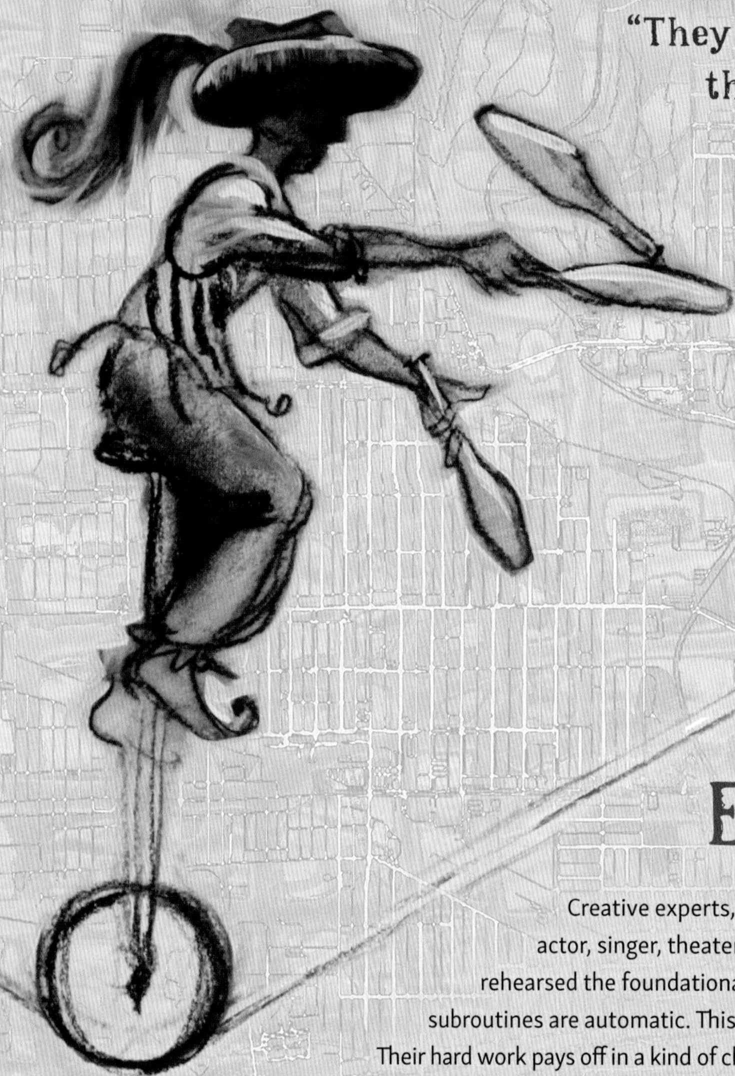

"They did everything by improvisation ... they knew by heart the opening and closing topics ... the conventional words or gestures which alerted the other actors to variations ..."

— Dario Fo, *Tricks of the Trade*

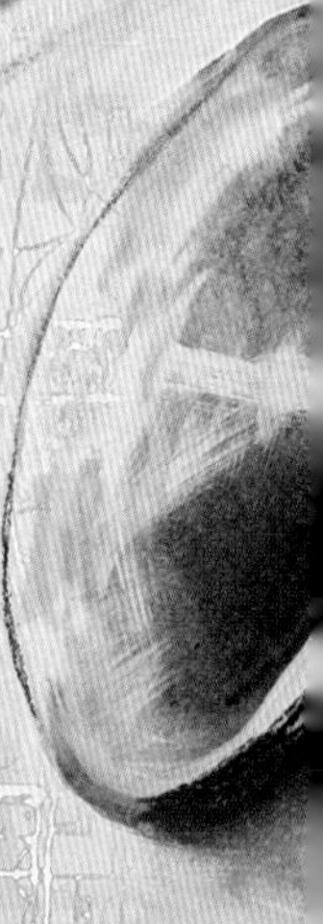

Creative Expertise

Creative experts, like Italian Nobel Prize-winning playwright, clown, actor, singer, theater director, and political activist Dario Fo, have rehearsed the foundational skills of their craft until the necessary subroutines are automatic. This allows them to perform "without thinking." Their hard work pays off in a kind of childlike spontaneity and playfulness.

True creative freedom requites mastery of one's craft. In Dario Fo's book, *Tricks of the Trade* (in Italian, literally "the actor's mini-manual"), he advises contemporary actors based on his deep knowledge of historical theatrical forms. Fo draws upon Commedia dell'arte, an improvisational Italian theatrical form dating back to the 1500s. Commedia dell'arte consists of a stock set of characters with established personalities and behaviors. All Commedia performers know (automatically) how Harlequin, Columbina, El Doctor, and the others may reasonably be expected to respond in a given situation, and this shared knowledge facilitates a kind of free improvisation in the moment.

The established conventions that Commedia dell'arte performers master have their analogue in many creative disciplines, where no set outcome is known at the beginning. The maker or performer embarks on a process of discovery equipped with an established set of tactics and strategies. The expert recognizes creative opportunities by making analogies with past experiences and prior knowledge.

In an interview, Sargent Ken Ebo of the Marine Corps Jazz Ensemble explained what Jazz and service in the Marine Corps have in common: "All instrumentalists ... feel that their instrument is an extension of themselves ... and improvisation is not just making it up as you go along, it's the ability to be creative within and around a known set of boundaries for which you've prepared a great deal."

A true master can respond gracefully to the unexpected. Jazz pianist Herbie Hancock recalled an incident when playing with the great trumpeter Miles Davis's band in the 1960s:

"It was a really hot night. The music was on. Right in the middle of Miles's solo, when he was playing one of his amazing solos, I played the wrong chord. Completely wrong, it sounded like a big mistake. And Miles paused for a second. And then he played some notes that made my chord right, that made it correct. Miles didn't hear it as a mistake. He heard it as something that happened. An event. And so that was part of the reality of what was happening at that moment. And he dealt with it. Since he didn't hear it as a mistake he felt it was his responsibility to find something that fit. That taught me a very big lesson, about not only music but about life."

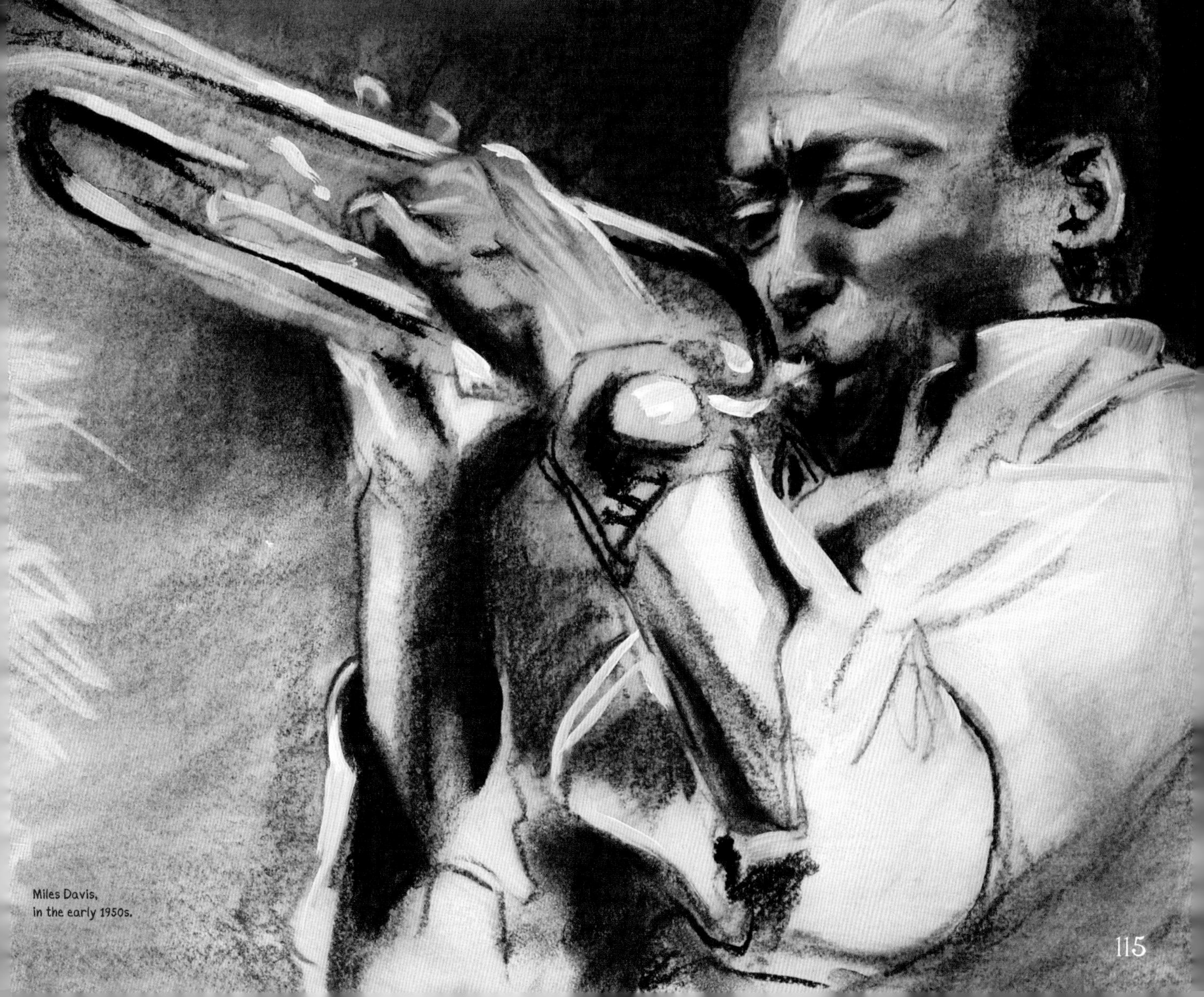

Miles Davis, in the early 1950s.

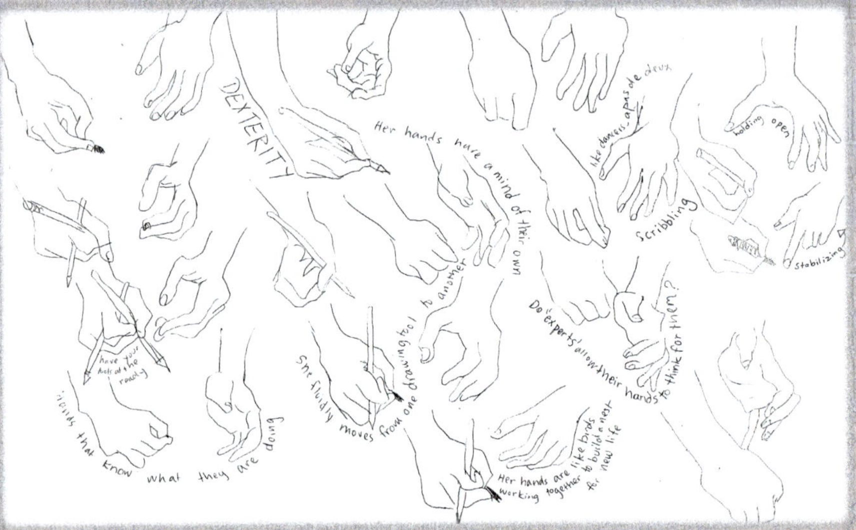

What Artists Do When They DRAW

EXPERTISE doesn't happen without years of dedication and commitment, even if you are Pablo Picasso or Miles Davis. Creative experts have established routines and procedures that facilitate discovery. By cultivating habits of consistent practice, it becomes possible to let go of conscious control, trust the process, and respond to the things that happen.

Several years ago I videotaped nine professional artists drawing in their studios to better understand their moment-to-moment processes. Artists' drawings differ from other kinds of drawings because they are often made for their own sake, rather than to solve an external problem. I recorded the first half-hour of a drawing, and viewed the video immediately afterward with the artists. The drawings looked very different from one another in scale, subject matter, and materials. Some were done from observation and some from imagination, memory, or external reference. I made my own drawings as I watched the videos, as a way of trying to understand the process. Despite differences in style, materials, and methods, the shape of the actual drawing process (if not the end result) was surprisingly consistent.

Most of the artists had a difficult time explaining their thinking and decision making, but at a certain point in the drawing process, all seemed to recognize "something starting to happen." A few talked about a kind of game, with its own rules that evolve as the drawing progressed. Random variations in the marks sparked the creation of new forms. Separate elements and areas were identified and defined. As marks accumulated, indications of borders and edges, figure and ground, began to emerge.

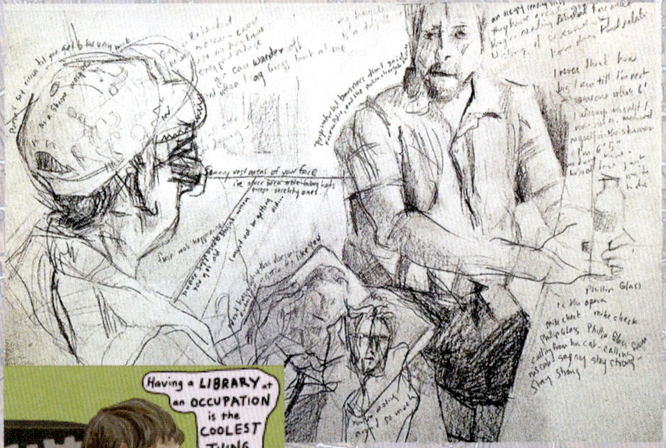

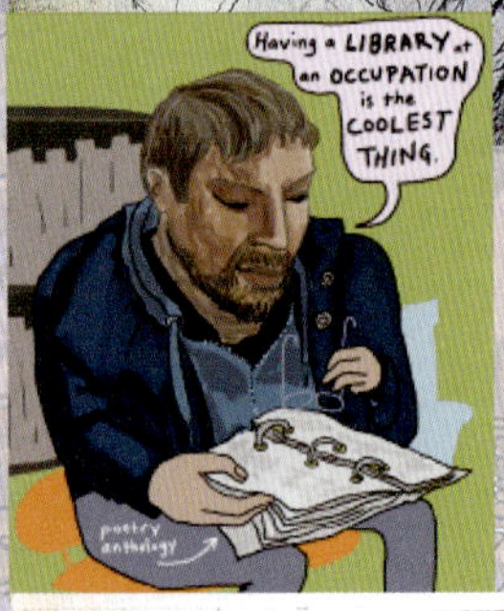

Above, my drawing from the video of artist/participant Sharon Rosenzwieg drawing.
Left, Sharon's actual drawing. Sharon makes comics based on people and experiences in her life.

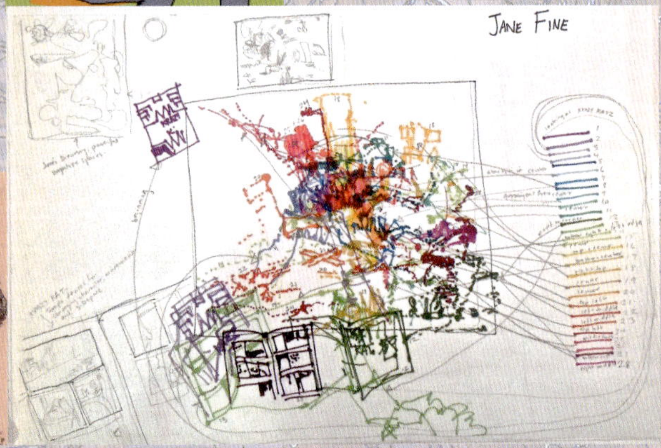

Right, my drawing from the video of artist/participant Jane Fine drawing.
Below, Jane Fine's drawing, *Bumping Uglies*. Jane makes drawings and paintings inspired by Krazy Kay and current events, among other things.

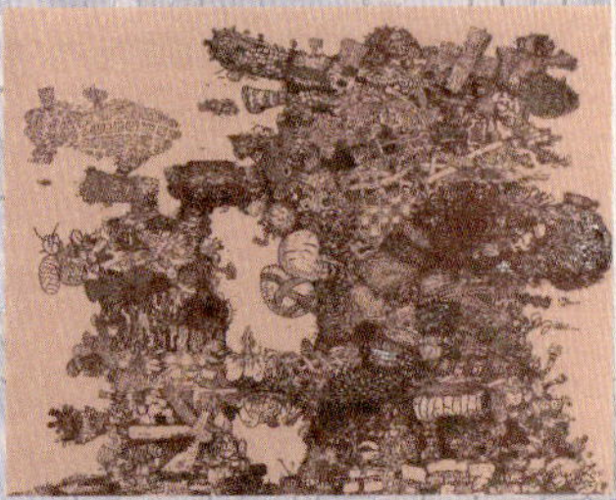

As I viewed the video recordings of the artists drawing over and over, I made drawings of their processes. I identified FIVE basic kinds of quick (3- to 5-second) ACTIONS artists made as they drew.

First Thoughts

The first marks tend to go down rapidly.

LOCATE a set of marks that lightly plot out the placement of key landmarks that will be developed in the course of the drawing.

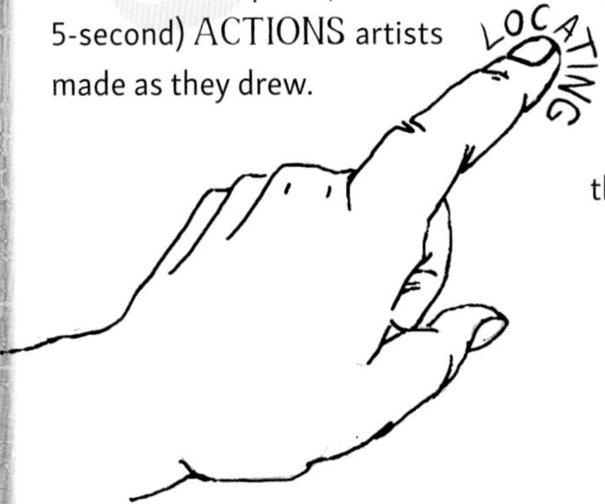

EXTEND: marks move outward from location marks into blank areas of the surface, indicating movement and direction, spatial relationships rather than details. Extending marks are open ended. Novices often skip over this phase of the drawing process, prematurely fixating on superficial details of their subject. Experts keep their marks open to allow for multiple revisions.

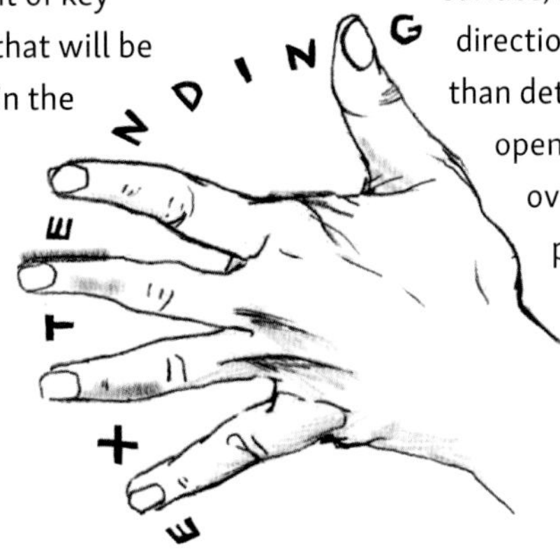

When the drawing talks back...

CONNECTING involves bridging or linking two separate areas to form a larger whole. Artists report that this is where they really start to respond to what the drawing seems to "want" or "need."

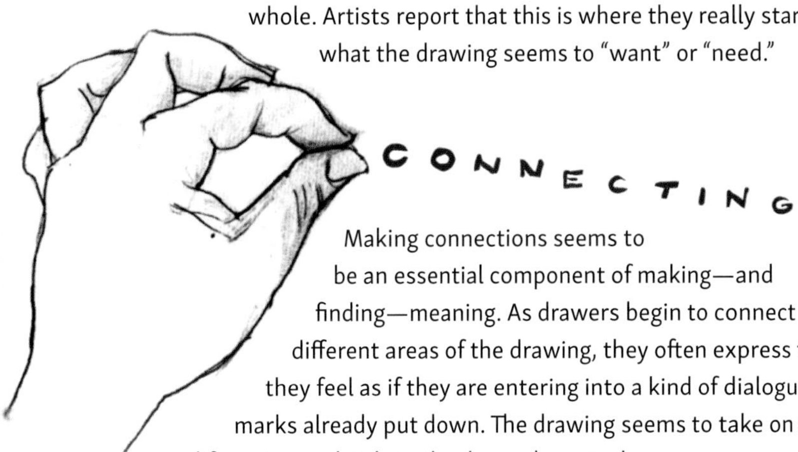

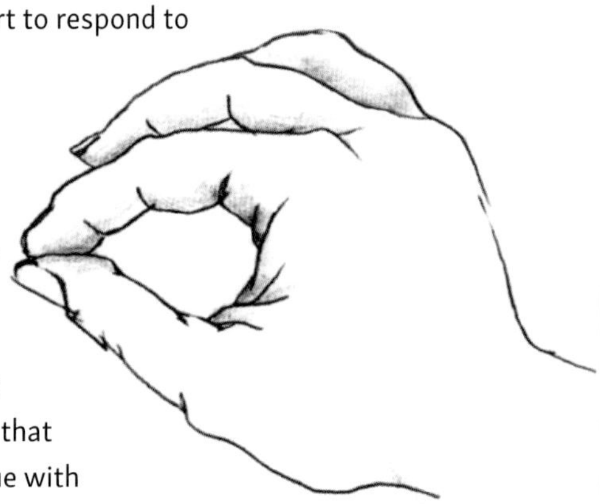

Making connections seems to be an essential component of making—and finding—meaning. As drawers begin to connect different areas of the drawing, they often express that they feel as if they are entering into a kind of dialogue with marks already put down. The drawing seems to take on an independent life, not completely in the drawer's control.

REINFORCE: refine, add detail, darken, or emphasize established areas of the drawing; define features; develop three-dimensional illusion, sense of depth.

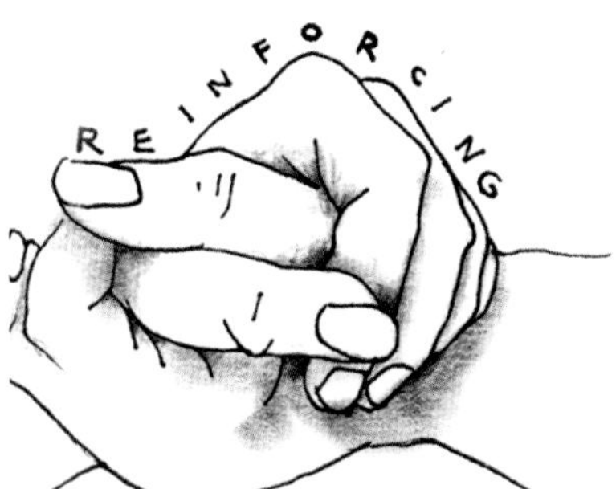

REVISE: The artist may choose to reverse earlier decisions through erasing or overdrawing, which might reintroduce ambiguity and invite multiple interpretations.

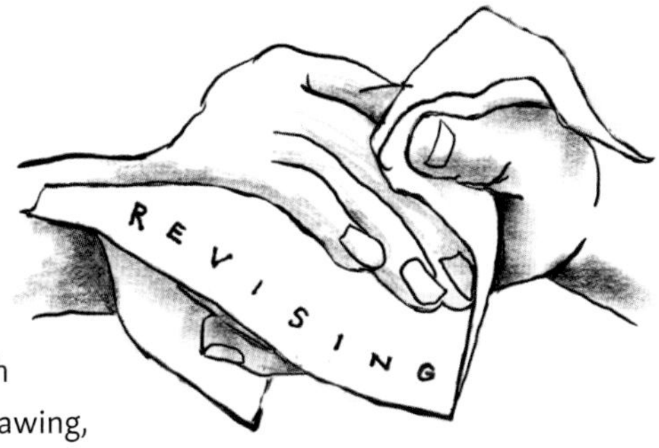

Think GLOBALLY Act LOCALLY

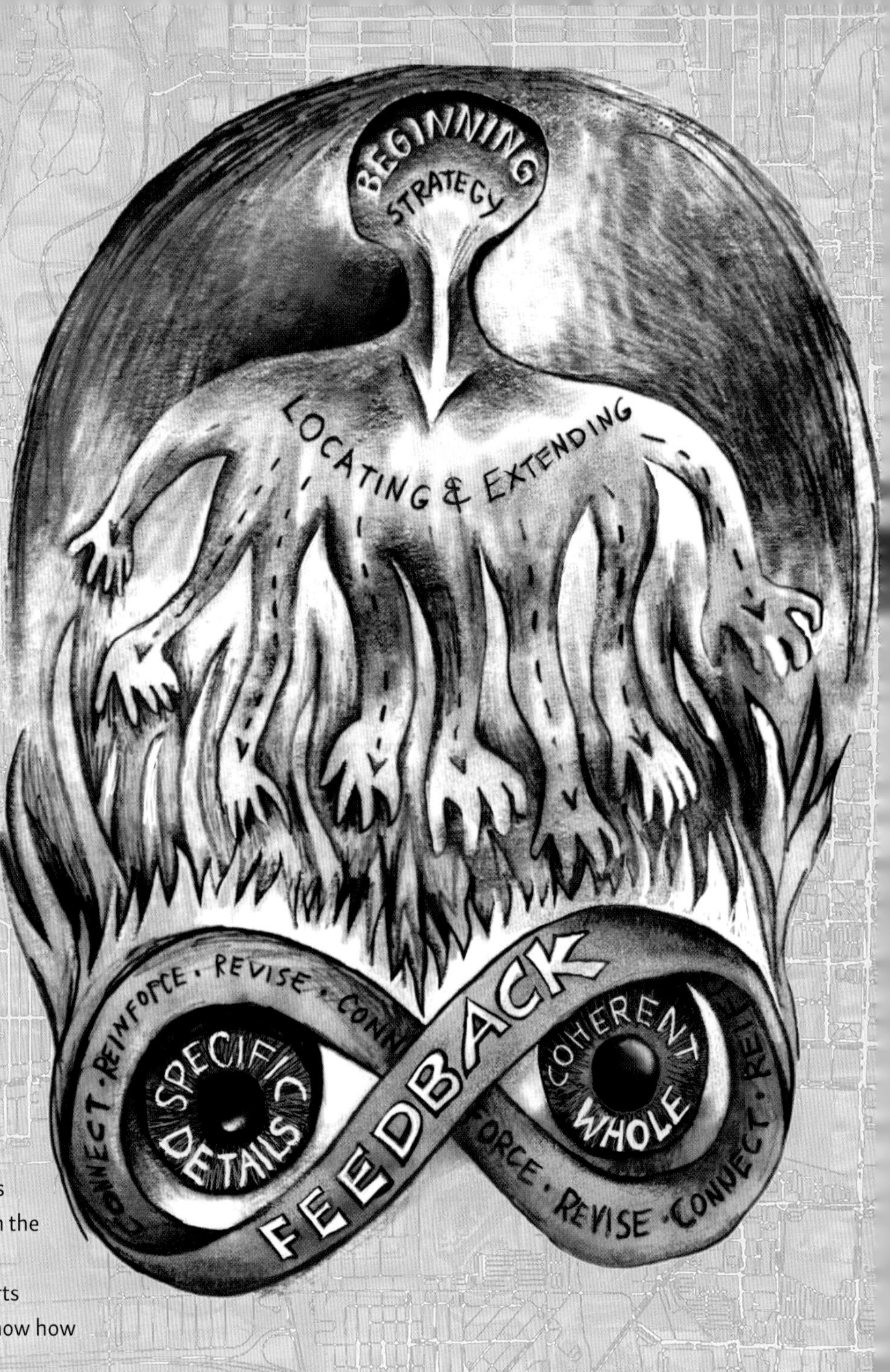

Experienced artists learn to balance focused activity on specific details with holistic awareness.

When artists draw, they tend to alternate between periods of concentrated activity in small areas, and jumps between areas. They divide their attention systematically from a focus on details to attention to larger relationships between parts.

Each skilled hand and eye has its own unique pattern of oscillation between looking and doing, action and reflection. These feedback loops drive the drawing forward and often have a regularity reminiscent of breath or heartbeat, the varying rhythms that pulse through living organisms.

One of the participants in my study, the comics artist Sharon Rosenzweig, explains that the pleasure of drawing comes "when the formless void of marks and erasures burp up something funny or alive." Experts are on the lookout for that "burp" and know how to make the most of it.

Observing an Expert

Michael Moore is one of the participants in my study of artists' drawing practices. A small, delicate bird's nest sits above his drawing table. Bach plays in the background as Michael begins to draw five separate groups of lines, which he varies by changing the movement of his hand. Repetitive, quick strokes stake out territory on the page. There is a practiced ease and confidence in his gestures. "I will definitely be putting myself in a situation where I have to work my way out of it," he says. He feels his way from one group of marks to the next, building the relationships between the separate groupings so that "the drawing becomes one whole drawing ... The relationship is crucial, one to the other."

Each time he dips his pen is an opportunity to reflect. He says, "the hand tells the eye where to go, and the eye tells the hand when to stop." Lines slowly accumulate. He layers multiple parallel lines on top of other shapes and explains: "They're used more to bring a feeling, or a sense of light and air into the work." He says that rather than working from observation of objects, he is working toward them, never quite getting to something clearly recognizable. During the retrospective interview, as he watches the lines build up he explains, "If you can draw air, you can draw things out of the air. You can pull things through the air. So what I know is that by using that light line, and drawing that light line over anything I want, over anyplace I want, I can begin to put air back into whatever is already drawn."

In the video, he turns the paper, building up tonal areas. Later, watching himself draw, Michael comments, "That's when you know you're really working … when you are driven by the drawing … People say it speaks to you. I've never heard it speak but it does drive you sometimes." He describes how the initial marks will eventually be absorbed into the whole as the drawing progresses. "The extraneous lines at the beginning are lines that need to be there in order to stimulate the rest of the drawing. But now … I'm trying to pull the lines together."

Just before I leave, Michael shows me an image of the Adam and Eve Panel, part of the *Gates of Paradise* by Lorenzo Ghiberti in Florence, Italy. The square bronze relief in real life is about the size of one of Michael's drawings. I would not have thought of this image in connection with his work, but at once it makes sense, not only as a visual fact—his drawings can feel like doorways into an ethereal realm—but also as a metaphor. Drawing can be a gateway into another level of experience, where boundaries are fluid and nothing has a name.

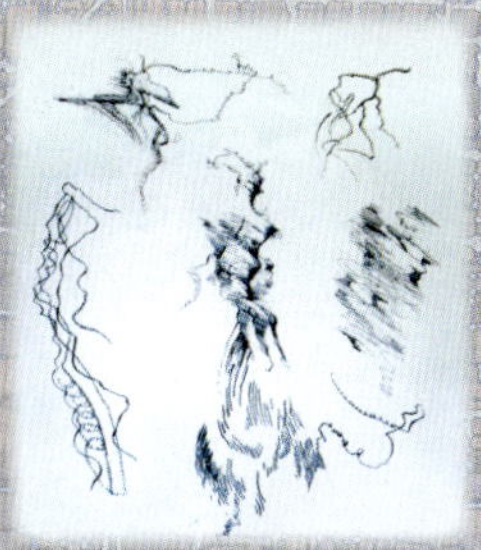

MICHAEL MOORE'S DRAWING METHOD

LOCATE five or six small yet varied scribbles in different areas of your paper. EXTEND out from these areas until you find ways to CONNECT them. As you build connections, new forms will suggest themselves. REINFORCE these forms by building up areas of tone. Stand back from your work periodically to see where you might need to REVISE to create a sense of overall coherence.

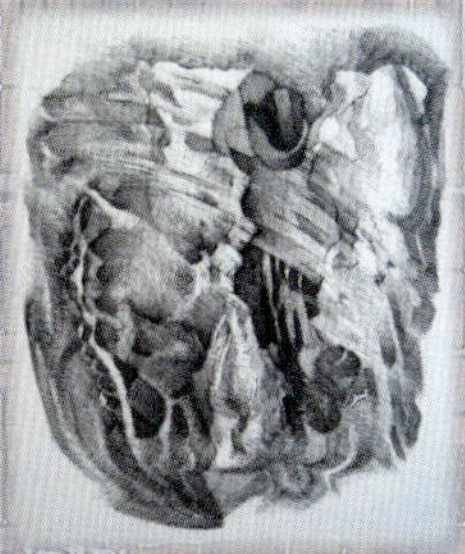

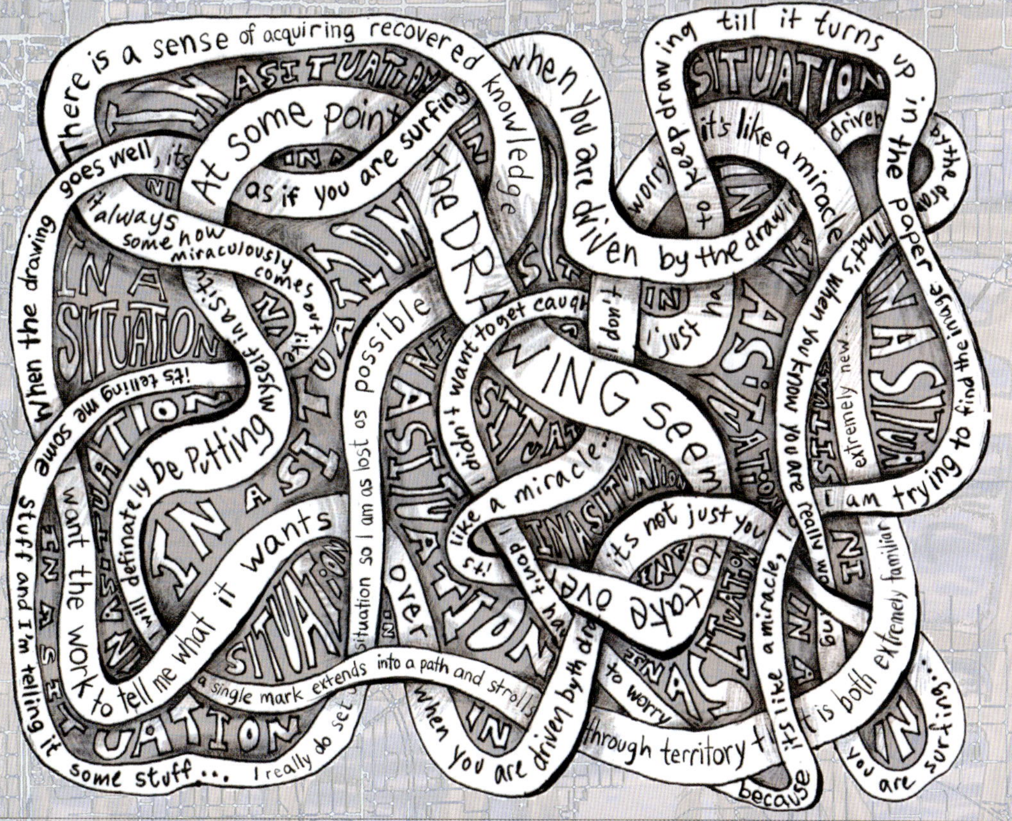

This drawing is based on retrospective interviews with the artists/participants in my study. Most artists mentioned searching for clues in specific parts of the drawing that could help guide its development. The quotes embedded in this drawing are from the critical period when the artists are "learning what the drawing is about." As Michael describes above, it is "when you are driven by the drawing."

"For it is not yet the memories themselves.
Not until they have turned to blood within us, to glance, to gesture,
nameless and no longer to be distinguished from ourselves—

Learning to Draw like an Expert

In art and design education, drawing technique is often sidelined in favor of efficiency or "free expression." But a firm foundation (knowing some tricks of the trade and practicing basic hand-eye coordination) can facilitate true freedom.

Access to a discipline specific "road map" can help beginners construct habits and routines that build on the past, so they don't have to re-invent the wheel before they begin their journey. Technical expertise is easier to achieve than creative expertise, but both can be taught and learned. Educators should provide their students with mastery experiences that develop both knowledge and confidence. It takes both to travel beyond the limits of the road map into uncharted territory to discover or invent something new.

As you accumulate many and varied drawing (and life) experiences, you can draw upon them as you encounter new challenges. Experts make analogies to figure out how to respond to the unknown or unexpected. When you come upon a novel situation or problem, you can ask yourself, "What is this like?" Over time, experiences and lessons learned are internalized, so you may access them without thinking, without analyzing why a particular move "feels right." And when you discover your inevitable errors, you have strategies on hand to help you revise, regroup, and try again, continually circling around understanding.

not until then can it happen that in a most rare hour the first word
of a verse arises in their midst and goes forth from them."

— Ranier Marie Rilke,
from *The Notebooks of Malte Laurids Brigge*

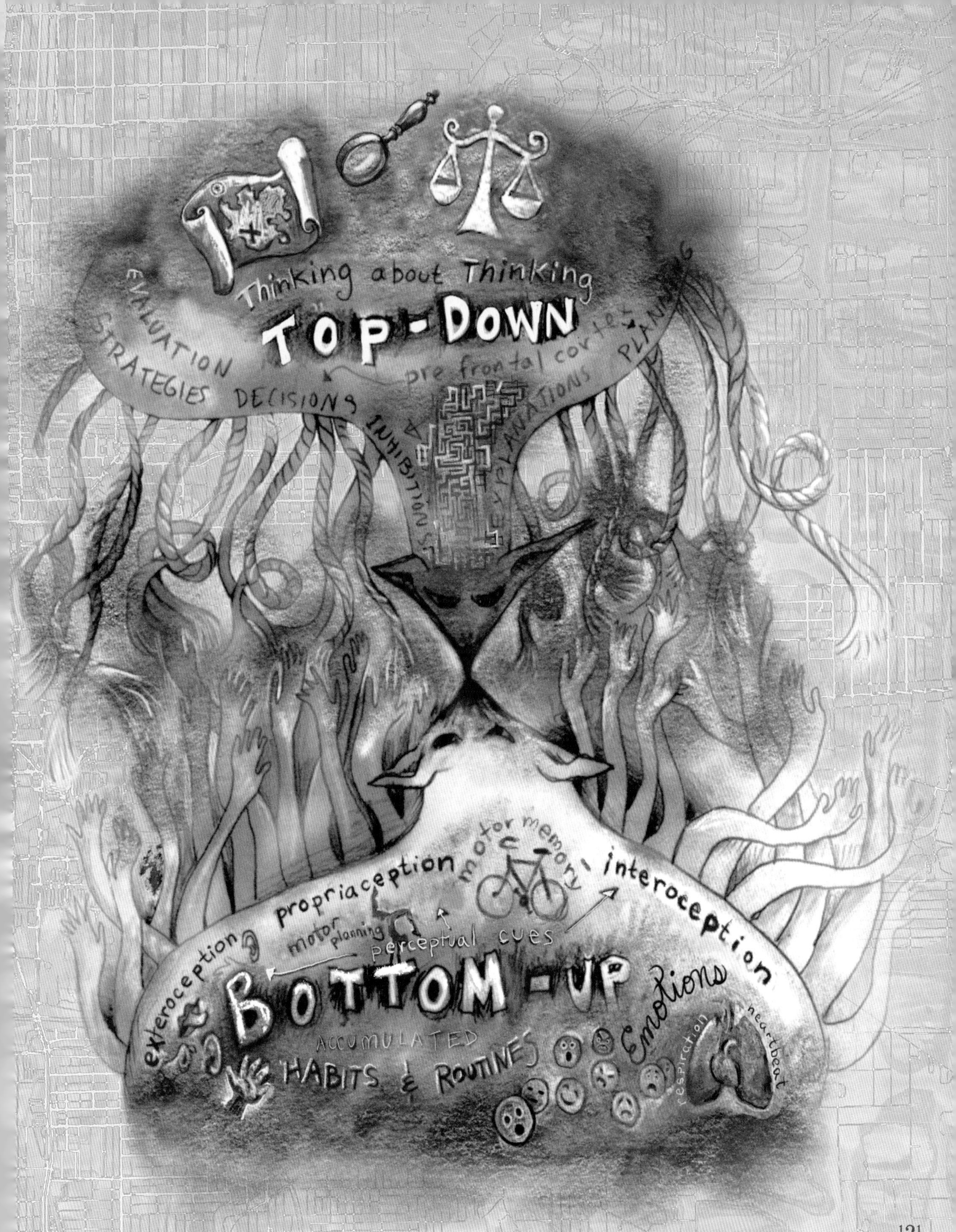
Thinking about Thinking
TOP-DOWN
EVALUATION
STRATEGIES
DECISIONS
pre frontal cortex
PLANNING
INHIBITIONS
EXPLANATIONS
propriaception
motor memory
interoception
motor planning
perceptual cues
exteroception
BOTTOM-UP
Emotions
ACCUMULATED
HABITS & ROUTINES
respiration
heartbeat

How to

Take a Point of View

Linear perspective = parallel lines converge

at one or more vanishing points on the horizon.

One-Point Perspective

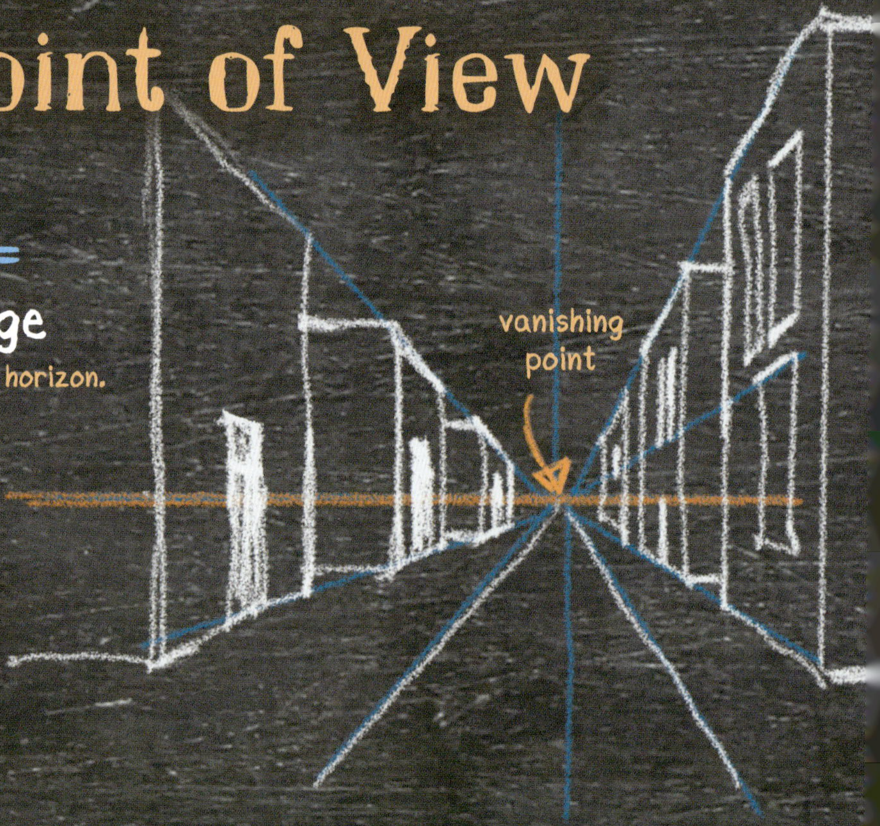

Two-Point Perspective

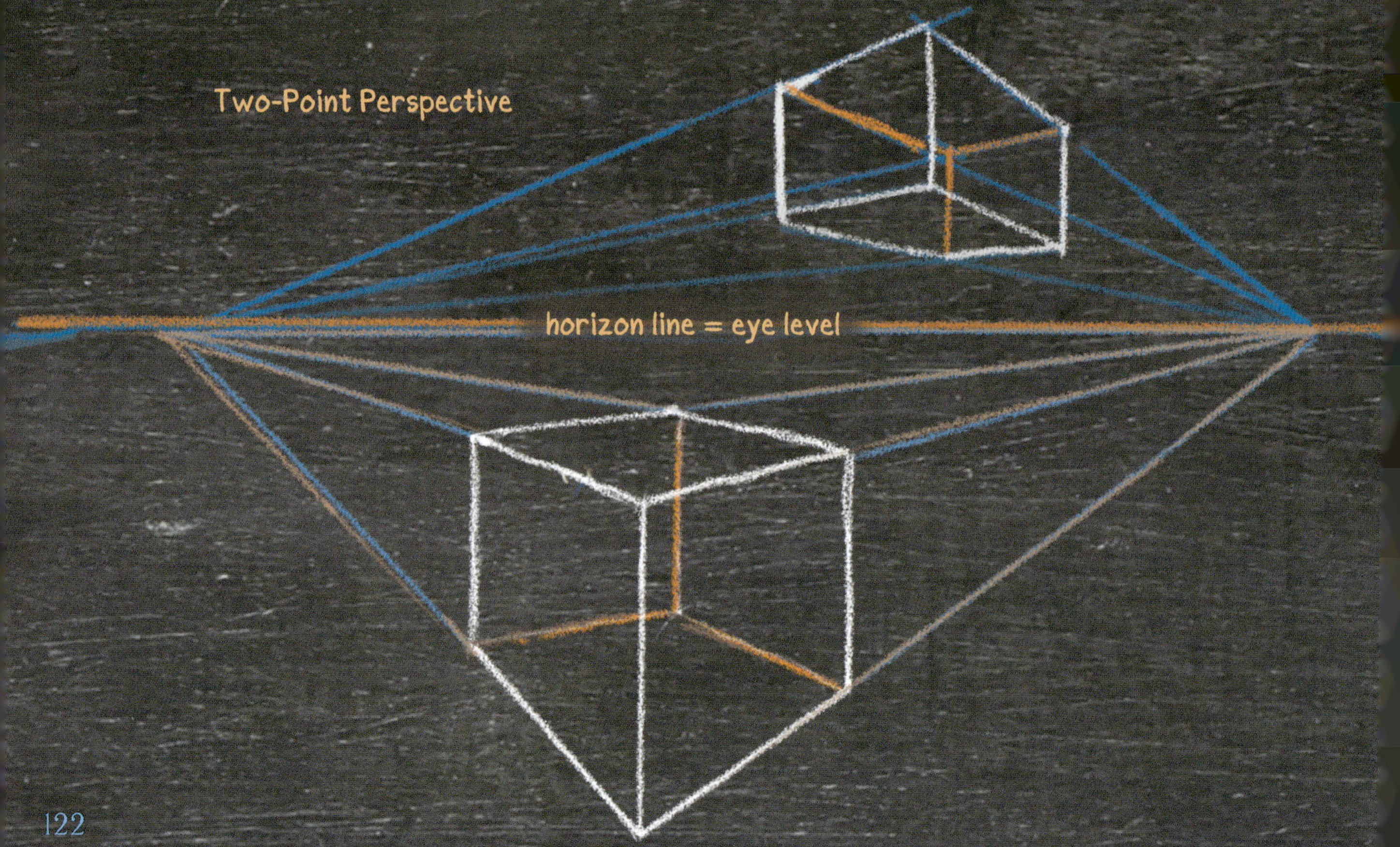

Bird's-Eye View

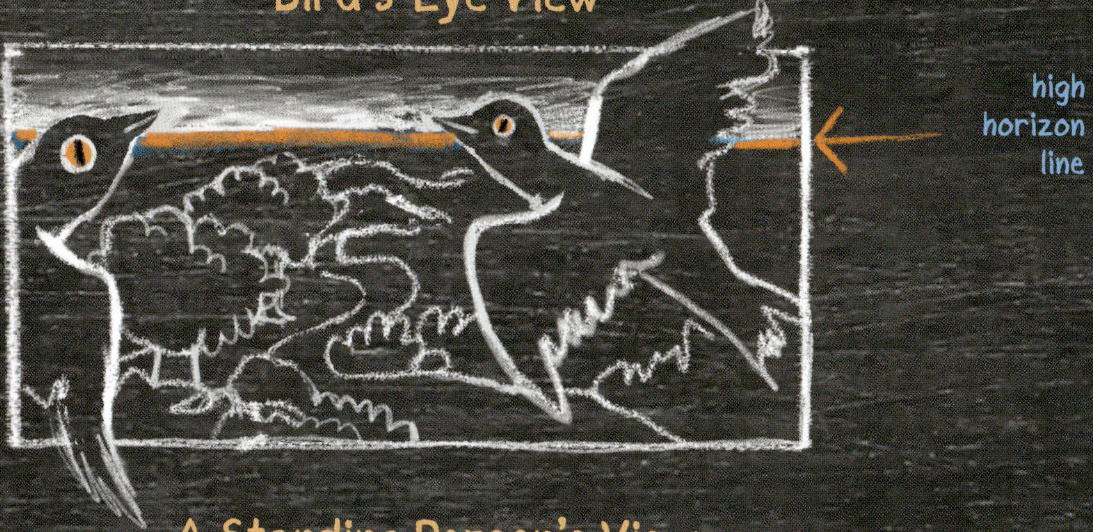

A Standing Person's View

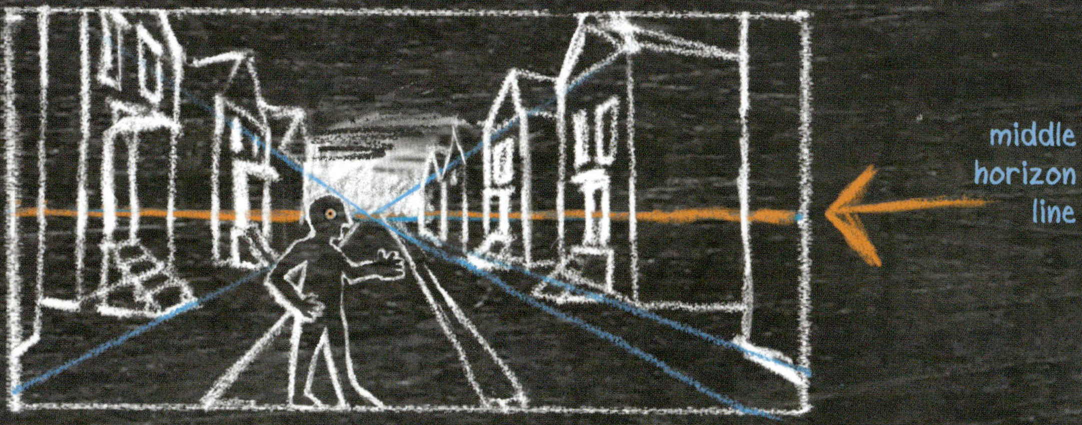

Worm's-Eye View

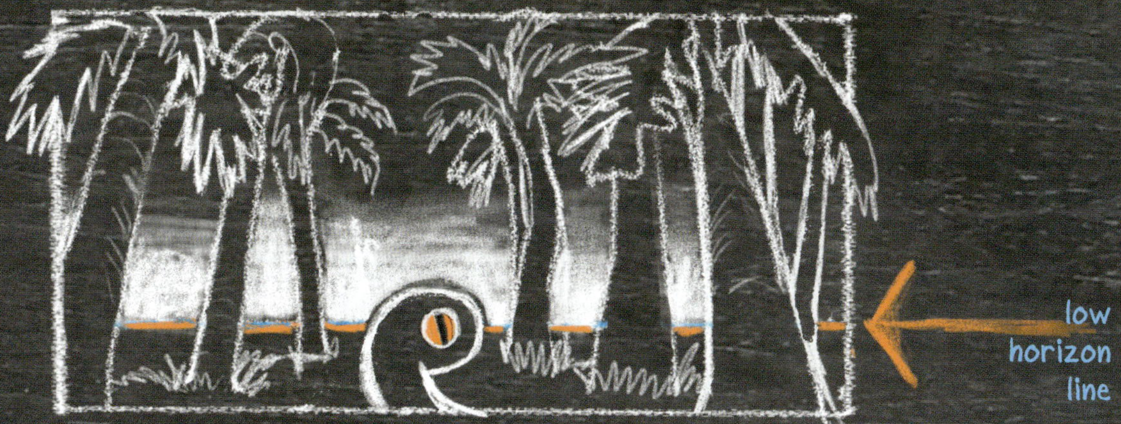

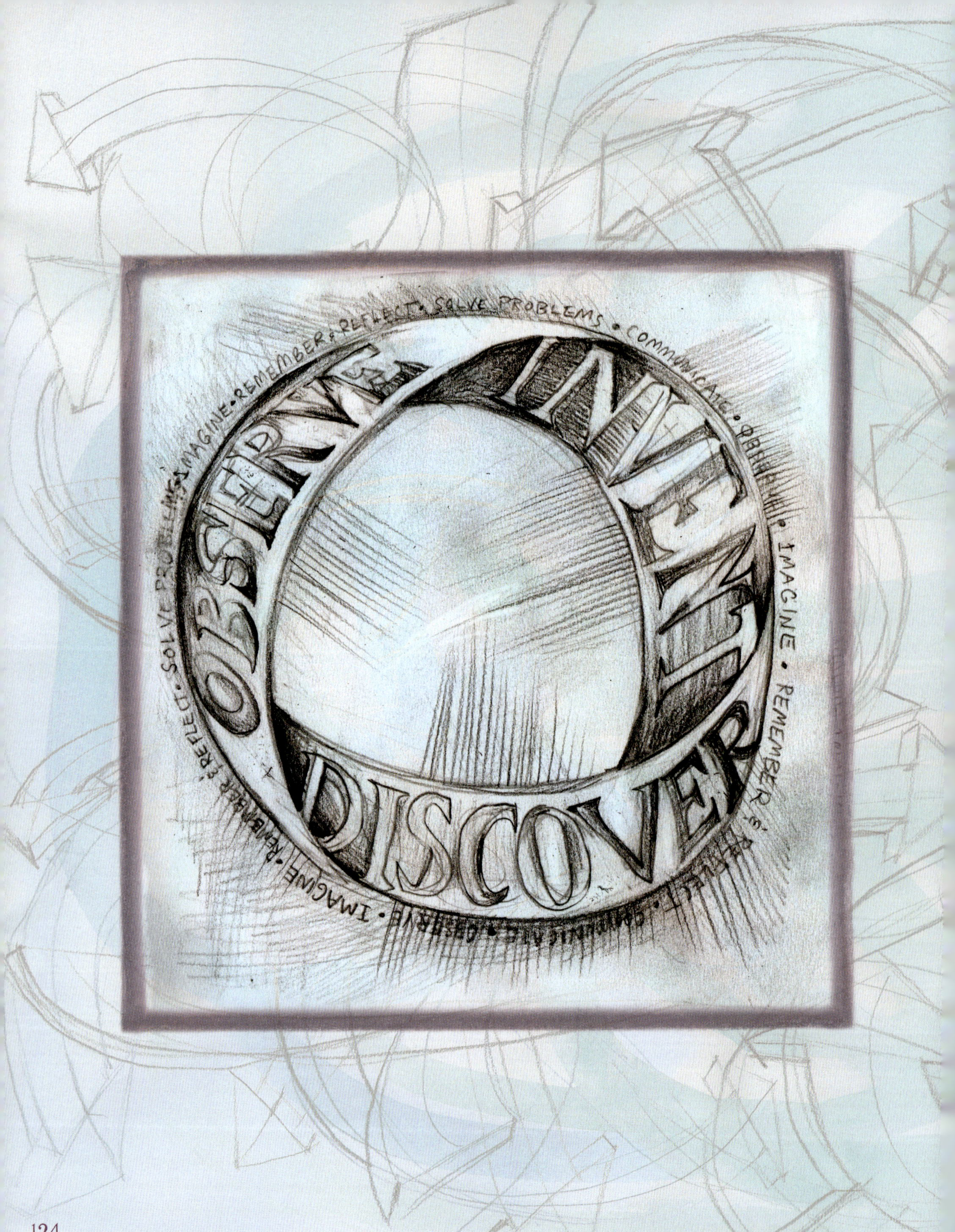
OBSERVE
INVENT
DISCOVER
IMAGINE • REMEMBER & REFLECT • SOLVE PROBLEMS • COMMUNICATE
IMAGINE • REMEMBER &
SOLVE PROBLEMS

chapter eight

Everybody Draw!

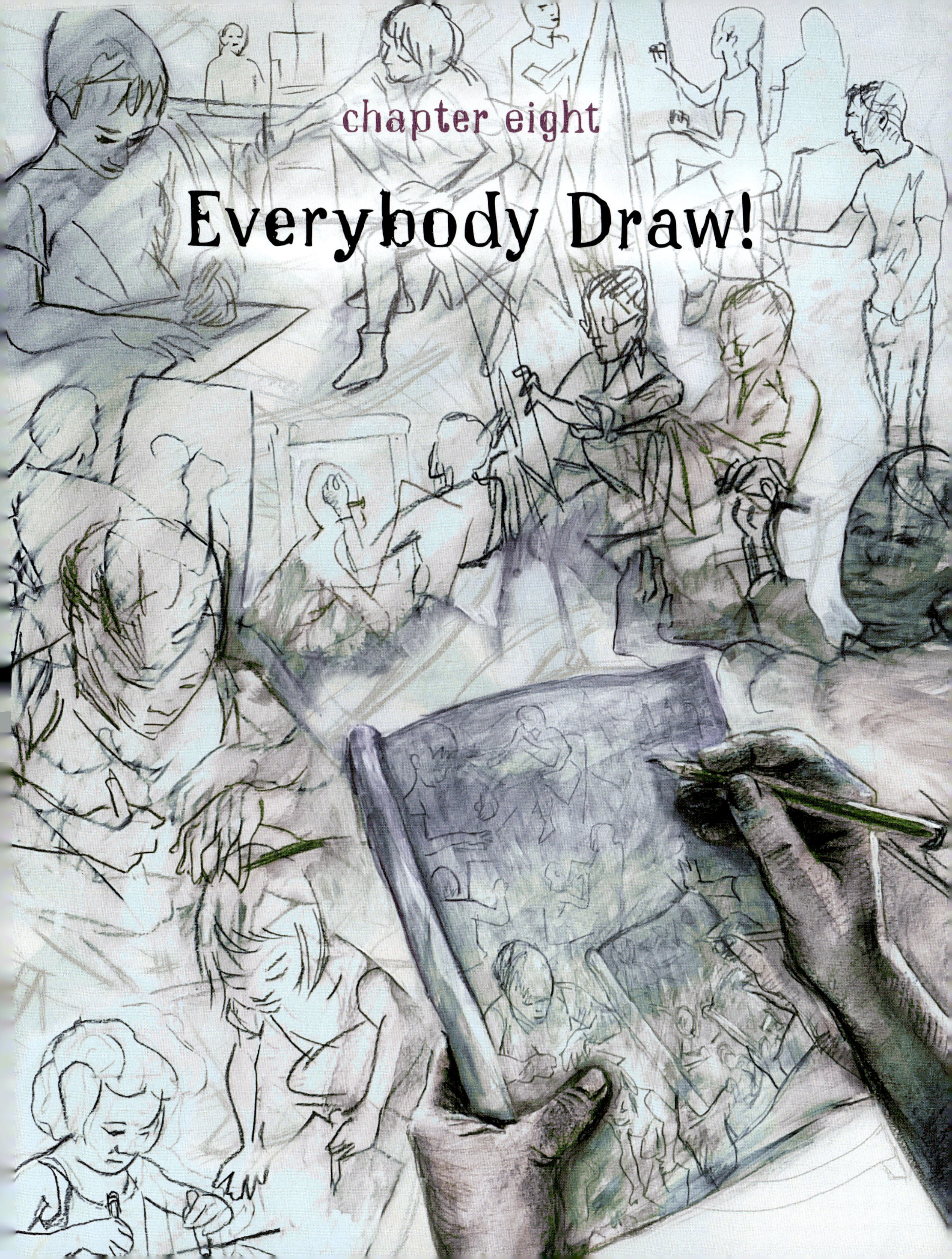

Let's count the WAYS we can draw OUT our

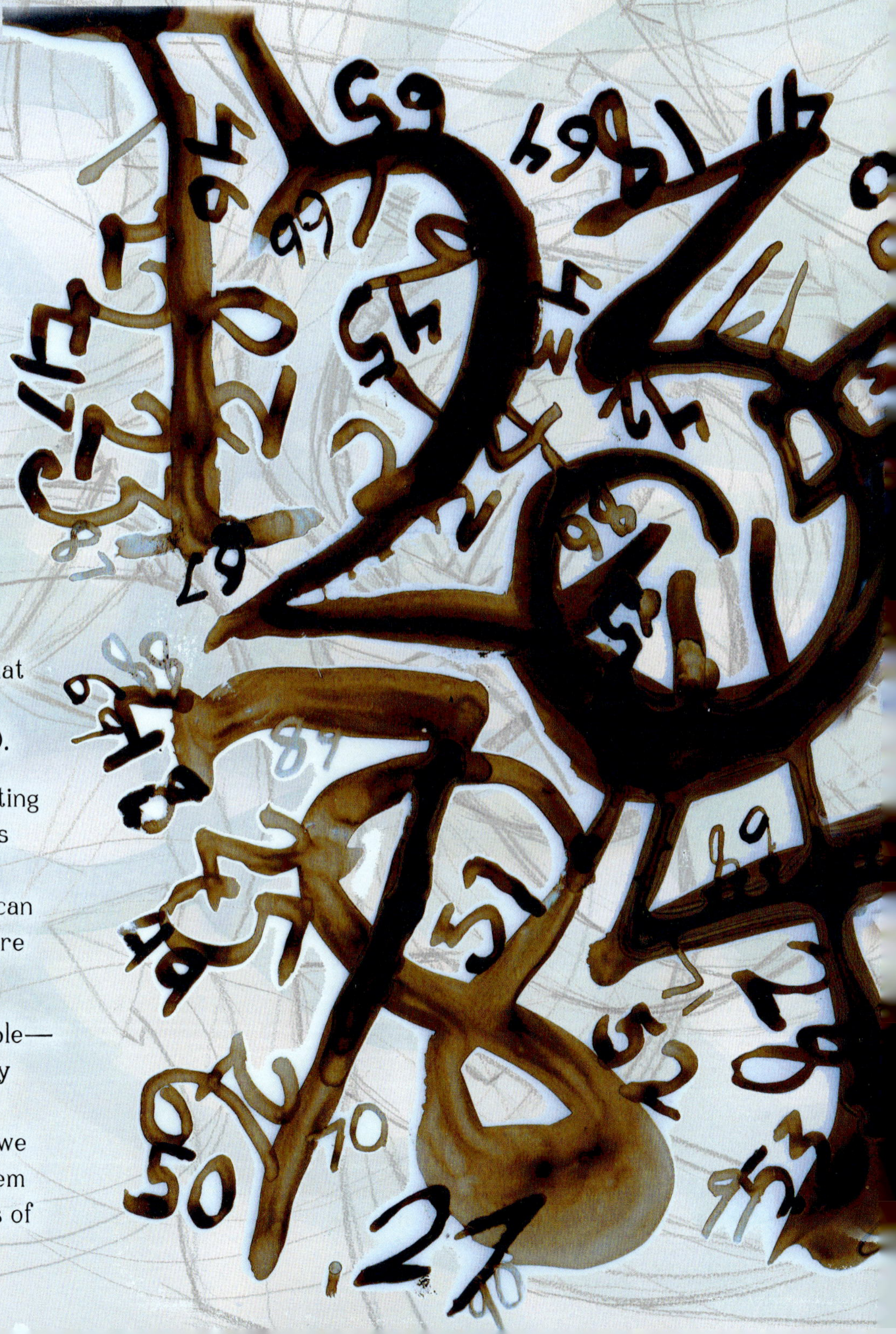

Drawing is for EVERYONE. It's not just a way of representing things that already exist (in the world or in our minds).

It's a way of constructing ideas and observations as much as a way of expressing them. We can all use drawing to figure things out.

It makes thinking visible—when we are not ready or not able to put our thoughts into words, we can sometimes put them down in arrangements of lines and marks.

THOUGHTS and draw IN the WORLD.

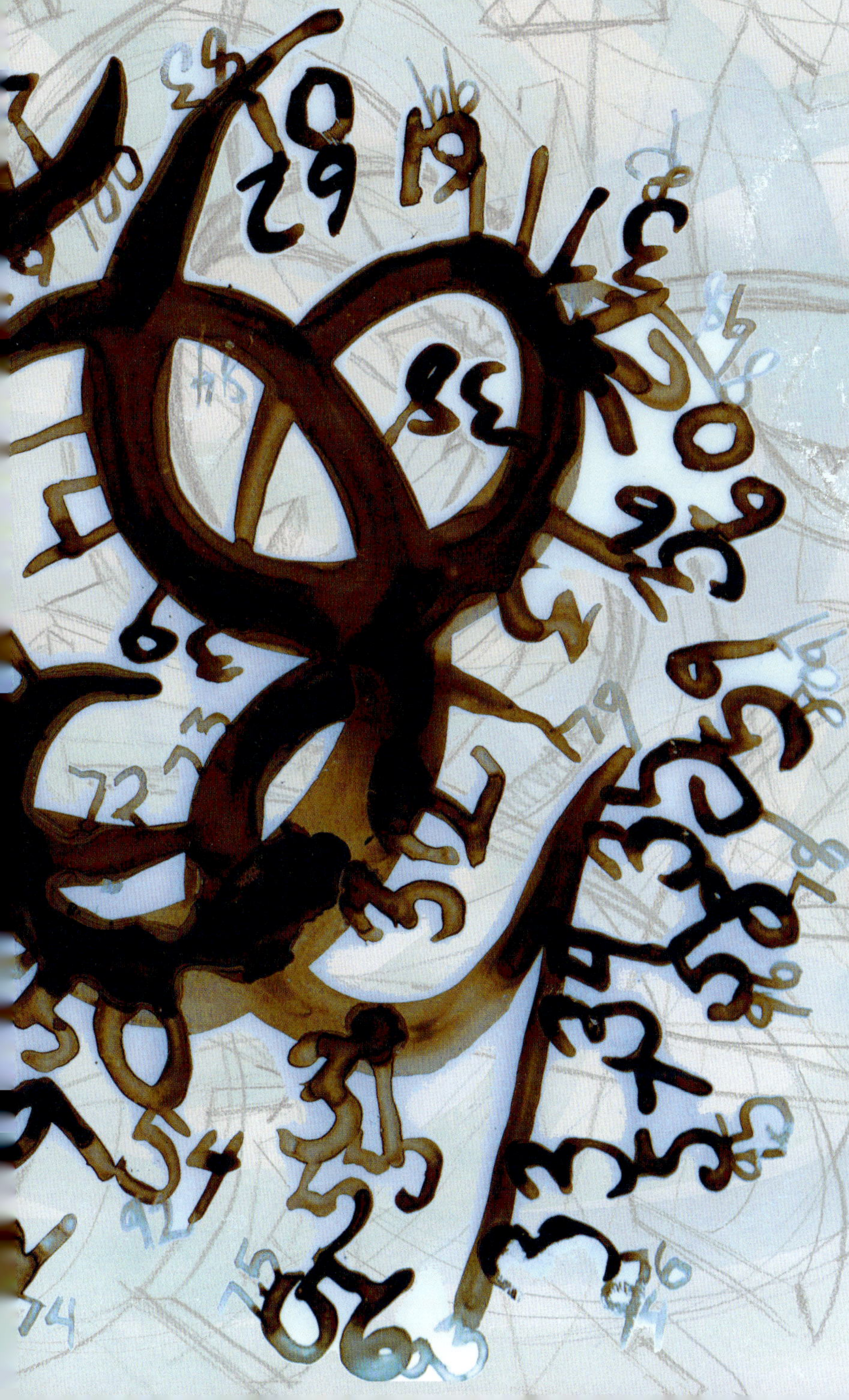

Very few five-year-olds will say they can't draw. Pretty much everyone starts out drawing. But many adults will tell you, sometimes without a trace of embarrassment, that they can't even draw a straight line. No problem! Why would you want to? Straight lines are not usually all that interesting. Sure, when you are just trying to get from point A to point B as quickly as possible, they can come in handy. But if you want to end up somewhere new, take the scenic route.

Most young children scribble for the pure joy and pleasure of seeing the traces of their actions on paper. Sometimes they invent a subject or story as they go along, on their own or when prodded by adults. The child knows and the adult sometimes must relearn that confusion and disorder can be an opportunity for surprise and discovery. Messy lines can lead you somewhere new, and sometimes they are just fun.

It would be wonderful to draw like Leonardo or even like the folks who draw Marvel Comics. But drawing benefits even people who don't draw like the experts. In fact, those who DON'T have strong visuospatial skills to begin with seem to benefit more from drawing than those who DO have high preexisting skills and strong internal mental models. The process of externalizing thought helps to support those who need it most.

"From around the age of six, I had the habit of sketching from life. I became an artist, and from fifty on began producing works that won some reputation, but nothing I did before the age of seventy was worthy of attention. At seventy-three, I began to grasp the structures of birds and beasts, insects and fish, and of the way plants grow. If I go on trying, I will surely understand them still better by the time I am eighty-six, so that by ninety I will have penetrated to their essential nature. At one hundred, I may well have a positively divine understanding of them, while at one hundred and thirty, forty, or more I will have reached the stage where every dot and every stroke I paint will be alive."

— Katsushika Hokusai,
Postscript to *One Hundred Views of Mount Fuji*, ca. 1834.

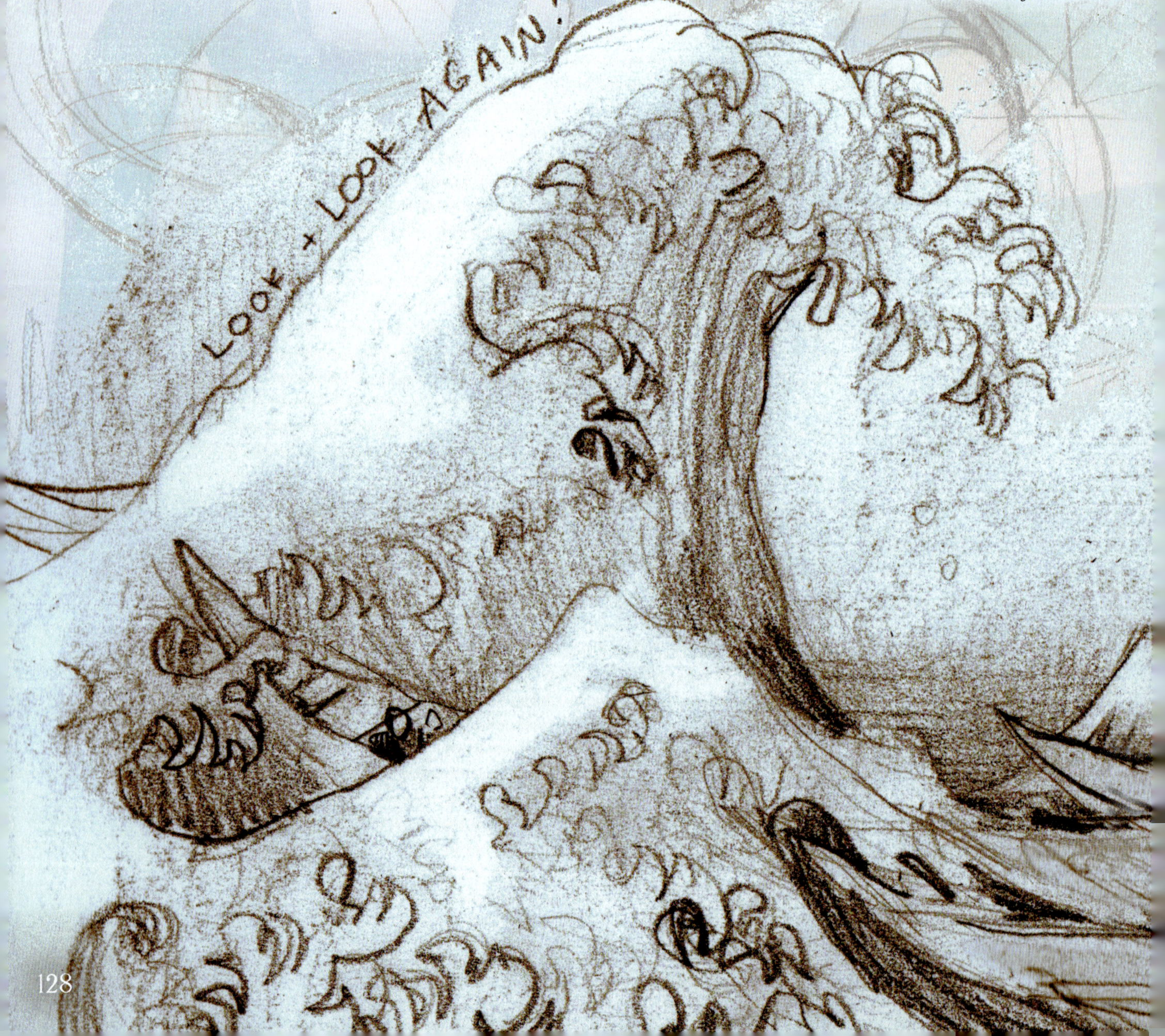

Learning to draw is a lifelong journey.

But using drawing as a way to generate and explore ideas and perceptions can happen all along the way, in sketchbooks and on napkins and in the margins of notebooks. If a great artist like Katsushika Hokusai felt he never quite reached his ideal we can't feel too bad about our own shortcomings. Our ideas and perceptions can be slippery—we aspire to grasp what is just out of reach. Hokusai remained ever hopeful and so can we.

These days, when we see something interesting, we tend to pull out our smartphones to capture it. That's okay, but as we snap the photo we are pulled away from the actual experience. At the same time, we imagine we've "got it," and are ready to move on. When we draw what we see, we give ourselves time to learn more about it and ourselves. "Why did this corner of the world capture my attention?" "What is really happening here?" We find there's always more to see; we've never totally "got it." We make time to allow a place or scene or experience to burrow deep into our minds so it might never be forgotten.

Drawing from observation or imagination helps wake us up to all that is available at any moment of our lives. In my experience, I may only sketch for a half-hour on a hike in the woods, or while sitting at my kitchen table, playing with whatever happens to come into my mind. Returning to the trail, or to the tasks of dishwashing, grading papers, or feeding my family, I feel so much more aware, as if I had been sleepwalking through my life until the minute I sat down to draw.

This drawing is based on Katsushika Hokusai's *The Great Wave of Kanagawa.*

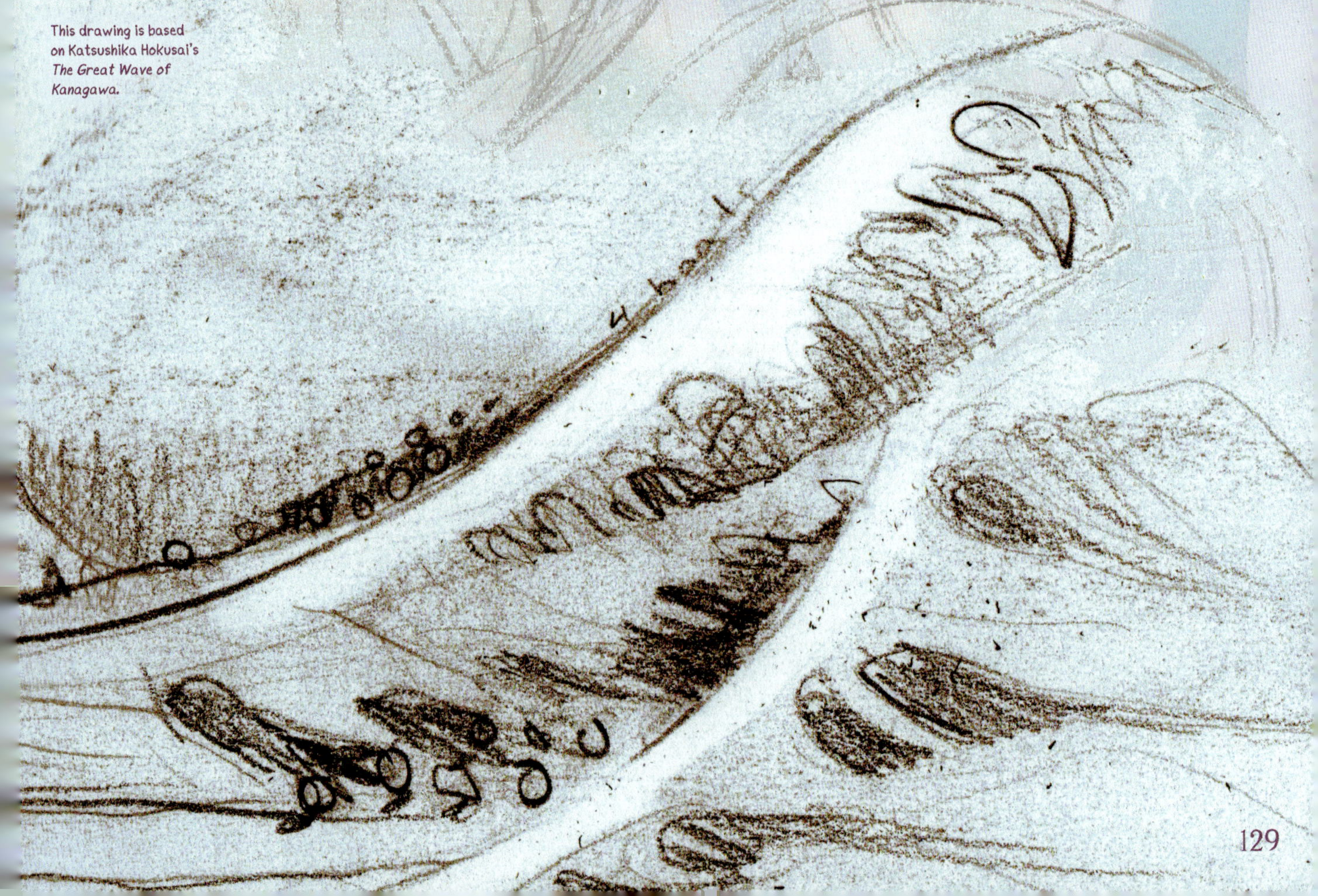

How to Draw

Drawing is more than the ability to transcribe what already exists, in our minds or in the world. We can also draw to discover or invent something new, never before seen or imagined. We all can learn how to convey complex information in a manner that supports inferences and reinterpretations by ourselves and others. People draw for many reasons: for a specific goal, as part of their professional practice, and sometimes just for fun. There are more approaches to drawing than there are reasons to draw. A number two pencil and copy paper work great, but digital tools have a place as well (I use both, almost everyday!). When we learn to draw, we learn to think strategically about our own thinking. We choose HOW we pay attention and WHAT we pay attention to. We choose to tighten or loosen conscious control over what our hands (and shoulders and arms) are doing. We choose when to speed up or slow down.

Technical MASTERY and

are not mutually exclusive. It may

COMBINE the two approache

Pay attention to what seem

Drawing to Learn...

... may be more important than learning to draw. These days we have so many other ways, these days to capture images that already exist. Digital photography and 3D drawing tools are as ubiquitous and handy as our cellphones; learning to render a preconceived scene or idea by hand may not justify all the time and hard work it requires. On the other hand, drawing to think and learn can be really valuable. (Even doodling may enhance listening and learning.)

As long as learners are confident they have (or can figure out) the drawing tools and techniques they need for the task at hand, drawing can increase emotional engagement and motivation. Learners should feel free to figure out their own ways to represent ideas, but have a safety net available as needed. Step-by-step, targeted guides, which are supportive rather than prescriptive, can be useful. I'm a big believer in how-to-draw books and have listed some of my favorites in the notes. There are also countless helpful video tutorials online on almost any drawing subject or technique imaginable.

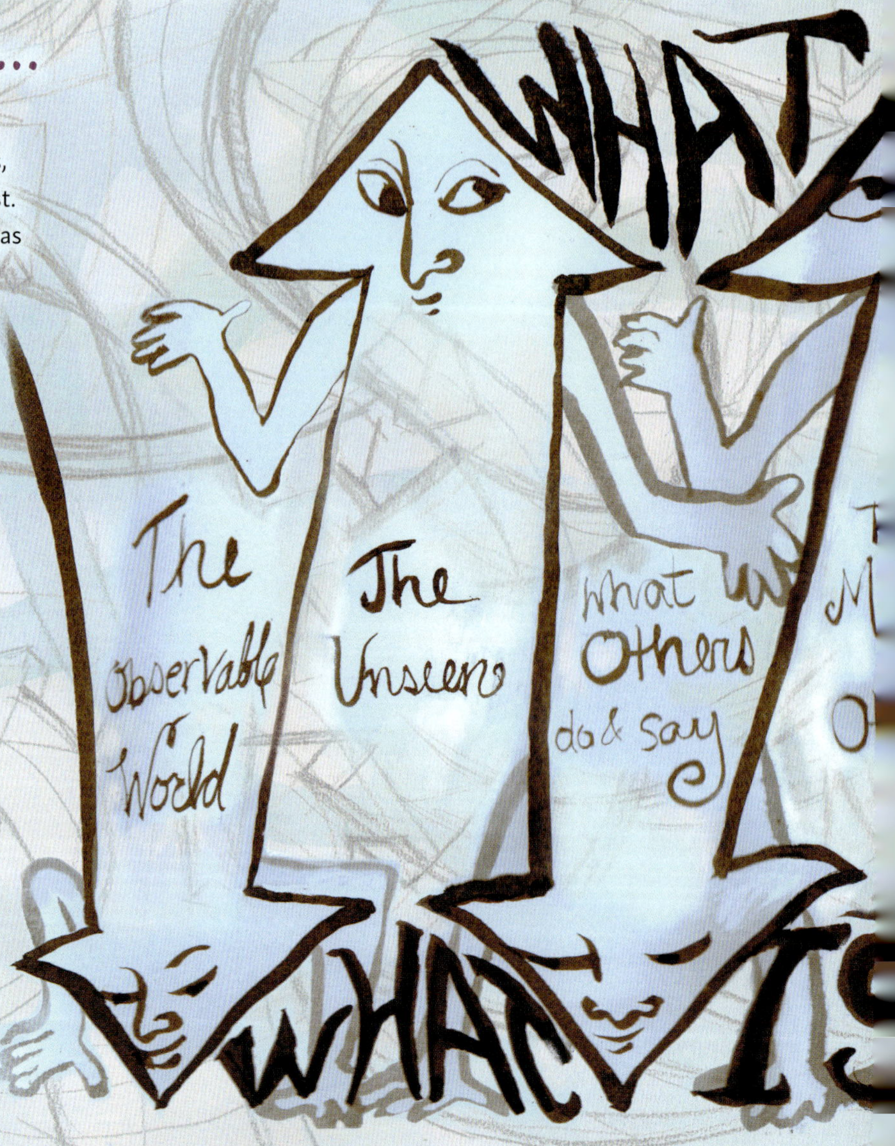

spontaneous EXPERIMENTATION

be most beneficial to ALTERNATE and

as you develop your drawing practice.

to be most HELPFUL in the moment.

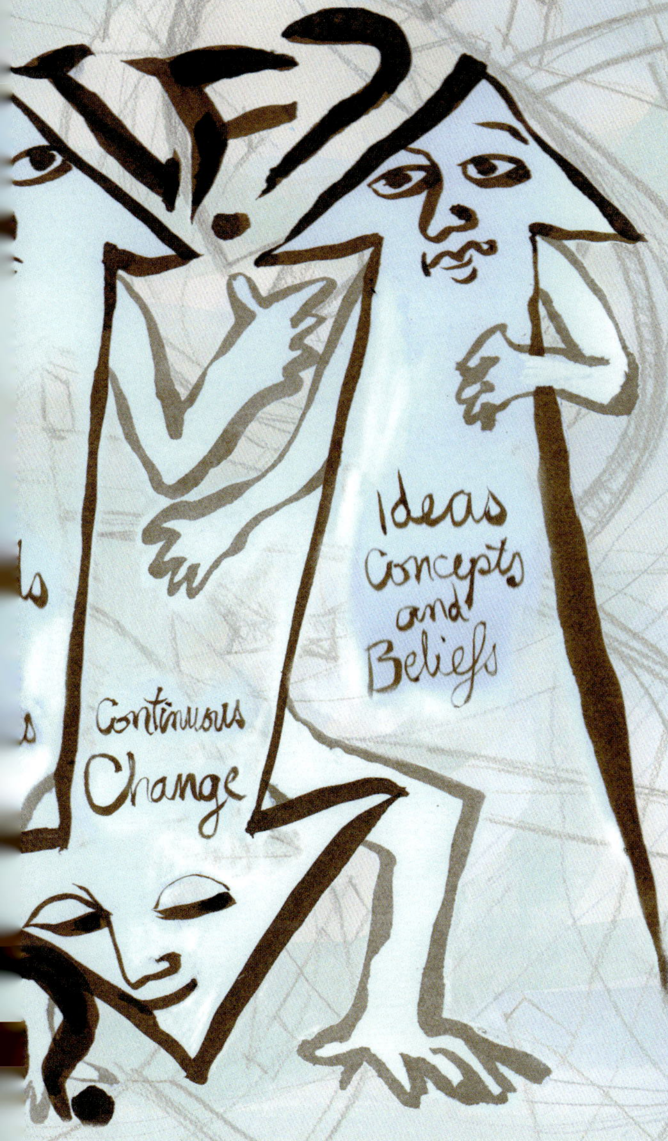

Learn Traditional Skills

Mastering a variety of techniques cultivates METACOGNITION, your ability to be aware of and make conscious choices about your own thinking processes. Tricks of the trade can help circumvent common beginner's errors. Most beginners place the eyes too high when they draw portraits. But once they learn the rule that eyes sit on an imaginary horizontal line halfway down the face, the portrait will look more naturalistic. Beginners often draw distant objects much larger than they appear. They tend to draw objects the relative size they know them to be, rather than their optical appearance. To create a sense of depth in a scene, allow and even exaggerate how elements in your drawings get smaller and less detailed as they recede into the distance.

These and similar techniques help beginners and more experienced drawers overcome common systematic errors. Most of these errors are due to innate, low-level operations in the visuospatial system; useful in everyday life, but not in the way when they creep into our drawings uninvited. Once we know to expect them, we can keep them at bay.

EXPERIMENTING and improvising with a range of methods and materials can release your imagination. You can use cross-modal aspects of perception and embodied cognition to give concrete form to invisible experiences and ideas, drawing how something sounds or feels, in a literal or metaphorical sense. Keep a sketchbook handy: it may become a valuable archive of your day-to-day ideas and observations that might otherwise fade from memory. Your sketchbook is a low-stakes arena in which to explore nascent interests and unexpected insights.

Learn from the masters. Collect and study drawings and paintings you admire and figure out how they work. Copy them in different ways. For example, instead of imitating them mark for mark, look for big shapes and action lines. Draw the implicit gesture and movement. Diagram the spatial relationships and major divisions of the drawing. Map how your eye moves through the drawing. Invent your own way of reinventing your favorite drawings (for examples, check out Picasso's fifty-eight versions of Velasquez's *Las Meninas*).

For more information on traditional (and not-so-traditional) drawing techniques, check out the resources listed in the notes for this chapter.

To Observe

Imagine you are a visitor from another planet. Focus on low-level information, such as shapes and patterns of light and dark. Forget that you have ever seen a flower or tree before, so you will be free to see this particular tree or flower in all its glorious individuality and uniqueness. Otherwise it is too easy to say to yourself, "Oh, it's a flower," and draw the one in your mind rather than the one in front of you.

Blind contour drawing, when you only look at your subject and don't look down at your paper, is a great way to warm up. Contour and gesture drawing are two complementary approaches that can work together, as long as you keep your gesture lines light and loose. (Review the exercises in chapter three.) Imagine your pencil tip is resting directly on your subject and draw with continuous line.

Use your pencil or pen to check for relative scale. Hold it out in front of you, with a straight arm. Line it up with your subject, checking proportions with the tip of your thumb and angles as you draw. This well-known technique helps control for common errors, such as locating the eyes too high on the forehead in portrait drawing. As you practice this trick it will eventually become automatic and you won't actually have to be holding your pencil out all the time. But even experienced drawers find this a helpful trick when they get stuck.

Drawing on location is a wonderful way to learn, stay motivated, and maybe make some new friends. Urban Sketchers is a global network of local groups, with chapters on every continent, from Singapore to Nairobi to Seattle, who meet weekly or monthly to go out and sketch together.

There are countless local life and portrait drawing groups all over the world that you can connect with via social media. Some years ago I had a few days to myself in Chiang Mai, Thailand, in between professional engagements. I was drawing with a friendly, diverse group in a local cafe within twenty-four hours of arriving.

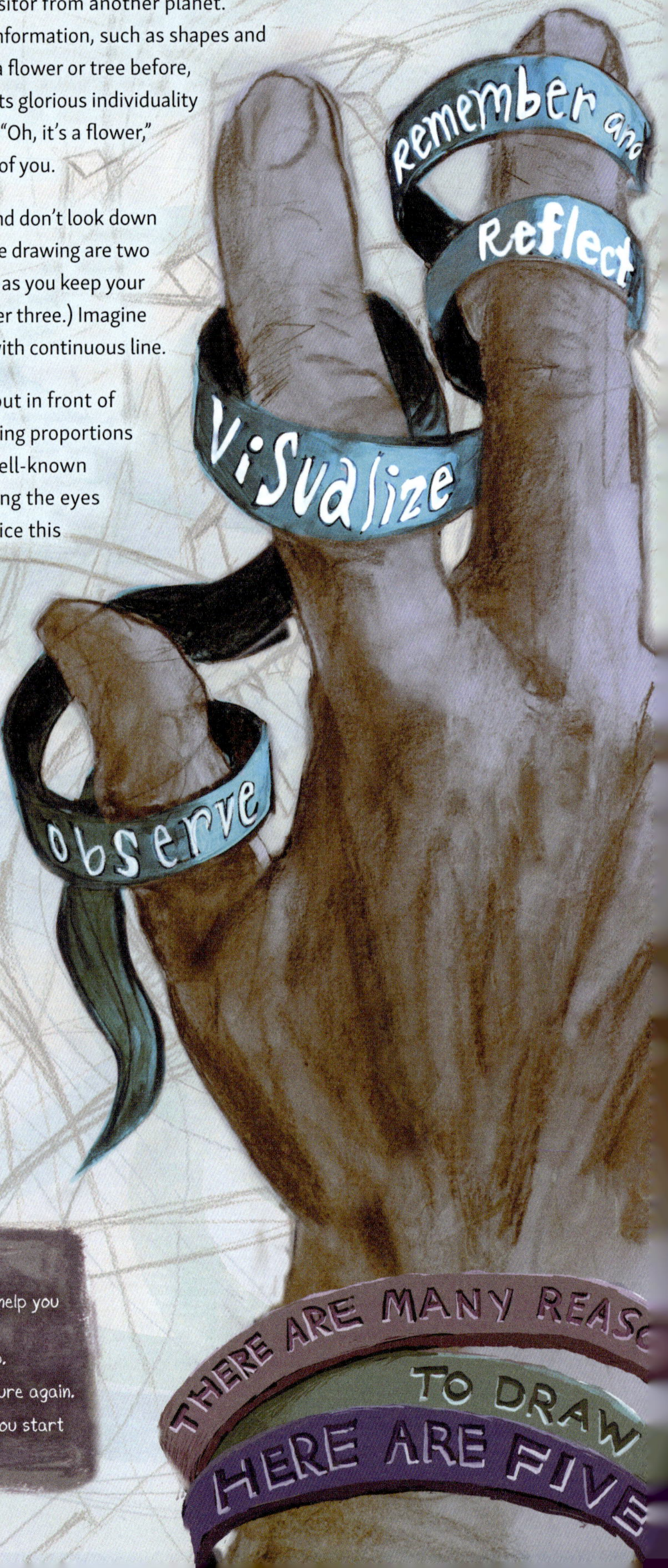

MORE IDEAS TO TRY:

- The in-between (negative) shapes are puzzle pieces that can help you see other shapes more accurately.
- Look for "Y" and "T" joints, articulating where forms overlap.
- Measure with your pencil held out in front of you. Then measure again.
- Map out large shapes and the location of key points before you start filling in the details.

To Visualize

When you draw from your imagination, you exercise spatial reasoning and visual memory. You develop your ability to create, rotate, and transform two- and three-dimensional mental models.

To gain confidence in your ability to draw from your imagination, work on hand-eye coordination. Practice drawing parallel straight lines. Draw simple shapes: rectangles, squares, circles, and eclipses. Practicing basic shapes and straight lines is like practicing scales on the piano.

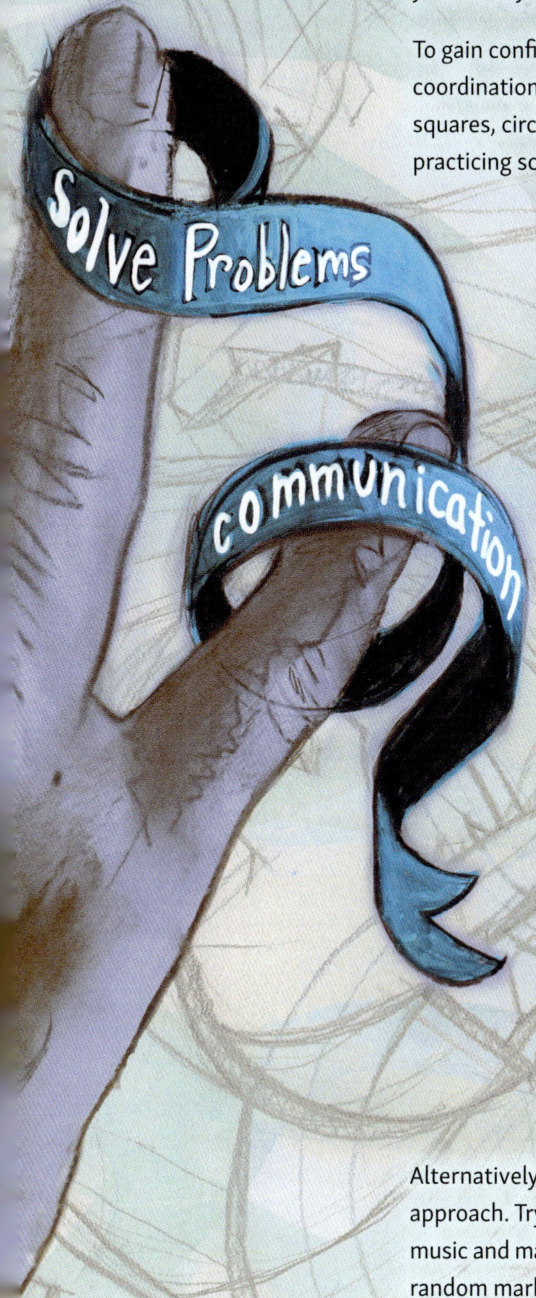

Once you feel comfortable drawing two-dimensional shapes, transform them into three-dimensional shapes. Almost anything you can imagine can be constructed from combinations of simple three-dimensional forms. Practice drawing cubes, spheres, pyramids, and cylinders and then combine them in different ways.

Nothing comes from nothing. Form hybrids from existing forms. If your goal is to create something that does not yet exist, you can start with things you already know, take them apart and combine them in new ways. Take known objects and creatures apart in your sketchbook; mix them up and put them together in different ways. Hybrid creatures with both human and animal characteristics are found in almost all cultures. You would like to invent a vehicle that can travel through the air and under the sea? Look at planes, hot air balloons, and submarines. You want to imagine what a city might be like on Mars? Look at ancient and modern cities in arid climates.

When parallel lines stay parallel, you have orthogonal perspective, used by architects and engineers to communicate with builders. Proportions stay constant. It is independent of the position of a hypothetical individual viewer. This is easier to master than linear perspective, and is a good way to get started.

Use linear perspective to explore or convey a scene from a particular point of view. Define the viewer's position in space relative to a scene in order to convey an mood or narrative. Traditional adventure comics (like Marvel) and manga are great references for exploring the narrative implications of varied points of view such as bird's-eye and worm's-eye (from above and from ground level).

Alternatively try an improvisational approach. Try putting on some favorite music and make some light and loose random marks across the drawing surface. Turn the paper occasionally. Let the drawing lead. Once marks cover most of the surface, respond to accidental shapes and forms as they emerge. You might see elements of landscapes, figures, or faces. Enjoy what shows up.

MORE IDEAS TO TRY:

- Make a few marks without looking at your paper. Gradually transform your 2D scribbles into 3D forms by erasing, overlapping, adding thickness to some lines, and occluding others.
- Begin with a nonvisual concept, perhaps just a single word, like liberty or justice. Translate it into visible form by focusing on its qualities: is it heavy or light? Rough or smooth? Huge or tiny? Aggressive or timid?
- Consider time. Think about beginnings, middles, and endings. What just happened? What will happen next?

To Remember and Reflect

Use drawing as a tool to remember and reflect on your ideas and experiences. If possible, set aside a few minutes at the end of the day to draw at least one idea or experience from that day in your sketchbook. Drawing from memory on a regular basis helps develop your visual memory over time. Taking the time to reconstruct an event from your daily life can help build visual resources that you can dip into when drawing for other purposes. You may find yourself noticing more aspects of your moment-to-moment experiences and ideas as they happen.

Comics, combining image and text, are an effective way to remember and reflect on your experiences. Comics are used in healthcare as a means for medical students, caregivers, and patients with no prior drawing training to reflect on their experiences. This form of reflection seems to help us process difficult or even traumatic events. Graphic memoirs, such as Alison Bechdel's *Fun Home* or Marjane Satrapi's *Persepolis*, can inspire you.

MORE IDEAS TO TRY:

- Select a meaningful quote. Play with the letters and add imagery that brings the quote to life.
- Draw a map of your day. How did it begin? What were highs and lows? Perhaps you encountered an oasis (coffee with a friend?) and/or roadblocks (perhaps during rush hour?)
- Draw a map of a larger section of your life's journey.

Historically, anthropologists used drawings along with written notes to capture observations and reflections in field journals. Despite the ubiquity of digital photography and video, there has been a recognition that drawing can facilitate reflective practices in a different and meaningful way. Anthropologist Andrew Causey, in *Drawn to See: Drawing as an Ethnographic Method*, offers a series of practical exercises to help social scientists use drawing as an aid to their research.

Infographics are another form to explore. You might diagram your day using flowcharts, Venn diagrams, or embellished web-like mind maps. Add details and images as they occur to you. Draw to reflect on larger issues of concern. For inspiration, take a look at sociologist, historian and civil rights activist W. E. B. Du Bois's gorgeous infographics (an example is given in the notes). He created visualizations of the lives of Black Americans in 1900.

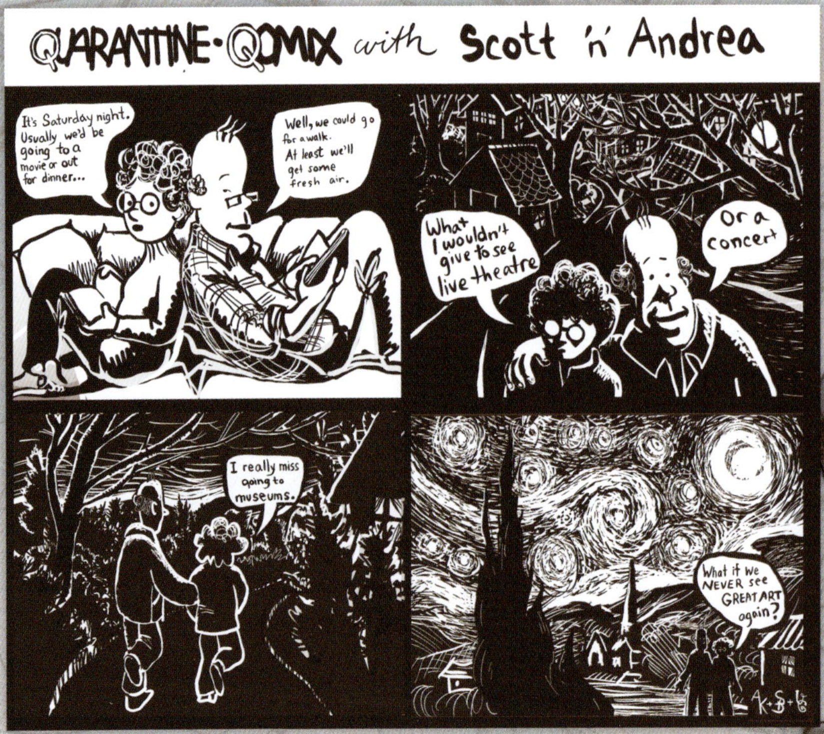

This was one of a series of cartoons my husband and I created as a response to the COVID-19 lockdowns of during the spring of 2020.

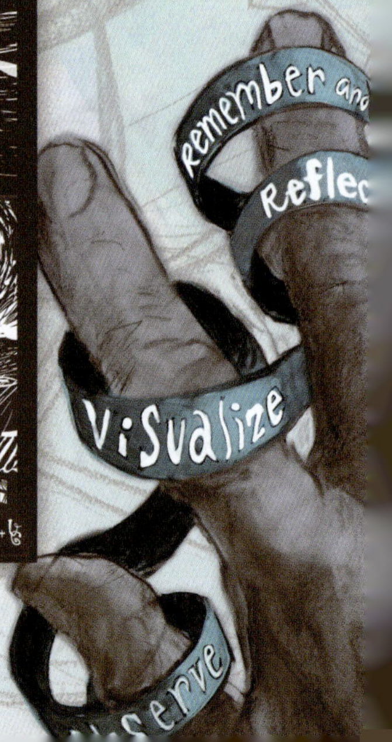

To Solve Problems

Drawing out your problems can help you solve them. Inventing visual metaphors for your problem, or pulling the elements apart and putting them back together in new ways, can lead to solutions that might otherwise be unimaginable. The act of drawing out your thoughts on paper makes it possible to see how things might fit together differently. Drawing becomes a way to ask questions, develop prototypes, and test possibilities.

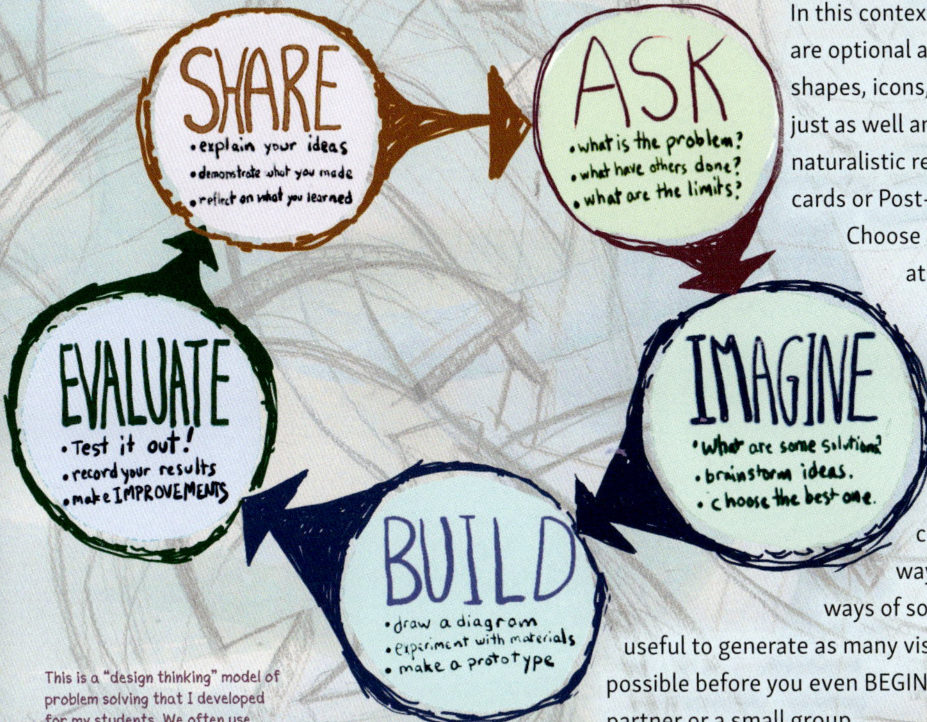

This is a "design thinking" model of problem solving that I developed for my students. We often use different forms of drawing as a way to prototype possible solutions to a variety of abstract and concrete problems.

In this context, sophisticated drawing techniques are optional and might even be distracting. Simple shapes, icons, symbols, and stick figures can work just as well and sometimes better than more naturalistic renderings. Keep piles of blank index cards or Post-its, pencils, and markers handy.

Choose a real-life issue you are grappling with at the moment. Take some index cards and visualize your problem in as many ways as you can. Make a diagram, cartoon, symbolic design, expressive abstraction or ... whatever else you can think of. Imagine the physical qualities, personality, and emotional characteristics of your problem. The more ways you visualize your problem, the more ways of solving it may present themselves. It's useful to generate as many visual representations of your problem as possible before you even BEGIN to think about solving it. Try this with a partner or a small group.

Let's say I'm having an issue with time management. I might start by drawing a droopy old-fashioned clock with a sad face. I think about all the things that eat up my time. (This is all hypothetical, of course.) I make an abstract drawing where a roundish shape is being pulled toward all four edges of the card like a trampoline. Then I draw two dogs engaged in a tug of war over a bone. I synthesize my ideas by drawing an anthropomorphic alarm(ed) clock that is on the verge of being torn apart by wild dogs. Now I have something that feels like an accurate portrayal of the problem. To find a solution, the personified clock shoos away some of the dogs, throws some bones out in a field to keep some others happy for a bit, and sets a timer, while one dog at a time comes in for dinner.

Through the process of re-representing my problem in different ways, I've begun maybe not to solve it in real life, but at least to imagine that a solution might be possible!

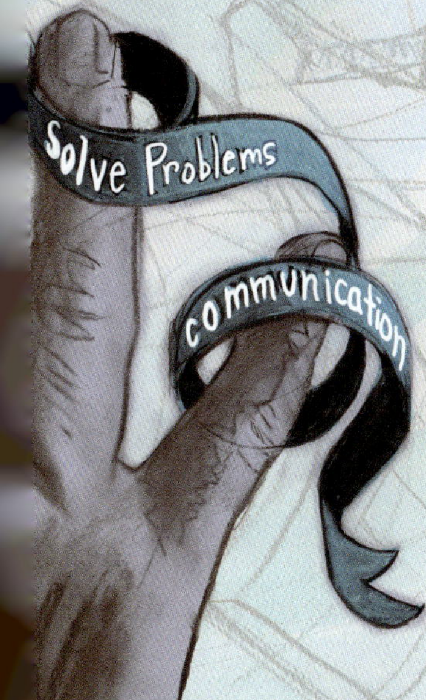

MORE IDEAS TO TRY:

- Warm up by creating visual metaphors for abstract conceptual verbs, such as: analyze, derive, emphasize, reconcile, fabricate, construct, etc. . . . Choose one word and represent it in different ways.
- Imagine the physical qualities, personality and emotional characteristics of your problem: is it thorny or slippery ... heavy or floating above your head, just out of reach ... explosive, or dark and gloomy ... squishy or hard as a rock?

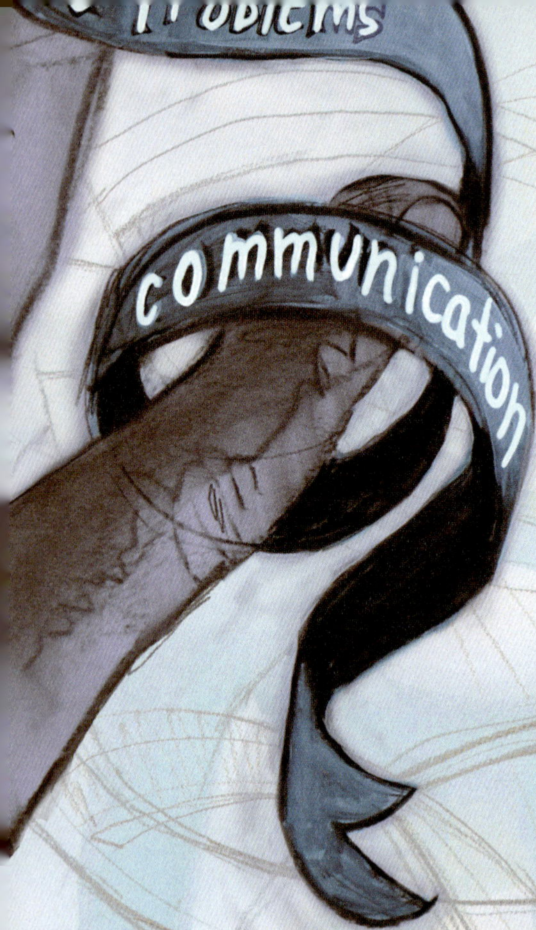

To Communicate

When we use drawing to communicate with others, context and purpose matters. Many domains have a preexisting visual vocabulary (such as in chemistry or football) that might be important and useful. Alternatively, you might get people's attention better by presenting your information in an unusual or unfamiliar way, with a diagram, cartoon, abstract image, or some combination of all three.

A good caricature is recognizable because it emphasizes distinctive features and eliminates distracting details. When drawing to communicate, it can be most effective to use simple, clear imagery and icons that everyone can make and understand, rather than more detailed renderings.

Gather information and ideas from groups of people by thinking through DRAWING TOGETHER. Find the biggest sheet of paper you can get your hands on and throw it up on the wall or lay it out a table or the floor. Before starting to work on the big piece, it helps to let everyone start on their own. Ask everyone the same question. It can be context specific, or as simple as: What are you curious about ... worried about ... excited about? (Pick one.) For idea generation, brainstorming works best when everyone in the group gets a chance to put their own individual thoughts on paper first. That way, everyone's ideas get seen, not just those of the boldest, most confident members of the group. Once everyone has made at least one drawing, compare and contrast them. There are many strategies to get the various ideas integrated into a single work. The group can categorize and arrange them in logical ways. One or more people can start drawing them out on the big paper. Then you draw connections and annotate with text, image, or both. This kind of group drawing can take place in a single session, or over an extended period of time. The drawing itself can function as a launching pad, library of ideas, or scrapbook; whatever works best for your group.

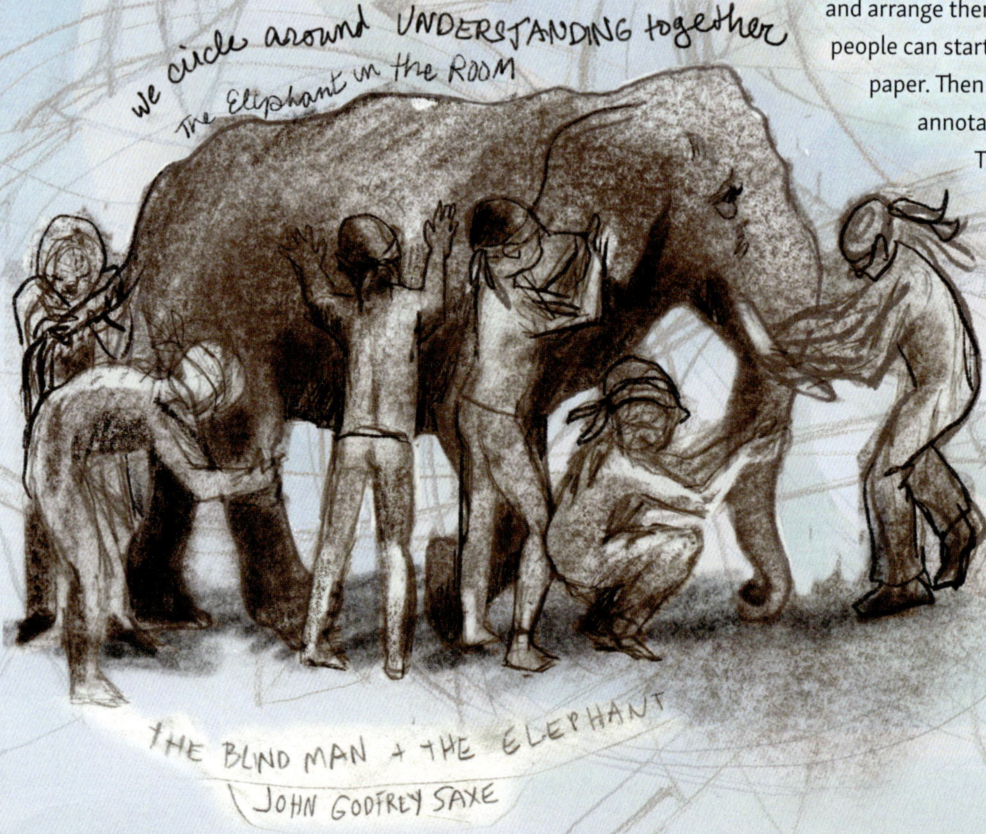

SKETCHNOTING resources can help anyone learn to make simple, clear drawings using basic shapes that communicate, regardless of prior drawing experience.

Further Questions...

Does drawing change the way you think, in a global and lasting way? Maybe, maybe not; it really depends on context. Cognitive and educational psychologists have repeatedly found that most people do not transfer learning from one domain to another unless they are explicitly instructed to do so. There are so many ways and reasons to draw that choices need to be tailored toward specific goals.

Drawing generally seems to improve mental focus and executive function, at least while we draw. Drawing might also improve mental flexibility and creative idea generation in more durable ways. Many have made the argument that drawing teaches us to see. Psychologists Aaron Kozbelt, Rebecca Chamberlain, and others have found artists' perceptual advantages persist even when they are not drawing. Beyond what we see, drawing can make visible thought processes that might otherwise be hidden from view.

The description of drawing detailed in these pages has correlates in many other domains. Any process of observation, discovery, or invention can involve making connections, combining parts to form new wholes, balancing attention to specific features while attending to underlying overall structures.

Visual perception, past experiences, and other sensory information, such as the movement of our bodies in space and inner awareness of our own heartbeat, influence what we see and notice. Drawing is the visible trace of the ways we think with our hands and bodies that we can leave behind. Marks and lines indicating awareness, action, and movement in a finished drawing allow a viewer, ourselves or others, to imaginatively reconstruct the drawing process.

Through drawing, we can learn to correct innate perceptual distortions and develop the ability to notice, question, and direct our attention and internal thoughts. We might become better equipped to observe, discover, invent, and solve problems in the arts, sciences, and everyday life.

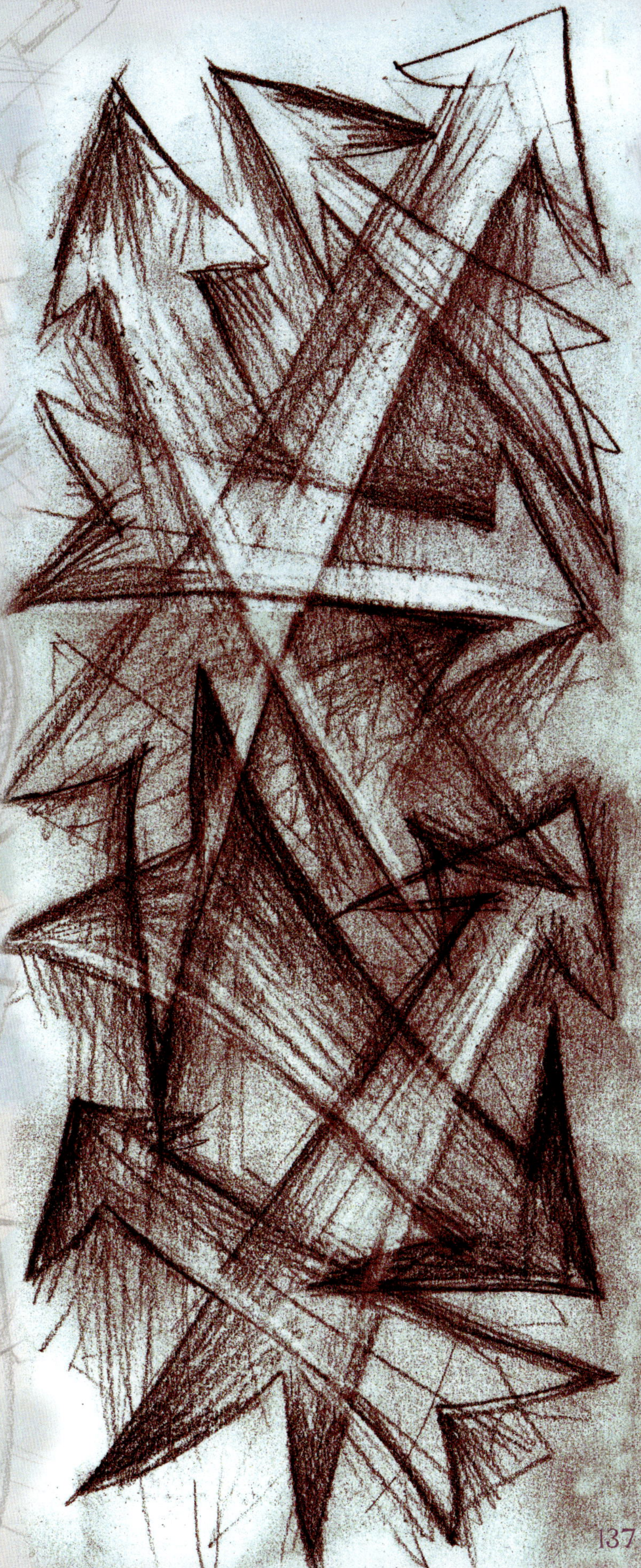

Why Draw?

(final answer… for now)

Drawing offers us a way to cultivate deeper knowledge of our own internal thoughts and of the world in which we find ourselves.

We discover that there is much more to observe and reveal than initially meets the eye.

We come to realize that we know and understand less than we think we do, but at the same time, we gain access to ideas and perceptions otherwise hidden from our conscious minds.

We are surprised by our own inventiveness.

Through regular practice and reflection, we can develop habits of mind, heart, and eye that keep curiosity alive.

Never be bored again.

There is always more to observe, discover, and invent.

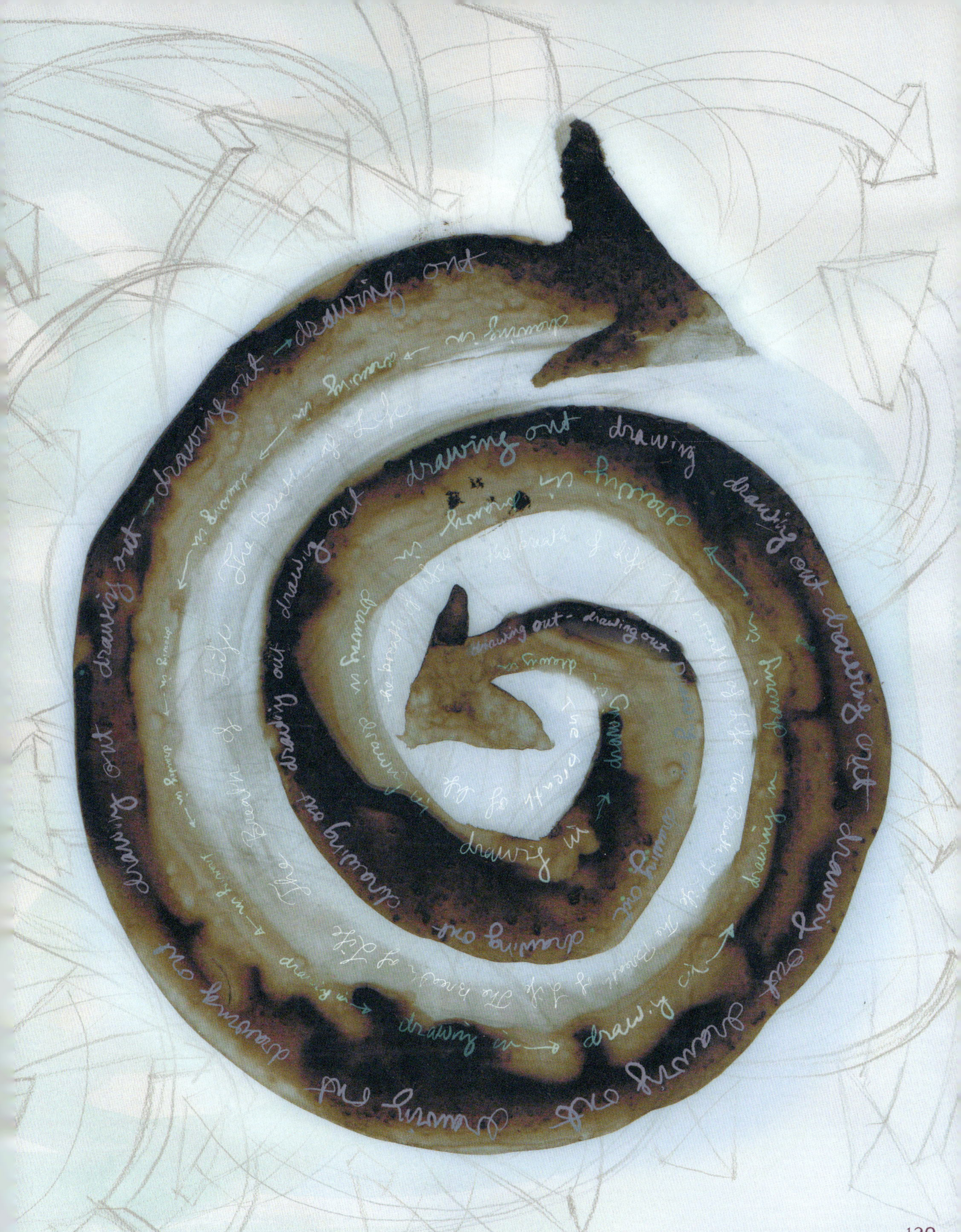
drawing out
drawing in
The Breath of Life

Notes

Cognitive scientists, evolutionary anthropologists, and other experts have shared the huge advances in their fields in books written for a lay audience as well as in academic journals. To learn more about the science I refer to in this book, please explore these resources. Any images I have included here are in the public domain unless otherwise noted and are reproduced with permission.

chapter one

The Evolution of Thought

Page 2

Thought and behavior—An understanding that cognition is situated, embodied, and action oriented has taken hold in the cognitive sciences over the past 25 years. The work of cognitive psychologist Barbara Tversky and colleagues, in particular, has greatly influenced my understanding of the relationship between thought and action. See Barbara Tversky, *Mind in Motion: How Action Shapes Thought* (New York: Hachette, 2019).

Drawing can be defined—as a process of intentional mark making, yet the word encompasses a diverse array of practices, from pencil on paper to stick in the sand. In "Nailing the Liminal: The Difficulties of Defining Drawing," artist and scholar Deanna Petherbridge writes: "Drawing . . . invites frustration or obsession in attempting to clarify something which is slippery and irresolute in its fluid status as performative act and idea; as sign, and symbol and signifier; as conceptual diagram as well as medium and process and technique. With many many uses, manifestations and applications." In *Writing on Drawing: Essays on Drawing Practice and Research*, ed. Steve Garner (Bristol: Intellect Books Ltd., 2008), 27.

Drawing makes thought visible—In the 1920s, Bauhaus artist and teacher Paul Klee wrote that in making art, "We learn to see what flows beneath; we learn the prehistory of the visible. We learn to dig deep and to lay bare. To explain, to analyse... Art does not reproduce the visible but makes visible." See *Notebooks, vol. 1: The Thinking Eye* (London: Lund Humphries, 1961), 69–74. Klee's teachings have influenced generations of artists and designers around the world.

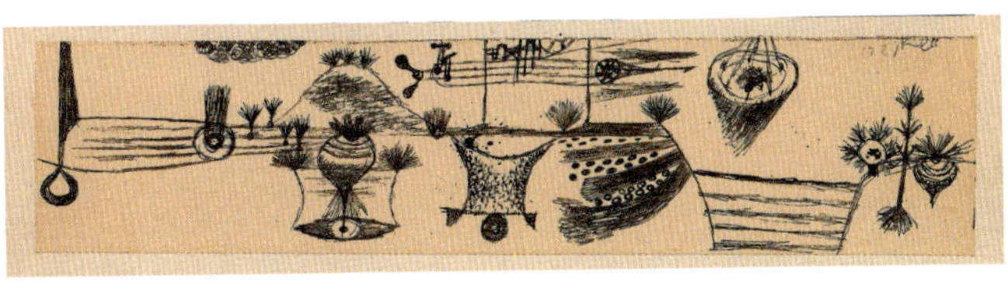

Paul Klee, "Garten Am Fluss," 1921 Wikimedia Commons http://commons .wikimedia.org/ Copyright: public domain.

Page 3

Our capacity for symbolic thought—In his book *Sapiens: A Brief History of Humankind* (New York: Random House, 2014), historian Yuval Harari puts the nature of human thought and behavior in an evolutionary context. Harari describes how we overcame our vulnerabilities (we are neither the strongest, the swiftest, nor the most agile) through our ability to cooperate in large groups. Symbolic thought made the construction of shared belief systems possible, which in turn facilitated large group cohesion.

Both predators and prey—Our cognitive architecture evolved to respond to the need to discriminate between predator and prey. Donna Hart and Robert Sussman, *Man the Hunted: Primates, Predators, and Human Evolution* (Boulder: Westview Press). See also Clark H. Barrett, "Adaptations to Predators and Prey," in *The Handbook of Evolutionary Psychology*, ed. David M. Buss (Hoboken, NJ: Wiley, 2015), 1–18.

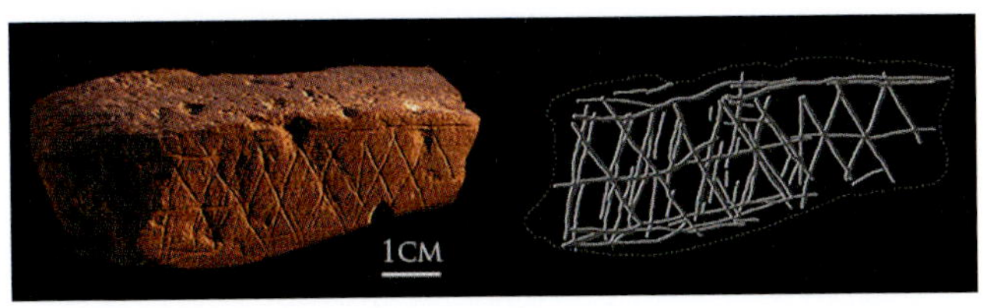

Photograph: Chris S. Henshilwood, https://api.ndla.no/image-api/raw/okerstein_blombosgrotten.jpg? Creative Commons.

Blombos Cave—Geometric drawings etched the wall of the Blombos Cave in South Africa over 70,000 years ago are the earliest traces of what anthropologists call "the cognitive revolution." They cite these drawings as oldest evidence left to us of the development of symbolic thought among modern humans. Even older evidence of intentional markings on rocks with an ochre crayon were found more recently at the Blombos Cave site. See Christopher S. Henshilwood et al., "Emergence of Modern Human Behavior: Middle Stone Age Engravings from South Africa," *Science* 295, no. 5558 (2002): 1278–1280. See also Christopher S. Henshilwood et al., "An Abstract Drawing from the 73,000-Year-Old Levels at Blombos Cave, South Africa," *Nature* 562, no. 7725 (2018): 115–118.

From Sulawesi, Indonesia, to Chauvet, France—The global spread of cave drawings that date back over 40,000 years has raised a question for modern anthropologists: did groups of humans independently invent similar iconography, often including the naturalistic portrayal of the animals they hunted, or did humans bring their drawing methods with them as they migrated across continents? See Wil Roebroeks, "Art on the Move," *Nature* 514, no. 7521 (2014): 170–171.

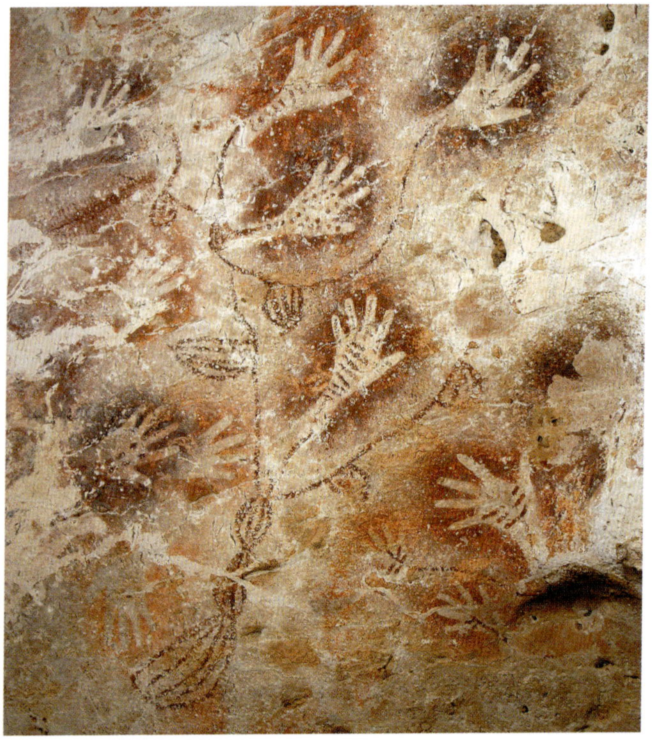

Painted ceiling from Gua Tewet, East Kalimantan, Indonesia, discovered in 1999 by Pindi Setiawan, Luc-Henri Fage, and Jean-Michel Chazine Photo courtesy of Luc-Henri Fage via Wiki Commons.

They often left their handprints behind—Handprints and stencils are found in ancient caves around the world dating back more than 40,000 years. They are sometimes seen in large collections such as at the Cueva de las Manos, Rio Pinturas, in Argentina (around 10,000 years old) and sometimes found alongside other drawings depicting humans and animals. There are numerous theories on what these hands mean: a few anthropologists theorize that some, with missing fingers and awkward positions, encode a sign language similar to those found among some hunter-gatherers today. See Ricardo Etxepare and Aritz Irurtzun, "Gravettian Hand Stencils as Sign Language Formatives," *Philosophical Transactions of the Royal Society* B 376, no. 1824 (2021): 20200205.

Page 4

Sketchnoting—Great resources to explore include Mike Rohde, *The Sketchnote Workbook: Advanced Techniques for Taking Visual Notes You Can Use Anywhere* (Berkeley: Peachpit Press, 2015). Sunni Brown accurately integrates insights garnered from cognitive science on the value of drawing out your thoughts in *The Doodle Revolution: Unlock the Power to Think Differently* (New York: Portfolio/Penguin, 2014). Christine Wodtke's book, *Pencil Me In: The Business Drawing Book for People Who Can't Draw* (Palo Alto: Cucina Media, 2017), is useful to anyone interested in sketchnoting, including people who already have drawing skills.

Our thoughts are not always under our direct control—For an overview of recent understandings of the complex relationships between cognitive control and automatic mental processes, see Jonathan D. Cohen, "Cognitive Control: Core Constructs and Current Considerations," in *The Wiley Handbook of Cognitive Control* (Hoboken, NJ: John Wiley and Sons, 2017), 1–28.

Page 5

What we experience as mind—Stephen M. Kosslyn and Olivier Koenig wrote, "The mind is what the brain does," in their book *Wet Mind: The New Cognitive Neuroscience* (New York: Free Press, 1992), 4. This book helped popularize the turn from mechanistic to biological understandings of human thought processes.

The cerebral cortex of our primate ancestors—Is there a qualitative difference between human and nonhuman minds? Frans de Waal, author of *Our Inner Ape: A Leading Primatologist Explains Why We Are Who We Are* (New York: Riverhead Books, 2005), has devoted much of his career to understanding the continuities between human and nonhuman minds. See also Frans de Waal, "Darwin's Last Laugh," *Nature* 460, no. 7252 (2009): 175–175. For the argument that our capacity for symbolic, abstract thought sets us apart from other animals, see Derek Penn, Keith Holyoak, and Daniel Povinelli, "Darwin's Mistake: Explaining the Discontinuity between Human and Nonhuman Minds," *Behavioral and Brain Sciences* 31, no.2 (2008): 109.

Glaciers—"How Old Is Glacier Ice?" 2021. *Usgs.Gov*, http://www.usgs.gov/faqs/how-old-glacier-ice?qt-news_science_products=0#qt-news_science_products.

Exaptation—The term "exaptation" was coined by evolutionary biologists Stephen Jay Gould and Elisabeth Vrba to describe their observation that "many features of organisms are non-adapted, but available for useful cooptation in descendants." "Exaptation—A Missing Term in the Science of Form," *Paleobiology* 8, no. 1 (1982): 4.

In considering the nature of human thought, they write:

> The two evolutionary phenomena that may have been most crucial to the development of complexity with consciousness on our planet (if readers will pardon some dripping anthropocentrism for the moment)—the process of creating genetic redundancy in the first place, and the myriad and inescapable consequences of building any computing device as complex as the human brain—may both represent exaptations that began as nonaptations . . . the codification of exaptation not only identifies a common flaw in much evolutionary reasoning-the inference of historical genesis from current utility. It also focuses attention upon the neglected but paramount role of nonadaptive features in both constraining and facilitating the path of evolution. (15)

Page 6

Thought is embodied and situated—The theory of situated cognition, a dynamic systems approach, developed in response to the idea that thinking is a computational process that takes place mainly within the brain. "Situated cognition" describes how human knowledge and understandings are created dynamically through ongoing interactions with our physical and sociocultural surroundings. "Embodied cognition" describes how conscious thoughts are the result of a complex series of top-down, bottom-up interactions, in which concepts and percepts are continually updated from multiple sources of information flowing between the brain, the whole body and surroundings. See Phillip Robbins and Murat Aydede, "A Short Primer on Situated Cognition," in *The Cambridge Handbook of Situated Cognition*, ed. Philip Robbins and Murat Aydede (Cambridge: Cambridge University Press, 2009), 3–9.

Page 7

Stream of consciousness—William James, often acknowledged as the father of the modern field of psychology, invented the phrase "stream of consciousness." See William James and Robert Drummond, *The Principles of Psychology* (New York: Henry Holt, 1890/1983).

For much of the twentieth century, James's understanding of human cognition was seen as outdated, and was superseded by mechanistic and computational models. Recently, James's model of thought as fluid and everchanging has found new resonance in biological models of the mind, such as Kosslyn and Koenig's 1992 book, *Wet Mind* (cited earlier). James's formulation of psychological principles was very influenced by Darwin's theory of natural selection, and sought to apply the idea of selective adaptation to mental functions. See Lucas McGranahan, *Darwinism and Pragmatism: William James on Evolution and Self-Transformation* (London: Routledge, 2017).

A river in which waters are always changing—The pre-Socratic philosopher Heraclitus said, "On those stepping into rivers staying the same other and other waters flow." It's not exactly the same as the common phrase "You can't step in the same river twice." The river only stays the same if the waters are always changing. Consciousness is maintained in a similar way, in a constant state of movement and flux. See Daniel W. Graham, "Heraclitus," in *Stanford Encyclopedia of Philosophy (Summer 2021 Edition)*, ed. Edward N. Zalta, https://plato.stanford.edu/entries/heraclitus/.

Page 8

New technologies have made it possible to begin to see inside the brain—For a good introduction to brain structure and function, see National Institute of Neurological Disorders and Stroke, "Brain Basics: Know Your Brain," http://www.ninds.nih.gov/Disorders/Patient-Caregiver-Education/Know-Your-Brain (accessed Dec. 1, 2021).

Functional magnetic resonance imaging (fMRI) and electroencephalogram (EEG) studies have been conducted on subjects engaged in a broad range of different kinds of mental activity, including drawing. Human fMRI studies are used to implicate specific brain structures, but can contain erroneous data because of motion artifacts. Techniques such as mental simulation, head constraints, and a fiber optic stylus have been used to overcome this limitation; however, fMRI does not provide precise temporal information. EEGs provide detailed temporal information, but give only a generalized sense of the particular brain structures activated by a given task.

Neuroscientists also learn about the brain through case studies—V. S. Ramachandran's research on phantom limbs and synesthesia is an example of neuroscience based on case studies. His book *The Tell-Tale Brain* covers his research and also posits some theories regarding experiences of beauty and art. See Vilayanur S. Ramachandran, *The Tell-Tale Brain: A Neuroscientist's Quest for What Makes Us Human* (New York: W. W. Norton, 2011).

Page 9

Neuroaesthetics is an emerging field—This field studies how "the complexity of aesthetic experience is reflected by the interplay between dynamic brain systems, whose neurofunctional organization may be modulated by different factors associated to objects, subjects and contexts of the aesthetic experience and can undergo rapid, plastic changes when these factors are manipulated." Louise P. Kirsch, Cosimo Urgesi, and Emily S. Cross, "Shaping and Reshaping the Aesthetic Brain: Emerging Perspectives on the Neurobiology of Embodied Aesthetics," *Neuroscience and Biobehavioral Reviews* 62 (2016): 57.

Dr. Anjun Chatterjee, professor of neuroscience and neuroimaging at the University of Pennsylvania, has written an accessible introduction to neuroaesthetics. See Anjun Chatterjee, *The Aesthetic Brain: How We Evolved to Desire Beauty and Enjoy Art* (New York: Oxford University Press, 2014).

Page 10

Goal-directed thought proceeds from the top down—In visual attention, top-down processes are driven by what someone is looking for, whereas bottom-up processes are driven by environmental stimuli. See Jan Theeuwes, "Top–Down and Bottom–Up Control of Visual Selection," *Acta Psychologica* 135, no. 2 (2010): 77–99.

Prefrontal cortex—"Cognitive control stems from the active maintenance of patterns of activity in the prefrontal cortex that represent goals and the means to achieve them." Earl Miller and Jonathan D. Cohen, "An Integrative Theory of Prefrontal Cortex Function," *Annual Review of Neuroscience* 24, no.1 (2001): 167–202.

Executive function—An influential meta-analysis of "193 functional neuroimaging studies of 2,832 healthy individuals" found "a superordinate cognitive control network in the brain. . . . A common pattern of activation was observed in the prefrontal, dorsal anterior cingulate, and parietal cortices across executive function domains, supporting the idea that executive functions are supported by a superordinate cognitive control network." Tara A. Niendam, Angela R. Laird, Kimberly L. Ray, Y. Monica Dean, et al., "Meta-Analytic Evidence for a Superordinate Cognitive Control Network Subserving Diverse Executive Functions," *Cognitive, Affective, and Behavioral Neuroscience* 12, no. 2 (2012): 241.

Our closest cousins—The gray matter (neurons) of the human prefrontal cortex (PFC) is proportionally 1.9 times greater than the macaque monkey and 1.2 times the size of the chimpanzee. When we measure subcortical white matter (glial cells, which connect neurons to each other), the disparity is even larger: 2.9 times greater than the macaque and 1.7 times greater than the chimpanzee. "Using tissue volume analyses, we show a disproportionately large amount of gray and white matter corresponding to PFC in humans compared with nonhuman primates." Chad J. Donahue, Matthew F. Glasser, Todd M. Preuss, James K. Rilling, and David C. Van Essen, "Quantitative Assessment of Prefrontal Cortex in Humans Relative to Nonhuman Primates," *Proceedings of the National Academy of Sciences* 115, no. 22 (2018): E5183.

Metacognition—"Metacognition refers to higher order thinking which involves active control over the cognitive processes. . . . Metacognitive strategies are sequential processes that one uses to control cognitive activities, and to ensure that a cognitive goal (e.g., understanding a text) has been met. These processes help to regulate and oversee learning, and consist of planning and monitoring cognitive activities, as well as checking the outcomes of those activities." Jennifer A. Livingston, "Metacognition: An Overview," *ERIC Document Reproduction Service*, no. ED47427 (2003): 2.

A lot can go wrong—The case of Phineas Gage taught neuroscientists about both the remarkable resilience of the brain and the crucial importance of the prefrontal cortex. Gage was a 25-year-old railroad construction foreman, and on September 25, 1848, he was the victim of a horrific accident: a sharp iron rod, over an inch thick and 40 inches long, was thrust into the front of his skull. In many ways, he fully recovered. Yet his personality had changed; his doctor, John Harlow, reported, "Gage was no longer Gage." His respect for social conventions had vanished completely. He lived for twelve more years, but his inability to act responsibly made it impossible for him to ever hold a similar job. When his skull was examined twenty years after his death, it was concluded that the main impact was in the frontal region, what we now call the PFC. More recently, Hana Damasio and colleagues reconstructed the injury based on photographs of Gage's skull. They found the main impact was to specific areas of the PFC. See Hana Damasio, Thomas Grabowski, Randall Frank, Albert M. Galaburda, and Antonio R. Damasio, "The Return of Phineas Gage: Clues about the Brain from the Skull of a Famous Patient," *Science* 264, no. 5162 (1994): 1102–1105. See also John M. Harlow, "Passage of an Iron Rod through the Head," *Bulletin of the Massachusetts Medical Society* 39, no. 20 (1868): 383.

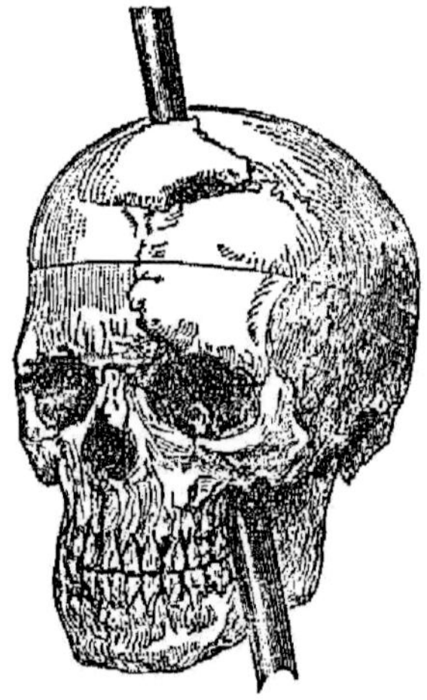

Diagram by John M. Harlow, M.D., Phineas Gage's doctor. (From "Passage of an iron bar through the head.")

Much thought flows from the bottom up—According to the American Psychology Association, bottom-up processing is "information processing in which incoming stimulus data initiate and determine the higher level processes involved in their recognition, interpretation, and categorization. . . . Typically, perceptual or cognitive mechanisms use bottom-up processing when information is unfamiliar or highly complex." See "Bottom-up processing," in *APA Dictionary of Psychology*, dictionary.apa.org/bottom-up-processing (accessed December 1, 2021).

Page 11

Emotion—Darwin laid out the evolutionary and biological basis for the fundamental emotions that we share with other animals: fear, anger, disgust, sadness, joy, and surprise. These fundamental emotions, said Darwin, emerge from even more fundamental drives toward pleasure and away from pain. See Charles Darwin, *The Expression of the Emotions in Man and Animals* (New York: Oxford University Press, 1998/1872).

There are multiple taxonomies of emotion. I am here relying on Paul Ekman, whose definition of the six basic emotions—joy, anger, fear, disgust, sadness, and surprise—has been widely adopted. Ekman also identified involuntary cross-cultural facial expressions that signal our emotions to others. See Paul Ekman, "Basic Emotions," *Handbook of Cognition and Emotion* 98, no. 45–60 (1999): 16.

Gary Fagin's guide to drawing facial expressions is also based on Paul Ekman's research. See Gary Faigin, *The Artist's Complete Guide to Facial Expression* (New York: Watson-Guptill, 2012).

Emotion can be generated and regulated by both top-down and bottom-up processes—Kevin Oschner and colleagues looked at top-down and bottom-up emotional responses and found there were multiple pathways in both directions: "Our data suggest that humans are emotional in part because of their intellectual—that is, cognitive—capacities. More broadly, the finding of separable bottom-up and top-down routes for generation of negative emotion provides a neural foundation for emotion theories positing multiple kinds of appraisal processes, some of which are bottom-up and triggered reflexively, and some of which are top-down and highly cognitive." Kevin Ochsner, Rebecca R. Ray, Brent Hughes, Kateri McRae, et al., "Bottom-Up and Top-Down Processes in Emotion Generation: Common and Distinct Neural Mechanisms," *Psychological Science* 20, no. 11 (2009): 1330.

Emotions are generated "by multiple neural systems, each supporting distinct types of emotion-relevant computations, different combinations of which will be engaged depending upon the nature of the stimulus and one's response." Laura Martin, Rebecca R. Ray, Brent Hughes, Kateri McRae, et al., "Explicit and Implicit Emotion Regulation: A Multi-Level Framework," *Social Cognitive and Affective Neuroscience* 12, no. 10 (2017): 1545.

Emotions put us in motion—Antonio Damasio divides emotive responses into three categories, "triggered by processing. myriad sensory stimuli such as tastes, smells, tactile, auditory, and visual stimuli" and "resulting from engaging drives (such as hunger or thirst) or motivations (such as lust and play) or emotions, in the more conventional sense of the term, which are action programs activated by confrontation with numerous and sometimes complex situations." Antonio Damasio, *The Strange Order of Things: Life, Feeling and the Making of Cultures* (New York: Pantheon Books, 2018), 101.

Damasio further writes, "Feelings then can be mental sensors of the organism's interior, witnesses of life on the fly." Antonio Damasio, *Looking for Spinoza: Joy, Sorrow, and the Feeling Brain* (Orlando, FL: Harcourt, 2003), 139.

We "feel our way"—This refers to a system of salience detection and response, anchored deep in an ancient part of the brain, in what has been called the limbic system. This is our emotional control center. Neuroscientist A. D. "Bud" Craig writes, "The unified representation of all salient conditions—represented as feelings—is in effect a representation of the entirety of the individual . . . a continuously updating series of global emotional moments . . . that incorporates predictive representations based on acquired internal models."A. D. Bud Craig, "The Sentient Self," *Brain Structure and Function* 214, nos. 5–6 (2010): 573. See also A. D. Bud Craig, "Interoception and Emotion: A Neuroanatomical Perspective," in *Handbook of Emotions*, ed. Michael Lewis et al. (New York: Guilford Press, 2010), 272–289; A. D. Craig, "How Do You Feel—Now? The Anterior Insula and Human Awareness," *Nature Reviews Neuroscience* 10, no. 1 (2009): 59–70; Hugo D. Critchley, "Neural Mechanisms of Autonomic, Affective, and Cognitive Integration," *Journal of Comparative Neurology* 493. no. 1 (2005): 154–166.

Page 12

"The life of reason—demands . . . a love of truth and a contempt for lying, a concern for accuracy in observation and inference, and a corresponding repugnance at error in logic or fact ... We define ourselves and orient our actions in the light of our situation as appraised. Characteristic orientations are associated with distinctive emotional dispositions, and both involve seeing the environment in a certain light; is it, for example, beneficial or harmful, promising or threatening, fulfilling or thwarting?"

Israel Scheffler, *"In Praise of the Cognitive Emotions," in In Praise of the Cognitive Emotions: And Other Essays in the Philosophy of Education* (New York: Routledge, 1991), 4.

Emotion and reason are in a dynamic relationship—"Investigations into the neural systems underlying human behavior demonstrate that the mechanisms of emotion and cognition are intertwined from early perception to reasoning." Elizabeth Phelps, "Emotion and Cognition: Insights from Studies of the Human Amygdala," *Annual Review of Psychology* 57 (2006): 27. See also Antonio Damasio, *The Feeling of What Happens: Body and Emotion in the Making of Consciousness* (New York: Harcourt Brace, 1999).

We are infovores—"Human beings are designed to be 'infovores.' It's a craving that begins with a simple preference for certain types of stimuli, then proceeds to more sophisticated levels of perception and cognition that draw on associations the brain makes with previous experiences. . . . If infovore behavior is so valuable to our species, one would expect the brain to have cellular and molecular mechanisms that encourage the acquisition of information. We believe we have identified such a system, and it is associated with a reward network that relies on the brain's natural opioids." Irving Biederman and Edward A. Vessel, "Perceptual Pleasure and the Brain: A Novel Theory Explains Why the Brain Craves Information and Seeks It through the Senses," *American Scientist* 94, no. 3 (2006): 247.

Page 13

Default mode network—The default mode network (DMN) comprises multiple brain areas, and "activates when individuals are engaged in internally focused tasks (i.e., those of a self-referential introspective nature, including autobiographical memory retrieval, envisioning the future, and conceiving the perspectives of others. However, the network also maintains high levels of metabolic activity at rest, in the absence of any task demands." "Default mode network," *APA Dictionary of Psychology*, dictionary.apa.org/default-mode-network (accessed December 1, 2021).

In an FMRI study of responses to art images, reasearch found that "DMN regions could be positively activated also in structured tasks, if those tasks involved self-referential thought or self-relevant information. . . . This mediates a sense of being 'moved,' or 'touched from within.'" Ed A. Vessel, Gabrielle Starr, and Nava Rubin, "Art Reaches Within: Aesthetic Experience, the Self and the Default Mode Network," *Frontiers in Neuroscience* 7 (2013): 258.

Neuroscientists describe mind-wandering as activation of the DMN, which goes online when we daydream, but is also associated with the generation of new ideas and connections. See Benjamin Baird Jonathan Smallwood, Michael D. Mrazek, Julia W. Y. Kam, et al., "Inspired by Distraction: Mind Wandering Facilitates Creative Incubation," *Psychological Science* 23, no. 10 (2012): 1117–1122.

Page 14

When we take the time to pay attention—Drawing is one of a variety of mindfulness practices, which may, over time, improve interoceptive accuracy and positively impact our physical and psychological health. *The Embodied Mind: Cognitive Science and Human Experience*, first published in 1991, lays out the relationship between cognitive science and Buddhist-influenced mindfulness practices. Francisco J., Varela, Evan Thompson, and Eleanor Rosch, *The Embodied Mind: Cognitive Science and Human Experience*, rev. ed. (Cambridge, MA: MIT Press, 2017).

chapter two
Below the Surface

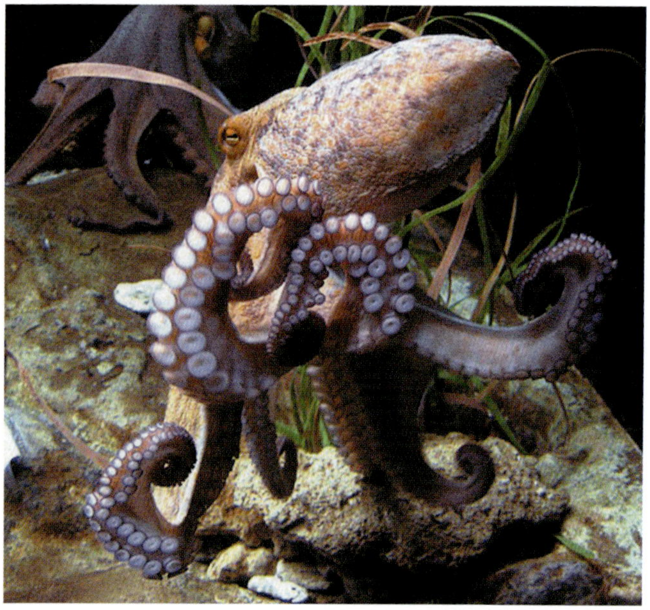

Octopus vulgaris Common Octopus — L'Aquarium de Barcelona. Photo by Anneli Salo (2007) Wiki Commons.

Page 18

The octopus—The size of the nervous system of the octopus is similar proportionally to a dog, yet is much more spread out in its body between its head and eight arms. Its intelligence (for example, its ability to learn and remember) "emerges from the octopus's embodied organization. The term 'intelligent embodiment' comes from robotics and refers to an approach to designing autonomous robots in which the behavior emerges from the dynamic physical and sensory interactions of the agent's materials, morphology and environment. Consideration of the unusual neurobiology of the octopus in the light of its unique morphology suggests that similar embodied principles are instrumental for understanding the emergence of intelligent behavior in all biological systems." Binyamin Hochner, "An Embodied View of Octopus Neurobiology," *Current Biology* 22, no. 20 (2012): R887–R892.

Philosopher of science Peter Godfrey-Smith objects to anthropomorphizing the octopus, emphasizing that they have come by their intelligence by a very different evolutionary process than humans:

In an octopus, the majority of neurons are in the arms themselves—nearly twice as many in total as in the central brain. The arms have their own sensors and controllers. They have not only the sense of touch but also the capacity to sense chemicals—to smell or taste. Each sucker on an octopus's arm may have 10,000 neurons to handle taste and touch . . . it is not clear where the brain itself begins and ends. The octopus is suffused with nervousness; the body is not a separate thing that is controlled by the brain or nervous system. The usual debate is between those who see the brain as an all-powerful CEO and those who emphasize the intelligence stored in the body itself. But the octopus lives outside both the usual pictures. It has a body—but one that is protean, all possibility; it has none of the costs and gains of a constraining and action-guiding body. The octopus lives outside the usual body/brain divide.

Peter Godfrey-Smith, "The Mind of an Octopus," *Scientific American Mind* 28, no.1 (2017): 62–69, http://doi.org/10.1038/scientificamericanmind0117-62.

Embodied—For a good introduction to the concept of embodied cognition, see Christie Aschwanden, "Where Do Thoughts Occur?" *Discover Magazine*, May 19, 2013, http://www.discovermagazine.com/mind/where-do-thoughts-occur.

Page 20

"We are least aware of what our minds do best"—Marvin Minsky was a cognitive and computer scientist, known as one of the pioneers of the field of artificial intelligence. He wrote, "The human brain performs its great variety of functions by exploiting the advantages of many different knowledge representations, reasoning methods, and other mechanisms. It is this diversity that enables us, when any part fails, to manage to do things in other ways. Marvin Minsky, *The Society of Mind* (New York: Simon and Schuster, 1985), 29.

Page 21

Our bodies constantly monitor the external and internal environments—Neuroscientist Antonio Damasio explains the evolutionary continuity between homeostatic processes in unicellular organims (such as the amoeba and paramecium depicted on these pages) and the most sophisticated and complex products of human cultures. Homeostasis, the steady maintenance of optimal functioning of living organisms, underlies the behavior of all organisms, including us. Sensations of pain and pleasure evolved 600 million years ago, along with the first nervous systems in living animals. These sensations motivate avoidance and attraction behaviors to maintain homeostasis and guide necessary adjustments See Antonio Damasio, *The Strange Order of Things: Life, Feeling, and the Making of Cultures* (New York: Pantheon, 2019).

Eric Kandel and other neuroscientists have unraveled mysteries of learning and memory by studying the lowly sea slug, Aplysia, a creature they love because its relatively few neurons (20,000 or so, compared to our 86 billion in the brain alone) are visible to the naked eye. Aplysia may be something like the last ancestor humans and octopuses had in common. See Eric Kandel, *In Search of Memory: The Emergence of a New Science of Mind* (New York: W. W. Norton, 2007).

Page 22

Body Language—Cognitive linguists George Lakoff and Mark Johnson propose that the "metaphors we live by," including abstract concepts like freedom or justice, are rooted in our bodily experiences. See George Lakoff and Mark Johnson, *Metaphors We Live By* (Chicago: University of Chicago Press, 1980). See also George Lakoff and Mark Johnson, *Philosophy in the Flesh: The Embodied Mind and Its Challenge to Western Thought* (New York: Basic Books, 1999).

Our internal thoughts and perceptions include so much more than words—Vinod Goel, in *Sketches of Thought* (Cambridge, MA: MIT Press, 1995), argues that sketches may provide a better model of human thought than a computer. The dense, rich, and ill-defined qualities of sketches make them fertile territory for new ideas because they mirror the richly layered, complex, and ill-defined characteristics of much of human thought. Goel borrowed Nelson Goodman's (1976) distinction between "repleteness" and "attenuation" to describe sketches. Natural language and sketching can both be ambiguous, undifferentiated, and expressive. Language is attenuated; sketching alone is replete. As Goodman said, "Any thickening or thinning of the line, its color, its contrast with the background, its size, even the qualities of the paper—none of these is ruled out, none can be ignored." Nelson Goodman, *Languages of Art: An Approach to a Theory of Symbols* (Indianapolis: Hackett, 1976),

228, 230. Because of "repleteness," sketches, like internal thoughts, can resist fixed meanings and generate new directions for further inquiry.

Page 23

We are often blind to our own ignorance—Steven Sloman and Philip Fernbach write, "Our point is not that people are ignorant. It's that people are more ignorant than they think they are. We all suffer to a greater or lesser extent, from an illusion of understanding." For more on how (and why) we think we know more than we really do, see Steven Sloman and Philip Fernbach, *The Knowledge Illusion: Why We Never Think Alone* (New York: Penguin, 2018), 8.

The "illusion of explanatory depth" is a category of common systematic cognitive errors: "People feel they understand complex phenomena with far greater precision, coherence, and depth than they really do. . . . The illusion is far stronger for explanatory knowledge than many other kinds of knowledge, such as that for facts, procedures or narratives. The illusion of explanatory knowledge is most robust where the environment supports real-time explanations with visible mechanisms." Frank Keil and Leonid Rozenblit, "The Misunderstood Limits of Folk Science: An Illusion of Explanatory Depth," *Cognitive Science* 26, no. 5 (2002): 521.

The Dunning-Kruger Effect—"This meta-ignorance (or ignorance of ignorance) arises because lack of expertise and knowledge often hides in the realm of the 'unknown unknowns' or is disguised by erroneous beliefs and background knowledge that only appear to be sufficient to conclude a right answer." David Dunning, "The Dunning–Kruger Effect: On Being Ignorant of One's Own Ignorance," in *Advances in Experimental Social Psychology*, vol. 44, ed. Mark Zanna and James Olson (San Diego: Academic Press, 2011), 247–296.

"We know more than we can tell"—Michael Polanyi started off as a chemist, publishing his first paper at 19. After making important contributions to both physical and social science, he turned his attention to the contribution of embodied cognition to the progress of scientific understandings of the world. In this work, he anticipated more recent discoveries by neuroscience: visceral neural simulation in response to observed events (for example, see chapter 5, "Mirror Neurons"). Polanyi wrote, "Physiologists long ago established that the way we see an object is determined by our awareness of certain efforts inside our body, efforts which we cannot feel in themselves. We are aware of these things going on inside our body in terms of the position, size, shape and motion of an object to which we are attending. In other words we are attending from these internal processes to the qualities of things outside. These qualities are what those processes mean to us." Michael Polyani, *The Tacit Dimension* (Chicago: University of Chicago Press, 1966), 13–14.

Holistic sense of reality—That the whole is more than the sum of its parts is one of the key defining principles of gestalt psychology. This principle is made visible in illusions, such as the Kanizsa triangle pictured to the right, which illustrates the Gestalt "Law of Closure." The psychologist Gaetano Kanizsa invented this graphic in 1955 to demonstrate Gestalt principles. In the Kanizsa triangle, we clearly see two triangles and three circles, even though technically there are only three Pacman-like shapes and three angled lines.

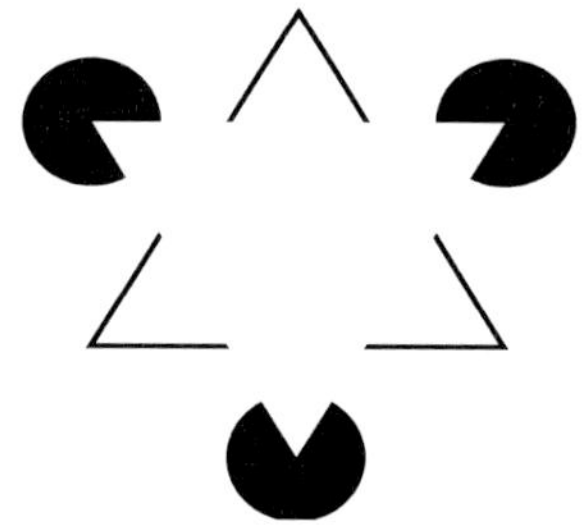

Created by Oleana Panasovska for the Noun Project (2021). https://thenounproject.com/term/kanizsa-triangle/.

Stephen Wiltshire—For a detailed description of Wiltshire's remarkable drawing abilities, read neuroscientist and writer Oliver Sacks's description of his meeting with the artist in his book *An Anthropologist on Mars*. Oliver Sacks, "Prodigies," in *An Anthropologist on Mars: Seven Paradoxical Tales* (New York: Vintage, 1995), 179–232.

Patients who have sustained brain damage—In *The Mind's Eye* and other books, Oliver Sacks tells stories of patients who were able to regain function and reinvent themselves in surprising ways after losing seemingly indispensable mental faculties. Oliver Sacks, *The Mind's Eye* (London: Picador, 2010).

Page 24

The automated procedures, habits, and routines—Automation (of routine tasks and activities) has its advantages. As Wendy Wood and Dennis Runger write in their literature review, "The Psychology of Habit": "Habits form through incremental experience and do not shift readily with changes in people's goals and plans. Also, by outsourcing action control to environmental cues, people have a ready response when distraction, time pressure, lowered willpower, and stress reduce the capacity to deliberate about action and tailor responses to current environments. Furthermore, habit systems are smart in the sense that they enable people to efficiently capitalize on environmental regularities." Wendy Wood and Dennis Runger, "The Psychology of Habit," *Annual Review of Psychology* 67 (2016): 313.

Page 25

When most of us learned how to walk—There is a growing appreciation for the importance of motor development within cognitive development. Developmental psychologist Karen Adolph and colleagues describe the advantage all motor actions have for researchers, as evidence of cognitive processes because they are directly observable, and this adds to a growing understanding of cognition as both embodied and embedded in the environment. Karen Adolph, Whitney G. Cole, Meghana Komati, Jessie S. Garciaguirre, et al., "How Do You Learn to Walk? Thousands of Steps and Dozens of Falls Per Day," *Psychological Science* 23, no. 11 (2012): 1387–1394.

"Infants' first steps while learning to walk reflect individual, idiosyncratic solutions: 'Steppers' take small, conservative steps to minimize disruptions to upright posture; 'fallers' lurch forward while their feet hurry to catch up; 'twisters' swing each leg around like a compass by twisting their trunk to generate angular momentum. . . . Within a few months, infants learn to exploit the pendular motions of their legs." Karen Adolph and Justine Hoch, "Motor Development: Embodied, Embedded, Enculturated, and Enabling," *Annual Review of Psychology* 70, no. 1 (2019): 146, https://doi.org/10.1146/annurev-psych-010418-102836.

We think we see a whole scene at once—The area of focus is called the *fovea*, and it allows you to see an area about the size of your thumbnail at arm's length. Our eyes must dart from spot to spot in milliseconds in order to "see" the whole scene. These ballistic eye movements are called *saccades*. Karl R. Gegenfurtner, "The Interaction between Vision and Eye Movements," *Perception* 45, no. 12 (2016): 1333–1357.

Page 26

Neuroscientists estimate—"Physiological studies of the cortex have shown the dominance and importance of the visual modality. Over much of the posterior half of the cortex, involving parts classifed as occipital, parietal and temporal, cells are visually responsive and some degree of retinotopic mapping is retained. A large number (30) of separate retinotopic maps, or visual areas, have been identifed. Cells in each map possess different response properties." John M. Findlay and Iain D. Gilchrist, *Active Vision: The Psychology of Looking and Seeing* (Oxford: Oxford University Press, 2003), 19.

David Williams, director of the University of Rochester's Center for Visual Science, states,"More than 50 percent of the cortex, the surface of the brain, is devoted to processing visual information. . . . Understanding how vision works may be a key to understanding how the brain as a whole works." His colleague, David Krill explains, "We mistakenly think of human vision like a camera. . . . We have this metaphor of an image being cast on the retina and we tend to think of vision as capturing images and sending them to the brain, like a video camera recording to a digital tap. . . . We learn to see. It's something we have spent our lives learning to do, so we can't imagine not understanding what we are seeing." Susan Hagan, "The Mind's Eye," *Rochester Review: University of Rochester* 74, no. 4 (2012): 35.

Interpretation of bodily sensations—Interoception is the perception of involuntary signals originating within the body, from multiple organ systems, including the heart, lungs, and gut. Individuals with more accurate subjective awareness of their internal bodily states (interoception) also report more intense emotions when viewing pleasant and unpleasant pictures. "Being in touch with your feelings" correlates across bodily and psychological self-perception. See Olga Pollatos, Klaus Gramann, and Rainer Schandry, "Neural Systems Connecting Interoceptive Awareness and Feelings," *Human Brain Mapping* 28, no. 1 (2007): 9–18.

"See like someone who has just been born!" Letter from Paul Cezanne to Jules Borely, 1902; quoted by Paul Smith, "Cezanne's 'Primitive' Perspective, or the 'View from Everywhere,'" *Art Bulletin* 95, no. 1 (2013): 102.

Drawing sound—There is a fascinating tradition of graphic notation in music. Product designer David Hall has collected some beautiful examples on his blog. "Graphic Notation: A Brief History of Visualising Music:" May 30, 2020, http://davidhall.io/visualising-music-graphic-scores/. See also Orfeo Overture, "Art and Music Collide in These 20 Stunning Graphic Scores," *Classic FM*, http://www.classicfm.com/discover-music/latest/graphic-scores-art-music-pictures/, accessed December 3, 2021.

Page 27

Bodily experiences—We construct visual metaphors that are grounded in bodily experiences. The Gestalt psychologist Rudolf Arnheim asked us to consider that "vision [is] a creative activity of the human mind" in his classic work *Art and Visual Perception* (Berkeley, CA: University of California Press, 1954/1974), 46.

Paul Cézanne—Cézanne's emphasis on the subjective experience of perception over the object perceived laid the foundation for cubism and other modern art movements. "Paul Cézanne died in October 1906 at the age of 67. In time he would be generally regarded as the most influential painter who had worked in the nineteenth century (e.g., Clive Bell, 1982; Clement Greenberg, 1993)." David Galenson and Bruce

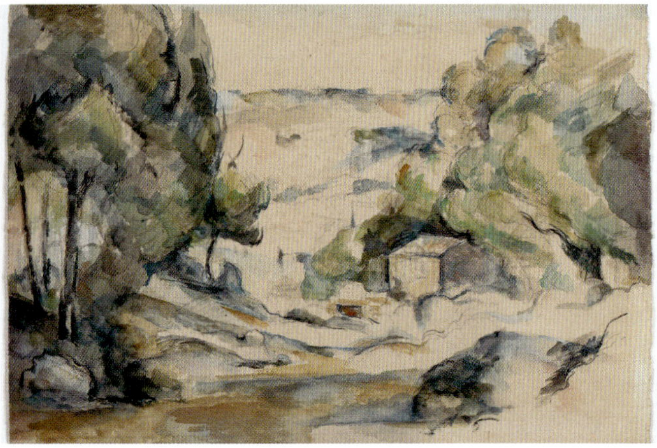

Paul Cezanne, Landscape in the Provence, *1860–1906, Cezannecatalogue.com, https://www.cezannecatalogue.com/ Copyright: Public Domain.*

Weinberg, "Creating Modern Art: The Changing Careers of Painters in France from Impressionism to Cubism," *American Economic Review* 91, no. 4 (2001): 1063–1071.

Phenomonology—"Phenomenology is the study of structures of consciousness as experienced from the first-person point of view." David Woodruff Smith, "Phenomenology," in *The Stanford Encyclopedia of Philosophy* (Summer 2018 edition), ed. Edward N. Zalta, plato.stanford.edu/entries/phenomenology/.

Merleau-Ponty—The French philosopher Maurice Merleau-Ponty explored the embodied nature of lived experience. He was influenced by earlier philosophers of existentialism (Jean-Paul Sartre and Simone de Beauvoir) and phenomenology (Edmund Husserl and Martin Heidegger) as well as Gestalt psychology, modern art, and literature. Stephanie Menase, in her foreword to a collection of essays by Merleau-Ponty, describes how the philosopher "complements this account of philosophy with a discussion of modern art in which he suggests that painters such as Cézanne likewise aim to make apparent to us the ways in which the emergence of the ordinary world in visual experience is 'strange and paradoxical.'" Stephanie Menase, foreword to *Maurice Merleau-Ponty: Basic Writings*, ed. Thomas Baldwin (London: Routledge, 2004), 14.

"Cézanne said that you should be able to paint the smell of trees." Maurice Merleau-Ponty, *The World of Perception* (London: Routledge, 2002), 3.

Page 29

We can reexamine them closely, pull them apart—"How is it that sketchers can see new things in their own sketches? One possibility is that they regroup the parts into new wholes, with different meanings. A protocol analysis of an experienced architect confirmed this hypothesis: regrouping parts of sketch drove detection of new features in sketches. Further, novices who adopted this strategy generated more interpretations of ambiguous sketches than those who didn't adopt the strategy." Masaki Suwa, Barbara Tversky, John Gero and Terry Purcell, "Seeing into Sketches: Regrouping Parts Encourages New Interpretations," in *Visual and Spatial Reasoning in Design II*, ed. J. S. Gero, B. Tversky and T. Purcell (Sydney: Key Centre of Design Computing and Cognition, University of Sydney, Australia, 2001), 207.

Draw into the present moment—Drawing can be experienced as one of many contemplative practices, and as such provides many of the same benefits. "What seems to matter is not so much the particular type of contemplative practice, but rather that it is applied with sustained effort." Boris Bornemann and Tania Singer, "Taking Time to Feel Our Body: Steady Increases in Heartbeat Perception Accuracy and Decreases in Alexithymia over 9 Months of Contemplative Mental Training," *Psychophysiology* 54, no. 3 (2017): 479.

The "sketchiness" of much of human thought—See Vinod Goel, *Sketches of Thought* (Cambridge, MA: MIT Press, 1995), 28.

chapter three
The Thinking Hand

Page 37

Down from the Trees—Neurologist Frank Wilson specializes in treating musicians' hand injuries. He details the parallel evolution of the human hand and brain in his book, *The Hand: How Its Use Shapes the Brain, Language and Human Culture* (New York: Vintage, 1999). He pulls together a wide range of research in primatology and his own anatomical expertise to show how hands, in tandem with the arm and shoulder, evolved in response to the needs of our primate ancestors' life in the trees. When our hominid antecedents came down from the trees to walk on two feet, the particular anatomy of their hands, wrists, arms, and shoulders were well suited to tool making and tool use, among other things. Wilson explains the advantages of the human hand has over the hands of nonhuman primates. We have greater freedom of movement, power, and control in our arms and hands, to be used as needed. Wilson, as a neurosurgeon, is particularly aware that this freedom also contributes to greater risk of physical injury to our hands, wrists, arms and shoulders.

How the paw became a hand—The physician John Napier called attention to two basic kinds of grips that we share with other primates: the power grip and the precise grip. We generally (but not always!) draw using a precise grip. See John Napier, "The Evolution of the Hand," *Scientific American* 207, no. 6 (1962): 56–65.

Page 38

Holding hands—Jung-Soon Moon and Kyung-Sook Cho, "The Effects of Handholding on Anxiety in Cataract Surgery Patients under Local Anaesthesia," *Journal of Advanced Nursing* 35, no. 3 (2001): 407–415.

Mens et Manus—"Head and Hand" in Latin: this is MIT's motto. "The craftsman at the anvil and the scholar with a book on the seal of the Massachusetts Institute of Technology embody the educational philosophy of William Barton Rogers and other incorporators of MIT as stated in their 1860 proposal . . . [that] call[s] for the most earnest co-operation of intelligent culture with industrial pursuits." MIT Libraries, "MIT History: Seal of the Massachusetts Institute of Technology," https://libraries.mit.edu/mithistory/institute/seal-of-the-massachusetts-institute-of-technology/ (accessed December 8, 2021).

Penfields' Homonculi—Penfield's visualization of cortical areas in the form of homunculi have been criticized recently as overly imaginative, obscuring the overlapping of synergistic neural pathways in the brain. Penfield's diagrams, however, still appear in neuroscience textbooks because the point they make regarding the division of sensory and motor cortices accord to body parts is still relevant. See Wilder Penfield and Theodore Rasmussen, *The Cerebral Cortex of Man: A Clinical Study of Localization of Function* (New York: Macmillan. 1950). See also Geoffrey D. Schott, "Penfield's Homunculus: A Note on Cerebral Cartography," *Journal of Neurology, Neurosurgery, and Psychiatry* 56, no. 4 (1993): 329.

Page 39

Affordances—In his influential 1979 text *The Ecological Approach to Visual Perception*, James Gibson provided a general theory of cognitive interaction between animals and their environments. "The affordances of the environment are what it affords the animal, what it provides or furnishes." See: J. J. Gibson, *The Ecological Approach to Visual Perception* (Hillsdale, NJ :Erlbaum, 1979/1986), 127. See also Eleanor J. Gibson and W. A. Collins, "The Concept of Affordances in Development: The Renascence of Functionalism," in *The Concept of Development: The Minnesota Symposia on Child Psychology*, vol. 15, ed. W. Andrews Collins (Hillsdale, NJ: Erlbaum, 1982), 55–81.

Abilities develop through interactions—The theory of distributed cognition calls attention to the ways in which we use our surroundings, including both the natural environment and human artifacts, to help us think. These external supports can also be social, symbolic, or physical. See Gavriel Salomon, ed., *Distributed Cognitions: Psychological and Educational Considerations* (Cambridge: Cambridge University Press, 1996).

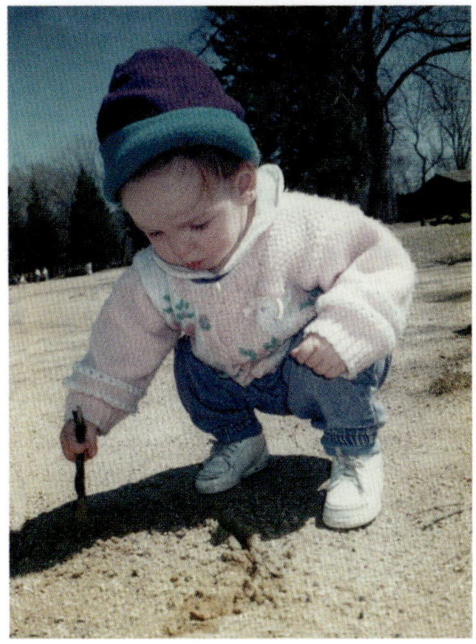

My daughter Anya at 18 months drawing a circle in the sand. She was very intent at making sure the line ended up where it began. Family photo.

Learning to act is learning to think—Developmental psychologist Esther Thelen pioneered an understanding of the interdependence of motor and cognitive development as an epigenetic phenomena. "We address specifically the developmental origins of cognition. . . . It has been widely acknowledged that all forms of human thought must somehow arise from the purely sensorimotor activities of infants. If we can show that 'knowing' cannot be separated from perceiving, acting, and remembering, then these processes are always linked. There is no time and no task when such dynamics cease and some other mode of processing kicks in. Body and world remain ceaselessly melded together." Esther Thelen, Gregor Schoner, Christian Scheier, and Linda B. Smith, "The Dynamics of Embodiment: A Field Theory of Infant Perseverative Reaching," *Behavioral and Brain Sciences* 24, no. 1 (2001): 1–34.

Page 40

Ziegfeld Follies—Performed from from 1907 to 1931 and produced by Florenz Ziegfeld on Broadway in New York City, the Ziegfeld Follies were a lavish combination of musical theater, vaudeville, burlesque, and minstrel shows, inspired by Parisian turn-of-the-century variety shows. See Ann Ommen van Der Merwe, *The Ziegfeld Follies: A History in Song* (Lanham, MD: Scarecrow Press, 2009), 8–12.

Page 41

Making is thinking—"Nobel laureates were significantly more likely to engage in arts and crafts avocations than Royal Society and National Academy of Sciences members, who were in turn significantly more likely than Sigma Xi members and the U.S. public. Scientists and their biographers often commented on the utility of their avocations as stimuli for their science." Robert Root-Bernstein, Robert, Lindsay Allen, Leighanna Beach, Ragini Bhadula, Justin Fast, Chelsea Hosey, Benjamin Kremkow et al., "Arts Foster Scientific Success: Avocations of Nobel, National Academy, Royal Society, and Sigma Xi Members," *Journal of Psychology of Science and Technology* 1, no. 2 (2008): 51–63.

Pens, pencils, and other handheld tools—As far as our brain is concerned, handheld tools become part of our body, extending our reach. "Recent advances have revealed that body representation is fundamentally multisensory, arising from the combination of many different sensory signals. These include classical 'senses,' such as touch and vision, and also much more specific signals, such as the flexion or extension of each muscle, which define the body's posture in space. . . . Our thoughts about what our body is are highly flexible, and track the multisensory inputs that the brain receives." Lucilla Cardinali Francesca Frassinetti, Claudio Brozzoli, Christian Urquizar, et al., "Tool-Use Induces Morphological Updating of the Body Schema," *Current Biology* 19, no. 12 (2009): R478–R479. See also Patrick Haggard and Matthew R. Longo, "You Are What You Touch: How Tool Use Changes the Brain's Representations of the Body," *Scientific American*, September 7, 2010, www.scientificamerican.com/article/you-are-what-you-touch/. See also Angelo Maravita and Atsushi Iriki, "Tools for the Body (Schema)," *Trends in Cognitive Sciences* 8, no. 2 (2004): 79–86.

Page 42

Froebel's Gifts—Friedrich Froebel (1782–1852) coined the term "kindergarten, and was an important pioneer in the development of "child-centered" education. Interestingly, his teacher, the Swiss educational reformer Johann Pestalozzi, is credited with including drawing for the first time as an essential subject to cultivate children's mental abilities, apart from its aesthetic or occupational value. See Tina Bruce, ed., *Early Childhood Practice: Froebel Today* (Thousand Oaks, CA: Sage, 2012); Clive Ashwin, "Pestalozzi and the Origins of Pedagogical Drawing," *British Journal of Educational Studies* 29, no. 2 (1981): 138–151.

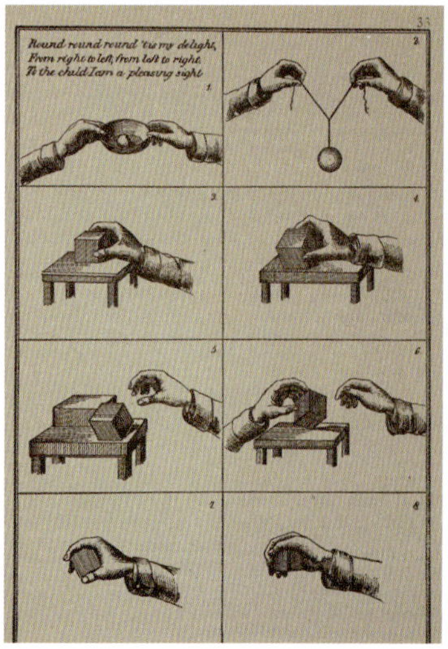

Friedrich Froebel, *Second Gift*, from *Royal Gifts for the Kindergarten, a manual for self-instruction* in Friedrich Froebel's *Principles of Education;* (1889) Library of Congress, https://www.loc.gov/ Copyright: Public Domain.

Sloyd—Swedish for "handicraft." Swedish educational sloyd was strongly influenced by the work of Uno Cygneus in Finland as well as earlier child-centered pedagogues such as Pestalozzi and Froebel. During the late nineteenth and early twentieth centuries, this pedagogy became influential among progressive thinkers and educators internationally, including William James and John Dewey in the United States. See Brynjar Olafsson, and Gisli Thorsteinsson, "The Intelligence of the Hands: Studying the Origin of Pedagogical Craft Education," *I-Manager's Journal on Educational Psychology* 5, no. 3 (Nov. 2012): 1–8.

As an art educator—See Andrea Kantrowitz, "K-12 Education," http://www.andreakantrowitz.com/-k-12-education.html (accessed December 13, 2021). See also Andrea Kantrowitz, "Drawing: A Matter of Life and Death," in *Thinking through Drawing: Practice into Knowledge, Proceedings of an Interdisciplinary Symposium* (New York : Teachers College Columbia University Art and Art Education Program, 2011), 118–119.

An experimental project—Our randomized control trial study involved over 800 third- through fifth-graders, and provided robust evidence of the impacts an interdisciplinary, hands-on curriculum could have, especially for children growing up in high-poverty communities. The children gained a significant advantage in math, as measured by their scores on standardized tests. Marisol Cunnington, Andrea Kantrowitz, Susanne Harnett, and Aline Hill-Ries, "Cultivating Common Ground: Integrating Standards-Based Visual Arts, Math and Literacy in High-Poverty Urban Classrooms," *Journal for Learning through the Arts* 10, no. 1 (2014): n1.

Studies by psychologist Dan Ariely and his colleagues—Michael I. Norton, Daniel Mochon, and Dan Ariely, "The IKEA Effect: When Labor Leads to Love," *Journal of Consumer Psychology* 22, no. 3 (2012): 453–460. See also Dan Ariely, *Payoff: The Hidden Logic That Shapes Our Motivations* (New York: Simon and Schuster, 2016).

Page 43

Table saws and hand tools—Matthew Crawford makes a passionate and personal argument for working with your hands in Shop Class as Soulcraft: An Inquiry into the Value of Work (New York: Penguin, 2009). He writes, "eBay is awash in such equipment [machine tools]. . . . It was in the 1990s that shop class started to become a thing of the past as educators prepared students to become 'knowledge workers.'"

Silicon Valley—Chris Weller, "Silicon Valley Parents Are Raising Their Kids Tech-Free—and It Should Be a Red Flag," *Business Insider*, February 18, 2018, http://www.businessinsider.com/silicon-valley-parents-raising-their-kids-tech-free-red-flag-2018-2.

Page 44

Gesture as a mode of communication precedes words—"There are a number of reasons to suppose that language evolved from manual gestures. . . . Studies of primate pre-motor cortex, and, in particular, of the so-called 'mirror system' suggest a double hand/mouth command system that may have evolved initially in the context of ingestion, and later formed a platform for combined manual and vocal communication. In humans, speech is typically accompanied by manual gesture, speech production itself is influenced by executing or observing hand movements, and manual actions also play an important role in the development of speech, from the babbling stage onwards." Maurizio Gentilucci and Michael C. Corballis, "From Manual Gesture to Speech: A Gradual Transition," *Neuroscience and Biobehavioral Reviews* 30, no. 7 (2006): 949–960. See also Michael Balter, "Animal Communication Helps Reveal Roots of Language," *Science* 22 (2002): 1569.

Babies point to what they want—"Infant pointing is best understood—on many levels and in many ways—as depending on uniquely human skills and motivations for cooperation and shared intentionality (e.g., joint intentions and attention with others). Children's early linguistic skills are built on this already existing platform of prelinguistic communication." Michael Tomasello, Malinda Carpenter, and Ulf Liszkowski, "A New Look at Infant Pointing," *Child Development* 78, no. 3 (2007): 705. See also George Butterworth, "Pointing Is the Royal Road to Language for Babies," in *Pointing: Where Language, Culture, and Cognition Meet*, ed. Sotaro Kita (Mahwah, NJ: Erlbaum, 2003), 33.

American Sign Language—"When called upon to carry the full burden of communication, gesture assumes a language-like form, with structure at word and sentence levels. However, when produced along with speech, gesture assumes a different form—it becomes imagistic and analog." Susan Goldin-Meadow, "The Role of Gesture in Communication and Thinking," *Trends in Cognitive Sciences* 3, no. 11 (1999): 419.

If we are asked to sit on our hands—Much of the evidence on the utility of gesture to solve problems concerns learning, such as this study: "We found that requiring children to gesture while learning the new concept helped them retain the knowledge they had gained during instruction. In contrast, requiring children to speak, but not gesture, while learning the concept had no effect on solidifying learning. Gesturing can thus play a causal role in learning, perhaps by giving learners an alternative, embodied way of representing new ideas. We may be able to improve children's learning just by encouraging them to move their hands." Susan Wagner Cook, Zachary Mitchell, and Susan Goldin-Meadow, "Gesturing Makes Learning Last," *Cognition* 106, no. 2 (2008): 1047.

Gesture itself helps to form new understandings—"When people talk, they gesture. We now know that these gestures are associated with learning—they can index moments of cognitive instability and reflect thoughts not yet found in speech. But gesture has the potential to do more than just reflect learning—it might be involved in the learning process itself." Susan Goldin-Meadow, "How Gesture Works to Change Our Minds," *Trends in Neuroscience and Education* 3, no. 1 (2014): 4–6.

Page 45

Mismatch between words and gestures—Susan Goldin-Meadow first used Piaget's conservation of volume task to look at the relationship between speech and accompanying gestures. Young children will say the same amount of water poured into two containers is different when the water level is higher in a tall narrow container than in a short wide container. When a child conveys the same information in gesture (he indicates the height of the water in each container by holding his hand at a higher or lower position), he has produced a gesture-speech match. Another child conveys the next stage of understanding through gesture (by spreading her hands apart to indicate the greater width of the shorter container) even though she still says there is more water in the tall container, she has produced a gesture-speech mismatch. When there is this kind of mismatch, the gesture reflects more advanced understanding than the verbal explanation. Susan Goldin-Meadow, *Hearing Gesture: How Our Hands Help Us Think* (Cambridge, MA: Harvard University Press, 2005), 27.

There is room to express nuance— The spatial reasoning that seems to be activated through gesture can be employed metaphorically to solve more abstract problems, as in this study of moral problem solving: "Requiring gesture during spatial tasks has been shown to catalyze the production of more sophisticated problem-solving strategies, allowing children to profit from instruction. Our data demonstrate that requiring gesture during moral reasoning tasks has similar effects, resulting in increased perspective taking ability subsequent to instruction." Leanne Beaudoin-Ryan and Susan Goldin-Meadow, "Teaching Moral Reasoning through Gesture," *Developmental Science* 17, no. 6 (2014): 984.

Page 46

Kimon Nicolaides—*The Natural Way to Draw: A Working Plan for Art Study* (Boston: Houghton Mifflin, 1969/1941).

"First thoughts"—"In all such drawings we recognize that the artist was working under the pressure of responsibility only to his own intelligence." Philip Rawson, *Drawing* (Philadelphia: University of Pennsylvania Press, 2016), 294–295.

Page 47

Of all the hand-held tools—James J. Gibson, *The Ecological Approach to Visual Perception* (Hillsdale, NJ: Erlbaum, 1986), 275.

Kimon Nicolaides—*The Natural Way to Draw*, 14.

Angela Brew—Angela Brew, "Learning to Draw: An Active Perceptual Approach to Observational Drawing Synchronising the Eye and Hand in Time and Space," PhD diss., University of the Arts London, 2015.

Page 48

Resistance—The sociologist Richard Sennett explores the nature of resistance in his book, *The Craftsman* (New Haven, CT: Yale University Press, 2008), 238: "Development of an intelligent hand does show something like a linear progression. The hand needs to be sensitized at the fingertip, enabling it to reason about touch. Once this is achieved, problems of coordination can be addressed. Integration of hand, wrist, and forearm then teaches lessons of minimum force. Once these are learned, the hand can work with the eye to look ahead physically, to anticipate and so to sustain concentration. Each stage, though challenging, grounds moving on to the next; but each is also an independent challenge."

chapter four

Imagine Other Worlds

Page 54

Our imaginations fill in gaps—See Bence Nanay, "Imagination and Perception," in *The Routledge Handbook of Philosophy of Imagination*, ed. Amy Kind (London: Routledge, Taylor and Francis Group, 2016), 124–134.

Page 61

Children invent answers—See Bipin Indurkhya, "Thinking Like a Child: The Role of Surface Similarities in Stimulating Creativity," in *AAAI Spring Symposium: Creativity and (Early) Cognitive Development* (Palo Alto, CA: AAAI Press, 2013).

Their guesses get more accurate—Alison Gopnik and Henry Wellman write: "Children learn about causal structure both through their own interventions on the world, for example, in exploratory play, and through observing the interventions of others, for example in imitation and informal pedagogy. . . . Intuitive theories are representations of the causal structure of the world." Gopnik and Wellman, "Reconstructing Constructivism: Causal Models, Bayesian Learning Mechanisms, and the Theory Theory," *Psychological Bulletin* 138, no. 6 (2012): 1085.

The lantern vs. the spotlight—Based on many years of experimental research with babies and their caregivers, the developmental cognitive psychologist Alison Gopnik and colleagues have greatly expanded our understanding of infant vs. adult consciousness: "Psychologists and neuroscientists have discovered that babies not only learn more, but imagine more, care more, and experience more than we would ever have thought possible. In some ways young children are actually smarter, more imaginative, more caring, and even more conscious than adults are." Alison Gopnik, *The Philosophical Baby: What Children's Minds Tell Us about Truth, Love, and the Meaning of Life* (New York: Random House, 2009), 5.

Page 56

Counterfactuals—See Ruth M. J. Byrne, "Counterfactual Thought," *Annual Review of Psychology* 67, no. 1 (2016): 135–157.

Inventing counterfactuals—Deena Weisberg and Alison Gopnik write, "Both young children and adults possess the extraordinary ability to imagine events and entities that they know full well are not real. . . . When learning, children consider alternative ways that the world could be; when planning, they consider alternative ways they could make the world be. In both cases, generating potential evidence patterns from counterfactual premises is crucial. Pretend play, because it engages the same set of cognitive abilities, provides valuable practice at doing precisely this sort of difficult mental task." Weisberg and Gopnik, "Pretense, Counterfactuals, and Bayesian Causal Models: Why What Is Not Real Really Matters," *Cognitive Science* 37, no. 7 (2013), 1377.

Early encouragement—Vera John-Steiner, in *Notebooks of the Mind: Explorations of Thinking* (Oxford: Oxford University Press, 1997), distills more than fifty interviews with highly accomplished creative individuals, across multiple disciplines in the arts and sciences. These interviews, along with historical materials, illuminate similarities in their life stories. John-Steiner finds that many individuals who go on to revolutionize their fields benefited from parents and other caring adults who encouraged them to follow passions and curiosities that emerged from their childhood play.

Page 57

Children with a rich fantasy life may be more empathic—See Melissa McInnis Brown, Rachel B. Thibodeau, Jillian M. Pierucci, and Ansley Tullos Gilpin, "Supporting the Development of Empathy: The Role of Theory of Mind and Fantasy Orientation," *Social Development* 26, no. 4 (2017): 951–964.

A life of their own—The developmental psychologist Marjorie Taylor writes: "I suspect that imagined entities become unruly only after the fantasies involving them are well established. . . . Performance becomes automatized with increasing expertise." Taylor, *Imaginary Companions and the Children Who Create Them* (Oxford: Oxford University Press, 1999), 251.

The invention of imaginary worlds in childhood may set the stage for creative endeavors later in life. See Michele Root-Bernstein and Robert Root-Bernstein, "Imaginary World-play in Childhood and Maturity and Its Impact on Adult Creativity," *Creativity Research Journal* 18, no. 4 (2006): 405–425.

The graphic novelist Lynda Barry—Lynda Barry, *Picture This* (Montreal: Drawn and Quarterly, 2010), 116.

The painter Philip Guston—Philip Guston, "Philip Guston Talking," in *Theories and Documents of Contemporary Art: A Sourcebook of Artists' Writings*, 2nd ed., ed. Kristine Stiles and Peter Selz (Berkeley: University of California Press, 2012), 250.

Pages 58–59

Gong Xian—A highly original seventeenth-century painter, Gong Xian integrated multiple past models with his own experience. He saw himself as "an intellectual painter." In her dissertation, Wang Chung-lan traces his philosophy of painting to the earlier Song dynasty master Guo Xi (1020–1090).

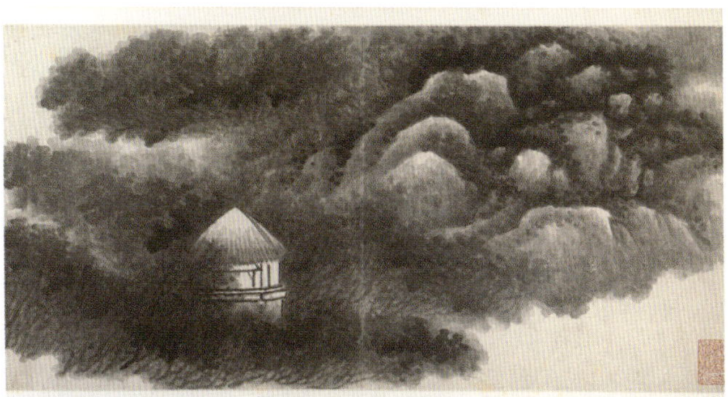

Gong Xian, from Landscapes of the Twelve Months, *1675–1695, Metropolitan Museum of Art, https://www.metmuseum.org/ Copyright: Creative Commons CC0 1.0 Universal Public Domain Dedication ("CC0 1.0 Dedication") http://www.metmuseum.org/art/collection/search/36130.*

Wang quotes Guo Xi's description of the different kinds of landscape paintings. The quotes are her translations from the original. Wang Chung-lan, "Gong Xian (1619–1689): A Seventeenth-Century Nanjing Intellectual and His Aesthetic World" (Yale University, 2005), 349–351.

Paracosm—The cognitive psychologist Margaret Wilson writes, "Mental structures that originally evolved for perception or action appear to be co-opted and run 'off-line,' decoupled from the physical inputs and outputs that were their original purpose, to assist in thinking and knowing. . . . These include symbolic off-loading, where external resources are used to assist in the mental representation and manipulation of things that are not present, as well as purely internal uses of sensorimotor representations, in the form of mental simulations." Wilson, "Six Views of Embodied Cognition," *Psychonomic Bulletin and Review* 9, no. 4 (2002): 626.

In ink or graphite, marks take on meanings—Philip Rawson begins his classic book by saying: "For a drawing's basic ingredients are strokes or marks which have a symbolic relationship with experience, not a direct, overall similarity with anything real. And the relationships between marks, which embody the main meaning of a drawing can only be read into the marks by the spectator, so as to create their own mode of truth." Dawson, *Drawing*, 2nd ed. (Philadelphia: University of Pennsylvania Press, 1969), 1.

Functional brain imaging reveals that we use the same parts of our brain—Imagination, perception, and memory rely on many of the same brain processes and structures. "Recent advances in cognitive neuroscience, including functional brain-imaging techniques, have shown that mental imagery makes use of much the same neural substrates as perception in the same sensory modality. Visual mental imagery seems to use the same two pathways (ventral or object processing, and dorsal or spatial processing) as perception. Defects in one or other pathway often, but not always, produce parallel deficits in both perception and imagery." Stephen Kosslyn, Giorgio Ganis, and William L. Thompson, "Neural Foundations of Imagery," *Nature Reviews Neuroscience* 2, no. 9 (2001): 635–642. These shared processes and structures seem to be the ones we use to make meaning out of our thoughts and perceptions: "Visual imagery and visual perception draw on most of the same neural machinery. . . . Cognitive control processes function comparably in both imagery and perception, whereas at least some sensory processes may be engaged differently by visual imagery and perception." Giorgio Ganis, William L. Thompson, and Stephen Kosslyn, "Brain Areas Underlying Visual Mental Imagery and Visual Perception: An fMRI Study," *Cognitive Brain Research* 20, no. 2 (2004): 226.

Each time we remember something—Memory is a set of complex interrelated processes, which integrate various brain structures that also play a role in perception and mental imagery. In episodic memory (the memory of specific events), we reconstruct our experiences each time we remember them. Our emotions, both at the time of the actual event and at the time of remembering, color our memories in ways that may distort their accuracy. The amygdala, responsible for the fear response, and the hippocampus, which connects emotion to memory, play an important role. These are both part of the limbic system, buried deep within the brain, which we share with all mammals. See Donna Rose Addis, Alana T. Wong, and Daniel L. Schacter, "Remembering the Past and Imagining the Future: Common and Distinct Neural Substrates during Event Construction and Elaboration," *Neuropsychologia* 45, no. 7 (2007): 1363–1377. See also Randy Buckner and Mark E. Wheeler, "The Cognitive Neuroscience of Remembering," *Nature Reviews Neuroscience* 2, no. 9 (2001): 624–634; Elizabeth A. Phelps, "Human Emotion and Memory: Interactions of the Amygdala and Hippocampal Complex," *Current Opinion in Neurobiology* 14, no. 2 (2004): 198–202.

Page 60

Apophenia—The tendency to perceive meaningful patterns where there may be none is associated with openness and loosening of top-down cognitive control. Apophenia is clinically associated with schizophrenic delusions. "Perceiving meaning in randomness and, more particularly, attributing mental states where none are indicated, may be important factors in the formation of paranormal and delusional beliefs"; yet positive schizotypy, "cognitive and perceptual aberrations, such as pseudohallucinations and deja vu, has been consistently associated with involvement in the arts." Sophie Fyfe, Claire Williams, Oliver J. Mason, and Graham J. Pickup, "Apophenia, Theory of Mind and Schizotypy: Perceiving Meaning and Intentionality in Randomness," *Cortex*, 44, no. 10 (2008): 1316–1325. In her study of artists' daily lives, Nicola Holt finds that "positive schizotypy predicted a range of cognitive and perceptual experiences (normative dissociation, inspiration and daydream-like cognition, but not experiences indicative of poor functioning, such as irrationality, negative affect or low self-esteem. This has important implications for conceptualizations of positive schizotypy, indicating that its expression is not always maladaptive, and that in some contexts it may be adaptive." Holt, "The Expression of Schizotypy in the Daily Lives of Artists," *Psychology of Aesthetics, Creativity, and the Arts* 13 (2019): 369. See also Christian Rominger, Elisabeth M. Weiss, Andreas Fink, Günter Schulter, and Ilona Papousek, "Allusive Thinking (Cognitive Looseness) and the Propensity to Perceive "Meaningful" Coincidences," *Personality and Individual Differences* 51, no. 8 (2011): 1002–1006.

Bias creeps in—The psychologist Raymond Nickerson defines the term as follows: "Confirmation bias . . . connotes the seeking or interpreting of evidence in ways that are partial to existing beliefs, expectations, or a hypothesis in hand." In Nickerson, "Confirmation Bias: A Ubiquitous Phenomenon in Many Guises," *Review of General Psychology* 2, no. 2 (1998): 175. Nickerson makes a distinction between deliberately making a case (the way a lawyer might) and making a case without being aware that one is doing so. He also makes a distinction between unmotivated and motivated biases, the former being more amenable to modification due to new and contradictory information. Confirmation bias influences psychological research as well: "Responders may inadvertently provide evidence for a working hypothesis by, in effect, accepting the assumption on which the questions or behavior are based and behaving in a way that is consistent with that assumption" (181). Numerology and witch-hunting are a couple of examples Nickerson gives of culturally widespread, real-life confirmation bias.

Confirmation bias may not always be a bad thing. The more we become aware of our bias and more accurate in our assessment of levels of uncertainty, the more useful such biases may be: "We suggest that confirmation bias is adaptive to the extent that agents have good metacognition, allowing them to downweight contradictory information when correct but still able to seek new information when they realize they are wrong." Max Rollwage and Stephen M. Fleming, "Confirmation Bias Is Adaptive When Coupled with Efficient Metacognition," *Philosophical Transactions of the Royal Society* B 376, no. 1822 (2021): 20200131.

"Look into the stains of walls"—Leonardo da Vinci, *Leonardo: Notebooks*, new ed., sel. Irma A. Richter, ed. Thereza Wells (Oxford: Oxford University Press, 2008), 173–174.

For decades, cardiac research focused on men—Charles F Emery, David J. Frid, Tilmer O. Engebretson, Angelo A. Alonzo, et al., "Gender Differences in Quality of Life among Cardiac Patients," *Psychosomatic Medicine* 66, no. 2 (2004): 190–197.

Female cardiac patients have . . . worse outcomes—"A large body of medical research suggests that women are less likely than men to survive traumatic health episodes like acute myocardial infarctions . . . gender concordance increases a patient's probability of survival and that the effect is driven by increased mortality when male physicians treat female patients." Brad N. Greenwood, Seth Carnahan, and Laura Huang, "Patient-Physician Gender Concordance and Increased

Mortality among Female Heart Attack Patients," *Proceedings of the National Academy of Sciences of the United States of America* 115, no. 34 (2018): 8569–8574.

Insufficient or biased training data—Kashmir Hill, "Wrongfully Accused by an Algorithm," *New York Times*, June 24, 2020 (updated August 3, 2020), http://www.nytimes.com/2020/06/24/technology/facial-recognition-arrest.html. See also Natasha Singer and Cade Metz, "Many Facial-Recognition Systems Are Biased, Says U.S. Study," *New York Times*, December 19, 2019, http://www.nytimes.com/2019/12/19/technology/facial-recognition-bias.html.

Page 61

Pareidolia—Joel L.Voss, Kara D. Federmeier, and Ken A. Paller, "The Potato Chip Really Does Look Like Elvis! Neural Hallmarks of Conceptual Processing Associated with Finding Novel Shapes Subjectively Meaningful," *Cerebral Cortex* 22, no. 10 (2012): 2354–2364.

Page 62

We are wired to jump to conclusions, thinking fast—Daniel Kahneman, in his book *Thinking, Fast and Slow* (New York: Macmillan, 2011), writes: "Most of our lives are spent in a default mood, all the decisions that are required are supplied by habits, once in a while there is an emergency, the senses realize it quickly and the fast thinking supplies an automated and instant response which in most cases is fully adequate. In this sense we do not depart from animals in general. However, our fast thinking is not always appropriate, and then the slow thinking takes over, but only reluctantly so, as it is always associated with a large effort."

Page 65

Las Meninas, by Diego Velazquez, is one of the most influential and analyzed paintings in Western European history. "Numerous underlying meanings that pertain to different fields of experience and which co-exist in one of the masterpieces of western art that has been the subject of the most numerous and most varied interpretations." "Las Meninas—The Collection—Museo Nacional Del Prado," https://www.museodelprado.es/en/the-collection/art-work/las-meninas/ad2cfc92-1f2c42ad-be46-e2ae0eaa0480.

Its composition plays upon the relationship between perception and imagination, reality and illusion. Are we, the viewers, playing the role of the king and queen, parents of the central figure of the princess, who are seen in the mirror in the back of the room? What painting is the artist, Velasquez himself, working on? Is it the painting we see before us, or something else . . . a portrait of the king and queen, or us, perhaps? I have spent days in front of this monumental painting myself, at the Prado in Madrid, which it never leaves. The size of the figures are at the viewer's scale and many, including the young princess and the artist himself, seem to be looking directly at us. The canvas itself is more or less at scale with the canvas Velasquez is working on within.

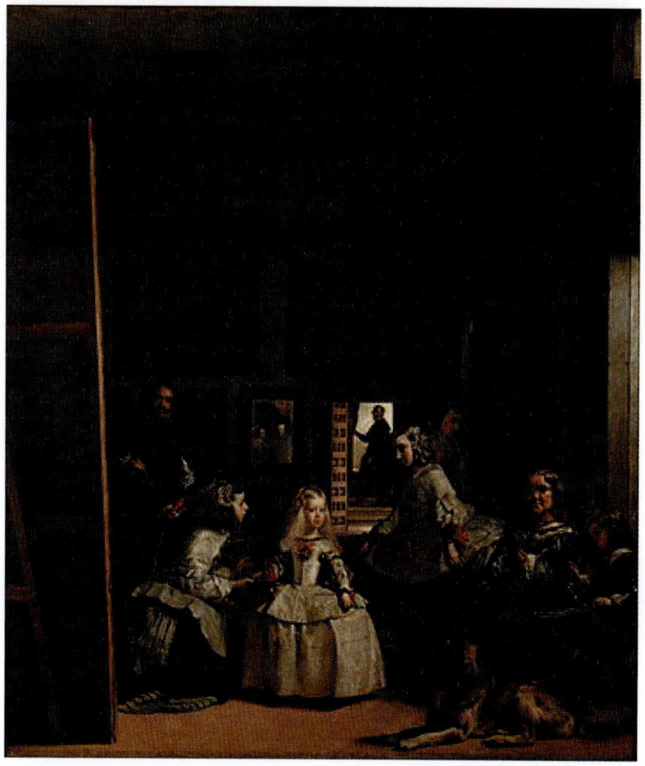

Diego Velázquez, *Las Meninas*, 1656. Oil on canvas 318 cm × 276 cm (125.2 in × 108.7 in). Museo del Prado, Madrid via *Wikimedia Commons*.

The reflexivity of the image has been explored by many artists, philosophers, and art historians. Picasso made a series of 58 paintings, dissecting, reinterpreting, and reimagining Velasquez's work in 1957. "Las Meninas (group), Highlights from the Collection, Museu Picasso," *The Website of Barcelona City*, http://www.bcn.cat/museupicasso/en/collection/mpb70-433.html.

The philosopher Michel Foucault wrote on the complexities of visibility and invisibility in *Las Meninas* in chapter 1 of *The Order of Things: An Archaeology of the Human Sciences* (New York: Vintage Books, 1973).

Page 66

Maxine Greene—Maxine Greene was a philosopher of education who advocated for arts education by championing the liberating power of the imagination to address social inequities and open up new posibilities in education and in the larger society. "To tap into imagination is to become able to break with what is supposedly fixed and finished, objectively and independently real. It is to see beyond what the imaginer has called normal or 'common-sensible' and to carve out new orders in experience. Doing so a person may become freed to glimpse what might be, to form notions of what should be and what is not yet." Maxine Greene, *Releasing the Imagination: Essays on Education, the Arts, and Social Change* (New York: Jossey-Bass, 1995), 19.

chapter five

Drawn Together

Page 73

Our ability to work together—The anthropologists Robert Boyd and Peter Richerson, in "Culture and the Evolution of Human Cooperation," *Philosophical Transactions of the Royal Society* B: Biological Sciences 364, no. 1533 (2009): 3281–3288, make a cogent (and influential) argument for the role of large-scale culturally mediated cooperation in the spread of the human race across the planet. They write:

> For better or worse, our ability to convert matter and energy into people in almost every terrestrial habitat has made us the Earth's dominant species. Most accounts of human evolution explain our ecological success as the result of superior cognitive abilities ... While it is probable that individual humans *are* smarter than other animals, we do not think this is the most important cause of our success. Think about what people have to know to survive and prosper in just one habitat where human foragers have flourished, the North American Arctic... Arctic foragers could make and do all the other things that they needed because they could make use of a vast pool of useful information available in the behavior and teachings of other people in their population...Scraps of individual insight and luck are spread widely to others, recombined with other scraps, and form the basis for additional innovations. (3282)

See also Joseph Henrich, "Cultural Group Selection, Coevolutionary Processes and Large-Scale Cooperation," *Journal of Economic Behavior and Organization* 53, no. 1 (2004): 3–35.

In *The Knowledge Illusion: Why We Never Think Alone* (New York: Penguin, 2018), Steven Sloman and Philip Fernbach write, "Individual intelligence is overrated. . . . We learn best when we're thinking with others. Some of the best teaching techniques at every level of education have students learning as a team" (18).

Drawing helped people cope with social isolation—The *New York Times* published a beautiful selection of drawings that were done in the darkest time of the pandemic in New York City, which experienced one of the first catastrophic episodes of the pandemic in the US during March and April of 2020. Antonio de Luca, Sasha Portis, and Adriana Ramic, "17 Artists Capture a Surreal New York from Their Windows," *New York Times*, April 16, 2020, http://www.nytimes.com/interactive/2020/04/16/nyregion/coronavirus-nyc-illustrators-window.html.

Heidi Edmundson is an emergency medicine consultant who has worked in the UK's National Health Service and as a consultant in emergency medicine at Whittington Health in London. She conducted weekly wellness sessions for her medical team during the height of the pandemic, which included drawing. She explained, "Drawing often enables people to express emotions that are difficult to say. For some drawing let them acknowledge or accept feelings that they were unaware that they had. Drawing together also created a shared experience. It was a fun task and there was always a lot of laughter—which not only bonds people, but can also reduce anxiety and blood pressure." Heidi Edmundson, "Covid-19: How Drawing Helped Us to Deal with the Pandemic," *BMJ Opinion*, August 6, 2020, blogs.bmj.com/bmj/2020/08/06/covid-19-how-drawing-helped-us-to-deal-with-the-pandemic/. The *Emergency Department Health and Wellbeing* animation compiled from these drawing sessions can be seen here: vimeo.com/435039026.

Prisoners who are held in solitary confinement—See Daniel Pforte, "Evaluating and Intervening in the Trauma of Solitary Confinement: A Social Work Perspective," *Clinical Social Work Journal* 48, no. 1 (2020): 77–86.

Depression may be a feature, not a bug, of our sociality—The analytical rumination hypothesis proposes that depression may have evolved as way to get us to step back and reevaluate a situation when we are not getting along well with the people around us. This may be adaptive because our survival depends so much on intergroup cooperation. (It's kind of like a time out.) Psychological researchers Magda Bartoskova and colleagues write: "89–98% of people who meet DSM criteria for major depression recover within a year of onset . . . and most of these remissions probably occur without treatment." Talk therapy has been shown to be at least as effective, if not more effective long term, because therapy provides a setting where an individual who is depressed can receive social support while working through the issues they may have with others. Magda Bartoskova, Marcela Sevcikova, Zachary Durisko, Marta M. Maslej, et al., "The Form and Function of Depressive Rumination." *Evolution and Human Behavior* 39, no. 3 (2018): 278.

Paul Andrews and J. Anderson Thomson Jr. write: "The analytical rumination (AR) hypothesis proposes that depression is an adaptation that evolved as a response to complex problems and whose function is to minimize disruption of rumination and sustain analysis of complex problems. It accomplishes this by giving episode-related problems priority access to limited processing resources, by reducing the desire to engage in distracting activities (anhedonia, and by producing psychomotor changes that reduce exposure to distracting stimuli." Paul Andrews and J. Anderson Thomson Jr., "The Bright Side of Being Blue: Depression as an Adaptation for Analyzing Complex Problems," *Psychological Review* 116, no. 3 (2009): 620.

See also Steven D. Hollon, "Is Cognitive Therapy Enduring or Antidepressant Medications Iatrogenic? Depression as an Evolved Adaptation," *American Psychologist* 75, no. 9 (2020): 1207.

Evidence-based talk therapies—In their review, Steven Hollon and colleagues conclude, "In the 50 years since it was first introduced, cognitive therapy has been shown to be as efficacious as antidepressant medications (on average) in the acute treatment of nonpsychotic depression, although some patients will do better on one than on the other. Moreover, patients treated to remission with cognitive therapy are less than half as likely to relapse following treatment termination as patients treated to remission with medications." Steven Hollon, Robert DeRubeis, Paul Andrews, and J. Anderson Thomson Jr., "Cognitive Therapy in the Treatment and Prevention of Depression: A Fifty-Year Retrospective with an Evolutionary Coda," *Cognitive Therapy and Research* 45, no. 3 (2021): 402–417, at 402.

Page 80

Newborns will fixate—Catherine J. Mondloch and colleagues found that "there appears to be a mechanism, likely subcortical, predisposing newborns to look toward faces. Changes in preferences at 6 and 12 weeks of age suggest increasing cortical influence over infants' preferences for faces." Catherine J. Mondloch, Terri L. Lewis, D. Robert Budreau, Daphne Maurer, et al., "Face Perception During Early Infancy," *Psychological Science* 10, no. 5 (September 1999): 419–422.

The "fusiform face area"—When we learn to become experts at recognizing specific birds or detecting cancer cells, we use that same area of our brain that we use to recognize familiar faces: "Acquisition of expertise with novel objects (greebles) led to increased activation in the right hemisphere face areas for matching of upright greebles as compared to matching inverted greebles. The same areas were also more activated in experts than in novices during passive viewing of greebles. Expertise seems to be one factor that leads to specialization in the face area." I. Gauthier, M. J. Tarr, A. W. Anderson, P. Skudlarski, and J. C. Gore, "Activation of the Middle Fusiform 'Face Area' Increases with Expertise in Recognizing Novel Objects," *Nature Neuroscience* 2, no. 6 (1999): 568. See also N. Kanwisher, J. McDermott, and M. M. Chun, "The Fusiform Face Area: A Module in Human Extrastriate Cortex Specialized for Face Perception," *Journal of Neuroscience* 17, no. 11 (1997): 4302–4311.

Most of us need no training—Prosopagnosia, or face blindness, results from dysfunction or damage to the fusiform gyrus. The portrait painter Chuck Close had prosopagnosia, as did the famous neuroscientist Oliver Sacks. Diverse conditions, such as depression, autism, schizophrenia, and Alzheimer's can also interfere with one's ability to recognize faces and facial expressions. See Andrea Albonico and Jason Barton, "Progress in Perceptual Research: The Case of Prosopagnosia," *F1000Research* 8 (2019), https://f1000research.com/articles/8-765.

"Own-race bias"—See Johnson, Kareem J., and Barbara L. Fredrickson, "'We All Look the Same to Me': Positive Emotions Eliminate the Own-Race Bias in Face Recognition," *Psychological Science* 16, no. 11 (2005): 875–881.

Predisposed to see faces—"Human face processing has a strong top-down component whereby sensory input with even the slightest suggestion of a face can result in the interpretation of a face," Jiangang Liu, Jun Li, Lu Feng, Ling Li, Jie Tian, and Kang Lee, "Seeing Jesus in Toast: Neural and Behavioral Correlates of Face Pareidolia," *Cortex* 53 (2014): 60.

Page 75

But that face facing me—Emmanuel Levinas, *Alterity and Transcendence*, trans. Michael Smith (New York: Columbia University Press, 1999), 24.

Page 76

We look each other in the eye—When the pupils in our eyes dilate or constrict, it can reveal important aspects of our thinking: The pupillary light "response is far more than a reflex, and reveals what you attend to, how you interpret what you see, and even what you think about." Sebastiaan Mathôt and Stefan Van der Stigchel, "New Light on the Mind's Eye: The Pupillary Light Response as Active Vision," *Current Directions in Psychological Science* 24, no. 5 (2015): 37.

Professional poker players—David Paredes (pictured at right) is a professional poker player and Harvard and NYU Law School grad who played a major role uncovering the UltimateBet online poker cheating scandal in 2008. He says early on in his poker career, he noticed that players' pupils stay steady when they get a good hand but tend to dart around when they don't. He started wearing sunglasses not only to hide his own eyes, but to be able to watch others surreptitiously. As well as providing comfort, the hoodie is useful in hiding the carotid artery, another involuntary "tell." Paredes's lifetime winnings to date are over $2.5 million. David Paredes, personal communication. See also Julio Rodriguez, "A Poker Life: David Paredes," Cardplayer.com, April 16, 2015, http://www.cardplayer.com/poker-news/18679-a-poker-life-david-paredes.

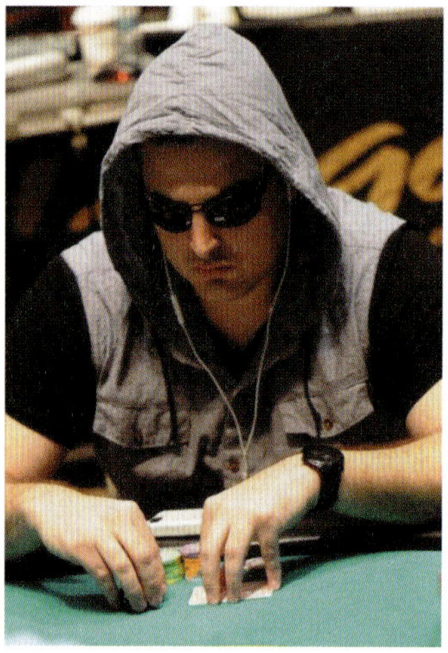

Photo courtesy of David Paredes.

The whites of our eyes (known as the "sclera")—See Michael Tomasello, *Becoming Human: A Theory of Ontogeny* (video), *PsychologicalScience*, May 23, 2019, The Fred Kavli Keynote Address, Association for Psychological Science Annual Convention, Washington, DC, http://youtu.be/BnbeleWvXyQ. See also Michael Tomasello, *Becoming Human: A Theory of Ontogeny* (Cambridge, MA: Belknap Press of Harvard University Press, 2019).

Page 77

Rats . . . will share a special treat—See Inbal Ben-Ami Bartal, Jean Decety, and Peggy Mason, "Empathy and Pro-social Behavior in Rats," *Science* 334, no. 6061 (2011): 1427–1430.

Humans and chimpanzees will cooperate for a common purpose—See Michael Tomasello, *Becoming Human: A Theory of Ontogeny* (video).

When others smile, yawn, or cough—See Thalia Wheatley, Olivia Kang, Carolyn Parkinson, and Christine E. Looser, "From Mind Perception to Mental Connection: Synchrony as a Mechanism for Social Understanding," *Social and Personality Psychology Compass* 6, no. 8 (2012): 589–606. "In summary, the current results suggest that friends are exceptionally similar to one another in terms of how they perceive, interpret, and react to the world around them, as reflected in unobtrusive measurements of mental processes as they unfold over time." Carolyn Parkinson, Adam M. Kleinbaum, and Thalia Wheatley, "Similar Neural Responses Predict Friendship," *Nature Communications* 9, no. 1 (2018): 8.

Diverse teams of people are often more creative and productive—In one study, diverse problem-solving teams were categorized by their prevailing ethos regarding cultural difference. Those who took a "polycultural" approach, embracing and learning from differences, scored highest. "Colorblind" teams, which disregarded difference, scored lowest, lower than culturally homogeneous teams. See Jaee Cho, Carmit T. Tadmor, and Michael W. Morris, "Are All Diversity Ideologies Creatively Equal? The Diverging Consequences of Colorblindness, Multiculturalism, and Polyculturalism," *Journal of Cross-Cultural Psychology* 49, no. 9 (2018): 1376–1401.

Multicultural acceptance may be passed down from mother to child. "When it comes to multicultural experience, its impact can extend beyond the self to also affect the next generation." Carmit T. Tadmor, Rony Berger, Alaina Brenick, Hisham Abu-Raiya, and Joy Benatov, "The Intergenerational Effect of Maternal Multicultural Experience on Children's Tolerance: An Example from Palestinians and Jews in Israel," *Journal of Cross-Cultural Psychology* 48, no. 9 (2017): 1342.

Page 78

When we mirror the body language—Thalia Wheatley, Adam Boncz, Ivan Toni, and Arjen Stolk, "Beyond the Isolated Brain: The Promise and Challenge of Interacting Mindsm," *Neuron* 103, no. 2 (2019): 186–188.

Mirror neurons—For an accessible discussion of mirror neurons, see: Marco Iacoboni, *Mirroring People: The New Science of How We Connect with Others* (New York: Farrar, Straus and Giroux, 2009). Our understanding of verbal language may have its origins in the mirror neuron system. Intentional gestures, including facial expressions, signify actions, prefiguring the spoken word. For an updated understanding of the mirror system which takes into account other higher level neural processes that help individuals understand one another, see U. Hasson and C. D. Frith, "Mirroring and Beyond: Coupled Dynamics as a Generalized Framework for Modeling Social Interactions," *Philosophical Transactions of the Royal Society B: Biological Sciences* 371, no. 1693 (2016): 20150366; Giacomo Rizzolatti and Michael A. Arbib,"Language within Our Grasp," *Trends in Neuroscience* 21, no. 5 (1998): 188–194.

Page 79

Appreciation of works of art—See D. Freedberg and B. Gallese, "Motion, Emotion and Empathy in Esthetic Experience," *Trends in Cognitive Sciences* 11, no. 5 (2007): 197–203. See also A. Pignocchi, "How the Intentions of the Draftsman Shape Perception of a Drawing," *Consciousness and Cognition* 19, no. 4 (2010): 887–898.

Kimon Nicolaides—Nicolaides encouraged his students to mentally simulate the model's actions. See Kimon Nicolaides, *The Natural Way to Draw: A Working Plan for Art Study* (Boston: Houghton Mifflin, 1941), 24.

Page 80

A cast of thousands—John Koenig invents a word for this idea in *The Dictionary of Obscure Sorrows*, a website, video collection, and book: "*sonder* n. the realization that each random passerby is living a life as vivid and complex as your own—populated with their own ambitions, friends, routines, worries and inherited craziness—an epic story that continues invisibly around you like an anthill sprawling deep underground, with elaborate passageways to thousands of other lives that you'll never know existed, in which you might appear only once, as an extra sipping coffee in the background, as a blur of traffic passing on the highway, as a lighted window at dusk." See *Sonder: The Realization That Everyone Has a Story* (video), youtu.be/AkoML0_FiV4, http://www.dictionaryofobscuresorrows.com/post/23536922667/sonder.

Improvisational comedians—This description of comedy improv is based on discussions over morning coffee with Scott Benjamin, magician/lawyer/reconteur/bon vivant—my partner in comics and in life. See *Quarantine-Qomix*, quarantine-qomix.weebly.com/.

Phillip Guston—See Musa Mayer, "Philip Guston and the Privilege of Writing Badly," *Columbia: A Journal of Literature and Art*, no. 13 (1988): 1–4.

In September 2020, after a summer of Black Lives Matter protests, the National Gallery of Art in Washington, DC, the Museum of Fine Arts in Boston, the Tate Modern in London, and the Museum of Fine Arts in Houston decided to delay a long-planned retrospective of Phillip Guston's work until 2024, "when its 'message of social and racial justice . . . can be more clearly interpreted.'" Three months earlier, they had announced, "Philip Guston's paintings have inspired generations of artists while also defying easy definition. . . . [this exhibition] will surely secure Guston's place in the pantheon of modern art, while reassessing his impact on the art of the present." According to the *Smithsonian Magazine*, "Responses to the postponement ranged from outrage to understanding, with critics and curators alternatively decrying the decision as 'cowardly,' 'extremely patronizing' and 'simply wrong.' . . . Guston's daughter, Musa Mayer, says she is 'saddened' by the decision, as her father's work strives to grapple with racism head-on. Referencing Guston's Jewish ancestry, she notes that his family fled Ukraine to escape persecution: In other words, he 'understood what hatred was.'"

See Isis Davis-Marks, "Understanding the Controversy Over Postponed Exhibition Featuring KKK Imagery," *Smithsonian Magazine*, September 29, 2020, http://www.smithsonianmag.com/smart-news/unraveling-controversy-over-postponed-art-exhibition-featuring-kkk-imagery-180975931/. See also: "*Philip Guston Now*: Statement from the Directors," nga.gov, June 27, 2019 (updated September 21, 2020), http://www.nga.gov/press/exh/5235.html.

Page 81

Cognitive psychologists Jennifer Drake and Ellen Winner—in a cross-cultural study of children recognized as exceptionally gifted in drawing, Drake and Winner found that "at the heart of artistic talent is the ability to master one's culture's representational conventions, whether the convention is Western-style realism in the case of Grace or Eitan, or Chinese-style allusionistic brush painting in the case of Yani." Drake and Winner were originally just looking at realistic drawing. In the course of their research, however, they discovered that drawing conventions, or schemata, are present and absorbed by gifted children in different forms in different cultural contexts. They wrote, "It is a mistake to be blinded by our Western eyes and see Western-style realism as the prime sign of artistic talent, when this style is but one of the many possible representational conventions that artistically gifted children master so early and so independently." Jennifer E. Drake and Ellen Winner, "Precocious Realists: Perceptual and Cognitive Characteristics Associated with Drawing Talent in Non-Autistic Children," *Philosophical Transactions of the Royal Society B: Biological Sciences* 364, no. 1522 (2009): 1452.

Page 82

Robert Beverly Hale—See Robert Beverly Hale, *Drawing Lessons from the Great Masters* (New York: Watson-Guptill, 1964).
The Mustard Seed Garden Painting Manual—The manual was compiled around 1679 (during Gong Xian's lifetime; see chapter 4). A. K'ai-ming Ch'iu wrote in 1951: "It is safe to say that for the last two centuries and a half, no book on Chinese painting has enjoyed wider circulation in China and Japan (as attested by its more than twenty editions). . . . It has received hearty welcome and most appreciative use by all beginners in Chinese painting since its first appearance." A. K'ai-ming Ch'iu, "The Chieh Tzu Yuan Hua Chuan (Mustard Seed Garden Painting Manual): Early Editions in American Collections," *Archives*

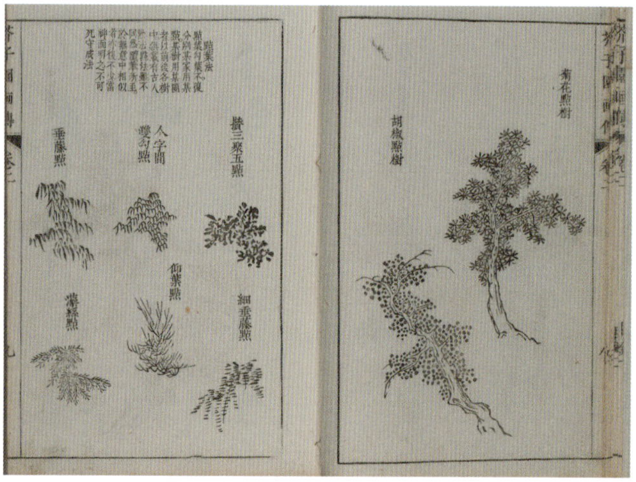

Two pages of Manual of Mustard Seed Garden, *1753, Wang, Gai (fl. 1677–1705), New York Public Library, http://digitalcollections.nypl.org/. Creative Commons CC0 1.0 Universal Public Domain Dedication ("CC0 1.0 Dedication").*

of the Chinese Art Society of America 5 (1951): 55–69. You can see the original here: http://archive.org/details/brooklynmuseum-o17617-mustard-seed-garden-a-chinese/brooklynmuseum-o17617i011-05.583_vol2_3_PS1.jpg.

Page 83

They have learned what to look for—Aaron Kozbelt, "Learning to See by Learning to Draw: Probing the Perceptual Bases and Consequences of Highly Skilled Artistic Drawing," *High Ability Studies 28*, no. 1 (2017): 93–105.

Page 90

A conversation with myself—Thirty drawing experts from diverse fields, such as design, art history, architecture, neuroscience, philosophy,and studio art, and from various backgrounds and cultures, including the US, UK, India, Poland, Italy and Germany, came to the conclusion that this "conversation with myself" is the starting point for a wide range of drawing practices at a "Thinking through Drawing" think tank held at the Metropolitan Museum in New York City in 2013.

Many artists have referred to the "intense" quality of the dialogue they have with their work. The writer and artist John Berger has written extensively on the first-person experience of drawing. His account is vivid and familiar to experienced drawers. See John Berger, *Berger on Drawing*, ed. Jim Savage (Aghabullogue, Co. Cork, Ireland: Occasional Press, 2005), 77.

chapter six

Thinking Space

Page 90

Spatial reasoning—David Lohman's formulation of spatial ability is widely cited in the literature on spatial reasoning and intelligence: "Spatial ability may be defined as the ability to generate, retain, retrieve, and transform well-structured visual images." David F. Lohman, "Spatial Ability and G," *Human Abilities: Their Nature and Measurement* 97, no. 116 (1996): 1. See also Barbara Tversky, "Visuospatial Reasoning," in *The Cambridge Handbook of Thinking and Reasoning*, ed. Keith J. Holyoak and Robert G. Morrison (Cambridge: Cambridge University Press, 2005), 209–240.

Analogies—Keith Holyoak defines an analogy as "an inductive mechanism based on structured comparisons of mental representations." Keith J. Holyoak, "Analogy and Relational Reasoning," in *The Oxford Handbook of Thinking and Reasoning*, ed. Keith J. Holyoak and Robert G. Morrison (Oxford: Oxford University Press, 2012), 234–259.

Page 91

Reasoning can be defined—Barbara Tversky writes that reasoning is going beyond the information given: "Going beyond the information given can also mean transforming the given information, sometimes according rules, as in deductive reasoning. Another way to go beyond the information given is to make inferences or judgments from it." Barbara Tversky, *Visuospatial Reasoning* (Cambridge: Cambridge University Press, 2005), 210.

Spatial reasoning includes—Mary Hegarty identifies two different components of spatial intelligence. The first component is "flexible strategy choice between mental imagery (or mental simulation more generally) and more analytic forms of thinking . . . such as task decomposition and rule-based reasoning. The second is meta-representational competence . . . which encompasses ability to choose the optimal external representation for a task and to use novel external representations productively." Mary Hegarty, "Components of Spatial Intelligence," *Psychology of Learning and Motivation* 52 (2010): 265.

In their taxonomy of spatial skills, Nora Newcombe and Thomas Shipley write, "Spatial information concerns shapes, locations, paths, relations among entities and relations between entities and frames of reference. . . . A variety of cognitive, neural and linguistic considerations motivate a

or no—and usually are able improve the drawing, to provide more information as to form and relations—it means something to them as most will go to design, it is easily understood as a situation they may encounter. More than many metrics it is objective mostly, and, if the answer is yes, you have a good drawing ! It is in fact what makes drawings "good." (May 2021, personal communication)

Page 97

Drawers can be taught—See Andrea Kantrowitz, Seymour Simmons, and Kimberly S. Sloane, "The Case for Drawing in the 21st Century," *FATE in Review*, Foundations in Art: Theory and Education, vol. 35 (Portland: Pacific College of Art, 2014).

Page 98

In a recent study of 682 art students—See Rebecca Chamberlain, "The Development of Expertise in the Visual Arts," in *The Science of Expertise: Behavioral, Neural, and Genetic Approaches to Complex Skill*, ed. D. Z. Hambrick, G. Campitelli, and B. N. Macnamara (New York: Routledge, 2017).

Pratt first-year art students—"Art students outperformed non-art students on drawing measures and some (but not all) visual-spatial tasks. This nuanced pattern of results broadly supports the notion that art students differ from non-art students in their ability to exert top-down control over attentional processing, but not in the phenomenology of low-level visual processing." Rebecca Chamberlain, Jennifer E. Drake, Aaron Kozbelt, Rachel Hickman, Joseph Siev, and Johan Wagemans, "Artists as Experts in Visual Cognition: An Update," *Psychology of Aesthetics, Creativity, and the Arts* 13, no. 1 (2019): 58.

Rebecca Chamberlain explains—Personal communication (email), 2021.

"Y" and "T" junctions—Aaron Kozbelt and colleagues gave their participants a detailed photographic portrait of Samuel Beckett. The participants were given 70 short pieces of tape to trace image on a clear plastic overlay—not enough to trace the entire image. The researchers found that non-artists would use the tape to outline the big shapes. Artists, in contrast, looked for places where internal forms overlapped, "Y" and "T" joints. See Aaron Kozbelt, Angelika Seidel, Amanda ElBassiouny, Yelena Mark, and David R. Owen, "Visual Selection Contributes to Artists' Advantages in Realistic Drawing," *Psychology of Aesthetics, Creativity, and the Arts* 4, no. 2 (2010): 93. In a second study, participants traced a photo of an elephant with 30 short pieces of tape, and again artists focused on internal "Y" and "T" junctions, where one form comes in front of another, whereas non-artists traced the flat outline of the large shapes. Justin Ostrofsky, Aaron Kozbelt, and Angelika Seidel. "Perceptual constancies and visual selection as predictors of realistic drawing skill." *Psychology of Aesthetics, Creativity, and the Arts* 6, no. 2 (2012): 124.See also Justin Ostrofsky and Aaron Kozbelt, "A Multi-Stage Attention Hypothesis of Drawing Ability," in *Thinking through Drawing: Practice into Knowledge: Proceedings of an Interdisciplinary Symposium on Drawing, Cognition and Education*, ed. Andrea Kantrowitz, Angela Brew and Michelle Fava (New York: Teachers College: Columbia University, 2011), 61–66.

Page 99

Drawing helps to coordinate widely dispersed neural circuits—Drawing experts spend more energy and recruit more widely dispersed neural resources to tackle more cognitively challenging tasks. So far, the evidence regarding artists and non-artists confirms this pattern. In their study, neuroscientists Bhattacharya and Petsche found significant differences between cortical integration patterns in artists and non-artists. The artists were found to have a much greater degree of long-range synchronization than non-artists. The researchers cited earlier studies that showed this kind of long-range coherence also occurs in the acquisition of bimanual motor skills, associative learning, and in gifted individuals as opposed to controls. In contrast to the popular notion that artists' creative thinking is "right-brained," both hemispheres were activated, with near-zero lag synchrony between them. See Joydeep Bhattacharya, "Increase of Universality in Human Brain during Mental Imagery from Visual Perception," *PLOS ONE* 4, no. 1 (2009): e4121, https://doi.org/10.1371/Journal.pone.0004121. See also Joydeep Bhattacharya and Hellmuth Petsche, "Drawing on Mind's Canvas: Differences in Cortical Integration Patterns between Artists and Non-Artists," *Human Brain Mapping* 26, no. 1 (2005): 1–14; Mara Kottlow, Elke Praeg, Christine Luethy, and Lutz Jancke, "Artists' Advance: Decreased Upper Alpha Power while Drawing in Artists Compared with Non-Artists," *Brain Topography* 23, no. 4 (2011): 392–402, https://doi.org/10.1007/s10548-010-0163-9.

Betty Edwards—Among the exercises Betty Edwards recommends is turning a drawing upside down to inhibit recognition and thus enhance accuracy. This has attracted the interest of psychologists who have been unable to replicate this and, in fact, found that turning an image upside down generally resulted in less accurate drawings. See Betty Edwards, *Drawing on the Right Side of the Brain: A Course in Enhancing Creativity and Artistic Confidence* (Los Angeles: J. P. Tarcher, 1979). For contradictory evidence, see Jennifer A. Day and Nicolas Davidenko, "Physical and Perceptual Accuracy of Upright and Inverted Face Drawings," *Visual Cognition* 26, no. 2 (2018): 89–99; Justin Ostrofsky, Aaron Kozbelt, Dale J. Cohen, Lauren Conklin, and Krista Thomson, "Face Inversion Impairs the Ability to Draw Long-Range, but Not Short-Range, Spatial

Relationships between Features," *Empirical Studies of the Arts* 34, no. 2 (2016): 221–233.

Two visual streams hypothesis—"The two visual systems hypothesis suggests processing of visual information into two distinct routes in the brain: a dorsal stream for the control of actions and a ventral stream for the identification of objects. Recently, increasing evidence has shown that the dorsal and ventral streams are not strictly independent, but do interact with each other. . . . The interactions between dorsal and ventral streams are important for controlling complex object-oriented hand movements, especially skilled grasp. . . . Physiological interconnections appear to be gradually more active as the precision demands of the grasp become higher." Vonne Van Polanen and Marco Davare, "Interactions between Dorsal and Ventral Streams for Controlling Skilled Grasp," *Neuropsychologia* 79 (2015): 186.

Kottlow and colleagues suggest that the practice of drawing might facilitate the integration of the ventral and dorsal pathways. Mara Kottlow, Elke Praeg, Christine Luethy, and Lutz Jancke, "Artists' Advance: Decreased Upper Alpha Power while Drawing in Artists Compared with Non-Artists," *Brain Topography* 23, no. 4 (2011): 400.

Page 100

Visuospatial intelligence is linked to creativity—David Lubinski, a psychologist who studies intellectually precocious youth, led a longitudinal study that found that spatial ability not only contributes added information to mathematical and verbal reasoning measures with respect to assimilating and utilizing knowledge in school and work settings, but also contributes to the generation of new knowledge or creative expression. See Harrison Kell and David Lubinski, "Spatial Ability: A Neglected Talent in Educational and Occupational Settings," *Roeper Review* 35, no. 4 (2013): 224.

"Without spatial ability, the psychological architecture supporting creative thought and innovative production is incomplete." Harrison J. Kell, David Lubinski, Camilla P. Benbow, and James H. Steiger, "Creativity and Technical Innovation: Spatial Ability's Unique Role," *Psychological Science* 24, no. 9 (2013): 1831–1836, at 1835.

Spatial . . . skills are not generally taught in a systematic way—Professional educators tend to score lowest on spatial intelligence tests, compared to professionals in a variety of STEM and non-STEM fields (such as business and law). Harrison Kell and David Lubinski, "Spatial Ability: A Neglected Talent in Educational and Occupational Settings," *Roeper Review* 35, no. 4 (2013): 219–230.

Spatial skills can be taught—and can be used in new situations: "To determine whether and to what extent training and experience can improve these skills, we meta-analyzed 217 research studies investigating the magnitude, moderators, durability, and generalizability of training on spatial skills. . . . Training effects were stable and were not affected by delays between training and post-testing. Training also transferred to other spatial tasks that were not directly trained." David Uttal, Nathaniel G. Meadow, Elizabeth Tipton, Linda L. Hand, et al., "The Malleability of Spatial Skills: A Meta-Analysis of Training Studies," *Psychological Bulletin* 139, no. 2 (2013): 352.

Drawing to learn in STEM education—See Sally P. W. Wu and Martina A. Rau, "How Students Learn Content in Science, Technology, Engineering, and Mathematics (STEM) through Drawing Activities," *Educational Psychology Review* 31, no. 1 (2019): 87–120.

For a practical application of drawing prompts in the context of an introductory engineering class, see Sally P. W. Wu and Martina A. Rau, "Effectiveness and Efficiency of Adding Drawing Prompts to an Interactive Educational Technology when Learning with Visual Representations," *Learning and Instruction* 55 (2018): 93–104.

Draw like an Engineer—Erin Riley is the Director, Engineering and Design Lab, at Greenwich Academy, a K–12 independent school for girls in Greenwich, Connecticut. She is also a Stanford Fab Learn Fellow and an artist. She writes: "Moving back and forth between 2D and 3D approaches encourages mental visualization and strengthens spatial skills. Providing opportunities to practice translating mental imagery into the physical world empowers makers." Erin Riley, "Think like an Architect, Draw like an Engineer: Teacher Guide" (2021), accessed December 22, 2021, from http://docs.google.com/document/d/1pki-2AhIYJzpUUgFS-ylgOBhEC7UpZiBv5HWj0wOWU/edit. See also Erin Riley, "Drawing: A Visual Language for Makers," FabLearn Fellows (blog), December 28, 2014, http://fablearn.stanford.edu/fellows/blog/drawing-visual-language-makers.

Page 102

The drawings on this page were inspired by the book by François Blanciak, *Siteless: 1001 Building Forms* (Cambridge, MA: MIT Press, 2008).

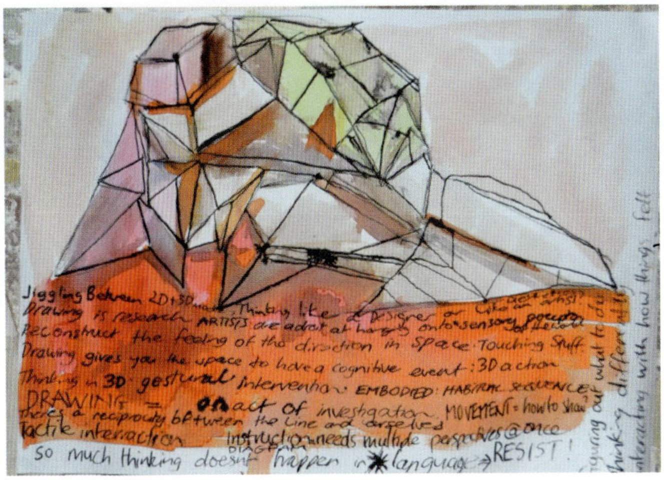

Drawing by an anonymous workshop participant.

"Drawing gives you the space to have a cognitive event."—This drawing was left behind in a master class that I taught at the 2015 "We All Draw": Thinking through Drawing Symposium in London. We made complicated origami boxes, and had participants work in pairs to document the deconstruction of the origami and then attempt to remake them using their drawings as a guide. This drawing says:

"Jiggling between 2D and 3D, Thinking like a designer or like an artist? (aesthetics) Drawing is research. ARTISTS are adroit at hanging onto sensory perception of the world. Reconstruct the feeling of the direction in space—touching stuff. Drawing gives you the space to have a cognitive event:3D action. Thinking in 3D, gestural intervention—EMBODIED: HABITUAL SEQUENCE. DRAWING = an act of investigation MOVEMENT = how to show Tactile interaction. Instruction needs multiple perspectives at once (DIAGRAM) so much thinking doesn't happen in* language—> RESIST! figuring out what to do. Thinking differently. Interacting with how things feel"

chapter seven

A Tool of Thought

Page 109

The first tools—Recent cognitive neuroscientific research suggests a common neural substrate for language and tool use and "important similarities in the way speech and tool-use networks are organized." Dietrich Stout and Thierry Chaminade, "Stone Tools, Language and the Brain in Human Evolution," *Philosophical Transactions of the Royal Society B: Biological Sciences* 367, no. 1585 (2012): 76.

"Increasingly complex prehistoric toolmaking methods through time offer insight into evolving capacities but require a robust interpretive framework linking archaeological evidence to specific behavioral and cognitive actions. . . . The adaptive complexity of grasp regulation in Paleolithic toolmaking invites comparison with the complex coordination of articulators (vocal cords, tongue, palate, lips) . . . 1) selection acting on either language or toolmaking abilities could have indirectly favored elaboration of neural substrates important for the other, and 2) archaeological evidence of Paleolithic toolmaking can provide evidence for the presence of cognitive capacities also important to the modern human faculty for language." Aldo Faisal, Dietrich Stout, Jan Apel, and Bruce Bradley, "The Manipulative Complexity of Lower Paleolithic Stone Toolmaking," *PLOS ONE* 5, no. 11 (2010): e13718, https://doi.org/10.1371/Journal.pone.0013718.

From an evolutionary perspective, this presents an ideal context for the co-option of existing neural substrates to support new behavioural phenotypes (i.e., "exaptation"). The intersection of language and praxis networks in Broca's area currently provides one of the best-known examples of such complex functional overlap in human neocortex.

Accumulating evidence is increasingly supportive of technological language origins, and goes a long way towards allaying concerns that the similarity in the hierarchical, combinatorial organization of the two domains is a superficial one or that the "imitative" learning of toolmaking skills is fundamentally distinct from intentional communication. In particular, evidence of intention attribution during the observation of stone toolmaking provides support for a "technological pedagogy" hypothesis, which proposes that intentional pedagogical demonstration could have provided an adequate scaffold for the evolution of intentional vocal communication. This hypothesis is consistent with the widespread view that increasing reliance on social learning and pedagogy was a key factor in hominin brain and cognitive evolution. (Stout and Chaminade, "Stone Tools, Language and the Brain in Human Evolution," 82)

Potters wheels were invented—See Megan Gambino, "A Salute to the Wheel," *Smithsonian Magazine*, June 17, 2009, http://www.smithsonianmag.com/science-nature/a-salute-to-the-wheel-31805121/.

A map or a calendar, a clock or a compass—The clock and the compass map a linear sequence onto a circle; they are material anchors that we use to help orient ourselves in time and space. Hutchins also considers cultural constructs, such as ticket queues, which are not physical objects but sets of conventionalbehaviors or rituals. A given artifact, either physical, social, or cultural, is not always a material anchor; according to Hutchins, there is a continuum. Sentence structure, in that it may stabilize a complex spatial and temporal organization, can be considered a kind of material anchor, though not, generally, single words, because they usually have a more direct, one-to-one relationship with a single concept. Edwin Hutchins, "Material Anchors for Conceptual Blends," *Journal of Pragmatics* 37, no. 10 (2005): 1555–1577, at 1573.

Mathematical notation systems—Kenneth Iverson developed APL, an important and influential computer programming language, in the 1960s. It is still in use today, and is notable for its use of special graphic symbols. Iverson quotes other pioneers in computer science to demonstrate that language and symbolic notation are tools of thought. He quotes George Boole, the nineteenth-century inventor of Boolean algebra, who "asserted 'That language is an instrument of human reason, and not merely a medium for the expression of thought, is a truth generally admitted.' Mathematical notation provides perhaps the best-known and best-developed example of language used consciously as a tool of thought." Iverson also quotes the philospher Alfred Whitehead: "By relieving the brain of all unnecessary work, a good notation sets it free to concentrate on more advanced problems, and in effect increases the mental power of the race." Kenneth E. Iverson, "Notation as a Tool of Thought," *Communications of the ACM* 23, no. 8 (1980): 444.

Our smartphones have become mega-tools—Contemporary British painter David Hockney was an early adopter of the smartphone as a high-end fine art drawing tool. See *David Hockney's i-Phone Paintings* (2009), http://improvisedlife.com/2009/11/09/david-hockneys-i-phone-paintings/.

Page 110

Living with uncertainty—See Baruch Fischhoff, Paul Slovic, and Sarah Lichtenstein, "Knowing with Certainty: The Appropriateness of Extreme Confidence," *Journal of Experimental Psychology: Human Perception and Performance* 3, no. 4 (1977): 552. See also Paul A. Mabe and Stephen G. West, "Validity of Self-Evaluation of Ability: A Review and Meta-Analysis," *Journal of Applied Psychology* 67, no. 3 (1982): 280.

Leverage uncertainty to build new knowledge—The extension of uncertainty in the drawing process to consider multiple alternative solutions seems to be an acquired skill that enables drawers to generate novel concepts. See Ilse M. Verstijnen, Cees van Leeuwen, G. Goldschmidt, Ronald Hamel, and J. M. Hennessey, "Sketching and Creative Discovery," *Design Studies* 19, no. 4 (1998): 519–546.

Managers were asked to sketch—Christian Muntwiler and Martin Eppler, "Showing What You Don't Know: The Effect of Visualization on Managers' Illusion of Explanatory Depth," *Academy of Management Annual Meeting Proceedings* (2019), issue 1.

Eliza Bobek asked 7th graders—"Visual explanations often included crucial yet invisible features. The greater effectiveness of visual explanations appears attributable to the checks they provide for completeness and coherence as well as to their roles as platforms for inference." Eliza Bobek and Barbara Tversky, "Creating Visual Explanations Improves Learning," *Cognitive Research: Principles and Implications* 1, no. 1 (2016): 1.

The drawing process—"Providing drawing activities likely helps students determine what they do not yet understand in the simulation and engage with these concepts when drawing and discussing content with peers." Sally. P. Wu and Martina A. Rau, "How Students Learn Content in Science, Technology, Engineering, and Mathematics (STEM) through Drawing Activities," *Educational Psychology Review* 31, no. 1 (2019): 103.

Social scientist Donald Schön studied five professions—engineering, architecture, management, psychotherapy, and town planning—to understand the way experts in a variety of fields were able to improvise rather than rely on espoused theory. In Schön's study of architects, he found they introduced uncertainty deliberately into their sketches to afford opportunities for discovery: "They will reflect-in-action on the situation's back-talk, shifting stance as they do so from 'what if?' to recognition of implications, from involvement in the unit to consideration of the total, and from exploration to commitment." Donald Schön, *The Reflective Practitioner: How Professionals Think in Action* (New York: Basic Books, 1983), 103.

Page 111

Experts' exploratory sketches—In "The Dialectics of Sketching," Gabriela Goldschmidt detailed the "oscillation of arguments which brings about gradual transformation of images" in architects' drawings. Using a talk-aloud protocol analysis method, Goldschmidt recorded the quick systematic alternation of "seeing as" and "seeing that"—in other words, interpreting (and reinterpreting) the gestalt of the figural elements in the sketch and imagining how they might be transformed. The intentional ambiguity of the sketcher's first thoughts allow for this consideration of alternatives. She quotes one of her participants: "I like fuzzy stuff. I can see in it more than I can in hard-lined things." Goldschmidt proposes that the "continuous production of displays pregnant with clues" in order to generate new ideas is unique to the drawing process, and does not occur in other kinds of visual production. Gabriela Goldschmidt, "The Dialectics of Sketching," *Creativity Research Journal* 4, no. 2 (1991): 123–143, at 140. See also Gabriela Goldschmidt, "Visual Analogy: A Strategy for Design Reasoning and Learning," *Design Knowing and Learning: Cognition in Design Education* (2001): 199–220.

Sketches allow for both intended and unintended ambiguities, affording opportunities for reinterpretation and restructuring. Fish and Scrivner wrote that "commonly found are blank spaces where the drawing fades away, multiple alternative contour lines (penitmenti) missing contour lines, wobbly lines. . . . One reason for such indeterminacies is the need to preserve alternatives." Indeterminate images spark thought. This is a strategy Fish and Scrivner detected in a wide variety of sketches of both artists and designers, from observation, memory, and invention. Indeterminacy, they wrote, "can provoke innate, unconscious recognition mechanisms to generate a stream of imagery." The more problematic an image is, they suggest, the more effective it may be in stimulating new ideas. Jonathan Fish and Stephen Scrivener, "Amplifying the Mind's Eye: Sketching and Visual Cognition," *Leonardo* 23, no. 1 (1990): 120.

Constructive perception—See Masuki Suwa and Barbara Tversky, "Constructive Perception: A Skill for Coordinating Perception and Conception," in *Proceedings of the Cognitive Science Society Meetings* (UC Merced: Cognitive Science Society, 2003); Suwa Masaki, Barbara Tversky, John Gero, and Terry Purcell. "Seeing into Sketches: Regrouping Parts Encourages New Interpretations," in *Visual and Spatial Reasoning in Design II*, ed. John S. Gero, Barbara Tversky, and Terry Purcell (Sydney: Key Centre of Design Computing and Cognition, University of Sydney, 2001), 207–219.

"Turn discomfort into inquiry"—Liz Lerman, *Hiking the Horizontal: Field Notes from a Choreographer* (Middletown, CT: Wesleyan University Press, 2014), 6.

Page 112

Bill Bradley—Wilson Conn, "Moments in March: Bill Bradley '65 led the Tigers to their only Final Four run in school history," *Daily Princetonian*, March 18, 2021, https://www.dailyprince tonian.com/article/2021/03/moments-in-march-bill-bradley -led-tigers-final-four-run. In 1965, John McPhee recounted that Bradley "tosses the ball into the basket over one shoulder, like a pinch of salt. Only when the ball is actually dropping through the net does he look around to see what has happened, on the chance that something might have gone wrong, in which case he would have to go for the rebound. That shot has the essential characteristics of a wild accident, which is what many people stubbornly think they have witnessed until they see him do it for the third time in a row." McPhee goes on to explain that this remarkable performance is due to his remarkably disciplined deliberate practice: "When Bradley, working out alone, practices his set shots, hook shots, and jump shots, he moves systematically from one place to another around the basket, his distance from it being appropriate to the shot, and he does not permit himself to move on until he has made at least ten shots out of thirteen from each location. He applies this standard to every kind of shot, with either hand, from any distance." John McPhee, "A Sense of Where You Are," *New Yorker*, January 25, 1965, https://www.newyorker.com/magazine/1965/01/23/a-sense-of-where-you-are.

Tyrone "Muggsy" Bogues—Tyrone Bogues with David Levine, *In the Land of Giants: My Life in Basketball* (New York: Little, Brown, 1994).

Page 113

Deliberate practice—Anders K. Ericsson, Ralf T. Krampe, and Clemens Tesch-Romer, "The Role of Deliberate Practice in the Acquisition of Expert Performance," *Psychological Review* 100, no. 3 (1993): 363. This research has been cited 12,586 times (according to a 2021 count by Google Scholar) and was popularized through Malcolm Gladwell's book, *Outliers*, as the "10,000 hours hypothesis." This popularization has become controversial in the nature vs. nurture debate. Ericsson and colleagues have defended it by reiterating that they are not denying that certain individuals have genetic advantages. They affirm, however, that specific kinds of targeted, strategic practice (not simply hours spent) are necessary to produce expert performance. Malcolm Gladwell, *Outliers: The Story of Success* (New York: Little, Brown, 2008); Anders K. Ericsson and Kyle W. Harwell, "Deliberate Practice and Proposed Limits on the Effects of Practice on the Acquisition of Expert Performance: Why the Original Definition Matters and Recommendations for Future Research," *Frontiers in Psychology* 10 (2019): 2396.

Automaticity—Across many different fields, once low-level, repetitive procedures and routines become automatic, the practitioner can devote full attention to the specific, unique characteristics of the task at hand. Automated perceptual habits and routines facilitate the drawing process. For example: "While creating drawings, the artist is continually focusing on small portions of a scene in order to reproduce it patch by patch, all the while keeping track of the larger organization of the object and the scene in order to place each element appropriately. Over thousands of hours of training, we suggest that this particular style of attention to the scene leads the artists to develop robust representations that are optimal for the step-by-step production of the drawing and the motor planning of hand movements." Florian Perdreau and Patrick

Cavanagh, "The Artist's Advantage: Better Integration of Object Information across Eye Movements," *i-Perception* 4, no. 6 (2013): 393.

Page 120

"They did everything by improvisation"—Dario Fo, *The Tricks of the Trade* (London: Routledge, 1991), 11.

"All instrumentalists . . ."—In an interview, trombonist and vocalist Staff Sgt. Ken Ebo said, "All instrumentalists . . . feel that their instrument is an extension of themselves . . . and improvisation is not just making it up as you go along, it's the ability to be creative within and around a known set of boundaries for which you've prepared a great deal . . . and that is right in line with the ethos of the Marine Corps." "How the US Marine Corps Jazz Ensemble Recruits with Music," *The World*, March 24, 2014, https://theworld.org/stories/2014-03-14/how-us-marine-corps-jazz-ensemble-recruits-music.

Page 115

Miles Davis—Herbie Hancock told this story multiple times. This telling was posted on YouTube by Old Town Improv Co.: https://www.youtube.com/watch?v=t-vItf0G05M.

Page 116

What artists do when they draw—I videotaped nine expert artists drawing in their studios. To define "consistent experts" in the realm of artistic drawing practice, I used three partial measures of drawing skill in contemporary terms. Sustained engagement in deliberate practice over many years, intentional choices regarding consistently evolving drawing methods, and professional recognition together were taken to identify contemporary artists' drawing expertise. This leads to a provisional definition in line with Galenson's category of "experimental innovators," artists whose achievements result from years of persistence rather than youthful flashes of genius. According to Galenson, experimental innovators persist in a focused line of inquiry. Their masterworks emerge from a long process of trial and error. See Andrea Kantrowitz, "A Cognitive Ethnographic Study of Improvisational Drawing by Eight Contemporary Artists," doctoral dissertation, Teachers College, Columbia University, 2014. See also David W. Galenson, *Old Masters and Young Geniuses the Two Life Cycles of Artistic Creativity* (Princeton, NJ: Princeton University Press, 2006).

Page 117

The images of hands on this page are reproduced by permission of the original publisher. © 2017, from "What Artists Do When They Draw," by Andrea Kantrowitz. Reproduced by permission of Taylor and Francis Group, LLC, a division of Informa plc.

Page 118

The skull on this page is reproduced by permission of the original publisher. © 2017, from "What Artists Do When They Draw," by Andrea Kantrowitz. Reproduced by permission of Taylor and Francis Group, LLC, a division of Informa plc. This permission does not cover any third-party copyrighted work which may appear in the material.

Through eye-tracking, Suhyun, Park, Louis Wiliams, and Rebecca Chamberlain found that artists switch into a different mode of seeing, moveing between features or objects. This is different from when they are looking "normally," suggesting that they choose to switch into a specific, learned mode of looking while drawing. Suhyun, Park, Louis Wiliams, and Rebecca Chamberlain, "Global Saccadic Eye Movements Characterise Artists' Visual Attention while Drawing," *Empirical Studies of the Arts* (2021).

Michelle Fava used eye-tracking to identify individual attentional patterns switching between local and global focus among her expert artist participants drawing activity. She found that drawing is a "skill that involves strategic use of visual deconstruction, comparison, analogical transfer and repetitive cycles of construction, evaluation and revision." Michelle Fava, "Understanding Drawing: A Cognitive Account of Observational Process," doctoral dissertation, Loughborough University, 2014.

Page 119

Michael Moore's drawings on this page are reproduced by permission of the artist.

The author's drawing is reproduced by permission of the original publisher. © 2017, from "What Artists Do When They Draw," by Andrea Kantrowitz. Reproduced by permission of Taylor and Francis Group, LLC, a division of Informa plc. This permission does not cover any third-party copyrighted work which may appear in the material.

Page 126

Technical expertise is easier to achieve than creative expertise—See Aaron Kozbelt and Andrea Kantrowitz, "Talent and Ability in Drawing and Visual Art," in *The Psychology of High Performance: Developing Human Potential into Domain-Specific Talent*, ed. Rena F. Subotnik, Paula Olszewski-Kubilius, and Frank C. Worrell (Washington, DC: American Psychological Association, 2019), 311–343.

This is the full passage from Rainer Maria Rilke, ***The Notebooks of Malte Laurids Brigge:***

For the sake of a few lines one must see many cities, men and things. One must know the animals, one must feel how the birds fly and know the gesture with which the small flowers open in the morning. One must be able to think back to roads in unknown regions, to unexpected meetings and to partings which one had long seen coming; to days of childhood that are still unexplained, to parents that one had to hurt when they brought one some joy and one did not grasp it (it was joy for someone else); to childhood illness that so strangely began with a number of profound and grave transformations, to days in rooms withdrawn and quiet and to mornings by the sea, to the sea itself, to seas, to nights of travel that rushed along on high and flew with all the stars—and it is not enough if one may think all of this. One must have memories of many nights of love, none of which was like the others, of the screams of women in labor, and of light, white, sleeping women in childbed, closing again. But one must also have been beside the dying, one must have sat beside the dead in the room with the open window and the fitful noises. And still it is not enough to have memories. One must be able to forget them when they are many, and one must have the great patience to wait until they come again. For it is not yet the memories themselves. Not until they have turned to blood within us, to glance, to gesture, nameless and no longer to be distinguished from ourselves-not until then can it happen that in a most rare hour the first word of a verse arises in their midst and goes forth from them.

(Rainer Maria Rilke, *The Notebooks of Malte Laurids Brigge: A Novel*, trans. Michael Hulse [New York: Penguin, 2009], 14)

Page 121

The author's drawing on this page is reproduced by permission of the original publisher. © 2017, from "What Artists Do When They Draw," by Andrea Kantrowitz. Reproduced by permission of Taylor and Francis Group, LLC, a division of Informa plc. This permission does not cover any third-party copyrighted work which may appear in the material.

chapter eight

Everybody Draw!

Page 127

They invent a subject or a story—See Judith Burton, "The Integrity of Personal Experience, or The Presence of Life in Art," *International Journal of Arts in Education* 3, no. 2 (2005): 9–23.

Marvel Comics—See Stan Lee and J. Buscema, *How to Draw Comics the Marvel Way* (New York: Simon and Schuster, 1984).

Page 128

Hokousai—quoted in Aaron Kozbelt and Yana Durmysheva, "Lifespan Creativity in a Non-Western Artistic Tradition: A Study of Japanese Ukiyo-e Printmakers," *International Journal of Aging and Human Development* 65, no. 1 (2007): 23–51.

Page 129

So it might never be forgotten—See Myra A. Fernandes, Jeffrey D. Wammes, and Melissa E. Meade, "The Surprisingly Powerful Influence of Drawing on Memory," *Current Directions in Psychological Science* 27, no. 5 (2018): 302–308.

Page 130

Even doodling may enhance listening—It is not yet clear whether or not any kind of doodling enhances learning (of nonrelated material), but multiple studies have found that certain kinds of structured doodling do help. It has been suggested that doodling may help because it serves to quiet the non-stimuli-related mental activity (the internal chatter Buddhists call the "monkey mind").

In a well-publicized study, Jackie Andrade found that doodling significantly helped participants recall relatively boring verbal information: "What mechanism might underlie the effect of doodling on concentration? One possibility is that doodling simply helps to stabilize arousal at an optimal level, keeping people awake or reducing the high levels of autonomic arousal often associated with boredom. . . . Future research using psychophysiological measures might pick up such effects. A more specific hypothesis is that doodling aids concentration by reducing daydreaming, in situations where daydreaming might be more detrimental to performance than doodling itself." See Jackie Andrade, "What Does Doodling Do?" *Applied Cognitive Psychology: The Official Journal of the Society for Applied Research in Memory and Cognition* 24, no. 1 (2010): 103.

Other studies have replicated Andrade's findings; however, one study found that only structured (as opposed to unstructured) doodling aided memory. See Jason Bruce Boggs, Jillian Lane Cohen, and Gwen C. Marchand, "The Effects of Doodling on Recall Ability," *Psychological Thought* 10, no. 1 (2017): 206.

Drawing can increase emotional engagement—Mary Immordino-Yang is a neuroscientist and former public school teacher who studies the impact of affect on learning: "When learning and knowledge are relatively devoid of emotion, when people learn things by 'rote' without internally driven motivation and without a sense of interest or real-world relevance, then it is likely that they won't be able to use what they learn efficiently in the real world." Mary H. Immordino-Yang, *Emotions, Learning, and the Brain: Exploring the Educational Implications of Affective Neuroscience* (New York: W. W. Norton, 2015), 28.

Page 131

Traditional skills—See D. W. Chan and Y. Zhao, "The Relationship between Drawing Skill and Artistic Creativity: Do Age and

Artistic Involvement Make a Difference?" *Creativity Research Journal* 22, no. 1 (2010): 27–36. "If we are to make a difference in young children's capacities for self-expression in the visual arts, we must facilitate the development of the necessary tools—the technical skill needed to express oneself and one's interactions with the world." Susan M Rostan, David Pariser, and Howard E. Gruber, "A Cross-Cultural Study of the Development of Artistic Talent, Creativity and Giftedness," *High Ability Studies* 13, no. 2 (2002): 151. See also Aaron Kozbelt, "Originality and Technical Skill as Components of Artistic Quality," *Empirical Studies of the Arts* 22, no. 2 (2004): 157–170.

Page 132

To Observe—Many more recent drawing manuals (including Betty Edward's *Drawing on the Right Side of the Brain*) borrow extensively from Kimon Nicolaides. So go directly to the source: Kimon Nicolaides, *The Natural Way to Draw: A Working Plan for Art Study* (Boston: Houghton Mifflin, 1969). An excellent more contemporary and inspiring text that includes a variety of master drawings with the artist's own work is Sarah Simblet's *Sketch Book for the Artist: An Innovative, Practical Approach to Drawing the World around You* (New York: DK Publishing, 2005).

Urban Sketchers—Urban Sketchers is an international nonprofit that connects drawing enthusiasts around the world, organizes an annual symposium, holds numerous workshops, and publishes a beautiful monthly newsletter, *Drawing Attention*, highlighting the work of individual members. These are their guiding principles: "1) We draw on location, indoors or out, capturing what we see from direct observation. 2) Our drawings tell the story of our surroundings, the places we live and where we travel. 3) Our drawings are a record of time and place. 4) We are truthful to the scenes we witness. 5) We use any kind of media and cherish our individual styles. 6) We support each other and draw together. 7) We share our drawings online. 8) We show the world, one drawing at a time." See Urban Sketchers, "Our Mission," http://www.urbansketchers.org/p/our-mission.html, accessed December 23, 2021.

For observational drawing with children, see Nancy Smith, *Observation Drawing with Children: A Framework for Teachers* (New York: Teachers College Press, 1998).

Page 133

To Visualize—*Drawing Ideas* is a really friendly, comprehensive, and well-designed manual by two professional designers. It includes clear instructions for drawing to visualize. Chapter 2, "Drawing Boot Camp," includes step-by-step guides to perspective, the human figure, light and shadow, and other topics. See Mark Baskinger and William Bardel, *Drawing Ideas: A Hand-Drawn Approach for Better Design* (New York: Watson-Guptill, 2013).

Scott Robertson and Thomas Bertling's book *How to Draw* is not only comprehensive, but also provides access to instructional videos, with QR codes. See Scott Robertson and Thomas Bertling, *How to Draw: Drawing and Sketching Objects and Environments from Your Imagination* (Culver City, CA: Design Studio Press, 2013).

For a less technical and more intuitive approach (less for designers and more for visual storytelling and comics), graphic novelist Lynda Barry has two books based on a class she teaches at University of Wisconsin Madison that are full of approachable and fun exercises to get your imagination started. See Lynda Barry, *Making Comics* (Montreal: Drawn and Quarterly, 2019); Lynda Barry, *Syllabus* (Montreal: Drawn and Quarterly, 2014).

Page 134

Remember and Reflect—See Alison Bechdel, *Fun Home: A Family Tragicomic* (New York: Houghton Mifflin Harcourt, 2007); Emil Ferris, *My Favorite Thing Is Monsters*, vol. 1 (Seattle: Fantagraphics Books, 2017); Marjane Satrapi, *The Complete Persepolis* (New York: Pantheon Books, 2007).

Comics is used in healthcare—"Graphic Medicine is a site that explores the interaction between the medium of comics and the discourse of healthcare. We are a community of academics, health carers, authors, artists, and fans of comics and medicine. The site is maintained by an editorial team under the direction of the Graphic Medicine International Collective" (http://www.graphicmedicine.org/). See also M. K. Czerwiec, Ian Williams, Susan Merrill Squier, Michael J. Green, Kimberly R. Myers, and Scott T. Smith, *Graphic Medicine Manifesto*, vol. 1 (State College, PA: Penn State Press, 2015).

Anthropologists use drawings—See Andrew Causey, *Drawn to See: Drawing as an Ethnographic Method* (Toronto: University of Toronto Press, 2017). See also Michael Taussig, *I Swear I Saw This: Drawings in Fieldwork Notebooks, Namely My Own* (Chicago: University of Chicago Press, 2011).

W. E. B. Du Bois's infographics—For W. E. B. Du Bois's infographics, see Whitney Battle-Baptiste and Britt Rusert, eds., *W. E. B. Du Bois's Data Portraits: Visualizing Black America* (San Francisco: Chronicle Books, 2018). See also Jackie Mansky, "W. E. B. Du Bois' Visionary Infographics Come Together for the First Time in Full Color," *Smithsonian Magazine*, November 15, 2018, http://www.smithsonianmag.com/history/first-time-together-and-color-book-displays-web-du-bois-visionary-infographics-180970826/.

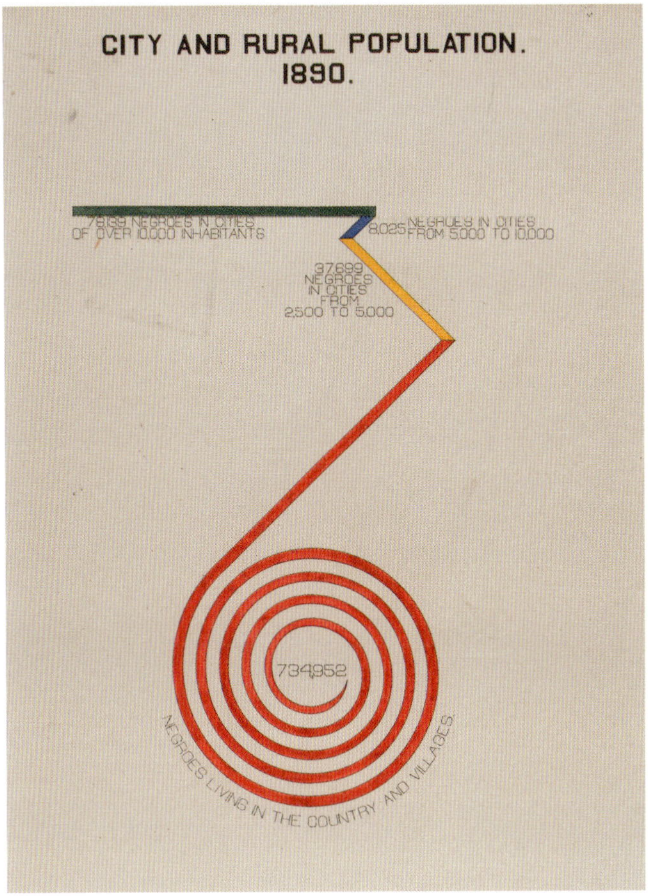

For W. E. B. Du Bois's Infographics, see: Whitney Battle-Baptiste, and Britt Rusert, eds. WEB Du Bois's Data Portraits: Visualizing Black America. *Chronicle Books, 2018.*

Quarantine Qomix—From the archives of the Qomix I made with my husband, Scott Benjamin, during the early months of the COVID-19 lockdown in spring 2020. See https://quarantine-qomix.weebly.com/.

Page 135

Design thinking—Design thinking has its origins in what was called "Design Science" in the 1950s at MIT. IDEO (a company out of Stanford University School of Design, known as the "d school") is credited with the development a widely used model, which they describe as a process of creative problem solving. See "What Is Design Thinking?" *IDEO U*, https://www.ideou.com/blogs/inspiration/what-is-design-thinking, accessed December 23, 2021.

Solve Problems—My "Thinking through Drawing" project partners—Michelle Darlington Fava and Angela Brew—and I developed a collaborative drawing problem-solving process that we have adapted and customized to suit the needs of a wide variety of audiences. Groups are formed on the basis on common themes and work to integrate their visual ideas. We've found, through conducting these workshops with diverse groups of people around the world, that in almost every context, possible solutions emerge almost spontaneously once the problem has been represented thoroughly in multiple ways.

For sketch-noting resources designed for problem solving in groups, see Dan Roam, *The Back of the Napkin: Solving Problems and Selling Ideas with Pictures* (New York: Portfolio, 2013).

Page 136

Communicate

Even when working in a group, start with individual drawings. For more on the pitfalls of group brainstorming and the advantages of individual brainstorming, see Adrian Furnham, "The Brainstorming Myth," *Business Strategy Review* 11, no. 4 (2000): 21.

Sketchnoting—See Notes for page 4, chapter 1.

Acknowledgments

Early in my doctoral research at Columbia University Teachers College, Barbara Tversky invited me into her cognitive studies seminar. That invitation opened up a world of possibilities that eventually led to the creation of this book. Together, my two dissertation advisors, psychologist Barbara Tversky and art educator Judith Burton, helped me analyze and build on relationships between their very different disciplines. Fellow grad student Nick Sousanis generously encouraged this work and inspired me by example (with his dissertation in comics form) since the first class we took together at Teachers College. I am deeply grateful to the artist participants in my doctoral research who shared their working practices with me, especially Michael Moore and Vicki Behm, along with lifelong friends and fellow artists Jane Fine and Sharon Rosenzweig. I am so grateful for the opportunity, while at Columbia, to develop the international Thinking through Drawing Project with Michelle Darlington and Angela Brew. I want to thank Emily Sheehan, Emma Falt, Rebecca Chamberlain, Marta Cabral, Matt Freeman, Sara Schneckloth, Seymour Simmons, and so many other Thinking through Drawing colleagues for the exchange of ideas and intellectual and moral support (not to mention fun!) we have enjoyed over the years. Thanks also to Kim Sloane at Pratt Institute who taught me much about the teaching of drawing.

I am also thankful to Victoria Loy and her colleagues at Singapore Teachers Academy of the Arts, who twice gave me the opportunity to work with dedicated, creative groups of art educators, and from whom I learned that the questions we ask as artist/teachers, and love of art and drawing in general, know no national or cultural boundaries. My gratitude also goes out to the students, from Singapore to the Bronx, from kindergarten to graduate school and in-service educators, of so many sociocultural backgrounds, from whom I have learned so much about art, drawing, and life.

My wise and brilliant friends Jessica Krash, Sara Wyman, Sean Justice, and my sister Barbara Kantrowitz, provided specific and invaluable feedback on various versions of the text, in addition to the helpful suggestions made by anonymous peer reviewers. Special thanks to SUNY New Paltz colleagues Josh Korenblat and Amy Papaelias, who gave me greatly appreciated design advice at key points along the way. Graphic design intern Hannah Taddonio made the final production process of this book possible, rendering my hand-drawn typefaces readable and helping produce the final version of this book.

There is no way to put into words the love and appreciation I feel for my family, who have supported this project in countless ways. My parents, Rosalind and Arthur Kantrowitz always encouraged me to go after my dreams. My two sisters, Barbara and Lore, have always been there for me in the best and worst of times. My daughters Anya and Sophia have watched and supported my journey with love and amusement, and continually remind me what is truly important in life. My wise and generous mother-in-law Doris attended to us all throughout this journey. And I can't imagine any of this without my loving husband Scott, who stood next to me every step of the way, buying groceries, debating ideas, my best editor and coach, how incredibly lucky I am to have him at my side.

About the Author

Andrea Kantrowitz, an artist and educator, is the Director of the Art Education Program at the State University of New York at New Paltz. She has lectured and led workshops on art and cognition internationally, and has twice served as a Singapore Ministry of Education Outstanding Educator in Residence. As a director of the Thinking through Drawing Project, founded during her doctoral studies at Teachers College, Columbia University, she co-organized 10 years of international drawing and cognition research symposia and workshops, in collaboration with colleagues from around the world. Before coming to Columbia University Teachers College as a doctoral student, she was a teaching artist in the New York City public schools for many years, involved in multiple local and national research projects. As a teaching artist with the Studio in a School organization, she co-developed and implemented an integrated art, math, and literacy curriculum for a federally funded Arts in Education Model Development and Dissemination (AEMDD) project. This project included a randomized control trial that demonstrated the impact of an integrated art curriculum for students growing up in poverty.

She holds a BA in Art and Cognition from Harvard University and a MFA in Painting from Yale. She has taught foundation drawing at Pratt Institute in Brooklyn and graduate courses in contemporary art at the College of New Rochelle. Prior to her work in K-12 education, she was the visual art foundation coordinator at the University of Wisconsin at Oshkosh. Her paintings have been exhibited nationally and are in many private collections. She has curated multiple exhibitions on themes of drawing, cognition, and the creative work of artist/educators. She is an artist member of The Painting Center in New York City, and her artwork is also represented by Kenise Barnes Fine Art. She lives, hikes, draws, and paints in the Hudson Valley, NY.